Biology, Society, and Behavior

Recent Titles in Advances in Applied Developmental Psychology
Irving E. Sigel, series editor

Two-Generation Programs for Families in Poverty:
A New Intervention Strategy
Sheila Smith, editor

Mastery Motivation: Origins, Conceptualizations, and Applications
Robert H. MacTurk and George A. Morgan, editors

Sibling Relationships: Their Causes and Consequences
Gene Brody, editor

Interacting With Video
Patricia M. Greenfield and Rodney R. Cocking, editors

Applied Developmental Science:
Graduate Training for Diverse Disciplines and Educational Settings
Celia B. Fisher, John P. Murray, and Irving E. Sigel, editors

Caribbean Families: Diversity Among Ethnic Groups
Jaipaul R. Roopnarine and Janet Brown, editors

Verbal Interaction and Development in Families with Adolescents
Manfred Hofer, James Youniss, and Peter Noack, editors

Children of the Dispossessed:
Far-West Preschoolers 30 Years On (2nd edition)
Barry Nurcombe, Susan-Lee Walker, and Philip DeLacey

Where Children Live:
Solutions for Serving Young Children and Their Families
Richard N. Roberts and Phyllis R. Magrab, editors

Partnerships in Research, Clinical, and Educational Settings
Roger Bibace, James Dillon, and Barbara Noel Dowds, editors

Communication: An Arena of Development
Nancy Budwig, Ina C. Uzgiris, and James V. Wertsch, editors

The Guided Acquistion of First Language Skills
Ernst L. Moerk, editor

Biology, Society, and Behavior: The Development of Sex Differences in Cognition

edited by

Ann McGillicuddy-De Lisi

and

Richard De Lisi

Advances in Applied Developmental Psychology, Volume 21
Irving E. Sigel, Series Editor

Ablex Publishing
Westport, Connecticut • London

Library of Congress Cataloging-in-Publication Data

Biology, society, and behavior : the development of sex differences in cognition / edited by Ann McGillicuddy-De Lisi and Richard De Lisi.
     p. cm. — (Advances in applied developmental psychology ; vol. 21)
     Includes bibliographical references and index.
     ISBN 1–56750–632–1 (alk. paper) — ISBN 1–56750–633–X (pbk.: alk paper)
     1. Cognition in children. 2. Cognition in adolescence. 3. Sex differences (Psychology) in children. 4. Sex differences (Psychology) in adolescence. I. McGillicuddy-De Lisi, Ann V. II. De Lisi, Richard. III. Advances in applied developmental psychology (1993) ; v. 21.
BF723.C5B475   2002
155.4'13—dc21   2001022177

British Library Cataloguing in Publication Data is available.

Library of Congress Catalog Card Number: 2001022177
ISBN: 1–56750–632–1
     1–56750–633–X (pbk.)

First published in 2002

Ablex Publishing, 88 Post Road West, Westport, CT 06881
An imprint of Greenwood Publishing Group, Inc.
www.ablexbooks.com

Printed in the United States of America

The paper used in this book complies with the Permanent Paper Standard issued by the National Information Standards Organization (Z39.48–1984).

10 9 8 7 6 5 4 3 2 1

We dedicate this book with all of our love to our children,
Brian, Michael, and Alex

Contents

Illustrations   *ix*

Foreword
Irving E. Sigel   *xi*

Acknowledgments   *xix*

Part I.   Introduction

1.   Causes, Correlates, and Caveats:
    Understanding the Development of Sex Differences in Cognition
    Diane F. Halpern and Simay Ikier   *3*

Part II.   Explanatory Constructs

2.   Sexual Selection and Sex Differences in Social Cognition
    David C. Geary   *23*

3.   Hormones, Brain, and Behavior:
    Putative Biological Contributions to Cognitive Sex Differences
    Roslyn Holly Fitch and Heather A. Bimonte   *55*

4.   Sex Differences in Motivation, Self-Concept, Career Aspiration,
    and Career Choice: Implications for Cognitive Development
    Allan Wigfield, Ann Battle, Lisa B. Keller, and Jacquelynne S. Eccles   *93*

Part III.   Domains of Human Cognition

5.   Gender Differences in Language Development
    Jean Berko Gleason and Richard Ely   *127*

6.   Sex Differences in Mathematical Abilities and Achievement
     Richard De Lisi and Ann McGillicuddy-De Lisi   *155*

7.   Maximization of Spatial Competence: More Important than Finding
     the Cause of Sex Differences
     Nora S. Newcombe, Lisa Mathason, and Melissa Terlecki   *183*

8.   Children's Gender Cognitions, the Social Environment,
     and Sex Differences in Cognitive Domains
     Carol Lynn Martin and Lisa M. Dinella   *207*

Part IV.   Summary and Conclusions

9.   Emergent Themes in the Development of Sex Differences in Cognition
     Ann McGillicuddy-De Lisi and Richard De Lisi   *243*

Author Index   *259*

Subject Index   *275*

About the Contributors   *281*

Illustrations

Figure 2.1. Physical male–male competition in the ruff (*Machetes pugnax*).   *28*

Figure 2.2. Bower building and behavioral male–male competition in the bowerbird (*Chlamydera maculata*).   *29*

Figure 2.3. Proposed sociocognitive modules.   *34*

Figure 2.4. Proposed pattern of relations among evolved but skeletal cognitive and brain systems, biased attentional, information processing, motivational, and activity patterns, and later cognitive and brain systems.   *37*

Figure 7.1. Effects of training on sex differences: One possibility.   *187*
Figure 7.2. Effects of training on sex differences: Another possibility.   *188*
Figure 7.3. Effects of training on sex differences. A threshold effect added.   *189*

Figure 8.1. Model of social environmental influences.   *211*

Foreword

Irving E. Sigel

This book, titled *Biology, Society, and Behavior: The Development of Sex Differences in Cognition,* edited by Ann McGillicuddy-De Lisi and Richard De Lisi, is the 21st volume in the Applied Development Psychology series dedicated to an in-depth discussion of fundamental issues in the field of developmental psychology.

Sex differences is a topic of interest for researchers and practitioners working in the biological, behavioral, and educational sciences because the more we can fathom the nature of the inequities women receive at the hands of their male counterparts, the sooner we can address them. I hope that such understanding will lead to a recognition of the bases of differences and acceptance of them as part of the nature of human variability without negative attributions.

Differences are not just justification for irrational prejudice, but rather require a rational and egalitarian perspective where the whole person is accepted with differences being part of everyone's human condition. To come to such understanding first requires an attitude of respect for individuality as a value, and second, the need to understand the bases for the inherent variability among all living creatures. It is a difficult lesson to learn that sources of individual differences between men and women, the topic of this volume, are rooted in complex evolutionary, biological, and sociocultural history. The untangling of this mystery can only come about by studying the sources of the differences and the way they are manifested in different situations. Of course, to accomplish these understandings requires careful study and reflection as to the state of the research capabilities available to investigators. However, there is a basic requirement whenever studies of differences between groups are undertaken—to face squarely what are inherent biases among investigators.

In the case of research in male–female differences, it is legitimate to ask what stereotypical beliefs investigators might have about women. There is no reason to think that researchers would not have conscious or unconscious biases about women. Might not a male investigator frame the differences between men and women differently than a female investigator? It seems to be the case that males have more negative beliefs about females' quantitative skills than their female counterparts. These differences between male and female investigators indicate how pervasive these beliefs are. Why would there be any differences between two scientists? My contention is that these differences are due to the basic belief system men have of women and women have of themselves, and, probably, the same holds true for women's views of men. These differences may be attributed by men and by women to the biological nature of females who were, in an evolutionary sense, dedicated to the reproductive functions, child care, and satisfying the sexual desires of males, while men evolved as the powerful protectors of women and traditional bread winners, providing food, shelter, and protection from enemies. It is not surprising to find that even in the year 2001, such beliefs are still held in different forms in many societies, even in the United States. Fundamentalist religious groups advocate the submission of women to their husbands. In Moslem countries, women are not allowed the same rights and privileges as men.

Men often judge women in terms of their sexual attractiveness or particular so-called feminine personality attributes, such as being deferential to men, or not too assertive or domineering. These traits are often valued more than their cognitive skills or managerial or entrepreneurial competence. In effect, women are considered inferior to men, especially in such cognitive areas as mathematics, understanding spatial relations, and abstract reasoning. Such male views in the aggregate may be shifting toward a more egalitarian acceptance of females as equals in the political, educational, and work venues, but this acceptance is more often in theory than in practice. There is still considerable evidence that such acceptance is somewhat begrudging and, therefore, not as pervasive and egalitarian as might be expected. Because males are still in positions of power in all spheres of society and continue to hold biased judgments regarding women, especially in the workplace, women will not be able to fulfill themselves on the basis of their competence. The reason for this is because men, who are in control of much of society's economic, political, and social power, do not want to lose their power and hence lose their social control. There is probably embarrassment that there are women in the society who are, in fact, more competent than they and hence threaten their prerogatives. Thus, women are denied equal opportunities to choose career paths that would satisfy their career aspirations. In addition, it is the case that even when women enter previously male-dominated occupations, the opportunities afforded them for assuming greater responsibility and authority are often limited. Women are often marginalized purely because of their sex.

These patronizing attitudes toward women are by no means of recent origin. From virtually time immemorial, women have been treated in many different ways, each with different forms of discrimination. In the so-called enlightened 20th century, when legislators created work rules for women and children, they defined for women the number of hours they could work, the time of day, and limited the occupations they could enter. It was with the belief that these folks needed protection and so different types of work rules were enacted. These rules were stated as necessary because women were exploited by employers precisely because they were, like the children, defined as naturally weak and in need of help.

There have been significant changes in such restrictions, enabling women to have more varied work opportunities. These rule changes were superficial and focused largely on the physical conditions of work, influencing entry into occupations such as police officer, firefighter, and airplane pilot—those that demand certain kinds of physical strength.

In spite of these changes, women generally were judged as less cognitively competent compared to men in mathematics and in dealing with spatial tasks such as navigation and map reading. Females also have been held to be less analytic thinkers than men. These are the reasons that some educational guidance counselors often steered female students away from fields such as engineering, natural and physical sciences, and computer technology. These beliefs persist today in spite of the fact that many females are now in a number of mathematics and science professions previously considered the sacrosanct domain of males (e.g., medicine, natural science, piloting aircraft). Each of these professions contradicts the stereotype of women as having lower levels of cognitive competence. The women who enter these fields are usually considered exceptions and are still discriminated against in terms of salary, opportunities for advancement, and above all, respect. In addition, female students often are still discouraged from entering these fields.

The question is, are judgments of women's cognitive competence based on sound evidence or are they part of a social stereotype of women? After all, in virtually every society, women are treated as second-class citizens. In extremely conservative Moslem countries, women are severely restricted in virtually every facet of their lives. In the Hebrew liturgy, there is a prayer that men recite thanking the Lord for not creating them as women.

Changes in women's status, rights, and privileges have undergone dramatic shifts to increasing egalitarian treatment, at least in many of the Western countries. However, the changes still have not created the equality that women feel is rightly due to them. As Halpern and Ikier state in chapter 1, "We (women) do not have to be the same to be equal."

This book addresses these issues during the early years of development, which set the stage preparing females for a future in which their competencies are recognized. However, the only way to examine the phenomenon of sex differences, to arrive at a seminal understanding of the issues involved, requires careful, thoughtful, and judicious examination of different perspectives emanating from scholarly research in the field. McGillicuddy-De Lisi and De Lisi set up a logical and psychological sequence that illustrates how various knowledge bases are required to understand the complexity of sex differences that contribute, as part of the whole, toward unraveling the mystery of the sex differences, especially the claims that females are less cognitively competent than males. Drawing on a group of experts in the fields of evolutionary, biological, educational, social, and developmental psychology to zero in on the central theme of sex differences in cognitive functioning, the editors have built a logic to create a coherent, conceptual, holistic framework to grasp fully the similarities and the differences between males and females.

The opening chapter by Halpern and Ikier sets the stage for the central question of why to study sex differences. They provide social, political, and psychological perspectives defining the issues inherent in research on studying sex difference. Among the valuable sections of the chapter is a section instructing readers how to read and think about research on sex differences. The guidelines include important caveats regarding the various technical aspects of research ranging from research design and measurement to interpretation and application of results. Another central issue that Halpern and Ikier discuss is the fact that there is resistance among feminists to the study of sex differences because of the potential harm that such studies can have on young women reading such research. Halpern and Ikier begin their essay with the following comments from prominent champions for women, broadcast on nationally televised interviews. Gloria Steinem and Gloria Allred stated, respectively, "It's really the remnant of anti-American crazy thinking to do this kind of research," and "This is harmful and damaging to our daughters' lives and our mothers' lives and I'm very angry about it." Why would two such prominent and intelligent women, who are so dedicated to women's issues, object to such research? Is it because the researchers will find that females do not perform well on cognitive measures and the findings might demoralize women? On the other hand, is it the fear that the research will provide scientific evidence supporting the social myths about women's cognitive inferiority relative to men? Alternatively, is the concern that the research will be conducted by researchers who are biased against females and so their research will reflect their bias? This latter thought may be based on the belief that many of the researchers in this area are men. The motivation of such opposition may not be evident, but the consequences of opposing this type of research because of its potential harm is a misreading of the nature of research.

Halpern and Ikier contend that Steinem and Allred are misguided about the aims of those studying sex differences. The error is in the assumption that such studies will have an effect on the young people reading about them. They grant that it is understandable that individuals who see themselves as victims of discrimination might accept the research findings as valid, which could lead to the self-fulfilling prophecy that, in fact, females are inferior to men. Although Halpern and Ikier provide clear arguments rebutting the critical claims, there is always the question of why should such research be done? Will it do more harm than good?

The study of sex differences is a legitimate issue because differences are discernible and do have social consequences. Why not find out what these differences mean? There is no doubt that these differences do exist. They are not inventions of the scientists. So what if they do in fact exist; why study these socially explosive topics? Those differences that are chosen as topics of study frame the argument. Studying sex differences in such areas as physical strength or hirsuteness pose no profound threat. But do they deal with a significant problem? When, however, sensitive areas as cognitive competence enter the fray, the emotions rise. Some feminists will see this type of study as an attempt to show differences in a negative light and hence lead to sustaining negative stereotypes of female competence, even though the findings are cloaked in scientific jargon.

An excellent analogy is the research on studies of intelligence between black and white people. Herrenstein and Murray (1994) authored *The Bell Curve*, a treatise supporting the notion that black Americans are intellectually inferior to whites. Their report engendered considerable controversy among social and behavioral scientists, many of whom argued that the research was flawed and revealed the racial bias of the authors toward African Americans. *The Bell Curve Wars*, edited by S. Fraser in 1995, contained critiques of *The Bell Curve* and detailed the errors and biases of the report. However, the Herrenstein and Murray volume was widely read and probably by racists seeking "scientific" confirmation of their already formed negative evaluations of African Americans. Herrenstein died before the book was published, but in spite of all the criticism, Murray continued to support the findings. Once such studies are published and available, there is no longer any control of their effects.

To avoid a repetition of such a misreading of research on group differences of any kind, including sex differences, the reader should read carefully the Halpern and Ikier chapter and follow their sage advice on how to judge the research among difference populations. They conclude the chapter by writing, "We do not have to be the same to be equal."

The reader may ask, of all the differences apparent between men and women, why focus on cognition? Here, again, we find the choice of topic discussed by Halpern and Ikier, who argue for such studies to deal with the stereotyping of women's cognitive abilities. It is only through such research that some of these difference questions may be cleared up. However, what if the research supports that sex differences do exist? Then one may ask, so what? The value of such findings should inform us as to reasons for the women's performance and it may well be, as in the case with black Americans, the differences are due to certain social factors that can be remedied through appropriated educational means. Thus, such research and its application demonstrate that the so-called stereotype is a function of some social or educational inequity and not inherent in the nature of women. However, what if the difference is due to some inherent condition? If that is the case, then the conclusion is well-stated; just being different does not preclude being equal.

We now come to the central issue of the book; why the focus on cognition? Cognition is a highly sensitive arena in which to engage in comparative research because it touches on a mental characteristic that is highly valued in our culture and presumed incompetence leads to considerable disservice to the population so designated.

As editor of the Applied Developmental Psychology series, I gladly accepted the suggestion of Ann McGillicuddy-De Lisi and Richard De Lisi to provide a forum to review the research on sex differences in cognition. They are ideally suited for this kind of review because of their long-standing interest and research in cognitive development. My hope was that their expertise will help dispel some of the mythology still existing in the fields of developmental psychology and education regarding male–female differences in cognitive abilities. Now is the time to address the mythology of women's inferiority with data and perspectives by experts in the field.

The reader may think my using the term mythology in reference to the sex difference issue is pejorative and biased. It is true that I am biased if that means seeking equal treatment of boys and girls in the educational system and men and women in the workplace. It is the case that opportunities for women in the workplace, in high-level educational enterprises, and in various political institutions reveal negative prejudgment of women's cognitive competence.

These are the arguments that preclude women the opportunity to undertake many high-level responsibilities (Sigel, 1996). Often, the language used to describe women is fraught with terms that are pejorative and demeaning. Evidence often used in such discussion is not based on reliable scientific inquiry but usually only anecdotes and hearsay. Therefore, my bias is the bias of one who favors the use of scientific data to support any social practice that is detrimental to the welfare of the person.

One way to counter the myth makers ideas, hopefully, is to provide an in-depth presentation of the latest scientific research to provide substantive information revealing what women are competent to do, and what they have difficulty doing. Ann McGillicuddy-De Lisi and Richard De Lisi created an integrated volume by instructing the authors how to shape the chapters so that they would flow one into the other. Their careful editorial monitoring resulted in the well-orchestrated set of chapters before you.

Halpern and Ikier, as mentioned previously, do set the stage instructing the reader how to interpret the research that follows. This is a critical issue, because they help in dealing with research that is contrary to one's expectations. Each contributor further refines the discussion, helping the reader to interpret the particulars of the research. This type of analysis requires in-depth understanding of how research is done and how it is reported.

Ann McGillicuddy-De Lisi and Richard De Lisi bring the experience with the field, expertise in the substantive methods of research, and a judicious respect for research, from its problem stating to its completion. They are indeed qualified to create this edited volume.

Although both are psychologists, their viewpoints are more than just a juxta-position of research from various disciplines; rather they come to the issue of sex differences from a holistic perspective that entails creating an integrative frame-work that is a guide for organizing the book. The chapters are organized in a pur-poseful way, beginning with Halpern and Ikier presenting the social and political issues.

Subsequent chapters involve a metatheoretical conceptualization, beginning with Geary's presentation, "a unifying framework based on principles of sexual selection for incorporating hormonal, experiential, as well as evolutionary influ-ences on human cognitive sex differences."

The next topic, by Fitch and Bimonte, focuses on the biological factors involved in the development of the individual. The search for the causative bio-logical factors, such as hormonal mechanisms, are offered as significant influ-ences on the masculinization and feminization of the brain and subsequent cog-nition. However, their perspective veers away from the simple quantitative argu-ment that developmental changes are additive to one that is more integrative. With the increasing knowledge emerging from neurobehavioral sciences, a con-ceptual shift has emerged in the study of sexual development. They write that "while acknowledging the biological basis of some sex differences in cognitive function, the neurobiological characterization of such differences is likely to prove so complex as to fundamentally undermine the straightforward interpreta-tion of task superiority."

The transition from the evolutionary and neurobiological perspective directly to the psychological realm follows in chapter 4 by Wigfield, Battle, Keller, and Eccles. They shift the discussion in two ways. First, they introduce the term gen-der differences instead of sex differences, drawing attention to the social psy-chological influences on male–female differences in cognition. The use of the term gender broadens the meaning of the sex differences construct to include the implication of social role that evolves from the biological features of sexuality. However, the authors seem to use the term interchangeably. No doubt, a reflec-tion of differences in terminology suggests a difference in context in which the issues are based. These authors provide a comprehensive discussion of the myr-iad of social influences that shape developing boys' and girls' motivation to learn, academic achievement, and self-concept, as well as career aspirations and career choices.

Three chapters follow that summarize the research in those areas most fre-quently cited as reflections of profound sex differences in cognition—language or verbal skills (Gleason and Ely), mathematics (De Lisi and McGillicuddy-De Lisi), and spatial relations (Newcombe, Mathason, and Terlecki). These cognitive skills have been believed to be influenced by genetics and hence presumably are irreversible. The general result of such beliefs have led to considerable inequity in how girls and boys have been treated in the classroom and even at home. What these chapters reveal is how naïve and over-simplified these so-called genetic hypotheses are, because their supporters fail to grasp the complexity of genetic influences. The research results clearly demonstrate the equivocal nature of the claims of male or female superiority in any cognitive domain.

But this is not the end of the story laid out by the editors. The next discussion by Martin and Dinella moves the analysis of sex differences into the level of the social environment, which implies cultural influence at a more distal level than dealt with in the early chapters on motivation.

The intellectual climax is in the final chapter, in which the editors succeed in generating the logic and basis for constructing a holistic model when they conclude, "We have models of evolutionary and ontogenetic processes that link biology, behavior, and society. The models are general and need refinement, but this can only occur if there is a willingness to view sex differences in cognitive functioning in such terms."

The readers are advised to read this book in sequence. That would be the only way to grasp the subtext that is crucial to follow the argument for constructing a holistic coherent model to understand the nature of sex differences in cognition.

REFERENCES

Fraser, S. (Ed.). (1995). *The bell curve wars: Race, intelligence, and the future of America.* New York: Basic Books.

Herrenstein, R. J., & Murray, C. (1994). *The bell curve.* New York: The Free Press.

Sigel, R. S. (1996). *Ambition and accommodation: How women view gender relations.* Chicago: University of Chicago Press.

Acknowledgments

The editors are grateful to the American Psychological Association for permission to reprint sociocognitive modules adapted from *Male, Female: The Evolution of Human Sex Differences* (p. 180), by D. C. Geary, 1998, Washington, DC: American Psychological Association, and to the National Council of Teachers of Mathematics for permission to reprint "Principles and Standards for School Mathematics—Electronic Version. Discussion Draft (1998)."

We would like to thank Rebecca W. Giagnacova and Lori Vitko for their assistance in preparation of the manuscript.

part I

Introduction

CHAPTER 1

Causes, Correlates, and Caveats: Understanding the Development of Sex Differences in Cognition

Diane F. Halpern
Simay Ikier

It's really the remnant of anti-American crazy thinking to do this kind of research.

—Gloria Steinem

This is harmful and damaging to our daughters' lives and our mothers' lives, and I'm very angry about it.

—Gloria Allred

These are the respective comments of Gloria Steinem, editor of *Ms. Magazine,* and Gloria Allred, prominent feminist attorney, during their televised interview with John Stossel on the ABC news special *Boys and Girls are Different* (ABC News, 1991). Their hostile and litigious remarks show the intensity of their feelings about the socially sensitive topic of cognitive comparisons between males and females.

SHOULD WE STUDY THE DEVELOPMENT OF COGNITIVE SEX DIFFERENCES?

There are controversies in virtually every field of research. But unlike most other areas in psychology and the other sciences, where the controversies usually concern the research methods and the way results are interpreted, when the topic is sex differences, the controversies include the question of whether the research should even be conducted. Is it simply too dangerous to even ask about sex differences in cognition? Gloria Steinem and Gloria Allred are not alone in their condemnation of this research question. There are many psychologists who agree that research on the development of cognitive sex differences should not be conducted because the results will be damaging to women (Hare-Mustin & Marecek, 1994). The concern that research on cognitive sex differences will be used against women and women's rights needs careful consideration before readers start their journey through the following chapters that dare to ask and seek answers to the many questions about cognitive sex differences.

The intense emotional response against the study of cognitive sex differences needs to be interpreted within the context of our current sociohistorical period. At this time in history, our most fundamental notions of what it means to be female or male are under attack on multiple fronts. In the United States, the affirmative action laws that were designed to correct past discrimination are now being challenged and discarded on the grounds that affirmative action is, itself, discriminatory. Emotions on this topic run high, and it is not unusual to find oneself on the same side of the affirmative action issue as someone else whose politics are the antithesis of one's own. Regardless of the outcome of research on cognitive sex differences, it is likely that the results will be used to argue both for and against the politically provocative topic of affirmative action. In other parts of the world, women are still denied basic human rights such as the right to vote and hold public office, and fair access to education. Throughout the corporate world, women are bumping their heads on glass ceilings and some companies have proposed special career tracks for "mommies." Thus, it is not surprising that spokespersons from the media, sciences, and political arenas are reacting with alarm to any study of the ways in which women and men are similar and different. No discussion of research in cognitive sex differences is complete without also considering its potential use and misuse to advance political agendas.

Even the most fundamental differences between males and females—their complementary roles in reproduction—are being questioned. Up to this point in history, both a female and a male were required to reproduce our species, but with the advent of test-tube babies, the active participation or physical presence of a man and a woman at the moment of conception is no longer necessary. Conception can readily take place in a petri dish, with a laboratory assistant handling the mechanics of uniting a sperm and an egg. Even a computerized robot could place sperm and eggs in a laboratory medium for later transplantation into a woman. But test-tube conceptions are minor harbingers of change. Dolly, the cloned sheep, has revolutionized some of our most basic truths about what it means to be female and male. For the first time in the history of the human race, cloning offers the possibility of asexual, single-parent reproduction. Although, adult females are still needed in the reproductive process because the uterus is an ideal place for the safe development of a cloned fetus, this may soon change making the participation of living humans in the act of procreation completely unnecessary. It is possible that the first cloned human already exists, and if not yet, then it seems likely that this unique individual soon will. Federal bans on cloning research can only drive these experiments underground or into countries where such laws do not exist.

The Women-Have-Less Fallacy

The allegation that women will be damaged by research findings is based on the unstated assumption that there will be a "winner" and a "loser" when male and female comparisons are made, and females will be the losers. As seen in the opening quotes by two prominent feminists, it is implicitly assumed that research on cognitive sex differences will be harmful to women because the data will show that females really are inferior to males. Halpern (2000) called the assumption that research on cognitive sex differences will reveal the true inadequacies of females the "women-have-less fallacy." A fallacy is an error or bias in the thinking process (Halpern, 1996). The fallacy in this example is the persistent (and unfounded) belief that research into the many questions of cognitive sex differences will reveal the cognitive deficits of women, or in other words, that women have "less" of some cognitive abilities than men do. Empirical studies have shown that this fear is unwarranted. A large body of research has documented the fact that for some abilities, there are on-average cognitive sex differences between women and men and, for other abilities, there are no sex differences. Sometimes, the differences favor women and sometimes they favor men, depending on the specific cognitive ability being studied and a host of other moderating variables including the age of the participants, the nature of the task, the historical and social context, and the response format. It seems that human cognition, like love, is a "many splendored thing." Sex differences are found for some of the multiple dimensions of human cognition, but there is no "winning" sex. The fears that women's cognition would emerge as inferior to men's has not been supported in the literature.

We urge readers to avoid the tendency to keep a tally on whether men or women are "ahead" in the cognitive sex differences scoreboard and instead to consider how, when, and why cognitive sex differences are found. A major challenge for every citizen in our increasingly fast-paced, highly technological, global community is the development of human intellect. An understanding of the ways in which females and males are similar and different in their cognitive abilities offers many potential benefits. Psychologists and other educators could use our knowledge of these differences to identify areas where additional or different types of education are needed (e.g., visuospatial skills training) or as a means of understanding the processes and mechanisms that underlie human cognition.

Stereotypes Are Us

Decades of research have documented the damning and ubiquitous effect of self-fulfilling prophecies (Rosenthal, 1966). There are multiple studies showing that researchers often communicate expectations about the participants' performance to participants without the researcher's conscious awareness, and these expectations have a profound effect on the actions, attitudes, and abilities of the person receiving the communication. Doesn't it follow that findings of sex differences will only increase the size of these differences because of the powerful influences of self-fulfilling prophecies? This is a reasonable concern, but it needs to be evaluated against the alternative position that prohibits research into the many questions of sex differences and similarities. Similarities and differences are always studied together because they exist as integrally as two sides of a coin. Researchers use the language of "differences" because of the data analytic techniques that we use, but it is not possible to study similarities without also studying differences, and vice versa. Every student who has taken a basic course in statistics can explain the logic of statistical tests that are designed to reject the null hypothesis and conclude that differences exist. Yet, with careful research and replications, the same experimental designs can be used to conclude that some differences are so small that they are, for all practical purposes, nonexistent.

Stereotypical beliefs about sex differences in cognition do not result from carefully conducted research—they flourish in the absence of any research findings. Sometimes these stereotypes have a basis in fact, which means that they reflect statistical differences between women and men. For example, it is commonly believed that the overwhelming majority of secretaries are females, and in fact, this is true, just as the fact that virtually every head of state in the world is male. Although there have been some strong women leaders in the past, they have always been few in number. Thus, any possible negative effects caused by the tendency to act in ways that make prior beliefs more likely to be true (i.e., self-fulfilling prophecies) can already be found in the absence of research.

Self-fulfilling prophecies can also lead to beneficial effects. If research were to show that everyone's cognitive abilities can improve with appropriate education, then these positive expectations about the outcome of education can be communicated to students and their teachers in ways that will improve learning for everyone. The news is good! All of the cognitive abilities discussed in this book can be improved with education, and everyone (except those who are so profoundly retarded that they are essentially uneducable) can improve. A skilled, educated, and thinking workforce is essential for every country, and none can afford to "write anyone off."

The role of stereotypes is a dominant theme in virtually every discussion of sex differences in cognition. Won't research on cognitive sex differences legitimize false stereotypes about men and women? Steele and his colleagues (1997; Steele & Aronson, 1995) have shown that negative stereotypes can decrease performance on cognitive tests when group membership is made salient (e.g., participants are asked to indicate their sex), the stereotype about one's group is negative (e.g., females are less able in math than males), performance on the test is important to the individual (e.g., scores will be used to determine college admissions), and the test is difficult. These are important studies, but this area of research, known as stereotype threat, is still new and there have been some statistically powerful studies in ecologically valid settings that have failed to find an effect for negative stereotypes (Stricker, 1998). Thus, it is not possible to make any strong conclusions until additional studies are published and psychologists have a better understanding of the way in which stereotype threat operates.

Regardless of the outcomes of this new line of research, it does seem that most of the stereotypes that we have about differences between men and women are relatively accurate (Swim, 1994). In general, people realize that female and male distributions overlap and that effect sizes vary over different sorts of abilities and depend on context variables. Given the surprising validity of most stereotypical beliefs, the fear that research would legitimize false stereotypes or that the knowledge gained from the research would somehow increase the size of any differences is unfounded.

Censorship is Senseless

Sex is a fundamental part of the identity of every individual. It is the primary way we categorize people into groups, and categorization is a basic cognitive activity in information processing. Information about the sex of an individual is implicitly and automatically processed, and it influences the way we think and feel about people. A clever series of experiments that require the rapid categorization of female- and male-related terms shows that these effects operate below the level of consciousness, even in people who honestly believe that they "have no prejudices" (Banaji & Hardin, 1996). Additionally, researchers found that when participants are provided with stereotypical information about fictional characters, the participants used the stereotypes to reduce the information processing demands of a memory task (Macrae, Milne, & Bodenhausen, 1994). The participants who could use their knowledge of stereotypes showed better performance on shared attention tasks than participants who did not have the stereotypes available. Thus, it could be argued that under some circumstances, the use of stereotypes is beneficial because it reduces the cognitive demands of a task. The automatic and unconscious use of stereotypes as categorical information is not meant to imply that stereotypes should be used to discriminate against anyone on the basis of his or her group membership or as an alternative for getting to know people as individuals. Stereotypes about males or females operate like any other categorization process, offering the greatest advantage when we have little personal knowledge about an individual.

Those opposed to research on cognitive sex differences would prefer that psychologists ignore the pervasive effects of one's sex and refrain from investigating the many research questions that are associated with being female or male. Censorship, even self-censorship, will not reduce prejudice or advance our understanding of powerful variables. Furthermore, censorship is not feasible. If researchers who care about social issues of equity and honest research abandon the field, then research on sex differences will be left to those investigators who would use results and interpret findings to advance their own political agenda. Examples of the misuse of research can be found in all extremes of the political spectrum, including advocates of biological politics, political correctness, and any position between or beyond these two extremes.

HOW TO READ AND THINK ABOUT RESEARCH ON SEX DIFFERENCES IN COGNITION

In reading and thinking about research on cognitive sex differences, readers are urged to adopt the amiable skepticism of a critical thinker—to examine the nature and strength of the evidence in support of research conclusions and to evaluate the appropriateness of the experimental design for the question it is being used to answer. We ask that you apply the same rigor in your standards for assessing the quality of research with outcomes that are consistent with your political proclivities as you use for those outcomes you do not like. Here are some caveats to keep in mind as you read and think about research into the many questions of cognitive sex differences.

In thinking about research on cognitive sex differences, two broad categories of variables are important. The category that is easier to conceptualize has to do with the adequacy of the research itself. Does the research design really address the question that is being investigated? The second broad category may be best thought of as everything outside of research design issues. In constructing an explanation, researchers weave explanatory nets where concepts are linked to each other, ideally in a logical way. This sort of explanatory structure is referred to as a nomological net. In thinking about these sorts of issues, it is often necessary to think beyond the research that is presented and to consider what is not included in the studies. Some examples of these two broad categories should help in making them clearer.

Questions Related to Research Design

In evaluating research in cognitive sex differences, there are many ways that the design, execution, and analysis of the research can bias results and interpretation of results. Readers with a strong background in research methods will recognize many of these potential pitfalls.

Are Correlational Designs Being Used to Support Causal Claims?

Sex differences research is almost always correlational in nature because we cannot randomly assign people to male or female categories or to the differential life experiences of a male or female. Although virtually every student of psychology knows the definition of the word "correlation," few are able to recognize the inherent weakness in correlational designs when they occur in natural contexts and seem to "make sense." As most readers know, a correlation between variables means that there is a relationship between them; it does not mean that variations in one of the variables caused the variations in the other variable.

Consider, for example, the finding that children who engage in more spatial activities, like play-time building with construction toys and playing spatial video games, have better spatial skills than those who spend less time engaged in spatial activities. Additionally, we know that boys spend more time in spatial activities than girls do and boys score considerably higher than girls on tests of visuospatial abilities (Baenninger & Newcombe, 1989). Doesn't it seem logical to conclude that boys are better, on average, at spatial tasks *because* they spend more time practicing these skills? To most people, this is a logical connection, and few recognize that this is a classic example of confusing correlation with cause. It is possible that children who are good at spatial skills choose to spend more time at spatial activities than those who are not as skilled. Thus, it may be just as likely that the superior spatial skill caused the additional time spent on spatial activities as the reverse relationship. Of course, other relationships are possible. Perhaps boys play with spatial toys more than girls because they receive more toys that support spatial play (e.g., Legos and building logs) and are better than girls (on average) at visuospatial tasks for some reason unrelated to the nature of their play. There is no way to determine from these data which of these possibilities is the best explanation for the finding that boys score higher on tests of visuospatial skills than girls do.

It is possible to use designs that allow for causal claims, such as the random assignment of participants to conditions, but such research is more likely to be used with nonhuman mammals and in drug and hormone studies than with ecologically valid tests of social hypotheses. Quasi-random designs are often used to infer cause, although causal inferences need to be made cautiously with these designs. For example, adult males who undergo hormone therapy may be compared to those who are not taking hormones, but unless specific drug studies are being conducted, we cannot randomly assign people to hormone therapy groups. Studies that manipulate social variables are usually quasi-experimental designs, which use already existing groups. Most researchers using quasi-experimental designs will ignore the fact that they do not have an appropriate research design to make strong causal claims, so it is left to the reader to be vigilant for this sort of oversight.

Is There a Strong Theoretical Basis for the Research?

Unfortunately, much of the research that investigates sex differences in cognition is of the "let's see if there is a difference" variety. This atheoretical approach is then followed with an "explanatory story" that is designed to make sense post hoc out of the findings. The rationale for any study should be clearly stated in the introduction, and ideally, when the study is proposed. There is nothing wrong with "fishing expeditions" as long as the researcher uses unexpected findings as the starting point for further studies that are designed to confirm or disconfirm a hypothesis that was suggested from an earlier study. A fishing expedition with a post hoc explanation of the finding needs multiple replications before it can be considered seriously. A related problem occurs when researchers get results that are opposite to what had been predicted before the study was conducted. Such unexpected results could be the signal for a new breakthrough that will change the direction of the field, or it could be the result of unsound, sloppy, or biased experiments. When research results are contrary to what was predicted by the dominant theory, the burden falls to the researcher to explain the inconsistencies. Paradigm shifts do occur, but we need to find consistent inconsistencies over time and across different studies for such a shift. This brings us to the next problem.

Are the Research Results Generalizable and Replicable?

One of the outcomes of sex differences research is that the results attract a great deal of media attention, which means that the results make their way into the belief systems of many people who have little or no understanding of the scientific method. For much of the general public, results from studies of sex differences become polarized into two categories—true for males and true for females—which in turn may make them think about and act differentially toward males and females. Few in the general public will consider the extent to which the findings can be generalized to all females and all males.

A good example of the problem of generalizability can be seen in the media coverage of the finding that there are many times more preadolescent males than females who are identified as mathematically precocious (Benbow, 1988). Mathematically precocious preteens are an interesting group of youngsters, but they are not representative of all boys or all girls. The sex differences among those who score in the middle ranges on mathematical achievement tests are much smaller than those found at the highest ends. Yet, many news reporters and their readers concluded that there are large sex differences in mathematical achievement in general, a conclusion that is not warranted given the use of extremely high scoring groups. Pronouncements about male and female abilities usually overlook the fact that there are exceptions to findings that are based on group means. A more accurate conclusion is that there are females with exceptional talent in mathematics, but there are fewer females than there are males in this elite group.

Cross-cultural research highlights the generalization bias by showing that the findings we assume to be universal often vary across cultures. We need to include various cultures in any study where we want to know about males and females (Best & Williams, 1993) to control for the effects of other factors such as socioeconomic development, religion, or any culture-specific stereotypes about males and females. Similarly, as the developmental approach that is taken in the following chapters show, a finding can also be specific to an age group, a context, a mode of presentation of stimuli, or the kind of instructions given in an experiment.

Are Comparable, Appropriately Standardized Instruments Being Used Across Groups?

When investigating the possibility of similarities and differences between the sexes, it is important that the materials be equally familiar to the members in each group and at a comparable level of difficulty. Although this may seem like a relatively easy condition to satisfy, in fact, the lack of comparable materials is a confounding variable in many studies. For example, if we want to study the development of verbal abilities in boys and girls across different language groups, it is extremely difficult to devise comparable instruments because words appear with different frequencies in different languages and many words have different connotations that vary across languages. Additionally, if a test is standardized on one group, for example children in the United States, it cannot be assumed to be equally valid or reliable if it is used for another group of children in a different country.

The problem of misuse of standardized instruments in studies of cognitive sex differences can be seen in Lynn's (1994) claim that females score lower on standardized intelligence tests. Standardized intelligence tests, as the name implies, are developed through repeated administration with a large sample from the population for which it is intended. The most frequently used intelligence tests, for example, the Weschler Adult Intelligence Scale, Revised (WAIS-R), were standardized so that they do not to show overall sex differences. During test development, any question that favored one sex was either discarded or balanced with a question that favored the other sex. Lynn (1994) showed his misunderstanding of standardization when he used a test that was standardized to show no sex differences to conclude that males score higher on these tests, and thus males are more intelligent. He then used this conclusion to further state that the reason males are smarter than females is that males have larger (and therefore superior) brains.

Are Conclusions Supported by Research Results?

Lynn's (1984) long leap from results, even if they had been valid, to brain size is unsupported. Astute readers will be quick to point out that even if men scored higher on intelligence tests and had larger brains, these are correlational data that do not permit any causal links between these two variables. Lynn failed to consider the fact that overall brain size includes brain areas that are not directly related to intelligence, so gross overall measures of brain size are not a quantification of the neural basis of intelligence. For example, recent research shows that males have a greater volume of cerebrospinal fluid and white matter (long axons). Female brains are denser in gray matter (neuronal cell tissue and dendrites) (Gur et al., 1999) and have larger and more bulbous corpus callosa, indicating better connectivity between the hemispheres (Allen, Richey, Chai, & Gorski, 1991). Thus, overall brain size does not differentiate between those structures that underlie cognition and those that do not, and in fact, a single measure of brain size misses the theoretically most important structural differences in female and male brains. In thinking about the results of research, it is important to consider how well the data support the conclusion.

Questions Related to the Conceptualization of Research

It is easier to look for routine problems in the design and execution of research than it is to consider the larger issues that relate to the way the research is conceptualized—the theoretical framework that drives the study in the first place and the way results are explained. Some examples follow.

Is the Theory That Is Being Tested Falsifiable?

This is a critically important question to ask about any research, but it is also easy to overlook this question because the researcher is not likely to mention it anywhere in the study. The criticism of unfalsifiable research has been leveled at some of the studies used to support evolutionary theories of cognitive sex differences. Evolutionary theories are very popular at this time because they offer a new way of thinking about old problems in psychology. The underlying premise for evolutionary theories is that humans have spent most of our time on earth in hunter–gatherer societies, and those skills and abilities that were adaptive in these societal arrangements can be used to explain modern cognitive sex differences. Males were the hunters in these societies, and thus had to travel long distances to track prey. Therefore, males developed neurocognitive systems that supported good spatial skills. Females, on the other hand, were responsible for childcare and the gathering of crops, so they developed superior skills for these tasks (e.g., good spatial memories). One criticism of this theory is that regardless of the empirical results from any study, it is always possible to explain how the results could have been useful to hunter–gatherer societies.

Cornell (1997) asked readers to imagine a society where the women were stronger, more aggressive, and more sexually active than the men. In short, the opposite of what we find in contemporary society. Could these opposite results be accommodated with evolutionary explanations? Her answer is a resounding "Yes!" After all, the females care for the young while the males are off hunting, so it is left to the females to protect the young. Naturally, they would be expected to be more aggressive, and because they are responsible for the children and their reproductive success depends on the quality of their mating partner, women would also be expected to be more sexually active because they have more to gain from successful reproductive mating. If the theory being investigated cannot be falsified, regardless of the experimental results, there is no test of the theory.

Has the Practical Size of the Effect Been Considered?

In any experiment, there can be a statistically significant difference between two groups, the effect size can account for a large proportion of the variability in the data (a statistical concept), and the finding can be of little practical significance. For example, when an experiment has good statistical power (it will detect differences between groups of subjects even when the differences are small), the more important question about the results is what do they mean in the real world? Interestingly, we often do not even know how to translate experimental findings into real world effects. Consider, for example, studies that use reaction times as measures of information processing speed or efficiency (e.g., Loring-Meier & Halpern, 1999). What does it mean in terms of everyday functioning to find that males (or females) perform some tasks fractions of a second faster than the other sex? Do these fractions of a second add up throughout the day so that, on average, males perform many more of these tasks than females or do the fractions of a second get "lost" in the many daily tasks that we all perform? These are important questions that are rarely considered.

Has the Researcher Confused "What Is" With "What Could Be"?

This is another question that is rarely addressed in studies of cognitive sex differences. Consider, for example, the finding that girls showed superior verbal learning when compared to boys (Kramer, Delis, Kaplan, O'Donnell, & Prifitera, 1997). In this study, the girls recalled more words from a categorizable list under a variety of delay conditions. The girls also were more likely to use clustering in free recall, an advanced strategy that showed differences in how the children learned and recalled the word lists. The unprompted use of semantic clustering in free recall by the girls does provide evidence for a superior verbal strategy, but we do not know if the boys would have performed as well as the girls if they had better told to use semantic clustering at recall. Perhaps the difference in the girl–boy performance on this task could be eliminated by instructing the boys to use the strategy that the girls used without prompting. Thus, we do not know if the finding that girls recalled more words than the boys (what is) would have also been true if the boys had been told what recall strategy to use (what could be).

Are There Research Findings That Are Not Being Reported in the Literature?

This is a question about what is missing. The difficulty in thinking about what is not present is that there is no way to determine if there is a systematic bias in what does not exist. Consider the following two possibilities:

1. Only a small percentage of the hundreds of thousands of studies in the research literature compare females and males because most researchers are not concerned with sex differences. In fact, an equal number of males and females are often used in experimental and control groups to "control for" any sex difference effects. It is impossible to know how many of these studies found sex differences, but the researchers never reported the differences or never bothered to test for differences between females and males. On the other hand, if every study routinely looked for sex differences, then a large number would be found "just by chance," thereby inflating the importance of sex as a variable.

2. It is also true that there are probably many studies that did not find sex differences and these failures to reject the null hypothesis were either omitted from the published study or never seriously considered for publication. This is the familiar "file drawer problem," so named in reference to a hypothetical number of studies that are stashed in file drawers, unpublished. Meta-analytic reviews of the literature often contain a file drawer "fail-safe" value—the statistically derived number of studies that found nonsignificance and were never published that would need to exist to alter a conclusion that there really are differences between males and females.

Is an Appeal to Ignorance Being Made?

An "appeal to ignorance" is another common thinking fallacy (Halpern, 1996). It is essentially a way of explaining a research outcome by saying that because we didn't find support for the explanation we were looking for (i.e., we do not have information, we are ignorant), then the explanation must be one that we did not look for. An example should help in understanding this. Consider research that finds sex differences in the performance on some test, for example, the quantitative section of the test used for admissions to graduate school—the Graduate Record Examination (GRE). Suppose further that researchers attempt to explain the finding that males score higher on this test by showing that males take more mathematics courses and the differences in course taking can account for the sex differences on the test. This is a reasonable hypothesis, except that it fails to work; even when students are matched on the number of mathematics courses they take in college, males score higher on this test (Willingham & Cole, 1997). Thus, based on this study, we cannot explain why males score higher on the GRE-Q. In other words, we are "ignorant" as to the cause of the difference.

There are some researchers who used the failure of social variables to explain group differences as evidence that the cause must be biological. This is essentially the argument used by Herrnstein and Murray (1994) in their explosive text, *The Bell Curve*. These authors did not study or manipulate biological variables, but concluded that biology is responsible for group differences in intelligence tests because they could not identify social variables that were responsible. In thinking critically about research on cognitive sex differences, readers need to keep this fallacy in mind as there are no clues in the research report to suggest that biological variables are being used as an explanation when these variables were never included in the study.

Are Simple Answers Being Offered for Complicated Questions?

It is a basic principle of the scientific method that simple answers are preferred over complex ones. Unfortunately, human cognition is too complex for simple explanations. Researchers often omit contradictory findings from their published reports, thus giving the impression that the explanation they are presenting is the only correct one. For example, there are many studies showing that some cognitive abilities fluctuate across the menstrual cycle in accord with monthly fluctuations in estrogen and progesterone (Hampson, 1990). These studies rarely cite any of the literature that shows the pervasive effects of stereotypes on performance, such as the studies conducted by Steele (1997) that were described earlier. Similarly, the papers that investigate the effects of stereotypes on performance usually omit any references to the hormone studies. Naïve readers would come away from any of these studies believing that they have "the answer" to the many questions about cognitive sex differences because findings that would contradict the explanation that was provided in the study were omitted. Human cognition is both biological and social in nature. There are no simple, unidimensional answers for complicated, multifaceted questions.

A PSYCHO-BIO-SOCIAL FRAMEWORK

The nature versus nurture dichotomy is ages old. Although many in the general public will argue if nature or nurture is responsible for any outcome, for most psychologists and educators, the question we pose is, "what proportion of the variance in cognitive sex differences can be attributed to nature or biological influences and what proportion can be attributed to nurture or socialization influences?" Most researchers will expect some proportional division between biological and social variables in which the numbers add to 100 percent, in part because this sort of partitioning of variance comes from the statistical techniques that we most frequently use. The problem with "the proportion of explained variance question" is that it assumes that "there is a number waiting to be discovered." It is as though researchers believe that there is a single true value that exists, and if we are clever in how we design our research, we will find that number.

There are many reasons why we cannot split causal mechanisms into two parts and assign a numerical value to each. Even "simple" distinctions like dividing variables into biological and environmental categories are impossible. Consider, for example, the fact that there are differences in female and male brains. The differences in brain structures could have been caused, enhanced, or decreased by environmental stimuli. Nutrition, for example, is an environmental factor with biological and behavioral consequences; a diet deficient in protein, especially in first year of life, will substantially reduce overall intellectual levels and affect development of brain structures, thus blurring the distinction between biology and environment (Mascie-Taylor, 1993). Brain size and structures remain plastic throughout life. Ungerleider (1995) used brain-imaging techniques to show changes in cortical representations that occurred after specific experiences. What we learn influences structures like dendritic branching and cell size; brain architectures in turn, support certain skills and abilities, which may lead us to select additional experiences. The interface between experience and biology is seamless. Biology and environment are as inseparable as conjoined twins who share a common heart. A psychobiosocial framework provides a more integrated way of thinking about a holistic process.

We are advocating for a psychobiosocial model of cognitive sex differences to replace the nature–nurture dichotomy. Any model of the multiple, sequentially interacting variables that cause and effect changes in hormone levels, brain structures and organization, the environments we select, and those that are correlated with our genetic predispositions, must recognize the way psychological, biological, and social variables operate reciprocally on each other. The nature–nurture dichotomy is, and always has been, false. Consider, for example, learning, which is both a social and a biological event. We are predisposed by our biology to learn some skills more readily than others; we are provided with different sorts of learning options; and we select experiences from our environment. Who can say where social variables turn into biological ones? It is because we are unable to label any variable as "fully nurture" or "fully nature" that we have eschewed the practice of using the term "gender " to refer to social variables and "sex" to refer to biological variables. We believe that the use of different labels to signal different types of influences only serves to reify the nature–nurture dichotomy and does not serve the field well. Unfortunately, there is no word in the English language that refers to the transaction of nature and nurture, but, despite the limitations of language, we caution against thinking that they are separable concepts.

Cognitive abilities do not progress independently of socioemotional development. Language and other cognitive skills are developed through human interactions and these interactions include emotional content communicated in a social setting. Thus, a full understanding of cognitive sex differences will also need to include the development of emotional understanding, which may be the first language to develop. In a recent study of preschool children, Bosacki and Moore (2000) found a positive relationship between scores on verbal skills tests and the ability to recognize and label emotions. Interestingly, this relationship was stronger for boys than for girls, suggesting that some variables might be more important in the development of boys' cognition than in girls' cognition, and vice versa. This is yet another demonstration of the general principle that there are multiple answers for a phenomenon as complex as sex and cognition.

SIMILARITIES AND DIFFERENCES

Females and males are similar in some ways and different in others. Thus, the better question is how and how much are males and females similar and different in their cognitive abilities. But the most theoretically important question is "why?" In reading the following chapters, keep in mind the familiar question about whether a glass is half full or half empty and the way this paradox applies to research in cognitive sex differences. The "half-full–half-empty" dispute is seen most clearly in cross-cultural studies where, inevitably, both cross-cultural similarities and differences are found.

Lummis and Stevenson (1990) investigated sex differences in mathematics and reading in Chinese, Japanese, and American children. In order to chart the development throughout the elementary school years, they used three age groups: kindergarten, first-year, and fifth-year elementary school children. Children in these three cultures were administered comparable and reliable tests of mathematical and reading ability and other cognitive abilities. The children's mothers were also questioned about whether they believed that their children were better at mathematics or reading and to indicate whether in general boys or girls are better at these tasks. Performance on cognitive tests showed no sex differences in reading ability, solving basic mathematical operations, knowledge of numbers, or mathematical and spatial concepts. But, boys outperformed girls in solving word problems, visual estimation of quantity, and visual transformations of geometric forms or scenes, which the researchers considered applications of mathematical concepts, and girls scored higher than the boys in coding, verbal memory, and auditory memory. Boys also had higher scores on tests of general information and spatial ability. Although the relative scores for the boys and girls were the same within each country, the results across countries showed differences in absolute achievement levels.

The mothers in all three countries rated girls as better in reading and boys as better in mathematics. Yet, there were no performance differences on the reading tests that were used and only selected differences in mathematics. Thus, the mothers across all the cultures had similar beliefs about the cognitive abilities of girls and boys, and only some of these beliefs were supported by actual differences in test performance. This complex pattern of results can be used to support the position that culture is important in determining cognitive sex differences or that it is not important depending on whether the reader focuses on within country or between country results. We hope that readers can see the glass as *both* half empty and half full as they read the following chapters. The study of cognitive sex differences is a fascinating area of scholarship that offers the possibility of advancing knowledge and providing new insights on individual and group differences and similarities in how we think and learn. Sex is only one of many ways in which people differ. We hope that through the study of sex differences and similarities that people will become more appreciative of the value of human variability. We also hope that one important message will come through to readers: We do not need to be the same to be equal.

REFERENCES

ABC News Special Presentation. (1991). *Boys and girls are different: Men, women and the sex difference.* New York: American Broadcasting Corporation.

Allen, L. S., Richey, M. F., Chai, Y. M., & Gorski, R. A. (1991). Sex differences in the corpus callosum of the living human being. *Journal of Neuroscience, 11,* 933–942.

Baenninger, M., & Newcombe, N. (1989). The role of experience in spatial test performance: A meta-analysis. *Sex Roles, 20,* 327–344.

Banaji, M. R., & Hardin, C. D. (1996). Automatic stereotyping. *Psychological Science, 7,* 136–141.

Benbow, C. P. (1988). Sex differences in mathematical reasoning ability in intellectually talented preadolescents: Their nature, effects, and possible causes. *Behavioral and Brain Sciences, 11,* 169–232.

Best, D. L., & Williams, J. E. (1993). A Cross-cultural viewpoint. In A. E. Beall & R. J. Sternberg (Eds.), *The psychology of gender* (pp. 215–248). New York: Guilford Press.

Bosacki, S. L., & Moore, C. (2000). Preschoolers' understanding of simple and complex emotions: Links with gender and language. Manuscript submitted for publication.

Cornell, D. G. (1997). Post hoc explanation is not prediction: Commentary on J. Archer. *American Psychologist, 52,* 1380.

Gur, R. C., Turetsky, B. I., Matsui, M., Yan, M., Bilker, W., Hughett, P., & Gur, R. E. (1999). Sex differences in brain gray and white matter in healthy young adults: Correlations with cognitive performance. *Journal of Neuroscience, 19,* 4065–4072.

Halpern, D. F. (1996). *Thought and knowledge: An introduction to critical thinking* (3rd ed.). Mahwah, NJ: Lawrence Erlbaum.

Halpern, D. F. (2000). *Sex differences in cognitive abilities* (3rd ed.). Mahwah, NJ: Lawrence Erlbaum.

Hampson, E. (1990). Estrogen-related variations in human spatial and articulatory-motor skills. *Psychoneuroendocrinology, 15,* 97–111.

Hare-Mustin, R. T., & Marecek, J. (1994). Asking the right questions: Feminist psychology and sex differences. *Feminism & Psychology, 4*(4), 531–537.

Herrnstein, R. J., & Murray, C. (1994). *The bell curve: Intelligence and class structure in American life.* New York: Freeman.

Kramer, J. H., Delis, D. C., Kaplan, E., O'Donnell, L., & Prifitera, A. (1997). Developmental sex differences in verbal learning. *Neuropsychology, 11*(4), 577–584.

Loring-Meier, S., & Halpern, D. (1999). Sex differences in visuospatial working memory: Components of cognitive processing. *Psychonomic Bulletin and Review, 6,* 464–471.

Lummis, M., & Stevenson, H. W. (1990). Gender differences in belief and achievement: A cross-cultural study. *Developmental Psychology, 26*(2), 254–263.

Lynn, R. (1994). Sex differences in intelligence and brain size: A paradox resolved. *Personality and Individual Differences, 17,* 257–271.

Mascie-Taylor, C. G. N. (1993). How do social, biological, and genetic factors contribute to individual differences in cognitive abilities? In T. J. Bouchard, Jr., & P. Propping (Eds.), *Twins as a tool of behavioral genetics: Life sciences research report* (pp. 53–65). New York: Wiley.

Macrae, C. N., Milne, A. B., & Bodenhausen, G. V. (1994). Stereotypes as energy-saving devices: A peek inside the cognitive tool box. *Journal of Personality and Social Psychology, 66*(1), 37–47.

Rosenthal, R. (1966). *Experimenter effects in behavioral research.* New York: Appleton-Century-Croft.

Steele, C. M. (1997). A threat in the air: How stereotypes shape intellectual identity and performance. *American Psychologist, 52,* 613–629.

Steele, C. M., & Aronson, J. (1995). Stereotype threat and the intellectual test performance of African Americans. *Journal of Personality and Social Psychology, 69,* 797–811.

Stricker, L. J. (1998). *Inquiring about examinee's ethnicity and sex: Effects on AP Calculus AB Examination performance* (Report No. 98-1). New York: The College Board.

Swim, J. K. (1994). Perceived versus meta-analytic effect sizes: An assessment of the accuracy of gender stereotypes. *Journal of Personality and Social Psychology, 66,* 21–36.

Ungerleider, L-G. (1995, November 3). Functional brain imaging studies of cortical mechanisms for memory. *Science, 270,* 769–775.

Willingham, W. W., & Cole, N. S. (1997). *Gender and fair assessment.* Mahwah, NJ: Lawrence Erlbaum.

part II

Explanatory Constructs

CHAPTER 2

Sexual Selection and Sex Differences in Social Cognition

David C. Geary

For the most part, the psychological study of cognitive sex differences has been an empirically driven endeavor, that is, sex differences were found on certain cognitive measures and the field has coalesced around these findings. Traditionally, the associated studies and theoretical models have focused on the advantage of men in the general domains of spatial and mathematical cognition and the advantage of women in verbal cognition (e.g., chapter 6; Halpern, 1992). The search for the origin of these sex differences has sometimes focused on biological factors, particularly sex hormones (chapter 3) (Kimura, 1999). Most theories, however, have focused on presumed culturally mediated (e.g., parental socialization) differences in the activities and experiences of boys and girls and later of men and women (chapter 7) (Baenninger & Newcombe, 1995; Eagly, 1987). The goal here is to provide a unifying framework based on the principles of sexual selection for incorporating hormonal, experiential, as well as evolutionary influences on human cognitive sex differences.

Sexual selection is an advantaged theoretical perspective for studying cognitive and other sex differences, for many reasons. The ultimate (evolutionary) and proximate (here and now, such as sex hormones) mechanisms associated with sexual selection have been studied in hundreds of species and are well understood (Andersson, 1994; Darwin, 1871). Basically, sexual selection provides a theoretical framework for understanding human cognitive sex differences in the context of sex differences found in other species and, at the same time, allows for hormonal, developmental, and experiential influences on the expression of these differences. Sex differences in social cognition will be discussed to illustrate the utility of the perspective of sexual selection. Discussion of a wide range of cognitive sex differences from the perspective of sexual and natural selection is provided by Geary (1998), and by Pinker (1994) for language, Gaulin (1992, 1995; see also Geary, 1995) for space, and Geary (1996) for mathematics. Before sex differences in social cognition are discussed, a brief overview of the basic mechanisms of sexual selection is in order and presented in the following section. The second section provides an evolutionary taxonomy of sociocognitive modules and the final section provides an overview of sexual selection as related to sex differences in these sociocognitive competencies.

SEXUAL SELECTION

Sexual selection refers to the processes associated with competition with members of the same sex and species (intrasexual competition) over mates and the processes associated with choosing mates (intersexual choice) (Darwin, 1871). Depending on reproductive and social dynamics, sexual selection can be manifest in terms of male–male competition, female–female competition, female choice, male choice, or some combination (Andersson, 1994; Geary, 1998). The following section briefly outlines these basic dynamics, whereas the second provides a few examples of intrasexual competition.

Mating or Parenting?

The dynamics of sexual selection are driven by the degree to which females and males focus their reproductive effort on parenting or on mating (Clutton-Brock, 1991; Trivers, 1972; Williams, 1966). The sex difference in reproductive effort, in turn, is related to sex differences in the potential rate of reproduction and to social and ecological influences on mating opportunities, in particular the operational sex ratio (OSR) (Clutton-Brock & Vincent, 1991; Emlen & Oring, 1977; Krebs & Davies, 1993). Reproductive rates and the OSR are related. They are described in separate sections below.

Reproductive Rates

Any sex difference in the potential rate of reproduction can create a sex difference in the relative emphasis on mating or on parenting. Most generally, the sex with the higher potential rate of reproduction invests more in mating effort than in parental effort, whereas the sex with the lower rate of reproduction invests more in parental effort than in mating effort (Clutton-Brock & Vincent, 1991). This pattern arises because members of the sex with the higher potential rate of reproduction can rejoin the mating pool more quickly than can members of the opposite sex and it is often in their reproductive best interest to do so (Parker & Simmons, 1996).

For species with internal gestation and obligatory postpartum female care, as with suckling in mammalian species, the rate with which females can produce offspring is considerably lower than the potential rate of reproduction of conspecific males (Clutton-Brock, 1991). At the same time, internal gestation and the need for postnatal care creates a strong female bias in mammals toward parental investment and results in a sex difference in the benefits of seeking additional mates (Trivers, 1972). Males can benefit, reproductively, from seeking and obtaining additional mates, whereas females cannot. Thus, the sex difference in reproductive rate, combined with offspring that can be effectively raised by the female, creates the potential for large female–male differences in the mix of mating and parenting, and this difference is realized in 95–97% of mammalian species. In these species, females can provide the majority of parental care effectively, and do so (Clutton-Brock, 1991). Female care, in turn, frees males to invest in mating effort, which typically takes the form of male–male competition over access to mates or for control of the resources (e.g., territory) that females need to raise their offspring.

Operational Sex Ratio

The OSR is defined as the ratio of sexually active males to sexually active females in a given breeding population at a given point in time, and is related to the rate of reproduction (Emlen & Oring, 1977). For instance, in a population where there are as many sexually mature females as there are sexually mature males—an actual sex ratio of 1:1—any sex difference in the rate of reproduction will skew the OSR. As noted, for mammalian species, males necessarily have a faster potential rate of reproduction and thus there are typically more sexually receptive males than sexually receptive females in most populations. This biased OSR creates the conditions that lead to intense male–male competition over access to a limited number of potential mates. Although these patterns are most evident in mammals, they are also found in many species of bird, fish, and reptile (Andersson, 1994), but are not limited to males.

When females have a faster rate of reproduction than males, then female–female competition is often more salient than male–male competition. As an example, consider the red-necked phalarope (*Phalaropus lobatus*), a polyandrous shorebird (i.e., females potentially have more than one mate) (Reynolds, 1987; Reynolds & Székely, 1997). In this species, males provide most or all of the parental care, specifically, the building of the nest and the incubation of the eggs; the fledglings fend for themselves once hatched. The high level of paternal care makes it possible for the female to pursue other mating opportunities, and she typically does. Once the clutch is laid, the female often leaves in search of another male. The crucial feature of this mating system is that females are ready to produce another clutch about one week after laying their first clutch, whereas the incubation time for males is close to three weeks. The result is that the effective rate of reproduction is potentially higher in females than in males and the

OSR is skewed such that there are typically more sexually receptive females than males at any given point in time. The limiting factor in the number of offspring that can be produced by any given female is thus the number of unmatched males, that is, males available to incubate her eggs.

In theory, the females of this species should show many of the characteristics that are typically associated with the males of species in which males compete for mates and, in fact, they do. Red-necked phalarope females are slightly larger than conspecific males, have a brighter plumage, fight with other females for access to males, and, once paired, guard their mates against competitors; males, in contrast, rarely threaten or attack one another (Reynolds, 1987). Moreover, the evolutionary consequences of female–female competition in this species are the same as those found in species with intense male–male competition. The most important of these consequences—and the principal force driving the evolution of female–female competition in the red-necked phalarope—is that the reproductive success of females is more variable than the reproductive success of males. Some females produce two clutches per breeding season, each with a different male, and many other females go unmated; unmated males, in comparison, are rare. In short, females who capitalize on the high level of paternal care produce more offspring than females who assist the male in clutch incubation. As long as the male can effectively incubate the eggs himself, selection—through differential reproduction—favors females who pursue and are successful in gaining additional mates; that is, females who invest more in mating effort than in parental effort.

It appears that the same basic mechanisms, that is a sex difference in potential reproductive rate and a skewed OSR, are the ultimate sources of the male focus on mating effort and the female focus on parental effort in the vast majority of mammalian species (Emlen & Oring, 1977; Parker & Simmons, 1996). However, the biology of internal fertilization and gestation are not the only factors that influence the potential rate of reproduction and the OSR in mammals, social and ecological factors are sometimes important as well. As an example, male callitrichid monkeys (*Callithrix*) have a higher potential rate of reproduction than conspecific females do. However, shared territorial defense, concealed ovulation, female-on-female aggression that drives away the males' potential mating partners, and twinning negate this physiologically based sex difference and result in a more balanced OSR, monogamy, and high levels of paternal investment (Dunbar, 1995; Geary, 2000).

In any case, the dynamics of sexual selection in humans, as with other species, turns on the degree to which women and men focus their reproductive efforts on mating or on parenting, in particular whether parental investment is evident in men. In fact, there is evidence that men throughout the world invest in the well-being of their children, albeit not to the same degree as women do (Geary, 2000). Paternal investment, in turn, makes sexual selection in humans more complicated than is the case in most other mammals. Not only are the standard features of male–male competition and female choice evident in humans, but so are female–female competition and male choice. With respect to sex differences in social cognition and their development, male–male competition and female–female competition appear to be more relevant than female choice and male choice and thus the following section focuses on intrasexual competition rather than on intersexual choice.

Intrasexual Competition

Intrasexual competition over mates, whether it is male–male competition or female–female competition, will result in the evolutionary emergence of sex differences for those traits that facilitate this competition (Andersson, 1994; Darwin, 1871). Studies of intrasexual competition have revealed that the associated sex differences can be physical, behavioral, or cognitive (including neural) and only affect those features actually involved in the competition (Geary, 1998). Moreover, these sex differences are often associated with developmental sex differences, illustrated as follows (Geary, 1999).

One of the more common expressions of intrasexual competition, as with the red-necked phalarope, involves physical threats and fights over access to mates or for control of the territory that members of the opposite sex need to raise offspring (e.g., nesting spots). The result is typically a sex difference in physical size and aggressiveness. The polygynous ruff (*Machetes pugnax*) provides one example of such competition among males and is illustrated in Figure 2.1. Of this species, Darwin stated:

The [polygynous] Ruff . . . is notorious for his extreme pugnacity; and in the spring, the males, which are considerably larger than the females, congregate day after day at a particular spot, where the females propose to lay their eggs. The fowlers discover these spots by the turf being trampled somewhat bare. Here they fight very much like gamecocks, seizing each other with their beaks and striking with their wings. The great ruff of feathers round the neck is then erected, and according to Col. Montagu "sweeps the ground as a shield to defend the more tender parts;" and this is the only instance known to me in the case of birds, of any structure serving as a shield. (Darwin, 1871, Part II, p. 41)

Sometimes the competition is more behavioral than physical, as is found in most species of bowerbird (Gilliard, 1969). In about three out of four of these species, the principal focus of male–male competition and female choice is bower building. The bower of one such species (*Chlamydera maculata*) was described by Darwin (1871) and is shown in Figure 2.2. More recently, the bower building of a related species, the satin bowerbird (*Ptilonorhynchus violaceus*), has been extensively studied by Borgia and his colleagues (Borgia, 1985a, 1985b; Collis & Borgia, 1992). These studies indicate that female choice of mating partners is strongly influenced by the complexity and symmetry of the male's bower, as well as by the number of decorations around the bower. Males thus compete

Figure 2.1. Physical male–male competition in the ruff (*Machetes pugnax*). From *The Descent of Man, and Selection in Relation to Sex* (Part II, p. 42), by C. Darwin, 1871, London: John Murray.

with one another through bower building and through the destruction of their competitors' bowers (Borgia, 1985a). The result is that about one out of six males sires most of the offspring, and these are the males with the most elaborate bowers and males who avoid (through male–male fighting) the destruction of their bower.

For satin bowerbirds, and many other species in which the nature of intrasexual competition differs, sex differences are also evident in growth patterns and activities during development (Darwin, 1871; Geary, 1998). These developmental sex differences directly reflect and are preparation for intrasexual competition. Male satin bowerbirds, for instance, mature many years after females have matured. During development, "young males spend a great deal of time observing older males at their bower, and practice bower building and display behaviors when the owner is absent from the bower site" (Collis & Borgia, 1992, p. 422). Young males also engage in play fighting, which provides the experience needed for dominance-related encounters in adulthood. The delayed maturation of male satin bowerbirds provides the opportunity to practice and refine the bower construction and physical competition skills that will be needed in adulthood. For this opportunity to be achieved, there must be inherent biases in the types of information young male bowerbirds attend, such as the activities of mature males and the social behaviors they are likely to imitate, suggesting some accompanying sex differences in brain and cognition.

In fact, in some species, intrasexual competition can be more dependent on cognitive and brain specializations than on behavioral or physical specializations. Gaulin and Fitzgerald have provided one of the best-documented examples of the influence of intrasexual competition on such differences (Gaulin, 1992; Gaulin & Fitzgerald, 1986, 1989); bird song is another example (Ball & Hulse, 1998; Hauser, 1996). The approach in these studies is to compare evolutionarily related species—those with a recent common ancestor—of voles (small rodents, *Microtus*). The comparison of species with a recent common ancestor is important because existing differences across related species cannot be attributed to their distant evolutionary history. Rather, these differences are more likely to reflect current differences in reproductive strategy or adaptations to different ecological niches (e.g., Grant & Grant, 1993). The primary difference across these species of vole is that some are monogamous and some polygynous. By comparing related species of monogamous and polygynous voles, Gaulin and Fitzgerald have studied the effects of sexual selection—which will operate more strongly in

Figure 2.2. Bower building and behavioral male–male competition in the bowerbird (*Chlamydera maculata*). From *The Descent of Man, and Selection in Relation to Sex* (Part II, p. 70), by C. Darwin, 1871, London: John Murray.

polygynous than in monogamous species (Andersson, 1994; Darwin, 1871; Geary, 1998)—on sex differences in spatial cognition and at least one underlying brain region.

In the polygynous meadow vole (*Microtus pennsylvanicus*), males compete with one another by searching for and attempting to mate with females who are dispersed throughout the habitat, rather than through physical contest. Prairie and pine voles (*Microtus ochrogaster, Microtus pinetorum*), in comparison, are monogamous and males do not search for additional mates, once paired. For meadow voles, intrasexual competition—through differential reproduction—will favor males who court the most females, which is possible only through an expansion of the home range. Thus, this form of male–male competition should result in larger home ranges for male than female meadow voles but no such sex difference should be evident in prairie or pine voles. Indeed, field studies indicate male meadow voles have home ranges that cover four to five times the area of the home ranges of females, but only during the breeding season and only in adulthood (Gaulin, 1992; Gaulin & Fitzgerald, 1986). The latter pattern indicates that the sex difference in the size of the home range is related to the reproductive strategy of the male (i.e., searching for females) and suggests that this difference is mediated by sex hormones. As predicted, the home ranges of male and female prairie and pine voles overlap and do not differ in size (Gaulin & Fitzgerald, 1986).

The sex difference in the size of the home range means that male meadow voles should have better developed spatial abilities—those abilities needed for navigation (Shepard, 1994)—than female meadow voles and male prairie and pine voles. Moreover, there should be no sex difference in the spatial abilities of monogamous prairie and pine voles. A series of laboratory and field studies confirmed these predictions. The polygynous male meadow vole shows better navigational skills than conspecific females and better navigational skills than the males of evolutionarily related monogamous species (Gaulin, 1992; Gaulin & Fitzgerald, 1986, 1989). An equally important finding is that this same pattern of differences is found for the overall and relative volume of the hippocampus, which supports spatial cognition, among other cognitive abilities (Jacobs, Gaulin, Sherry, & Hoffman, 1990). The hippocampus of male meadow voles is larger than that of female meadow voles and larger than that of male prairie and pine voles.

Although these examples have focused on male–male competition, the same effect is evident for female–female competition. Intrasexual competition results in the evolutionary elaboration and an hormonally influenced proximate expression of those traits associated with this competition, whether the traits are physical, behavioral, cognitive and neural, or some combination (Andersson, 1994; Geary, 1998). Moreover, based on the principles of sexual selection, sex differences are predicted in only those areas that are directly related to intersexual choice and intrasexual competition, although natural selection could result in sex differences as well. Enhanced spatial abilities in males are not expected in all species, only species in which males have larger territories or use these territories in more complex ways than conspecific females, which includes humans, at least for navigation in unfamiliar territory (e.g., Geary, 1998). When females have larger territories or use territories in more complex ways than males, a female advantage is expected.

Studies of the brown-headed cowbird (*Molothrus ater ater*) nicely illustrate this point (Sherry, Forbes, Khurgel, & Ivy, 1993). Brown-headed cowbirds are brood parasites, that is, females lay their eggs in the nests of other species who then hatch and feed the cowbird nestlings. Female cowbirds must utilize the home range in more complex ways than male cowbirds because the females must locate suitable hosts for their eggs. Moreover, many hosts will only accept cowbird eggs after they have started laying eggs of their own. Thus, female cowbirds not only need to locate potential hosts, they must remember their locations and return to them at suitable times. The sex difference in the spatial demands of reproduction should then result in a larger hippocampus in female relative to male cowbirds. This is exactly the pattern found by Sherry and his colleagues (Sherry et al., 1993). As with voles, no sex differences in hippocampal size were found for species of monogamous birds—where males and females share a home range—that are evolutionarily related to the cowbird (e.g., the red-winged blackbird, *Agelaius phoeniceus*).

SOCIAL COGNITION AND THE EVOLUTION OF THE HUMAN MIND

As noted earlier, the study of human cognitive sex differences has been largely driven by empirical findings, not theory-driven predictions. The principles of sexual selection enable theoretically driven predictions about the loci of human cognitive sex differences and thus provides a broader perspective than is typically employed for understanding these differences (Gaulin, 1992). In short, sex differences are predicted for those physical, behavioral, cognitive, and neural traits that facilitate intrasexual competition and intersexual choice (Buss, Larsen, Westen, & Semmelroth, 1992; Geary, 1998). Nonetheless, a common objection to evolutionary theories of human sex differences is that they are post hoc "just so stories" (Halpern, 1997). Certainly, care must be exercised when constructing models of evolutionary influences on human functioning, but, at the same time, it must be recognized that the vast literature on sexual selection in other species and the use comparative studies place empirically derived constraints on evolutionary models (e.g., Foley & Lee, 1989).

As an example, comparative studies of primate species, including humans, have consistently found relations among the size of the neocortex, the length of the developmental period, and the species' social system (Barton, 1996; Dunbar, 1993; Joffe, 1997; Sawaguchi, 1997). Neocortex size—after controlling for body size—is largest in those species that live in the most complex social systems and these same species have the longest developmental periods. These comparative patterns suggest that social factors, such as social competition, contributed to the evolution of mind and brain and that a long developmental period is needed to practice and refine the associated social skills, as with male satin bowerbirds. Sawaguchi's analysis revealed that neocortex size across primate species is related to the intensity of intrasexual competition, suggesting that one important feature of the complexity of a species' social system is the intensity of the competition for mates. The latter conclusion is an inference based on the principles of sexual selection and the empirical finding across species that as the intensity of intrasexual competition increases, the size of the neocortex increases as well. In short, the principles of sexual selection and comparative studies provide necessary constraints on evolutionary models of human sex differences. When these principles and constraints are used judiciously, the associated explanations of human sex differences are not simply "just so stories."

The author used this comparative approach and principles of evolutionary selection, combined with empirical studies in cognitive anthropology, cognitive neuroscience, ethnobiology, and psychology, to develop a taxonomy of evolved human cognitive competencies (Geary, 1998). In this taxonomy, evolved cognitive competencies are conceptualized as systems of domain-specific modules for processing information about other people, flora and fauna in the local ecology, and for moving about, representing (e.g., navigating), and using (e.g., tools) resources in the physical world (see Geary, 1998; Geary & Bjorklund, 2000). These modules correspond to the notions of folk psychology, folk biology, and folk physics. The following section describes the taxonomy for sociocognitive competencies (i.e., folk psychology) and the second section presents a model for how these competencies might be elaborated during development. The last section of the chapter describes the application of this taxonomy and developmental model to human sociocognitive sex differences.

Sociocognitive Modules

A current and yet unresolved debate in evolutionary psychology and the cognitive neurosciences centers on whether human cognitive competencies are inherently specified (e.g., Elman et al., 1996; Pinker, 1994, 1997). One perspective is that the human mind is a constellation of domain-specific modules that have been shaped by natural selection to address specific and recurring problems of adaptation in ancestral environments (Tooby & Cosmides, 1995). In this view, evolved domains, such as language, emerge from genes that code for the construction of modular neurocognitive systems that process domain-specific information (Pinker, 1994, 1997). Although not always emphasized, this position is consistent with an epigenetic expression of these genes; that is, gene expression is contingent on exposure to evolutionarily expectant information (Geary & Bjorklund, 2000; Gelman & Williams, 1998; Greenough, Black, & Wallace, 1987). An alternative view is that the functional capacity of the human neocortex is initially underspecified, resulting in a general-purpose learning organ. From this perspective, language and other domains of mind emerge from an interaction between innate general purpose learning mechanisms and environmental experiences that act to shape the associated neuronal circuits (Elman et al., 1996).

The assumption is that there is some degree of inherent specificity to the human mind and brain, but that the associated competencies are elaborated and adapted to local conditions during development (see the section "Ontogenetic Development and Sex Differences in Brain and Cognition"). As noted previously, inherent specificity can be understood as a system of hierarchically organized cognitive modules, that is, brain and cognitive systems that process domain specific information (Tooby & Cosmides, 1995). The focus is on the sociocognitive modules shown in Figure 2.3, which in turn can be subdivided into individual-level and group-level systems. The associated taxonomy was developed based on studies of the forms of information, such as facial expressions and gestures, used in social communication across species and on associated patterns of group dynamics, such as group fission and fusion

Individual-Level Modules

The function of individual-level modules is to moderate the dynamics of one-on-one social interactions, to develop and maintain long-term relationships with kin and friends (i.e., nonkin), to support attempts to obtain social and material resources from other people, and to avoid being exploited by other people. Before discussion of the modules that support these functions, brief mention is needed of differences between relationships with kin and friends, as these differences are relevant to several later described sex differences.

Kin-based relationships are found across many species, ranging from invertebrates to primates, and are understood in terms of inclusive fitness (e.g., Altmann et al., 1996; Hamilton, 1964). Inclusive fitness refers to an individual's overall genetic contribution to the next generation, which is represented by the combination of one's children and the children of kin (e.g., nephews). Natural selection will strongly favor individuals who aid kin in ways that facilitate their reproduction and survival because the reproductive success of kin will perforce increase the altruist's genetic contributions to the next generation (Hamilton, 1964, 1975). More simply, selection pressures will quickly favor individuals who selectively provide social and material support to their kin (Hamilton, 1975). The primary distinction between the social relationships among kin and among friends is reciprocity. Relationships with kin are not always reciprocal, whereas long-term friendships are defined by reciprocity (Hartup & Stevens, 1997; Trivers, 1974). Of friends, Hartup and Stevens concluded that children "and adults of all ages

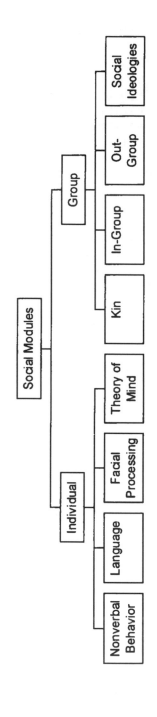

Figure 2.3. Proposed sociocognitive modules.
Adapted from *Male, female: The evolution of human sex differences* (p. 180), by D. C. Geary, 1998, Washington, DC: American Psychological Association. Reprinted with permission.

consider these relationships to be marked by reciprocation, that is, *mutuality*—the giving and taking, and returning in kind or degree. On this basis, we argue that the friendship deep structure . . . is best described as 'symmetrical reciprocity'" (Hartup & Stevens, 1997, p. 356).

The sociocognitive modules that support relationships with kin, friends, and competitors include the ability to read nonverbal communication signals and facial expressions, language, and theory of mind (Adolphs, 1999; Brothers & Ring, 1992; Leslie, 1987; Moscovitch, Winocur, & Behrmann, 1997; Premack & Woodruff, 1978; Pinker, 1994). Language and theory of mind appear to be of central importance in human social relationships (Povinelli & Preuss, 1995). Most generally, theory of mind represents the ability to "mind read" or make inferences about the intentions, beliefs, emotional states, and likely future behavior of other individuals (Baron-Cohen, 1995; Gopnik & Wellman, 1994). Facial processing and the processing of other nonverbal forms of communication (e.g., body posture), along with changes in vocal intonation and language itself, appear to provide the basic information that feeds into theory of mind. At the same time, these signals (e.g., facial expressions) modulate the dynamics of one-on-one social interactions, providing cues to the on-line emotional states and intentions of other people and sometimes to manipulate and deceive other people.

Of these, language and theory of mind appear to be the most highly developed, evolutionarily. Other primates respond to conspecific facial expressions, vocalizations, and body language (Hauser, 1996) but none of these primates, or any other species for that matter, has a vocal communication system as complex as human language (Pinker, 1994). Theory of mind is also highly elaborated in comparison to other primates. In fact, most primates—except perhaps other great apes but this is debated (e.g., Povinelli & Preuss, 1995; Premack & Woodruff, 1978)—do not show consistent evidence of a theory of mind. These findings are important because they provide a link between the earlier described comparative studies of social complexity and brain size (Barton, 1996) and the proposed sociocognitive modules. Rilling and Insel's (1999) neuroimaging study of individuals from 11 primate species indicated that the human neocortex is larger than expected, based on overall body and brain size, in just those areas that support human language (i.e., the left temporal cortex) and theory of mind (i.e., portions of the prefrontal cortex) (see Adolphs, 1999; Baron-Cohen, Ring, Moriarty, Schmitz, Costa, & Ell, 1994). These patterns support the position that social competition and cooperation contributed to the evolution of the human mind and brain, particularly the evolutionary elaboration of the neurocognitive systems that support language and theory of mind.

Group-Level Modules

In addition to specialized modules for maintaining and regulating dyadic relationships and interactions, there are almost certainly complementary systems—the group-level modules shown in Figure 2.3—designed to parse the social universe. Bugental (2000) provides a model of the potential cognitive mechanisms underlying this parsing. However it is achieved, the parsing of people into social groups appears to reflect the previously described categorical significance of kin, the formation of in-groups and out-groups, and ideologically based social identification, as exemplified by nationality, religious affiliation, and so forth (Alexander, 1979; Geary, 1998). The proposal is that coalition-based competition is essential to understanding the evolution and expression of social parsing, especially as related to in-groups and out-groups and associated ideologies (Alexander, 1990; Geary, 1998). In other words, one function of social parsing is to facilitate the formation of competition-related coalitions.

In preindustrial cultures, and most likely during the course of human evolution, functional group size appears to be constrained by the number of individuals with whom personal relationships can be maintained without the existence of formal laws and a formal police force to enforce these laws (Dunbar, 1993). The size of such groups varies in response to the opportunities and demands of the local habitat that supports the group (Alexander, 1990), but typically does not exceed 150 to 200 individuals (Dunbar, 1993). The individuals who comprise these groups are typically kin and share beliefs, such as origin myths, that not only distinguish them from other groups but often, if not always, assign special significance to their own group (Brown, 1991).

Cognitive constraints (e.g., on the number of people with whom personal relationships can be maintained) on the functional size of social groups and ecological constraints that resulted in competition over limited resources are likely to have contributed to the evolution of an in-group/out-group social psychology (Alexander, 1979); this form of social parsing almost certainly predated the emergence of hominids (Goodall, 1986). In-groups and out-groups are defined by differing social and moral ideologies that favor in-group members—kin and friends—and, under extreme conditions, devalue and even dehumanize out-group members. In fact, one important condition for effective competition against an out-group is the disengagement of the emotional and moral mechanisms that appear to be designed to reduce conflict and foster cooperation within in-groups. Although some level of in-group conflict is anticipated—especially when there are no current competing out-groups—it appears that emotional reactions, such as guilt and empathy, moderate this conflict in the service of mutually beneficial cooperative exchanges (Trivers, 1971).

When directed toward out-groups, the same moderating emotional reactions would result in a competitive disadvantage. In other words, when the competition between groups affected reproduction and survival—and it likely did in throughout the course of human evolution (Alexander, 1990; Chagnon, 1988; Keeley, 1996)—individuals who were able to dehumanize, in extreme cases, members of out-groups were likely at a competitive advantage. Stephan's (1985) review of the social psychology of intergroup relations supports this position, as do numerous studies on the social identification processes underlying group formation and competition (e.g., Sherif, Harvey, White, Hood, & Sherif, 1961). Humans readily form in-groups and out-groups and process information about members of these groups in ways that are favorably biased toward the in-group, particularly when the comparisons are made between competing groups. Moreover, "anticipated competition caused in group members to feel more hostility toward the out-group than did anticipated cooperation" (Stephan, 1985, p. 675); the seminal *Robbers Cave* experiment nicely illustrates the process of in-group/out-group formation and intergroup competition (Sherif et al., 1961).

An in-group/out-group social psychology that likely evolved in the context of competition between relatively small kin-based groups more likely than not provided the foundation for the evolution of social ideologies (Alexander, 1990). These ideologies are particularly important, because they appear to be the basis for the formation of large nation-states, that is, the social organization of individuals who have never met, and never will, and thus are unable to develop one-on-one personal relationships (Geary, 1998). Such ideologies define the mutual self-interest of individuals who comprise groups that are larger than functional villages in preindustrial societies and are the basis for large-scale between-group conflict. In fact, the competitive advantage associated with group size was the likely pressure, after the emergence of language and shared belief systems (e.g., origin myths), that resulted in the evolution of the tendency of humans to form and rally around such ideologies (Alexander, 1990). In support of this view is the finding that people show an enhanced endorsement of in-group ideologies and harsher evaluations of out-group members under conditions that imply a threat to one's mortality (Arndt, Greenberg, Pyszczynski, & Solomon, 1997).

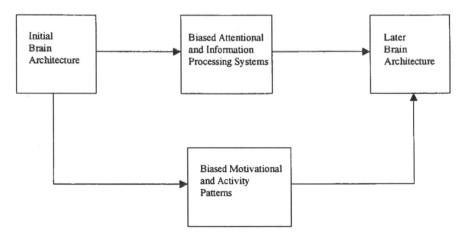

Figure 2.4. Proposed pattern of relations among evolved but skeletal cognitive and brain systems, biased attentional, information processing, motivational, and activity patterns, and later cognitive and brain systems.

Ontogenetic Development and Sex Differences
in Brain and Cognition

Evolution will relentlessly select for a short developmental period and there-fore faster reproduction, unless there are strong advantages to maturational delays; these advantages must reproductively outweigh the risk associated with death before the age of reproduction. Comparative studies suggest that the basic adaptive benefit of delayed maturation is the accompanying ability to refine the physical, social, cognitive, and neural competencies that support survival and reproduction in adulthood (Mayr, 1974). The earlier described relation between neocortex size and length of the developmental period supports the view that one function of delayed maturation is to allow juveniles to practice and refine the sociocognitive competencies associated with survival and reproduction (e.g., competing for mates) in adulthood (Geary, 1999; Joffe, 1997). An extended developmental period is also related to enhanced tool use in some species and greater knowledge of the local ecology, both of which facilitate later foraging (Byrne, 1995; Geary, 1998).

For humans, play, social interactions, and exploration of the environment and objects appear to be the mechanisms through which these emerging competen-cies, including the sociocognitive competencies shown in Figure 2.3, are prac-ticed and refined during development (e.g., Pellegrini & Smith, 1998). In theory, these child-initiated activities provide experiences with the social, biological (e.g., prey species), and physical world that interact with underlying genetic sys-tems to produce the physical, social, cognitive, and neural phenotypes that were associated with the survival and reproduction of our ancestors (Geary, 1998; Scarr & McCarthy, 1983). In other words, child-initiated social play and explo-ration are intimately linked to cognitive and neural development, in that these activities result in the environmental experiences that are an integral part of the epigenetic processes that result in adult phenotypes (Greenough et al., 1987). The basic pattern is shown in Figure 2.4, whereby the initial, or skeletal, architecture of evolved modules is associated with motivational, attentional, information pro-cessing, and activity biases. These biases result in child-initiated experiences that further shape neurocognitive systems such that these systems are adapted to the local ecology (e.g., the local language) (Geary, 1998; Gelman & Williams, 1998).

When considered in the context of sexual selection, developmental sex differ-ences are expected only in those areas in which the reproductive activities of males and females differ (Geary, 1999). As described below, female–female com-petition is more interpersonal, involving relational aggression, than is male–male competition (Crick, Casas, & Moser, 1997). For this reason and others described later, early sex differences, favoring girls, are expected and found in the associ-ated sociocognitive domains, such as the processing of facial expressions (Haviland & Malatesta, 1981). An early bias in the focus on and processing of such cues would provide the experiences necessary to practice and refine the skills needed to effectively compete in the subtle and complex dynamics of female–female competition in adulthood.

At a more proximate level, it is expected that the expression of the accompanying sex differences in motivational, attentional, activity, and information-processing biases, as well as underlying sexually dimorphic brain structures, will be related to prenatal and circulating hormone levels (see chapter 3) (Geary, 1999; Kimura, 1999). Sex differences in attentional and information-processing biases and associated motivational and activity differences are predicted to interact with prenatal sexual dimorphisms in brain structure and with circulating sex hormone levels in ways that will lead to the emergence, or increase in magnitude, of sex differences in brain and cognition. Stated differently, the prediction is that cognitive sex differences will result from a hormonally moderated epigenetic process (Gilbert, Opitz, & Raff, 1996). The epigenetic process results from an interaction between hormonally induced cognitive and behavioral biases that act on early cognitive and brain sex dimorphisms such that the resulting experiences further modify the associated sex differences in social, cognitive, and brain systems.

HUMAN SEX DIFFERENCES

The primary goal in this section is to use the system of sociocognitive competencies shown in Figure 2.3, in combination with the principles of sexual selection, as the theoretical framework for organizing sex differences research in the associated domains. However, to fully understand the utility of this approach, brief discussion of sexual selection in humans is required.

Sexual Selection

In addition to the earlier mentioned fact that men throughout the world show some level of parental investment, thus creating the conditions for the evolution of female–female competition in humans (Geary, 2000), the social structure of our hominid ancestors is highly relevant to interpreting current sociocognitive sex differences.

Hominid Social Structure

In most species of primate, females stay in their birth group—they are the philopatric sex—and males migrate to other groups, as a mechanism of inbreeding avoidance. The social structure of these species is centered on coalitions of related females who defend territory and important food sources (e.g., fruit trees) from coalitions of other females (Wrangham, 1980). Males of these species tend not to form coalitions but compete one-on-one with other males to become the dominant (i.e., reproductive) male of the female coalition. Humans and all other great apes are an exception to this pattern, as males, not females, are the philopatric sex (Manson & Wrangham, 1991). Consistent with the social structure found in other great apes, in the majority of preindustrial human cultures, men stay in their birth group and women migrate to the group of their husband (Pasternak, Ember, & Ember, 1997). A recent study of sex differences in genetic variability in 14 such cultures indicated a "higher female than male migration rate (through patrilocality, the tendency for a wife to move into her husband's natal household)" (Seielstad, Minch, & Cavalli-Sforza, 1998, p. 278).

There are two critical corollaries to this pattern. First, because coalition formation is most common in the philopatric sex, coalition-based intrasexual competition was likely to have been much more common in our male than in our female ancestors. In fact, coalition-based male–male competition is common in the chimpanzee (*Pan troglodytes*), a close relative, and is found to some degree in all human cultures in which group-level conflict is found (Geary, 1998; Goodall, 1986; Keeley, 1996). Large-scale coalition-based female–female competition, in contrast, has not been documented for any culture that has been studied, or in other great apes (Geary, 1998; Manson & Wrangham, 1991). Second, it is very likely that our female ancestors were forced to develop social alliances with nonkin more frequently than were our male ancestors, given that they migrated to the social group of their male mates. The development of relationships with nonkin likely provided a system of social support for our female ancestors. In extant societies, greater social stability is associated with improved health and reduced mortality risks for children (Geary, 1998, 2000). If this same pattern was evident during the course of human evolution, then social, cognitive, and emotional mechanisms associated with developing and maintaining relationships with nonkin were more likely to have been elaborated in hominid females than males.

If so, then sex differences, favoring women, should be found for many, perhaps all, of the individual-level sociocognitive competencies shown in Figure 2.3, that is, language, the processing of facial and nonverbal communication signals, and theory of mind. This is because relationships with nonkin are generally less stable than those with kin and likely require a higher level of social competencies to develop and maintain. Pressures for refined social competencies in turn would result in the evolutionary elaboration of the supporting sociocognitive competencies. Sex differences are also predicted in social motives, with women more than men favoring equality and reciprocity in interpersonal relationships—the features of relationships that characterize friendships, that is, relationships with nonkin (Hartup & Stevens, 1997).

Intrasexual Competition

The nuances of intrasexual competition are many and complex. Detailed discussion of these nuances has been presented elsewhere (see Andersson, 1994; or Geary, 1998), but the observation that certain general features of intrasexual competition are more common for one sex than the other has important implications for the development of sex differences in human social cognition. As found in nearly all other species in which males compete for mates, male–male competition in humans is focused on issues of social dominance and resource control and often involves a physical component (Andersson, 1994; Geary, 1998). For humans, this competition occurs within and between groups. Beginning in childhood and extending throughout the lifespan, boys and men form relatively large in-groups, most typically to compete with other groups of males (e.g., sports) (Lever, 1978), and compete for status—the ability to influence other boys and men—within these groups. Once the resulting dominance hierarchy is formed, the behavior of boys and men becomes cooperative and focused on competing with the out-group (for an example see Savin-Williams, 1987). As noted earlier, this male–male competition is common in preindustrial societies and is related to reproductive issues (Chagnon, 1988; Keeley, 1996). In this view, the rough and tumble play of boys and the sex difference, favoring boys, in the engagement in group-level competition (e.g., team sports) are a reflection of evolved mechanisms that result in the practice and refinement of competencies associated with the forms of male–male competition—one-on-one and coalition based—that prevailed during human evolution (Geary, 1998, 1999).

Although girls and women do occasionally compete physically, they do so much less frequently than do boys and men (Geary, 1998); there are also qualitative differences (e.g., in focus and intensity) in this physical competition (Savin-Williams, 1987). More typically, girls and women compete relationally, that is, they back bite, shun, and ridicule their competitors (called relational aggression) (Crick et al., 1997). One function of this competition is to make these competitors look unattractive ("she's a real slut") to males and perhaps drive these women out of the social group, thus making them unavailable as mating partners to the men in the group (Buss, 1994; Geary, 2000). Another function appears to be to disrupt the formation of the above-mentioned network of interpersonal support (Geary, 1999).

One possibility is that this form of female–female competition evolved, in part, in the context of polygynous marriages—polygyny is very common in preindustrial societies and almost certainly throughout human evolution (Murdock, 1981). In these contexts, co-wives compete for the attention and resources of their husband. A recent study of polygynous versus monogamous marriages in a pastoral society in Tanzania provides some support for this thesis (Sellen, 1999), as do other studies of similar societies (e.g., Borgerhoff Mulder, 1990). Most generally, children of polygynous marriages show poor growth patterns and thus increased morbidity and mortality risks than do children of monogamous marriages. These conditions would promote female–female competition over the husband's resources, as gaining control of additional resources would improve the health of and reduce the mortality risks to her children. In any case, relational aggression would still be expected over potential mates, even in monogamous societies (Geary, 2000). This is because all men are not equal in terms of their value as potential mates and female–female competition is expected and found over the most desirable mates (Buss, 1994).

Sex differences in the nature of intrasexual competition are predicted to result in sex differences in the sociocognitive competencies that support this competition. Sex differences in the nature of in-group and out-group dynamics are expected, with greater in-group bias and hostility toward the out-group in boys and men than in girls and women. Relational aggression would again favor the evolutionary and developmental elaboration of the individual-level sociocognitive competencies more in girls and women than in boys and men, as this form of aggression is focused on interpersonal relationships. The nature of intrasexual competition would also operate to create a sex difference in social motives, with boys and men being more concerned with issues of social dominance than girls and women.

Social Cognition

The first and second sections that follow provide a brief review of respective sex differences in the individual-level and group-level sociocognitive competencies shown in Figure 2.3. The final section provides discussion of social motives and developmental issues.

Individual-Level Modules

As predicted, there are sex differences, largely favoring girls and women, in most, perhaps all, of the individual-level sociocognitive modules shown in Figure 2.3 (see also chapter 8). Relative to boys and men, girls and women show advantages for a number of basic language-related skills. More frequently than boys and men, girls and women show standard grammatical structure and a correct pronunciation of language-sounds in their utterances; have a better memory for words; are better at generating strings of words; and are better at discriminating basic language sounds (e.g., consonants and vowels) from one another (Block, Arnott, Quigley, & Lynch, 1989; Halpern, 1992, 1997; Halpern & Wright, 1996; Hampson, 1990; Hyde & Linn, 1988; Kimura, 1999). Girls and women also show many fewer pauses (e.g., filled with "uhh") in their utterances than do boys and men (Hall, 1984), and, at the same time, boys and men manifest language-related disorders, such as stuttering, two to four times more frequently than do girls and women (Tallal, 1991).

Girls and women also show consistent advantages over boys and men in the ability to read facial expressions and nonverbal communication signals. The most ambitious and comprehensive study of these differences was conducted by Rosenthal and his colleagues (Rosenthal, Hall, DiMatteo, Rogers, & Archer, 1979; see also Buck, Savin, Miller, & Caul, 1972). The associated test—Profile of Nonverbal Sensitivity (PONS)—was initially administered to 492 high school students, but in follow-up studies the entire PONS or portions of it were administered to more than 4,000 other individuals, including elementary and junior high school students, college students, and older adults from a variety of occupations. Testing was also done on three or more samples of individuals from Australia, Canada, Israel, and New Guinea and smaller numbers of individuals were assessed in Northern Ireland, Mexico, New Zealand, Hong Kong, West Germany, and Singapore.

Across these samples, girls and women showed an advantage over boys and men for accuracy in judging emotion cues—when the cues were assessed separately—based on facial expressions, body posture, and vocal intonation. The magnitude of the overall advantage of girls and women did not vary with age and was moderate in size; about 2 out of 3 girls and women outperformed the average same-age boy or man on these measures (Rosenthal et al., 1979). The advantage of girls and women was found in all nations in which three or more samples were obtained—Australia, Canada, the United States, Israel, and New Guinea—and was of the same general magnitude in all of these nations (Hall, 1984). When facial, body language, and vocal intonation cues are presented simultaneously, about 17 out of 20 girls and women are more accurate at decoding the emotion cues of another individual than is the average same-age boy or man (Hall, 1984). This finding is of considerable practical significance, as these combined cues represent a more accurate assessment of nonverbal decoding skills in "real world" settings.

Nonetheless, there are some contexts in which men are as skilled, perhaps more skilled, than women in reading facial expressions and some other cues (e.g., vocal intonation). It appears that men are relatively more sensitive to negative-emotion cues signaled by other men, especially anger, than they are to the same cues signaled by women or to more positive-emotion cues signaled by men (Rosenthal et al., 1979; Rotter & Rotter, 1988). Two studies conducted by Rotter and Rotter (1988) found that women were consistently more accurate than men in judging the emotion cues signaled by the facial expressions of other women and men, when these expressions conveyed the emotions of disgust, fear, or sadness. Men, in contrast, were more accurate than women in detecting an angry expression on the face of other men, especially if the expression was directed toward them. The latter finding might be interpreted as an evolved sensitivity to the facial cues associated with male–male competition.

Theory of mind goes at least one step beyond the ability to "read" facial expressions and other nonverbal communication cues (Baron-Cohen, 1995). Among other things (e.g., making inferences about the intentions of other people), theory of mind represents the ability to infer whether the emotions signaled by these facial expressions are or are not an accurate reflection of the actual emotional state of the individual. In other words, people often signal or suppress emotion cues independent of their actual emotional state (e.g., with social deception).

Sensitivity to the social and emotion cues signaled by nonverbal behavior and the ability to make inferences about the underlying emotional state of another individual are thus two relatively distinct classes of ability.

Sex differences research on theory of mind is less extensive and conclusive than the just described studies of language and sensitivity to facial and nonverbal communication signals. Most theory of mind studies have not assessed sex differences because, according to Baron-Cohen and colleagues, the associated tests are not sensitive enough to detect subtle individual differences, including sex differences (Baron-Cohen, Jolliffe, Mortimore, & Robertson, 1997). A few studies, nonetheless, suggest an advantage of girls and women in the ability to make inferences about the emotional states of other people and to adjust their social behavior accordingly (Banerjee, 1997; Baron-Cohen et al., 1997; Happé, 1995). Moreover, it has been hypothesized that a lack of theory of mind is a defining characteristic of autism (Baron-Cohen, 1995) and three to four times more boys and men are diagnosed as autistic than are girls and women (Klinger & Dawson, 1996). Although not definitive, these studies suggest that a sex difference, favoring girls and women, may exist for certain aspects of theory of mind.

Group-Level Modules

Sex differences in patterns of relationships with kin have been discussed in a variety of contexts by Geary (1998) and Pasternak et al. (1997). The discussions here focus specifically on sex differences in the dynamics of in-group/out-group social psychology and adherence to group ideologies. Recall, on the basis of coalition-based male–male competition, the prediction is that boys and men will show more cohesive in-groups, including ideologically formed in-groups, and more hostility toward out-groups than girls and women. However, these differences are only anticipated during periods of group-level competition. Unfortunately, sex-differences research in this area is meager, in comparison to the quantity of studies on individual-level sociocognitive sex differences. The research that has been conducted suggests that boys and girls and men and women are more similar than different (Davis, Cheng, & Strube, 1996; Schaller, 1992). Both boys and girls as well as men and women readily form in-groups and out-groups and generally make judgments about in-group members that are more favorable than their judgments about out-group members (e.g., Schaller, 1992). Under conditions that implicitly or explicitly provide a reminder of one's mortality (e.g., being exposed to issues associated with death), both men and women show a marked increase in their endorsement of the in-group's social ideology and more negative attitudes toward people who question this ideology (Arndt et al., 1997).

Nonetheless, it appears that sex differences in the dynamics of in-group and out-group formation do emerge under some conditions and as early as the preschool years (e.g., Benenson, 1993; Bugental, 2000; Davis et al., 1996; Yee & Brown, 1992). Relative to girls and women, boys and men appear to exert more intense social pressures on in-group members to adhere to group norms and typical group behaviors. These differences are evident in childhood play (e.g., boys tease other boys more intensely about interacting with girls than vice versa) (Maccoby, 1988), in the context of competitive sports (Savin-Williams, 1987), and in attitudes in adulthood (e.g., toward homosexuality) (Geary, 1998). Moreover, boys and men appear to develop relatively more negative attitudes about out-group members during periods of competition and conflict and are less likely to compromise during conflict than are girls and women (Davis et al., 1996; Towson, Lerner, & de Carufel, 1981; Yee & Brown, 1992). In other words, in comparison to girls and women, boys and men appear to be relatively intolerant of in-group members who deviate from group norms and more readily develop agonistic attitudes and behaviors toward out-group members. There has been little research on sex differences in adherence to social ideologies during periods of group conflict and thus it is not currently known if sex differences exist on this dimension.

Social Motives and Development

On the basis of the sex difference in hominid social structure, girls and women are predicted to favor greater levels of reciprocity and equality in social relationships—those motives associated with the maintenance of relationships with nonkin (Hartup & Stevens, 1997)—than are boys and men. On the basis of the general cross-species pattern of male–male competition over mates and because male–male competition has almost certainly been more intense than female–female competition throughout human evolution (Geary, 1998), the prediction is that boys and men will evince more dominance-related social motives than girls and women. Studies of these motives across age levels and societies support these predictions. The social relationships that develop among girls are more consistently communal—manifesting greater empathy, more concern for the well-being of other girls, more nurturing, intimacy, social/emotional support, concern for equality and so on—than are the relationships that develop among boys, whereas relationships among boys are more consistently instrumental or agentic—more concern for the establishment of dominance and control of group activities (e.g., Feingold, 1994; Knight & Chao, 1989; Maccoby, 1988; Savin-Williams, 1987; Whiting & Edwards, 1988).

As predicted in the developmental section, many of the sociocognitive sex differences are evident early in life, are manifested in social and play patterns, and some of these have been linked to prenatal exposure to sex hormones. For instance, a greater orientation of girls toward people is evident in infancy and likely results from and contributes to the sex differences in individual-level sociocognitive competencies (Haviland & Malatesta, 1981; McGuinness & Pribram, 1979). One indicator of orientation toward other people is the duration of eye contact. Haviland and Malatesta noted that "there is no doubt that girls and women establish and maintain eye contact more than boys and men. The earliest age for which this is reported is one day" (Haviland & Malatesta, 1981, p. 189). Although many girls engage in group-level competition, as in team sports, many more boys than girls engage in these activities and by adolescence are more intensely focused in these contexts than are same-age girls (Lever, 1978; Savin-Williams, 1987). In fact, the sex difference in preferred social organization, that is, girls and women favoring dyadic interactions and boys and men favoring group-level interactions, is evident as early as 3 years (Benenson, 1993; Yee & Brown, 1992). The research of Berenbaum and Snyder (1995) suggests that the sex difference in this preferred social organization is influenced by prenatal exposure to male hormones, as appears to be the case with some other primates (Wallen, 1996).

CONCLUSION

The principles of sexual selection provide a new and advantaged approach to the study of human cognitive sex differences. The primary advantages include a theoretical framework that enables us to systematically search for the connections and precursors to observed sex differences and the only perspective that allows these differences to be understood in the context of sex differences found in other species (Darwin, 1871). The latter is useful because the principles of sexual selection have provided a fruitful framework for the study of sex differences in literally hundreds of other species (Andersson, 1994). The evolutionary (e.g., male–male competition) and proximate (e.g., sex hormones) mechanisms associated with sexual selection are thus well understood. There is every reason to believe that these same principles will provide a useful tool for studying human cognitive sex differences (Gaulin, 1992; Geary, 1998). In fact, the mechanisms associated with sexual selection are arguably better understood than the mechanisms associated with other theoretical approaches to human sex differences. In any case, a complete understanding of human cognitive sex differences will require careful consideration of sexual, and in some cases natural, selection, even if other mechanisms (e.g., gender stereotypes) (Eagly, 1987) are also shown to contribute to these differences.

This chapter demonstrated why this is so. Rather than organizing sex differences in terms of empirical findings, the approach was to use a proposed taxonomy of evolved cognitive modules to provide an a priori framework for organizing what is known of sex differences in sociocognitive competencies (Geary, 1998). The framework was then combined with the principles of sexual selection and intrasexual competition, in particular, to make predictions about the loci of sex differences in sociocognitive competencies, including developmental sex differences. With respect to the latter, the specific prediction is that sex differences in intrasexual competition and intersexual choice will be mirrored in early sex differences in play styles, social motives, cognitive biases, and so forth, especially in slow developing species (Geary & Bjorklund, 2000). In theory, these early biases enable boys and girls to practice and refine those physical, social, and cognitive competencies that were associated with the reproductive demands of our adult ancestors (Geary, 1999).

Existing empirical research is consistent with many of these predictions, such as the prediction—based on relational aggression and the hominid social structure—that girls and women will outperform boys and men on many of the sociocognitive competencies associated with individual relationships (e.g., reading facial expressions). A corollary prediction is that these sex differences will be evident developmentally and they in fact are: In infancy, girls show a greater orientation to other people and by 3 years of age favor a dyadic rather than a group-level social organization (Benenson, 1993; Haviland & Malatesta, 1981). In other cases, extant research was not conclusive. Sex differences, favoring girls and women, in theory of mind were predicted, but current studies do not provide definitive support for a sex difference in this area, although they are highly suggestive.

In short, sexual selection not only provides a framework for interpreting currently known sex differences, it also generates many testable predictions about other sex differences. As an example, future studies could easily pursue the prediction of a sex difference in theory of mind and the corollary prediction that any sex difference in theory of mind may vary with social context. For instance, if the hominid social structure and relational aggression resulted in a greater elaboration of theory of mind in our female than our male ancestors, then women should be especially skilled on theory of mind tasks that involve relationship formation and competition with other women. Similarly, if coalition-based male–male competition resulted in an in-group/out-group social psychology that facilitated this competition, then sex differences are expected in patterns of in-group formation and degree of hostility toward the out-group. Again, context is expected to be important in the demonstration of any such sex differences. Sex differences are expected to be the largest (e.g., in ease of coalition formation and willingness to compromise with the out-group) in contexts involving fairly large groups and competition over a prized resource (e.g., Sherif et al., 1961). Based on the assumption that the function of a long developmental period is to enable the practice and refinement of survival and reproduction related competencies, the just described sex differences are excepted in childhood as well.

REFERENCES

Adolphs, R. (1999). Social cognition and the human brain. *Trends in Cognitive Sciences, 3*, 469–479.

Alexander, R. D. (1979). *Darwinism and human affairs*. Seattle, WA: University of Washington Press.

Alexander, R. D. (1990). *How did humans evolve? Reflections on the uniquely unique species*. Museum of Zoology (Special Publication No. 1). Ann Arbor: The University of Michigan.

Altmann, J., Alberts, S. C., Haines, S. A., Dubach, J., Muruthi, P., Coote, T., Geffen, E., Chessman, D. J., Mututua, R. S., Saiyalel, S. N., Wayne, R. K., Lacy, R. C., & Bruford, M. W. (1996). Behavior predicts genetic structure in a wild primate group. *Proceedings of the National Academy of Sciences USA, 93*, 5797–5801.

Andersson, M. (1994). *Sexual selection.* Princeton, NJ: Princeton University Press.

Arndt, J., Greenberg, J., Pyszczynski, T., & Solomon, S. (1997). Subliminal exposure to death-related stimuli increases defense of the cultural worldview. *Psychological Science, 8*, 379–385.

Baenninger, M., & Newcombe, N. (1995). Environmental input to the development of sex-related differences in spatial and mathematical ability. *Learning and Individual Differences, 7*, 363–379.

Ball, G. F., & Hulse, S. H. (1998). Birdsong. *American Psychologist, 53*, 37–58.

Banerjee, M. (1997). Hidden emotions: Preschoolers' knowledge of appearance-reality and emotion display rules. *Social Cognition, 15*, 107–132.

Baron-Cohen, S. (1995). *Mindblindness: An essay on autism and theory of mind.* Cambridge, MA: MIT Press/Bradford Books.

Baron-Cohen, S., Jolliffe, T., Mortimore, C., & Robertson, M. (1997). Another advanced test of theory of mind: Evidence from very high functioning adults with autism or Asperger syndrome. *Journal of Child Psychology and Psychiatry, 38*, 813–822.

Baron-Cohen, S., Ring, H., Moriarty, J., Schmitz, B., Costa, D., & Ell, P. (1994). Recognition of mental state terms: Clinical findings in children with autism and a functional neuroimaging study of normal adults. *British Journal of Psychiatry, 165*, 640–649.

Barton, R. A. (1996). Neocortex size and behavioural ecology in primates. *Proceedings of the Royal Society of London B, 263*, 173–177.

Benenson, J. F. (1993). Greater preference among females than males for dyadic interaction in early childhood. *Child Development, 64*, 544–555.

Berenbaum, S. A., & Snyder, E. (1995). Early hormonal influences on childhood sex-typed activity and playmate preferences: Implications for the development of sexual orientation. *Developmental Psychology, 31*, 31–42.

Block, R. A., Arnott, D. P., Quigley, B., & Lynch, W. C. (1989). Unilateral nostril breathing influences lateralized cognitive performance. *Brain and Cognition, 9*, 181–190.

Borgerhoff Mulder, M. (1990). Kipsigis women's preferences for wealthy men: Evidence for female choice in mammals? *Behavioral Ecology and Sociobiology, 27*, 255–264.

Borgia, G. (1985a). Bower destruction and sexual competition in the satin bower bird (*Ptilonorhynchus violaceus*). *Behavioral Ecology and Sociobiology, 18*, 91–100.

Borgia, G. (1985b). Bower quality, number of decorations and mating success of male satin bower birds (*Ptilonorhynchus violaceus*): An experimental analysis. *Animal Behaviour, 33*, 266–271.

Brothers, L., & Ring, B. (1992). A neuroethological framework for the representation of minds. *Journal of Cognitive Neuroscience, 4*, 107–118.

Brown, D. E. (1991). *Human universals.* Philadelphia, PA: Temple University Press.

Buck, R. W., Savin, V. J., Miller, R. E., & Caul, W. F. (1972). Communication of affect through facial expression in humans. *Journal of Personality and Social*

Psychology, 23, 362–371.

Bugental, D. B. (2000). Acquisition of the algorithms of social life: A domain-based approach. *Psychological Bulletin, 126*, 187–219.

Buss, D. M. (1994). *The evolution of desire: Strategies of human mating.* New York: Basic Books.

Buss, D. M., Larsen, R. J., Westen, D., & Semmelroth, J. (1992). Sex differences in jealousy: Evolution, physiology, and psychology. *Psychological Science, 3*, 251–255.

Byrne, R. (1995). *The thinking ape: Evolutionary origins of intelligence.* New York: Oxford University Press.

Chagnon, N. A. (1988, February 26). Life histories, blood revenge, and warfare in a tribal population. *Science, 239*, 985–992.

Clutton-Brock, T. H. (1991). *The evolution of parental care.* Princeton, NJ: Princeton University Press.

Clutton-Brock, T. H., & Vincent, A.C. J. (1991, May 2). Sexual selection and the potential reproductive rates of males and females. *Science, 351*, 58–60.

Collis, K., & Borgia, G. (1992). Age-related effects of testosterone, plummage, and experience on aggression and social dominance in juvenile male satin bowerbirds (*Ptilonorhynchus violaceus*). *Auk, 109*, 422–434.

Crick, N. R., Casas, J. F., & Mosher, M. (1997). Relational and overt aggression in preschool. *Developmental Psychology, 33*, 579–588.

Darwin, C. (1871). *The descent of man, and selection in relation to sex.* London: John Murray.

Davis, L. E., Cheng, L. C., & Strube, M. J. (1996). Differential effects of racial composition on male and female groups: Implications for group work practice. *Social Work Research, 20*, 157–166.

Dunbar, R. I. M. (1993). Coevolution of neocortical size, group size and language in humans. *Behavioral and Brain Sciences, 16*, 681–735.

Dunbar, R. I. M. (1995). The mating system of callitrichid primates: I. Conditions for the coevolution of pair bonding and twinning. *Animal Behaviour, 50*, 1057–1070.

Eagly, A. H. (1987). *Sex differences in social behavior: A social-role interpretation.* Hillsdale, NJ: Lawrence Erlbaum.

Elman, J. L., Bates, E. A., Johnson, M. H., Karmiloff-Smith, A., Parisi, D., & Plunkett, K. (1996). *Rethinking innateness: A connectionist perspective on development.* Cambridge, MA: Bradford Books/MIT Press.

Emlen, S. T., & Oring, L. W. (1977, July 15). Ecology, sexual selection, and the evolution of mating systems. *Science, 197*, 215–223.

Feingold, A. (1994). Gender differences in personality: A meta-analysis. *Psychological Bulletin, 116*, 429–456.

Foley, R. A., & Lee, P. C. (1989, February 17). Finite social space, evolutionary pathways, and reconstructing hominid behavior. *Science, 243*, 901–906.

Gaulin, S. J. C. (1992). Evolution of sex differences in spatial ability. *Yearbook of Physical Anthropology, 35*, 125–151.

Gaulin, S. J. C. (1995). Does evolutionary theory predict sex differences in the brain? In M. S. Gazzaniga (Ed.), *The cognitive neurosciences* (pp. 1211–1225). Cambridge, MA: Bradford Books/MIT Press.

Gaulin, S. J. C., & Fitzgerald, R. W. (1986). Sex differences in spatial ability: An evolutionary hypothesis and test. *American Naturalist, 127*, 74–88.

Gaulin, S. J. C., & Fitzgerald, R. W. (1989). Sexual selection for spatial-learning ability. *Animal Behaviour, 37,* 322–331.

Geary, D. C. (1995). Sexual selection and sex differences in spatial cognition. *Learning and Individual Differences, 7,* 289–301.

Geary, D. C. (1996). Sexual selection and sex differences in mathematical abilities. *Behavioral and Brain Sciences, 19,* 229–284.

Geary, D. C. (1998). *Male, female: The evolution of human sex differences.* Washington, DC: American Psychological Association.

Geary, D. C. (1999). Evolution and developmental sex differences. *Current Directions in Psychological Science, 8,* 115–120.

Geary, D. C. (2000). Evolution and proximate expression of human paternal investment. *Psychological Bulletin, 126,* 55–77.

Geary, D. C., & Bjorklund, D. F. (2000). Evolutionary developmental psychology. *Child Development, 71,* 57–65.

Gelman, R., & Williams, E. M. (1998). Enabling constraints for cognitive development and learning: Domain-specificity and epigenesis. In D. Kuhn & R. S. Siegler (Vol. Eds.), *Cognition, perception, and language, Vol. 2* (pp. 575–630). W. Damon (Gen. Ed.), *Handbook of child psychology* (5th Ed.). New York: Wiley.

Gilbert, S. F., Opitz, J. M., & Raff, R. A. (1996). Resynthesizing evolutionary and developmental biology. *Developmental Biology, 173,* 357–372.

Gilliard, E. T. (1969). *Birds of paradise and bower birds.* London: Weidenfeld and Nicolson.

Goodall, J. (1986). *The chimpanzees of Gombe: Patterns of behavior.* Cambridge, MA: The Belknap Press.

Gopnik, A., & Wellman, H. M. (1994). The theory theory. In L. A. Hirschfeld & S. A. Gelman (Eds.), *Mapping the mind: Domain specificity in cognition and culture* (pp. 257–293). New York: Cambridge University Press.

Grant, B. R., & Grant, P. R. (1993). Evolution of Darwin's finches caused by a rare climatic event. *Proceedings of the Royal Society of London B, 251,* 111–117.

Greenough, W. T., Black, J. E., & Wallace, C. S. (1987). Experience and brain development. *Child Development, 58,* 539–559.

Hall, J. A. (1984). *Nonverbal sex differences: Communication accuracy and expressive style.* Baltimore, MD: The Johns Hopkins University Press.

Halpern, D. F. (1992). *Sex differences in cognitive abilities* (2nd Ed.). Hillsdale, NJ: Lawrence Erlbaum.

Halpern, D. F. (1997). Sex differences in intelligence and their implications for education. *American Psychologist, 52,* 1091–1102.

Halpern, D. F., & Wright, T. M. (1996). A process-oriented model of cognitive sex differences. *Learning and Individual Differences, 8,* 3–24.

Hamilton, W. D. (1964). The genetical evolution of social behavior. II. *Journal of Theoretical Biology, 7,* 17–52.

Hamilton, W. D. (1975). Innate social aptitudes of man: An approach from evolutionary genetics. In R. Fox (Ed.), *Biosocial anthropology* (pp. 133–155). New York: John Wiley & Sons.

Happé, F. G. E. (1995). The role of age and verbal ability in the theory of mind task performance of subjects with autism. *Child Development, 66,* 843–855.

Hartup, W. W., & Stevens, N. (1997). Friendships and adaptation in the life course. *Psychological Bulletin, 121*, 355–370.

Hauser, M. D. (1996). *The evolution of communication.* Cambridge, MA: MIT Press/Bradford Books.

Haviland, J. J., & Malatesta, C. Z. (1981). The development of sex differences in nonverbal signals: Fallacies, facts, and fantasies. In C. Mayo & N. M. Henley (Eds.), *Gender and nonverbal behavior* (pp. 183–208). New York: Springer-Verlag.

Hyde, J. S., & Linn, M. C. (1988). Gender differences in verbal ability: A meta-analysis. *Psychological Bulletin, 104*, 53–69.

Jacobs, L. F., Gaulin, S. J. C., Sherry, D. F., & Hoffman, G. E. (1990). Evolution of spatial cognition: Sex-specific patterns of spatial behavior predict hippocampal size. *Proceedings of the National Academy of Sciences USA, 87*, 6349–6352.

Joffe, T. H. (1997). Social pressures have selected for an extended juvenile period in primates. *Journal of Human Evolution, 32*, 593–605.

Keeley, L. H. (1996). *War before civilization: The myth of the peaceful savage.* New York: Oxford University Press.

Kimura, D. (1999). *Sex and cognition.* Cambridge, MA: Bradford Books/MIT Press.

Klinger, L. G., & Dawson, G. (1996). Autistic disorder. In E. J. Mash & R. A. Barkley (Eds.), *Child psychopathology* (pp. 311–339). New York: Guilford Press.

Knight, G. P., & Chao, C.-C. (1989). Gender differences in the cooperative, competitive, and individualistic social values of children. *Motivation and Emotion, 13*, 125–141.

Krebs, J. R., & Davies, N. B. (1993). *An introduction to behavioural ecology* (3rd Ed.). Oxford: Blackwell Science Ltd.

Leslie, A. M. (1987). Pretense and representation: The origins of "theory of mind." *Psychological Review, 94*, 412–426.

Lever, J. (1978). Sex differences in the complexity of children's play and games. *American Sociological Review, 43*, 471–483.

Maccoby, E. E. (1988). Gender as a social category. *Developmental Psychology, 24*, 755–765.

Manson, J. H., & Wrangham, R. W. (1991). Intergroup aggression in chimpanzees and humans. *Current Anthropology, 32*, 369–390.

Mayr, E. (1974). Behavior programs and evolutionary strategies. *American Scientist, 62*, 650–659.

McGuinness, D., & Pribram, K. H. (1979). The origins of sensory bias in the development of gender differences in perception and cognition. In M. Bortner (Ed.), *Cognitive growth and development: Essays in memory of Herbert G. Birch* (pp. 3–56). New York: Brunner/Mazel.

Moscovitch, M., Winocur, G., & Behrmann, M. (1997). What is special about face recognition? Nineteen experiments on a person with visual object agnosia and dyslexia but normal face recognition. *Journal of Cognitive Neuroscience, 9*, 555–604.

Murdock, G. P. (1981). *Atlas of world cultures.* Pittsburgh, PA: University of Pittsburgh Press.

Parker, G. A., & Simmons, L. W. (1996). Parental investment and the control of selection: Predicting the direction of sexual competition. *Proceedings of the Royal Society of London B, 263*, 315–321.

Pasternak, B., Ember, C. R., & Ember, M. (1997). *Sex, gender, and kinship: A cross-cultural perspective*. Upper Saddle River, NJ: Prentice-Hall.

Pellegrini, A. D., & Smith, P. K. (1998). Physical activity play: The nature and function of a neglected aspect of play. *Child Development, 69*, 577–598.

Pinker, S. (1994). *The language instinct*. New York: William Morrow.

Pinker, S. (1997). *How the mind works*. New York: W. W. Norton & Co.

Povinelli, D. J., & Preuss, T. M. (1995). Theory of mind: Evolutionary history of a cognitive specialization. *Trends in Neuroscience, 18*, 418–424.

Premack, D. & Woodruff, G. (1978). Does the chimpanzee have a theory of mind? *Behavioral and Brain Sciences, 1*, 515–526.

Reynolds, J. D. (1987). Mating system and nesting biology of the red-necked phalarope *Phalaropus lobatus*: What constrains polyandry? *Isis, 129*, 225–242.

Reynolds, J. D., & Székely, T. (1997). The evolution of parental care in shorebirds: Life histories, ecology, and sexual selection. *Behavioral Ecology, 8*, 126–134.

Rilling, J. K., & Insel, T. R. (1999). The primate neocortex in comparative perspective using magnetic resonance imaging. *Journal of Human Evolution, 37*, 191–223.

Rosenthal, R., Hall, J. A., DiMatteo, M. R., Rogers, P. L., & Archer, D. (1979). *Sensitivity to nonverbal communication: The PONS test*. Baltimore, MD: The Johns Hopkins University Press.

Rotter, N. G., & Rotter, G. S. (1988). Sex differences in the encoding and decoding of negative facial emotions. *Journal of Nonverbal Behavior, 12*, 139–148.

Savin-Williams, R. C. (1987). *Adolescence: An ethological perspective*. New York: Springer-Verlag.

Sawaguchi, T. (1997). Possible involvement of sexual selection in neocortical evolution of monkeys and apes. *Folia Primatologica, 68*, 95–99.

Scarr, S., & McCarthy, K. (1983). How people make their own environments: A theory of genotype→environment effects. *Child Development, 54*, 424–435.

Schaller, M. (1992). In-group favoritism and statistical reasoning in social inference: Implications for formation and maintenance of group stereotypes. *Journal of Personality and Social Psychology, 63*, 61–74.

Seielstad, M. T., Minch, E., & Cavalli-Sforza, L. L. (1998). Genetic evidence for a higher female migration rate in humans. *Nature Genetics, 20*, 278–280.

Sellen, D. W. (1999). Polygyny and child growth in a traditional pastoral society: The case of the Datoga of Tanzania. *Human Nature, 10*, 329–371.

Shepard, R. N. (1994). Perceptual-cognitive universals as reflections of the world. *Psychonomic Bulletin & Review, 1*, 2–28.

Sherif, M., Harvey, O. J., White, B. J., Hood, W. R., & Sherif, C. W. (1961). *Intergroup conflict and cooperation: The Robbers Cave experiment*. Normal, OK: Institute of Group Relations, University of Oklahoma.

Sherry, D. F., Forbes, M. R. L., Khurgel, M., & Ivy, G. O. (1993). Females have a larger hippocampus than males in the brood-parasitic brown-headed cowbird. *Proceedings of the National Academy of Sciences USA, 90*, 7839–7843.

Stephan, W. G. (1985). Intergroup relations. In G. Lindzey & E. Aronson (Eds.), *Handbook of social psychology: Volume II: Special fields and applications* (pp. 599–658). New York: Random House.

Tallal, P. (1991). Hormonal influences in developmental learning disabilities. *Psychoneuroendocrinology, 16*, 203–211.

Tooby, J., & Cosmides, L. (1995). Mapping the evolved functional organization of mind and brain. In M. S. Gazzaniga (Ed.), *The cognitive neurosciences* (pp. 1185–1197). Cambridge, MA: Bradford Books/MIT Press.

Towson, S. M. J., Lerner, M. J., & de Carufel, A. (1981). Justice rules or ingroup loyalties: The effects of competition on children's allocation behavior. *Personality and Social Psychology Bulletin, 7*, 696–700.

Trivers, R. L. (1971). The evolution of reciprocal altruism. *Quarterly Review of Biology, 46*, 35–57.

Trivers, R. L. (1972). Parental investment and sexual selection. In B. Campbell (Ed.), *Sexual selection and the descent of man 1871–1971* (pp. 136–179). Chicago, IL: Aldine Publishing.

Trivers, R. L. (1974). Parent-offspring conflict. *American Zoologist, 14*, 249–264.

Wallen, K. (1996). Nature needs nurture: The interaction of hormonal and social influences on the development of behavioral sex differences in rhesus monkeys. *Hormones and Behavior, 30*, 364–378.

Whiting, B. B., & Edwards, C. P. (1988). *Children of different worlds: The formation of social behavior.* Cambridge, MA: Harvard University Press.

Williams, G. C. (1966). *Adaptation and natural selection: A critique of some current evolutionary thought.* Princeton, NJ: Princeton University Press.

Wrangham, R. W. (1980). An ecological model of female-bonded primate groups. *Behaviour, 75*, 262–300.

Yee, M. D., & Brown, R. (1992). Self-evaluations and intergroup attitudes in children aged three to nine. *Child Development, 63*, 619–629.

CHAPTER 3

Hormones, Brain, and Behavior: Putative Biological Contributions to Cognitive Sex Differences

Roslyn Holly Fitch
Heather A. Bimonte

Anyone who has attended a 17-week ultrasound in a healthy pregnancy is familiar with the query, "Do you want to know the sex?" If the answer is yes, a simple visual inspection of the fetal profile (if baby cooperates) is typically sufficient to satisfy curiosity. However, a more reliable indication of fetal sex is provided through amniocentesis, in which the chromosomal profile of the fetus is assessed (in most cases, for reasons other than sex determination). Although expectant parents waiting to pick nursery room colors know that ultrasound sex-determination may or may not be reliable, amniocentesis is almost definite. The reason is that chromosomes determine gonadal sex and, in all but a few developmentally anomalous conditions, gonadal sex determines phenotypic sex.

HORMONAL MECHANISMS OF ACTION ON THE BRAIN

XX or XY?

In early fetal mammalian development, the gonadal system is equipotential or "indifferent." At this developmental time point, the sexual characteristics of the fetus are not yet established. However, a genetically normal fetus will carry either an XX or XY sex chromosome pair. It is the presence or absence of the Y chromosome (and more specifically, a gene on the Y chromosome) that will determine the path of ongoing sexual differentiation. If the Y-chromosome gene coding for testis determination factor (TDF) is transcribed, then the production of this protein induces development of the indifferent gonads on a masculine path (Berta et al., 1990). As the primordial gonads begin to differentiate into testes, they also begin to secrete hormones that further promote the masculine phenotype, including müllerian regression factor (a peptide hormone that induces regression of feminine gonadal structures) and testosterone (a steroid hormone, which continues to be secreted throughout life).

So what factors determine a feminine developmental path? Until recently, it was believed that the female developmental path occurred simply because active induction of the male path did not. Accordingly, terms such as "hormonally neutral" and "default" were used to describe differentiation of the female (e.g., see Lisk & Suydam, 1967). Yet ongoing evidence suggests that normal growth of the ovaries may also depend on the presence of an ovary-determining gene, as well as estrogen secreted from primordial ovarian tissue (Eicher & Washburn, 1983; Wilson, George, & Griffen, 1981), and researchers have suggested that estrogen (presumably of ovarian origin) plays an active role in feminization of the brain (e.g., Dohler et al., 1984a and b; Dohler, 1991; Hendricks, 1992; Toran-Allerand, 1976, 1992). This evidence of androgenic as well as estrogenic effects on neurobehavioral systems is reviewed. We begin, however, with a short overview of hormonal mechanisms of action on the brain. This provides a framework within which the developmental mechanisms underlying neurobiological sex differences, which may in turn influence cognitive sex differences, can be considered.

Gonadal Steroids, Steroid Metabolism, and Alpha-Fetoprotein

Androgens comprise a category of chemically related hormones produced primarily in the testes in the male, and in the adrenal cortex of both sexes; the ovaries also produce small amounts. As stated previously, testicular androgens are the primary catalyst for masculine sexual differentiation in mammals (see Breedlove, 1992, or Toran-Allerand, 1986 for review). Moreover, there are a number of different androgens that exert masculinizing effects in different regions and at different times in development. They may be metabolized from one form to another before acting at the cellular level. For example, testosterone can be intraneuronally converted (aromatized) to estradiol in a variety of species (see Toran-Allerand, 1986, for review). This "locally biosynthesized" estrogen may act on estrogen receptors within neuronal nuclei. This mechanism appears to play a critical role in the masculinization process for many mammalian species. Specifically, androgens such as testosterone are secreted by the testes, but can then be converted to estrogen within individual cells before exerting developmental effects. This metabolic pathway led to surprising observations that high levels of estrogen in development can masculinize many neural and behavioral features.

One might ask why females are not inherently "masculinized" by maternal cross-placental estrogen and/or estrogen from their own ovaries. In rodents at least, females are protected from estrogen-based masculinization via a blood-born protein called alpha-fetoprotein (AFP) (Raynaud, Mercier-Bodard, & Balieu, 1971). AFP, which is present during the perinatal period, binds to circulating estrogen and is thought to prevent it from entering the neuron as freely as unbound estrogen (although small amounts of estrogen may pass into the neuron while bound to AFP) (see Toran-Allerand, 1986). Evidence suggests that maximal levels of AFP are seen in rat brain on gestational day 18, and that AFP declines to low levels by postnatal day seven when its synthesis appears to "switch off" (e.g., Ali & Sahib, 1983). Hence, female rodents are "protected" from the potentially masculinizing effects of estrogen by AFP from late gestation through about postnatal day seven.

Interestingly, masculinizing effects of androgens on the brain typically occur in rodents during this same late prenatal/early neonatal time-frame (e.g., Rhees, Shryne, & Gorski, 1990a and b; Wagner & Clemens, 1989). As sensitivity to the masculinizing effects of androgens ends, and as AFP levels fall in rodents, the ovaries become active (around postnatal day seven) (Mannan & O'Shaughnessy, 1991; Sokka & Huhtaniemi, 1995; Weniger, Zeis, & Chouraqui, 1993), and begin to secrete estrogen and progesterone. Accordingly, evidence suggests that ovarian effects on brain and behavior occur much later in life than the early masculinizing effects of androgens (see Fitch & Denenberg, 1998, for review). The potential relevance of temporal differences in testicular and ovarian effects to neurobehavioral systems, which, in turn, may have differing developmental time-frames are considered further in later sections.

Steroid Receptors and Steroid Effects on Neural Growth

How does the secretion of steroid hormones (including both testicular androgen and ovarian estrogen) influence ongoing development of the brain? Systemically released steroids are carried through the bloodstream, move into local neurons, and bind to intraneuronal nuclear receptors in target brain areas where they ultimately alter neuronal genomic expression (see Toran-Allerand, 1986, or McCarthy, 1994 for review). Thus, the topography of steroid effects on the brain is largely mediated by the distribution and binding affinity of specific receptor types (i.e., estrogen receptors, androgen receptors, etc.). Further, receptor distributions appear to differ as a function of age and sex (e.g., Brown, MacLusky, Shanabrough, & Naftolin, 1990; Kuhnemann, Brown, Hochberg, & MacLusky, 1994; Miranda & Toran-Allerand, 1992).

The effects of steroid binding may be expressed as alterations in regional cell growth, proliferation, or death, which may, in turn, influence cell number, size, and packing density. Early migrational patterns, dendritic growth, and neuronal myelination may also be altered. Accumulated evidence suggests that "sexual differentiation of the brain" reflects interacting steroid effects on many such neural parameters. Moreover, the interaction of hormonal effects on multiple parameters at different points in development most likely induce changes in neural circuitry and function that are not merely quantitative (i.e., is a structure larger or smaller in males or females?) but qualitative (for reviews see Breedlove, 1992; McCarthy, 1994; Tobet & Fox, 1992; Toran-Allerand, 1986).

Indeed, the inherently complex nature of developmental neuroendocrine effects cautions us in the interpretation of reported sex differences for unidimensional measures (such as size of neural structures or performance on specific tests). Certainly, meaningful interpretations can be drawn from some sex differences, such as in the size of the spinal nucleus of the bulbocavernosus (SNB). This nucleus contains spinal motorneurons that enervate the muscles of the penis. Accordingly, the SNB contains more and larger neurons in male as compared to female rats. This sex dimorphism is mediated by early exposure to androgen (see Breedlove, 1992). The implication of such a sexual dimorphism is relatively straightforward. However, as one moves to more complex sex effects (e.g., in size of the corpus callosum or on higher-order cognitive tasks), it becomes far more difficult to make straightforward interpretations. Indeed, the mechanisms that relate structure to function in the human brain per se, much less those that relate neural sex differences to cognitive sex differences, are still poorly understood.

Organizational versus Activational Effects of Steroid Hormones

Mechanisms of hormone action traditionally have been divided into organizational effects that seem to occur early in development and are permanent, even if hormones are removed (as compared to activational effects that seem to occur later in development and are transitory, thereby depending upon the presence of the hormone at the time of assessment). Within this framework, sex differences in neuroanatomy were largely assumed to reflect the permanent organizing effects of steroids present during early development. Conversely, many sexually dimorphic behaviors (e.g., sexual behaviors in rodents) appeared to be dependent on circulating hormones because they could be induced through exogenous administration of sex steroids. Still other behavioral effects appeared to be primarily dependent on the early hormonal milieu (e.g., reduced rough and tumble play following early testosterone removal in the male) (Meaney, 1988). In experimental animal studies, activational and organizational influences are somewhat easier to separate than in human studies, because both early and circulating hormone levels can be independently manipulated. Even so, ongoing research indicates that although early hormonal exposure appears to play a significant role in mediating sexually differentiated behavior, these effects may be further augmented or influenced by activational effects (e.g., see Beatty, 1992). This interactive model reflects, in part, the fact that activating (or circulating) hormones are acting on a differentiated neural substrate and a "male" versus "female" brain is unlikely to respond to the same circulating hormones in the same way (e.g., Beatty & Beatty, 1970).

Moreover, accumulated evidence has blurred the organizational/activational dichotomy. Specifically, the temporal distinction that categorized hormonal effects during early development as organizational and hormonal effects in adulthood as activational has been called into question. Nonconforming data include observations of estrogenic activation of sexual behavior in female rat pups as young as six days (Williams, 1986a), as well as changes in neuroanatomy following postpubertal hormone manipulations (Bloch & Gorski, 1988; Bimonte, Fitch, & Denenberg, 2000a and b; Bimonte, Mack, Stavnezen, & Denenberg, 2000; Pappas et al., 1979; Rodriguez-Sierra, 1986). Some researchers have suggested that the primary organizational/activational distinction now depends on whether induced changes represent permanent or transient effects, whenever in life they occur (see Arnold & Breedlove, 1985, or Williams, 1986b, for discussion). Classification of hormonal effects is complicated further by accumulating evidence of neurophysiological and neurochemical plasticity in the female brain, reflecting neural sensitivity to endogenous hormonal fluctuation (e.g., Becker & Cha, 1989; Frankfurt, Gould, Woolley, & McEwen 1990; Woolley, Gould, Frankfurt, & McEwen, 1990). Specifically, it appears that fluctuations in some neurophysiological features occur in response to ovarian hormone cyclicity. Although these effects reasonably could be excluded from a review on neural sex differences because they are transient and not "permanent features," they nevertheless certainly constitute a part of what makes the female brain distinct (or differentiated) from the male brain. Moreover, because these "permanently cyclic" features have potentially important relevance to the interpretation of sex differences in cognitive function, we include these findings in the discussion (see the section on "Activational Hormone Effects on Cognition in Human and Animal Studies").

PERMANENT HORMONE EFFECTS
ON NEUROBEHAVIORAL MEASURES

Although recognizing the difficulty inherent to separation of organizational and activational hormonal effects on neural and behavioral measures, we nevertheless attempt to cull and review hormone effects that appear to be permanent and are mediated by some period of developmental exposure to gonadal hormones. In this section, we review some of the known permanent effects of androgens on behavior and structure, followed by a discussion of permanent estrogen effects on behavior and structure. Finally, we note that the temporal developmental window for sensitivity to permanent neurobehavioral effects of ovarian hormones seems to be much later than for testicular hormones. Neurobehavioral effects that appear to be transient and mediated largely by circulating hormones are discussed further in the section on activational hormone effects.

Neurobehavioral Effects of Androgens in Human Studies

Developmental androgen effects have been reported for human cognition, as well as sexual orientation and aggression (see Collaer & Hines, 1995, for review). Some of the earliest work in this area derived from studies of human clinical populations with anomalous hormonal exposure. For example, a small percentage of girls are born with a condition known as congenital adrenal hyperplasia (CAH), in which the adrenal glands produce excessive amounts of androgen. Indeed, in some cases the androgenization is sufficiently severe to require corrective surgery on the genitalia. Behavioral studies on CAH girls have indicated a general pattern of enhanced spatial skills and reduced verbal fluency, consistent with more "male-like" cognitive patterns (e.g., Leveroni & Berenbaum, 1998). In addition, males born with androgen insensitivity syndrome (characterized by a complete lack of sensitivity to endogenous androgens), appear phenotypically as females and show cognitive patterns of higher verbal than spatial processing (a pattern more typical of females). Such data has bolstered the view that early exposure to androgens may contribute to the apparent male advantage on some spatial tasks. More recent studies confirm this association; for example, by demonstrating that prenatal androgen levels are positively correlated with later mental rotation skill in girls (e.g., Grimshaw, Sitarenios, & Finegan, 1995).

The developmental sequelae through which early exposure to varying levels of hormones ultimately translates to behavioral differences are quite difficult to characterize. For example, few neuroimaging studies have been performed that directly link structural and functional (behavioral) effects associated with androgen exposure. Although some gross structural evidence of sex differences in the human brain have been reported, for example, in asymmetry of the plenum temporale (Kulynych et al., 1994) and size of the interhemispheric fiber tract and the corpus callosum (see Bishop & Wahlsten, 1997, for review), the contribution of androgen exposure to such effects is unclear. Moreover, the functional significance of these structural sex differences is largely unknown. For these reasons, many researchers have turned to the use of animal models to study hormonal effects on behavior to elucidate underlying neurodevelopmental mechanisms that ultimately may contribute to sex differences in cognition in humans.

Androgen and Behavioral Effects in Animal Studies

It has been demonstrated in rodents that males and females differ on a large number of nonreproductive behaviors, including aggressiveness and rough and tumble play, and that many of these behaviors are influenced by neonatal exposure to testosterone (for review see Beatty, 1992). With respect to cognitive behavior, female rats normally learn an active avoidance response more quickly than males, whereas males tend to outperform females on passive avoidance. Moreover, female rats treated neonatally with testosterone and primed with testosterone prior to testing appear to be indistinguishable from males in avoidance learning behavior (see Van Haaren, Van Hest, & Heinsbroek, 1990 for review). However, circulating testosterone may not be critical to this sex difference because other researchers have reported that early neonatal exposure to androgen alone is sufficient to induce a male-like pattern of active avoidance learning in female rats (Denti & Negroni, 1975). Avoidance behavior in male rats can also be demasculinized. Specifically, prenatal exposure to the androgen-receptor blocker cyproterone acetate, followed by postnatal castration, resulted in males with female-like avoidance behavior in adulthood (Scouten, Grotelueschen, & Beatty, 1975).

With respect to spatial learning, male rats typically do better than females. In general, neonatal castration of males or exposure of females to androgens reverses this adult sexually dimorphic pattern (Dawson, Cheung, & Lau, 1975; Joseph, Hess, & Birecree, 1978; Stewart, Skavarenina, & Pottier, 1975). More recently, Roof (1993b) reported that male rats performed significantly better than females on both the radial arm and Morris water maze. Roof also found that neonatal treatment with testosterone improved spatial ability in female rats to male levels, an effect expressed as early as 21 days of age. Consistent with this, Roof and Havens (1992) reported that neonatal treatment with testosterone led to a male-like pattern of hippocampal anatomy (as measured by size and asymmetry of granule cell layers) and improved maze learning in female rats. Moreover, maze performance correlated significantly with the size of hippocampal granule cell layers (Roof, 1993a).

In a related series of studies, Williams and colleagues manipulated specific components of the extra-maze testing environment and showed that male and female rats use different strategies and rely on different cues in maze learning (e.g., Williams, Barnett, & Meck, 1990; Williams & Meck, 1991). Williams also showed that estrogen plays a major role in influencing the development of spatial ability in rats by implanting estradiol into the hippocampus or cortex of neonatally castrated males. This reinstated male-like maze learning behavior. These findings support a developmental role for estrogen biosynthesis from testosterone in sexual differentiation of the rat cerebral cortex.

Sex differences in cerebral organization are also seen in nonhuman primates. Clark and Goldman-Rakic (1989) reported that intact male monkeys made fewer errors than intact females in learning a visual object discrimination reversal task. Lesions to the orbital prefrontal cortex disrupted the ability of males, but not females, to perform the task. Furthermore, females given perinatal androgen treatment performed like normal males, and were similarly disrupted by the lesion. Interestingly, this male advantage does not generalize across ages and visual learning tasks, since 3-month-old male monkeys were slower to learn a set of visual discriminations than were age-matched females (Bachevalier, Hagger, & Bercu, 1989). In this study, testosterone levels were obtained from males and estradiol levels from females. These hormone levels were correlated against learning scores. Within the three-month-old male monkey group, the rank-order correlation was .95; the higher the testosterone, the slower the learning. There were no other significant correlations. The interpretation was that high testosterone levels temporarily slowed the maturation of the neural systems underlying visual discrimination because by six months of age no sex differences or hormone-behavior correlations were found. A later study showed that ablation of inferior temporal cortex depressed visual discrimination scores in three-month-old female monkeys, but did not affect age-matched males (Bachevalier, Brickson, Hager, & Mishkin, 1990), an effect that is apparently mediated by testosterone exposure (Hagger & Bachevalier, 1991). These results agree with the interpretation that testosterone delayed maturation of neural systems underlying the visual discrimination task (see also Bachevalier & Hagger, 1991).

Neural Effects of Androgen in Animal Studies

In animal studies, evidence has clearly shown that neonatal testosterone is involved in sexual differentiation of the brain. Although many studies have demonstrated significant androgenic effects on subcortical structures (e.g., the sexually dimorphic nucleus of the preoptic area of the hypothalamus) (see Gorski, 1984), we focus on a summary of androgenic effects on the cerebral cortex and hippocampus. These are more likely to be relevant to reports of human cognitive sex differences.

Diamond and colleagues (e.g., Diamond, Dowling, & Johnson, 1981) reported that certain regions of the cortex are significantly thicker in the right hemisphere than in the left in male rats, whereas females show a nonsignificant trend toward asymmetry in the opposite direction (see also Kolb, Sutherland, Nonneman, & Whishaw, 1982; Stewart & Kolb, 1988). This effect appears to be mediated at least partly by androgen exposure because neonatally gonadectomized male rats fail to show the R–L pattern of cortical asymmetry seen in intact males (Diamond, 1991; Stewart & Kolb, 1988). The male cortical thickness pattern is also reversed by prenatal stress (Fleming, Anderson, Rhees, Kinghorn, & Bakaitis, 1986; Stewart & Kolb, 1988), which depresses and shifts the gestational day 18 testosterone surge in fetal male rats (Ward & Weisz, 1980). Moreover, the masculinizing effect of androgens on cortical asymmetry in rats appears to be mediated by conversion to estrogen because perinatal exposure to the aromatase blocker ATD (1,4,6 androstatriene-3,17-dione) reversed the adult cortical thickness pattern in males (Diamond, 1991). Furthermore, sex differences have been demonstrated in the dendritic branching patterns of prefrontal cortical cells in rats, and these patterns appear to be influenced by gonadal hormonal exposure during early development (Kolb & Stewart, 1991). In addition, cortical thickness of the binocular subfield of occipital cortex (Oc1B) is significantly greater in male rats as compared to females (Seymoure & Juraska, 1992). There are also sex differences in the apical branching of Oc1B and Oc1M (monocular subfield) neurons, wherein females have longer dendrites, terminal branches, and bifurcating branches. Reid and Juraska (1992) confirmed the sex difference in binocular cortical thickness. They also reported that this effect reflects higher numbers of neurons and glial cells in males, with no sex differences in soma size or neuronal density. More recently, Reid and Juraska (1995) found sex differences in synaptic junctions in this region, with the higher number of neurons in male cortex relating to higher numbers of synaptic junctions.

Neonatal androgen has also been shown to affect the development of cortical neurotransmitter systems. Indeed, monoamine systems innervating anterior cortex in intact female rats develop earlier than in males or androgen treated females (Stewart, Kuhnemann, & Rajabi, 1991). Evidence suggests that sex differences in development of frontal cortical catecholamine systems may derive from prenatal biosynthesis of estrogen from testosterone (Stewart & Rajabi, 1994).

With respect to the hippocampus, Juraska (1991) reported sex differences in hippocampal dendritic anatomy that vary in direction as a function of rearing environment, and are influenced by early androgen exposure. Roof (1993a) also found sex differences in the granule cell layers of the hippocampus in rats, and found that this effect is modulated by early exposure to testosterone.

The data clearly demonstrate that testosterone exerts developmental effects on many aspects of the brain in experimental animal studies. Although the specific relationships among neural and behavioral effects remains unclear, it seems reasonable to presume that some of the reported neural effects of androgens are tied to some of the behavioral effects reported. Because animal studies provide tight experimental control of most environmental variables, and because social and societal influences on sex-specific behavior and neurobiology would appear less pronounced in an experimental animal preparation, it seems reasonable to conclude that sexually dimorphic developmental hormonal factors contribute to at least some portion of sex-based variance in cognitive behavior as reported in the human literature and as addressed in this issue.

Neurobehavioral Effects of Estrogen in Human Studies

As discussed earlier, the traditional model of sexual differentiation presumes that exposure—or lack of exposure—to androgen is the critical factor that determines expression of the male or female neurobehavioral phenotype. However, accumulated evidence suggests that the secretory products of the ovaries, primarily estrogen, are also critical to the normal development of the female brain. As such, a growing interest in the neurobehavioral role of estrogen, and potential effects of estrogen on sexually differentiated neurobehavioral features, has recently emerged.

As one example, a large amount of controversy has surrounded the frequently cited report that females have a more bulbous corpus callosum (CC) (the fiber tract inter-connecting the cerebral hemispheres) as compared to males

(Delacoste-Utamsing & Holloway, 1982; but see Bishop & Wahlston, 1997). To the extent that this presumed sex difference might be mediated by hormonal exposure, the traditional assumption would be that such exposure specifically revolves around the presence or absence of androgen during early development. Consider, however, the additional observation that sex differences in CC size are highly dependent on age. Specifically, anterior regions in the callosa of women were seen to increase in size even through their 50s, whereas male anterior callosal measures appeared to peak in their 20s to 30s and decline in size thereafter (Cowell, Allen, Zalatimo, & Denenberg, 1992). These differences in gross anatomy may reflect, in part, observations of cellular cytoarchitectural components of the anterior corpus callosum that continue to develop well into adulthood in women but not men (Aboitiz, 1996).

But what is the cause for these divergent age-by-sex trends in callosal morphology? One obvious connection is that male androgen levels begin to decline in their 20s to 30s. In women, these years typically include active childbearing and nursing followed by a gradual decline in ovarian activity until menopause (typically in the 50s). Thus, high levels of estrogen in the early childbearing years may have an inhibitory effect on female CC growth. This inhibition may decline with gradual reductions in estrogen levels through mid-adulthood (discussed in Cowell et al., 1992). In addition to these differing CC developmental trends in early to middle adulthood, evidence suggests that the anterior CC in women declines in width to the size seen in men by the seventh decade of life (i.e., after menopause). These combined results suggest that estrogen plays a complex, multidimensional role in the neurophysiology of the CC across the female life span. Further, such an interpretation of complex, multidimensional hormone effects is supported by evidence from animal studies showing that developmental exposure to testosterone leads to a larger callosum in early adulthood, whereas developmental exposure to ovarian estrogen inhibits CC size when measured in early adulthood (Bimonte, Fitch, & Denenberg, 2000a and b; Bimonte, Mack, Stavnezer, & Denenberg, 2000; Fitch & Denenberg, 1998 for review).

Neurocognitive studies assessing the role of ovarian hormones have further revealed significant effects of estrogen decline in middle adulthood, and estrogen replacement therapy after menopause. Indeed, evidence suggests that estrogen depletion and replacement modulate a wide array of cognitive, emotional and neurophysiological factors (e.g., Kampen & Sherwin, 1994; Paganini-Hill & Henderson, 1994; Schneider, Farlow, Henderson, & Pogoda, 1996). These activational effects of estrogen on cognitive behavior are discussed in later sections.

Evidence from participants with endocrine dysfunction also suggests an active role for ovarian hormones in normal female development. For example, it has long been known that women with Turner's syndrome (a genetic disorder characterized by one X chromosome and ovarian dysgenesis) show a wide array of phenotypic alterations and cognitive deficits, most notably in spatial ability (e.g., Buchanan, Pavlovic, & Rovet, 1998; Ross et al., 1995). In addition, research has shown that the brains of girls with Turner's syndrome are characterized by a variety of anomalies in parietal cortex and hippocampus (e.g., Murphy et al., 1993; Reiss et al., 1995). Whether or not these cortical effects are mediated, at least in part, by anomalous developmental exposure (or lack of exposure) to estrogen, and whether or how they relate to observed cognitive deficits, remains to be determined.

Estrogen and Behavioral Effects in Animal Studies

Consistent with the human research literature, animal research literature is also characterized by emergent evidence of a role for ovarian hormones (specifically estrogen) in sexual differentiation of the female brain and behavior. For example, prepubertal ovariectomy (OVX) has been shown to alter female nonreproductive behavior in a male-typical direction using a variety of paradigms. Early removal of the ovaries decreased open field behavior in adult female rats (Blizard & Denef, 1973; Denti & Negroni, 1975; Stewart & Cygan, 1980), decreased activity in a plus maze (Leret, Molina-Holgado, & Gonzalez, 1994; Zimmerberg & Farley, 1993), depressed active avoidance performance (Denti & Negroni, 1975), and decreased behavioral responsiveness to amphetamine (Forgie & Stewart, 1994). These effects are consistent with emerging evidence that developmental exposure to the secretory products of the ovaries (e.g., estrogen) plays a critical role in human female neurocognitive development.

Neural Effects of Estrogen in Animal Studies

Accumulating evidence from animal studies also demonstrates a significant role for estrogen in feminization of neuromorphological structure. One of the most compelling series of studies to support this claim has shown that early developmental exposure to estrogen is critical for normal development of the female rat CC (Bimonte, Fitch, & Denenberg, 2000a and b; Bimonte, Mack, Stavnezer, & Denenberg, 2000; Fitch, Cowell, Schrott, & Denenberg, 1991; Mack et al., 1993). Specifically, it has been found that females receiving prepubertal OVX exhibit significantly larger CC in adulthood. Interestingly, these prepubertal OVX effects can be reversed by estrogen replacement—either thrrough an estrogen implant or by ovary transfer—relatively late in life (Bimonte, Fitch, & Denenberg, 2000a and b; Bimonte, Mack, Stavnezer, & Denenberg, 2000; Mack et al., 1993). Finally, and perhaps most intriguing of all, is the finding that early exposure to estrogen appears to be essential for the female brain to respond normally to estrogen in adulthood, as measured by CC responsiveness to an adult ovary transfer or estrogen implant (Bimonte, Fitch, & Denenberg, 2000b). This latter finding suggests that the apparent life-long sensitivity of the female brain to estrogen may in fact be an organizational feature of the female brain that is set early in development by exposure to ovarian secretions.

There is other evidence that estrogen exposure has significant neuroanatomical effects. For example, neonatal treatment with an estrogen antagonist or estrogen mRNA antisense has been shown to reduce the volume of the sexually dimorphic nucleus of the preoptic area (SDN-POA) in female rats (Dohler et al., 1984a and b; McCarthy, Schlenker, & Pfaff, 1993). Prepubertal OVX has been found to increase cortical thickness (Diamond, Johnson, & Ehlert, 1979; Stewart & Kolb, 1988), whereas OVX followed by estrogen treatment decreased cortical thickness (Pappas, Diamond, & Johnson, 1979) relative to OVX only. One study found prepubertal OVX to alter patterns of asymmetry in cortical thickness (Diamond, Dowling, & Johnson, 1981), although another group failed to replicate this finding (Stewart & Kolb, 1988). Prepubertal OVX was also found to prevent a female-typical loss of dendritic spines in the visual cortex of rats (Munoz-Cueto, Garcia-Segura, & Ruiz-Marcos, 1990). Together, these findings demonstrate that ovarian hormones in fact have a significant influence on brain neurophysiology, which may ultimately be linked to behavior.

Moreover, a different set of temporal parameters appears to apply to feminization as compared to masculinization. The sensitive period for permanent structural and behavioral ovarian effects does not end by day 10 in female rodents, as generally appears to be true for androgen effects in males, but, depending on the system under study, appears to extend much later in life. Many of the ovarian manipulations just cited were not performed until the late neonatal or prepubertal period, but nevertheless exerted significant (and apparently permanent) effects on brain and behavior (e.g., Fitch et al., 1991; Forgie & Stewart, 1994; Mack et al., 1993; Munoz-Cueto et al., 1990; Pappas et al., 1979; Stewart & Cygan, 1980). Some estrogen manipulations were even performed postpubertally (in adulthood) and were still found to exert apparently permanent effects on brain structure (Bimonte, Fitch, & Denenberg, 2000a and b; Bimonte, Mack, Stavnezer, & Denenberg, 2000; Bloch & Gorski, 1988; Pappas et al., 1979; Rodriguez-Sierra, 1986). These findings suggest a sensitive period for ovarian effects on neurophysiology that extends up to or around puberty in rodents. Indeed, for some neurobehavioral systems, sensitivity to estrogen may extend throughout life.

Finally, other significant effects of ovarian steroids on neurophysiology and neurochemistry have been seen in the adult female brain that are largely nonpermanent (i.e., are transient or activational). These are further discussed in the following section.

Neurobehavioral Associations: Implications for Human Cognitive Sex Differences

We reviewed evidence showing that both testicular androgens and ovarian estrogens exert significant developmental effects on brain and behavior resulting in the expression of sex differences. These effects have been most clearly demonstrated in animal studies, although evidence of hormonal associations with cognitive behavior in humans supports the view that the latter effects are also influenced (at least in part) by intermediary hormone effects on brain physiology. Accordingly, there is ample evidence of sex differences in neuromorphological features, brain organization, and incidence of neurodevelopmental disorders in humans, and the evidence reviewed here supports the view that these effects may reflect, at least in part, differential hormonal exposure. Finally, it appears likely that such neurobiological effects are related to observed sex differences in cognitive behavior in humans.

For example, sex differences in language recovery following left-hemisphere damage have been consistently observed, with females showing significantly better recovery (McGlone, 1980). Sex differences in the magnitude of the right ear advantage (REA) for the discrimination of verbal material have also been reported, with males showing a larger and more consistent REA (Kimura & Harshman, 1984), indicating greater functional asymmetry. Sex differences have been reported in the pattern of cerebral blood flow during the performance of verbal tasks (Wood, Flower, & Naylor, 1991), in asymmetry as measured by fMRI during verbal tasks (Shaywitz et al., 1995), and in structural asymmetry of the right and left plenum temporale as measured by MRI (Kulynych et al., 1994). These results all support the existence of sex differences in the pattern of cerebral organization, particularly for language related functions, with males generally demonstrating greater asymmetry than females. These effects speak in turn to a hormonal role in establishing cerebral organization of language functions.

These observed sex differences in interhemispheric function may be further associated with reported sex differences in CC morphology (Cowell et al., 1992; Witelson, 1991; see also Bishop & Wahlston, 1997). For example, it has been shown in women that certain lexical and rhyming tasks involve activation of right and left language centers in the frontal lobe, which sends fibers through the anterior CC (Shaywitz et al., 1995; Wood et al., 1991). In men, these same tasks are associated primarily with activation of the left hemisphere, which would suggest the need for a different pattern of interhemispheric connections as compared to women.

Animal studies further support the general notion of hormonally mediated effects on cerebral organization, specifically by demonstrating hormonally mediated differences in the maturation rate of specific cortical regions that in turn critically influence the cognitive effects of lesioning these regions (e.g., Bachevalier et al., 1989; 1990; Bachevalier & Hagger, 1991; Clark & Goldman-Rakic, 1989; Kolb & Cioe, 1996). Geschwind and Galaburda (1985) postulated that differential androgen exposure in utero may influence the development of cerebral organization, particularly for language, and further suggested that exposure to androgens may render the male brain more susceptible to adverse effects following developmental injury. Other studies suggest that female hormones may protect the brain from the deleterious consequences of cortical damage (Roof et al., 1993). This accumulated evidence of sex differences in early hormonal exposure, neural maturation, brain organization, and response to focal brain injury, may further relate to reports of a higher incidence of language and reading impairments among males as compared to females (e.g., Finucci et al., 1983; Gualtieri & Hicks, 1985; Niels & Aram, 1986; Vogel, 1990), although this observation remains controversial (Shaywitz et al., 1990).

Sex differences in the neurobiological consequences of aging have also been observed in humans. For example, sex differences in age-related decreases in cortical volume have been observed. Specifically, volumetric decrements with aging are greater in men than women in the frontal and temporal cortices (Cowell et al., 1994; Murphy et al., 1996). In the parietal cortex and hippocampus, decrements are greater in women than in men (Murphy et al., 1996).

The consequences of these findings for cognitive sex differences has yet to be fully elucidated. However, it is apparent that the multidimensional nature of hormonal effects on neurobiology and behavior—that diverge with the timing and nature of hormonal exposure, and further interact with injury, aging, and experience across the lifespan—are not likely to provide us with evidence of unidimensional sex differences that can be interpreted in straightforward and simplistic ways.

ACTIVATIONAL HORMONE EFFECTS ON COGNITION IN ANIMAL AND HUMAN STUDIES

Up to this point, we have discussed evidence that many male and female patterns of brain and behavior, and therefore also the expression of sex differences, are permanently influenced by gonadal hormone exposure during early life. Such effects are typically considered the critical descriptors of sexual differentiation. Thus, any behaviors that can be influenced by exogenous administration of hormones—defined as "activational" or transient effects—are typically not considered essential to characterization of sex differences in the brain. This thinking rests on the reasonable assumption that the adult brain is a relatively fixed substrate (at least until old age). Thus masculine features, as determined by early androgen exposure, might be considered to be "set" and subject to an inevitable emergence through a normal developmental trajectory. Feminine features, historically thought to be determined by an absence of androgen during critical early developmental periods, would similarly be expected to emerge along an inevitable developmental trajectory. The mechanisms allowing early steroid effects to emerge at later points in brain development remains somewhat unclear. Nevertheless, the assumption has been that sexually dimorphic features are "set" or imprinted following early androgen exposure (or lack thereof), and that, where such differences exist, they can be reliably measured via brain and/or behavior once the adult state is achieved. As such, little regard has been given to circulating hormonal status at the time of non-reproductive behavioral evaluations in both animal and human research.

However, the assumptions that (1) androgen exposure or lack thereof is the critical defining factor of permanent sex differences, (2) the adult brain is defined by a fixed state, and (3) activational hormone effects are not relevant to sex differences in the brain, have all been recently challenged. The latter two assumptions have specifically been challenged by a series of animal studies demonstrating that a variety of neurobiological features of the female brain are influenced by cyclic hormonal status. For example, OVX and estrogen replacement in adulthood were found to alter dendritic spine density of ventromedial hypothalamic neurons in female rats, and this measure was found to vary endogenously across the estrous cycle (1990). Similarly, exposure to pulsatile estrogen was shown to potentiate dopaminergic and behavioral response to AMPH in female but not male rats. This responsiveness also was found to vary across the estrous cycle (Becker, 1990; Becker & Cha, 1989; Castner & Becker, 1990; Forgie & Stewart, 1994). Adult OVX has been shown to increase dendritic arbor of pyramidal neurons in parietal cortex (Stewart & Kolb, 1994), as well as a decrease hippocampal dendritic spine density (Gould, Frankfurt, Woolley, & McEwen, 1990). The latter effect can be blocked by concurrent treatment with estrogen and progesterone, and has also been shown to vary across the estrous cycle (Woolley et al., 1990; Woolley & McEwen, 1992).

What relevance do these findings have to sex differences in the brain and, more specifically, to sex differences in cognition? These data show that some neurophysiologic and neurochemical parameters of the female brain vary with fluctuating levels of ovarian hormones. As such, they suggest that "chronic cyclicity" is not merely a feature of the hypothalamic–pituitary–gonadal axis in females, but that cyclicity per se has new-found importance to accurate characterization of the female brain. Indeed, these findings may collectively challenge the assumption that the adult brain can be considered, and experimentally assessed, as a fixed or completely stable substrate. Accordingly, several studies have shown that the expression of cognitive sex differences in adulthood (i.e., as seen in spatial memory) is affected by hormonal status at the time of testing (e.g., Galea, Kavaliers, Ossenkopp, & Hampson, 1995). As research in this area has expanded, evidence has also indicated that fluctuating levels of androgens may affect cognitive function in males (e.g., Goudsmit, Van de Poll, & Swaab, 1990). It should be recognized that the effects of activational hormones on cognitive behavior represents an emergent area of neuroscientific research. Many of the studies reviewed in this chapter are quite recent and some are contradictory. Clearly, further research is required before the links between neurophysiology and the expression of cognitive sex differences can be fully understood.

Circulating Estrogen Effects on Spatial Ability in Women

Due to the unethical nature of manipulating hormonal status in humans for the purpose of experimental assessment, researchers have been resourceful in investigating the activational effects of gonadal hormones in humans. The methods employed for such investigations have included assessments of healthy pre-menopausal women at different phases of the menstrual cycle, menopausal women with or without hormone replacement therapy, and anti-estrogen and anti-androgen treated female and male transsexuals.

Studies investigating performance across the menstrual cycle in women have demonstrated subtle transient effects of ovarian hormones on tasks that require spatial ability (Chiarello, McMahon, & Schaefer, 1989; Fedor-Freybergh, 1977; Hampson, 1990a and b; Hampson & Kimura, 1988; Hartley et al., 1987; Komnenich et al., 1978; Phillips & Sherwin, 1992a; Silverman, & Phillips, 1993). In general, women exhibited a slight decrease in spatial task performance during the midluteal or pre-ovulatory stages of the menstrual cycle, when circulating estrogen levels were highest, and better performance during menses, when estrogen and progesterone levels were lowest.

Because both estrogen and progesterone fluctuate with the menstrual cycle, and some menstrual phases are characterized by simultaneous high estrogen and progesterone levels (i.e., midluteal) or low estrogen and progesterone levels (i.e., menstrual), it is difficult to determine the relationship between each specific hormone and the observed effects on spatial cognition from assessments across the menstrual cycle. There are findings, however, that link the ovarian hormone estrogen, specifically, to the observed fluctuations in spatial ability across the menstrual cycle. For example, several researchers cleverly assessed women at the pre-ovulation phase, when estrogen levels peaked and progesterone levels were at their nadir (Broverman et al., 1981; Hampson, 1990a; Komnenich, Lane, Dickey, & Stone, 1978). In these studies, a decrement in spatial performance was exhibited during the pre-ovulation phase, serving to illustrate that elevated estrogen levels alone may be associated with the observed decline in spatial performance. In addition, quadratic trend analyses revealed that Space Relations Test scores were related to estradiol levels in a curvilinear, inverted U-shape function; optimal spatial performance was demonstrated when estradiol levels were in the intermediate physiological range, and lower scores were exhibited when estradiol levels were minute or high (Hampson, 1990a; see also Nyborg, 1983).

It should be noted that there is inconsistency in the findings of spatial cognition fluctuation across the menstrual cycle. Some studies, for example, have demonstrated that spatial test scores were better at non-menstrual, higher estrogen phases of the cycle (Chiarello et al., 1989; Phillips & Sherwin, 1992a; Postma, Winkel, Tuiten, & van Honk, 1999). Still others reported no change in spatial task performance as related to hormone fluctuations of the menstrual cycle (Gordon & Lee, 1993; Ho, Gilger, & Brink, 1986). As Phillips and Sherwin point out (1992a), the inconsistency in these results may be due, in part, to methodological differences between studies. Such differences include categorizing a subject's cycle phase by techniques that are less reliable than hormone assays, such as counting backward or forward from menses onset or relying on basal body temperature to predict ovulation or hormone level (discussed in Halpern, 1992). Also, perhaps some discordance in the literature is due to the extensive variability in the cognitive requirements of the numerous spatial tasks employed, which ultimately may be a reflection of the complex nature of spatial processing in general (see Halpern, 1992).

Circulating Androgen Effects on Spatial Ability in Men

Recent work has also provided evidence that circulating testosterone is related to indices of human spatial ability. For example, baseline assessments of untreated transsexuals demonstrated an expected sex difference, with genetic males outperforming genetic females. However, adult hormone treatment reversed this sex difference. Indeed, androgen treatment improved performance of genetic females, whereas anti-androgen plus estrogen administration to genetic males resulted in a decline in spatial performance (Slabbekoorn et al., 1999; Van Goozen et al., 1994; Van Goozen et al., 1995). It should be noted that the latter effect was not replicated (Slabbekoorn et al., 1999).

Data further suggest that androgenic effects on spatial cognition may be dose dependent. Indeed, lower androgen levels in men, and higher androgen levels in women, may be optimal for performance on tests requiring spatial ability. For example, androgen administration improved spatial cognition in older men (Janowsky, Oviatt, & Orwoll, 1994) who exhibit a decline in testosterone levels (Morley, Kaiser, Hajjar, & Perry, 1997). Young males with testosterone levels below the average exhibited better performance on spatial tasks than those with levels above the average. Further, spatial ability has been related to seasonal fluctuations in testosterone levels (see Kimura & Hampson, 1994, for review). Others have found that testosterone levels in young men were positively correlated with spatial task performance, but not verbal ability (Silverman, Kastuk, Choi, & Phillips, 1999). In addition, for some spatial tasks, women with higher levels of testosterone outperformed women with lower levels of testosterone, and men with lower testosterone levels outperformed men with higher testosterone levels (Gouchie & Kimura, 1991). Male athletes (with supposed higher androgen levels than nonathletic men) also performed significantly lower than the national sample norms on a spatial task (Lord & Leonard, 1997). Other work showed that women athletes (with supposed higher androgen levels than nonathletic women) outperformed men athletes on spatial cognition tests (Lord & Garrison, 1998).

Thus, as with estrogen, the accumulated data suggest a curvilinear relationship between circulating testosterone level and spatial ability. That is, an intermediate testosterone level may be optimal for spatial performance. Whether testosterone's effects on spatial ability act directly or via conversion to estrogen has yet to be determined.

Circulating Estrogen Effects on Spatial Ability in Rodents

Animal models provide an excellent means to study a phenomenon, such as spatial ability, while minimizing variables that are difficult to control in human studies, such as sociocultural biases. Abundant evidence has demonstrated that sex differences on spatial learning and memory tasks in rodents are influenced by the adult gonadal hormone milieu. For example, Galea et al. (1995) found male superiority on the spatial Morris water maze when males were compared to females during their higher, but not lower, estrogen cycle phase. Other rodent studies have also demonstrated variations in spatial performance across the estrous cycle (Burke & Broadhurst, 1966; Diaz-Veliz, Soto, Dussaubat, & Mora, 1989; Farr et al., 1995; Frye, 1995; Galea et al., 1995; Markus & Zecevic, 1997; Warren & Juraska, 1997). In general, females performed better at estrous, when estrogen levels were lower, and worse at diestrous and proestrous, when estrogen levels were higher. However, not all rodent studies report fluctuations in spatial cognition across the estrous cycle (Berry, McMahan, & Gallagher, 1997; Stackman, Blasberg, Langan, & Clark, 1997).

Estrogen administration has been shown to improve the spatial performance of aged male and aged or young adult ovariectomized female rodents on tests such as the radial-arm maze, and to positively affect performance on tasks which may not be spatially dependent, such as active avoidance and T-maze alternation (Bimonte & Denenberg, 1999; Daniel, Fader, Spencer, & Dohanich, 1997; Diaz-Veliz, Urresta, Dussaubat, & Mora, 1991; Fader, Hendricson, & Dohanich, 1998; Luine & Rodriguez, 1994; Luine, Richards, Wu, & Beck, 1998; O'Neal, Means, Poole, & Hamm, 1996; Packard & Teather, 1997; Rissanen, Puolovali, Van Groen, & Riekkinen, 1999; Singh, Meyer, Millard, & Simpkins, 1994; Williams, 1996). In addition, some data suggest that different memory types are differentially influenced by the ovarian hormonal milieu in adulthood. For example, Daniel et al. (1999) demonstrated that the presence of ovarian hormones facilitated working memory but was detrimental to reference memory as assessed on the spatial radial-arm maze. Accordingly, estrogen replacement improved performance of ovariectomized rats specifically on the working memory portion of the radial-arm maze, and, in addition, physiologically moderate levels of estradiol facilitated performance of ovariectomized rats as working memory load increased (Bimonte & Denenberg, 1999; Luine et al., 1998).

Circulating Androgen Effects on Spatial Ability in Rodents

Although less research has been done to assess circulating testosterone influences on spatial ability in rodents, the available data indicate that high levels of testosterone at the time of test are detrimental to spatial ability. For example, impaired retention of spatial information has been demonstrated in young and middle-aged male rats, but not old-aged male rats (who have presumably undergone a decline in testosterone levels) when treated with testosterone prior to testing (Goudsmit et al., 1990; Roof, 1993b). It is noteworthy that, as discussed earlier in this chapter, high physiological levels of testosterone present during the neonatal period nevertheless facilitate adult performance on these same spatial tasks.

Verbal Memory and Fluency: Relationships Between Performance and Circulating Sex Steroid Levels

Because the reported sex difference in verbal abilities favors females, it has generally been expected that higher levels of estrogen and progesterone in women would facilitate performance on tasks assessing verbal ability. Supporting this view, one study found verbal fluency to be enhanced during the midluteal phase (when estrogen and progesterone levels were high), as compared to menses (when both hormone levels were low) (Hampson, 1990b).

Further support that circulating ovarian hormone levels affect memory function comes from studies assessing menopausal women with or without hormone replacement therapy. A woman undergoes menopause, on the average, between 49–52 years of age (Meites & Lu, 1994). Menopause is characterized by permanent cessation of cyclic ovarian activity and by estrogen and progesterone levels that are lower than any phase of the menstrual cycle, comparable to levels of an ovariectomized young woman (Judd, 1984; Meites & Lu, 1994). Memory decline is one of the many effects of menopause. Estrogen replacement has been shown to ameliorate some deficits in memory and cognitive function associated with menopause (Sherwin, 1994, 1998 for review), although not all studies found that estrogen replacement therapy benefits cognitive functioning or prevents age-related memory decline (for critical reviews see Haskell, Robinson, & Horwitz, 1997; Yaffe, Sawaya, Lieberburg, & Grady, 1998).

As with the menstrual cycle studies, the menopausal studies do not form a unified picture. This may be due, in part, to methodological factors. Most of the studies assessing menopausal women were observational, with only a few using a randomized, double-blind procedure (for review see Sherwin, 1998). In addition, between studies there was great variability in the subject pool, in the cognitive tests administered, and in the hormone treatment regimens (discussed in Haskell, Robinson, & Horwitz, 1997). Another important factor may be that several studies combined surgically and naturally menopausal women without reference to whether the groups differed, or there was no mention of menopause etiology. Indeed, a recent assessment found that surgically menopausal women had lower verbal memory scores than naturally menopausal women (Nappi et al., 1999).

Sherwin and colleagues have performed some very resourceful and well-controlled studies assessing the efficacy of hormone replacement. In three studies, women were assessed on several spatial and verbal cognitive tasks before and after total abdominal hysterectomy with bilateral ovariectomy for benign disease (Phillips & Sherwin, 1992b; Sherwin, 1988; Sherwin & Phillips, 1990; see Sherwin, 1994 and 1998 for reviews). Surgically menopausal women that received postovariectomy supplementation with estrogen plus androgen, estrogen alone, or androgen alone either maintained or improved immediate and delayed verbal memory scores pre- to postoperatively. In contrast, ovariectomized women that did not receive hormone replacement exhibited a decline in immediate and delayed verbal memory pre- to postoperatively. Interestingly, in these and other studies, although benefits were seen on verbal abilities and memory, there were no hormone-related changes on visual memory tasks (i.e., Caldwell & Watson, 1952; Kampen & Sherwin, 1994; see Sherwin, 1994, 1998 for reviews). Yet, more recent studies found that estrogen replacement therapy did protect against longitudinal decline in short-term visual memory (Resnick, Metter, & Zonderman, 1997; Resnick, Perry, Parry, Mostofi, & Udell, 1998).

Taken together, the cumulative data suggest that the memory decline exhibited in healthy menopausal women may be due, in part, to the cessation of ovarian function and subsequent lack of hormone release. Controlled clinical trials assessing menopausal women indicate that hormone replacement therapy may have positive effects on specialized cognitive functions such as verbal fluency and memory.

Finally, observations that estrogen may affect verbal fluency and memory are further supported by studies of transsexuals. Male-to-female transsexuals given estrogen performed better on short-term verbal memory, but not spatial ability, compared to those not given estrogen (Miles, Green, Sanders, & Hines, 1998). Limited research also suggests that androgen may be related to verbal ability. Indeed, androgen administration decreased verbal fluency, but increased spatial ability, in female-to-male transsexuals (Van Goozen et al., 1994), whereas a follow-up study showed no androgenic effects on verbal fluency (Slabbekoorn et al., 1999).

Estrogen Replacement Therapy and Alzheimer's Disease in Women

Evidence suggests that the estrogen deficiency associated with menopause also contributes to the cognitive decline and neurodegeneration associated with the development of Alzheimer's disease and age-related dementias in women (Birge, 1996; Simpkins, Singh, & Bishop, 1994). Consistent with this assertion, many studies have reported that estrogen replacement improves cognition, memory, and symptoms of dementia in women with Alzheimer's disease and senile dementia-Alzheimer's type (Birge, 1996; Fillit, 1994; Fillit et al., 1986; Haskell et al., 1997; Henderson, Paganini-Hill, Emanuel, Dunn, & Buckwalter, 1994; Henderson, Watt, & Buckwalter, 1996; Honjo et al., 1995; Ohkura, Isse, Akazawa, Hamamoto, Yaoi, & Hagino, 1995). It should be noted that although most studies report positive effects, some have found no benefits of estrogen therapy (see Haskell et al., 1997; Yaffe et al., 1998 for reviews).

Several reports provide evidence that estrogen replacement delays the onset or reduces the risk of developing Alzheimer's disease and related dementias in women (Kawas et al., 1997; Paganini-Hill & Henderson, 1996; Stephenson, 1996; Tang et al., 1996). In addition, studies have also found that the frequency of estrogen use was lower in women with Alzheimer's disease compared to women free of the disease, even after controlling for variables such as age, age at menopause, and education (Baldereschi et al., 1998; Henderson et al., 1994). Finally, estrogen replacement has been shown to enhance responsiveness to the cholinesterase inhibitor tacrine, as measured by cognitive assessment in women diagnosed with Alzheimer's disease (Schneider et al., 1996).

Postulated Mechanisms of Action for Circulating Gonadal Hormone Effects on Cognition

The neurobiological mechanisms that mediate circulating (transient) gonadal hormone effects on cognition are not, as yet, fully understood. However, it is clear that circulating gonadal hormones affect neurotransmitter systems and neural substrates subserving learning and memory function. For example, there are data demonstrating that the cholinergic and hippocampal systems are intimately linked to learning and memory processes (Beuzen, Belzung, & Roullet, 1994; Drachman & Leavitt, 1974; Eckerman, Gordon, Edwards, MacPhail, & Gage, 1980; Ikegami, 1994; Jaffard & Meunier, 1993; Jarrard, 1995). Accordingly, rodent studies have shown that ovarian hormones influence cholinergic receptor populations and function (see McEwen et al., 1997, for review) as well as mediates dendritic spine density in the CA1 region of the hippocampus (an effect possibly involving NMDA receptors) (reviewed in Woolley, 1998, and McEwen et al., 1997). Such findings may provide a mechanism whereby gonadal hormones affect learning and memory in both sexes and, thus, the expression of sex differences in cognition.

Other work has indicated that estrogen and nerve growth factor receptors are colocalized in forebrain regions, and that they may regulate each other (see Toran-Allerand et al., 1999, for review). For example, in some neurons, nerve growth factor increases estrogen receptor mRNA and estrogen binding. Conversely, estrogen increases trkA mRNA and decreases p75NTR mRNA (Toran-Allerand et al., 1999). Additionally, brain serotonin levels are affected by alterations in ovarian hormone levels, as seen in studies assessing activity across the estrous cycle and in ovariectomized rats treated with estrogen and progesterone (see McEwen et al., 1997, for review).

These cumulative findings demonstrate that ovarian hormones have widespread effects in the brain, including regions that mediate learning and memory. Thus, it is no surprise that ovariectomy or cessation of ovarian function in adulthood affects cognition. However, the research to date has only begun to decipher the neurobiological mechanisms underlying the many observed cognitive effects. The complexity of sex differences and hormone effects on brain and behavior may speak to the inconsistent research findings, as discussed. This inconsistency does not render the findings invalid or undermine the importance of gonadal hormone effects on brain functioning. Rather, it a sign that gonadal hormones exert multidimensional effects that are so complex that, in some cases, they may only be observed under certain experimental conditions.

IMPLICATIONS FOR THE STUDY OF SEX DIFFERENCES IN COGNITION

Differences in Performance as Measured by Group Means

The overwhelming majority of experimental research on hormonally mediated sex differences has centered on the role of early exposure to androgen. Animal research, for example, has demonstrated permanent effects of neonatal androgen exposure on virtually every sexually dimorphic cognitive task that has been assessed (see Beatty, 1992, or Van Haaren, Van Hest, & Heinsbroek, 1990, for review). Such findings have served as the basis for an assumption that biological sex differences are mediated primarily by the degree of early developmental exposure to androgen. This assumption has provided a theoretical framework for ongoing experimentation, and has also facilitated the interpretation of sex differences by asserting that the key variable in establishing such differences could be characterized along a unidimensional continuum (i.e., more or less androgen).

The view that early androgen exposure served as the key determinant in establishing sex differences was clearly supported by experimental evidence and played a critical ongoing role in elaborating our understanding of the sexual differentiation process. However, evidence reviewed here shows that ovarian hormones also affect neuromorphology and cognitive behavior in females (see Fitch & Denenberg, 1998, for review). Moreover, ovarian hormone effects in females have a significantly later period of action when compared to androgen effects in males. Evidence of ovarian effects further includes significant neurophysiological changes in the adult female brain, including neural regions shown to relate to learning and memory, in response to circulating ovarian hormones. These combined findings point to the existence of orthogonal masculine and feminine neurodevelopmental processes. This has critical repercussions for our interpretation of, and approach to, human cognitive sex differences. For example, orthogonal developmental processes might be expected to lead to *qualitative,* rather than *quantitative,* differences in adult male and female brain organization and cognitive function (see also Halpern, 1992). Thus, the presence of active masculinizing versus feminizing influences in development may contribute to divergent patterns of brain organization in men and women, which may be expressed not merely as mean differences in group performance but as fundamental sex differences in neurocognitive processing that may not be readily quantifiable.

As an example of the complex and multidimensional form of some sex differences, we refer to the work of researchers who have looked beyond differences in mean scores of cognitive performance. When we measure spatial navigation behavior in male and female rats, it is tacitly assumed that we are measuring a unidimensional, stable, underlying neurobehavioral process. However, evidence suggests that male and female rats utilize fundamentally different strategies in some forms of maze learning and that reliance on a particular strategic approach is influenced by early hormonal exposure (see Williams & Meck, 1991). Similarly, a recent study found that adult male and female rats showed no differences in overall memory scores on a maze-learning task, but showed significant sex differences in search strategy while solving the task when components of search behavior were further examined (Bimonte & Denenberg, 2000). Such results speak to the existence of underlying sex differences in cognitive processing that can be masked easily when looking at overall performance scores, and just as easily can produce misleading interpretations of sex differences that are seen for some overall performance scores.

Similarly, a behavioral measure may not show a mean sex difference and yet reveal a completely different pattern of brain–behavior correlations. For example, Witelson showed that men and women in the same hand preference category (nonconsistent right handers) had disparate neuroanatomical profiles as measured by regional callosum size and various other cortical measures (e.g., Witelson, 1991).

The existence of sex differences in cognitive strategies and brain–behavior relationships sounds a cautionary note regarding the interpretation of sex differences in single measures, such as test scores. The typical interpretation of such a result is that one sex is, however slightly, superior to the other on some meaningful neurobehavioral feature. However, there is enormous complexity inherent to developmental processes characterized by different hormonal effects, with different periods of temporal sensitivity, acting on different steroid receptor populations that vary with age and sex, acting in turn on neural substrates that have already been affected by prior hormonal exposure. This leads to a picture of neurobiological sex differences that are so complex as to cast doubt on any simple interpretation of observed sex differences in performance on cognitive tasks.

Mathematical Models of Group Difference and Variance

Accumulating evidence also suggests that male and female scores on cognitive tests are not always characterized by equivalent distributions and variances, as assumed within most statistical models (Feingold, 1995). For example, one study reported that female scores on a mental rotation test were bimodal; 80% of the women scored approximately the same as the male group, and a second group of women (20%) scored much lower than the men and remaining women (Kail, Carter, & Pelligrino, 1979; see also Favreau & Everett, 1996). Such an observation, although rarely addressed by traditional statistical tests, could reflect the fact that female performance on visuo-spatial tasks appears to fluctuate on the basis of estrogen exposure (e.g., Hampson, 1990a and b), with the implication that a constantly changing subset of normally cycling women tested at any given time might show depressed performance on such a task. Such an interpretation contrasts with the views that (1) there is a fixed subpopulation of women whose visuospatial ability is always lower than the male average, or (2) as a population, women have lower mean performance than men.

The previous discussion is concerned with variation in individual female performance across the menstrual cycle. A different phenomenon is that a much higher overall population variance in measures of performance on cognitive tasks has been observed for males as compared to females (e.g., Lubinski & Benbow, 1992). This is consistent with evidence of a much higher proportion of males at the high end of the cognitive spectrum (e.g., genius categories) (Benbow, 1988), as well as at the low end (e.g., having neurodevelopmental disorders including retardation, autism, dyslexia, and language disorders) (Finucci et al., 1983; Gualtieri & Hicks, 1985; Neils & Aram, 1986; Spinillo et al., 1995; Vogel, 1990). Commenting on this phenomenon, Geschwind and Galaburda (1985) suggested that males may be "at risk" for both cognitive disability and genius due to an early exposure to a "male factor," which was most likely testosterone.

Another possibility is that ovarian hormones are actively involved in promoting effective reorganization following neurodevelopmental trauma and, hence, also may act to reduce cognitive variance in the female population. Findings that support this view include evidence that estrogen has protective effects against the onset, recurrence and severity of certain mental disorders such as schizophrenia (see Sherwin, 1998, or Seeman & Lang, 1990) as well as memory loss and Alzheimer's disease after menopause. Within the animal literature, progesterone has been shown to act as a neuroprotectant against cerebral trauma in female rats (Roof, Duvdevani, & Stein, 1993). These findings may be related to observations that female premature infants show better recovery than male premature infants following intracranial hemorrhage, as measured by IQ (Raz et al., 1995).

The concept that estrogen may play a protective role in females could account for the smaller number of females in the lower tails of cognitive distributions, although it does not account for observations of lower incidence of cognitive "genius" in females. Perhaps the plasticity resulting from ovarian effects and chronic cyclicity carries (statistically) a cognitive "price." Restriction of range at one end of the distribution may cause a restriction at the other end as well. Moreover, endogenous estrogen does not appear to "protect" against all neurofunctional disorders. For example, women suffer more frequently than men from certain syndromes such as depressive disorder. The basis for these differing effects is not well understood and clearly requires further empirical study.

In sum, we must recognize that developmental hormonal factors influence group cognitive performance and variability as a function of sex and, moreover, that the developmental role of ovarian hormones influences patterns and variability of female cognitive performance (both individual variability across time, as well as the population variance) in ways that have not been, to date, thoroughly addressed at a theoretical level or studied empirically.

CONCLUSION

Traditional models of sexual differentiation have emerged from the data showing a powerful influence of testosterone on differentiation of the male phenotype in mammals. Accordingly, the work of researchers in this area has rested on the assumption that testosterone exposure represents the single overriding hormonal factor that ultimately distinguishes the male from the female neurobehavioral phenotype. The conceptual and empirical repercussions of this assumption to other fields of research (particularly those pertaining to sex differences in brain and behavior) have been profound.

In this chapter, we have reviewed evidence of neurobehavioral androgenic effects, along with evidence that ovarian hormones also play a key role in sexual differentiation of the brain. The latter findings prompt a modification of the traditional model of sexual differentiation, specifically the addition of an active developmental role for ovarian hormones. This conceptual shift has significant implications for the study of neurobehavioral sex differences. First, it belies the notion that male and female neurobehavioral development can be regarded as subject to quantitative, unidimensional developmental influences (i.e., more or less androgen) expected to produce neurobehavioral features that differ unidimensionally along a continuum (i.e., are males or females "bigger or smaller," "better or worse"). Indeed, evidence suggests that the developmental pathways of neural masculinization and feminization differ in qualitative ways, resulting from the interacting influence of different hormones at different times on different neural substrates. Furthermore, evidence that the female brain is characterized by cyclic plasticity for some neurobehavioral features has profound implications for the notion that meaningful interpretations about sex effects can be drawn from cognitive tests administered at a single time point. Finally, the authors acknowledge that although the evidence reviewed points convincingly toward a biological basis for some sex differences in cognitive function, the neurobiological characterization of such differences is likely to prove so complex as to fundamentally undermine straightforward interpretations of task superiority. Indeed, an evolutionary perspective would suggest that biological features differentiating male and female brains are subject (like all biologically determined features) to selective pressure, and, therefore, must confer potentially different but nonetheless ideal features to both the female and male brain.

REFERENCES

Aboitiz, F. (1996). Corpus callosum morphology in relation to cerebral asymmetries in the post-mortem human. Paper presented at The NATO Advanced Study Institute for the Role of the Corpus Callosum in Sensory Motor Integration: Anatomy, Physiology and Behavior; Individual Differences and Clinical Applications. Castelvecchio, Lucca, Italy.

Ali, M., & Sahib, M. K. (1983). Changes in alpha-fetoprotein and albumin synthesis rates and their levels during fetal and neonatal development of the rat brain. *Brain Research, 282,* 314–317.

Arnold, A. P., & Breedlove, S. M. (1985). Organizational and activational effects of sex steroids on brain and behavior: A reanalysis. *Hormones and Behavior, 19,* 469–498.

Bachevalier, J., Brickson, M., Hagger, C., & Mishkin, M. (1990). Age and sex differences in the effects of selective temporal lobe lesions on the formation of visual discrimination habits in rhesus monkeys (*Macaca mulatta*). *Behavioral Neuroscience, 6,* 885–899.

Bachevalier, J., & Hagger, C. (1991). Sex differences in the development of learning abilities in primates. *Psychoneuroendocrinology, 16,* 177–188.

Bachevalier, J., Hagger, C., & Bercu, B. B. (1989). Gender differences in visual habit formation in 3-month-old rhesus monkeys. *Developmental Psychobiology, 22(6),* 585–599.

Baldereschi, M., Di Carlo, A., Lepore, V., Bracco, L., Maggi, S., Grigoletto, F., Scarlato, G., & Amaducci, L. (1998). Estrogen-replacement therapy and Alzheimer's disease in the Italian Longitudinal Study on Aging. *Neurology, 50,* 996–1002.

Beatty, W., & Beatty, P. (1970). Hormonal determinants of sex differences in avoidance behavior and reactivity to electric shock in the rat. *Journal of Comparative and Physiological Psychology, 73,* 446–455.

Beatty, W. W. (1992). Gonadal hormones and sex differences in nonreproductive behaviors. In A. Gerall, H. Moltz, & I. L. Ward. (Eds.), *Handbook of behavioral neurobiology* (Vol. 11, pp. 85–128). New York: Plenum Press.

Becker, J. B. (1990). Direct effect of 17B-estradiol on striatum: Sex differences in dopamine release. *Synapse, 5,* 157–164.

Becker, J. B., & Cha, J. (1989). Estrous-cycle variation in amphetamine induced behaviors and striatal dopamine release assessed with microdialysis. *Behavioral Brain Research, 35,* 117–125.

Benbow, C. P. (1988). Sex differences in mathematical reasoning ability in intellectually talented pre-adolescents: Their nature, effects and possible causes. *Behavioral and Brain Sciences, 11,* 169–183.

Berry, B., McMahan, R., & Gallagher, M. (1997). Spatial learning and memory at defined points of the estrous cycle: Effects on performance of a hippocampal-dependent task. *Behavioral Neuroscience, 111,* 267–274.

Berta, P., Hawkins, J. R., Sinclair, A. H., Taylor, A., Griffiths, B. L., & Goodfellow, P. N. (1990). Genetic evidence equating SRY and the testis-determining factor. *Nature, 348,* 448–450.

Beuzen, A., Belzung, C., & Roullet, P. (1994). Drug effects in a radial maze designed for dissociation of cues used by mice. *Pharmacology, Biochemistry and Behavior, 48,* 23–29.

Bimonte, H. A., & Denenberg, V. H. (1999). Estradiol facilitates performance as working memory load increases. *Psychoneuroendocrinology, 24,* 161–173.

Bimonte, H. A., & Denenberg, V. H. (2000). Sex differences in vicarious trial-and-error behavior during radial-arm maze learning. *Physiology and Behavior, 68*(4), 495–499.

Bimonte, H. A., Fitch, R. H., & Denenberg, V. H. (2000a). Adult ovary transfer counteracts the callosal enlargement resulting from prepubertal ovariectomy. *Brain Research, 872*(1–2), 254–257.

Bimonte, H. A., Fitch, R. H., & Denenberg, V. H. (2000b). Neonatal estrogen blockade prevents normal callosal responsiveness to estradiol in adulthood. *Developmental Brain Research, 122*(2), 149–155.

Bimonte, H. A., Mack, C. M., Stavnezer, A. J., & Denenberg, V. H. (2000). Ovarian hormones can organize the rat corpus callosum in adulthood. *Developmental Brain Research, 121*(2), 169–177.

Birge, S. J. (1996). Is there a role for estrogen replacement therapy in the prevention and treatment of dementia? *Journal of the American Geriatric Society, 44,* 865–870.

Bishop, K., & Wahlsten, D. (1997). Sex differences in the human corpus callosum: Myth and reality. *Neuroscience and Biobehavioral Reviews, 21,* 581–601.

Blizard, D., & Denef, C. (1973). Neonatal androgen effects on open-field activity and sexual behavior in the female rat: The modifying influence of ovarian secretions during development. *Physiology and Behavior, 11,* 65–69.

Bloch, G. J., & Gorski, R. A. (1988). Estrogen/progesterone treatment in adulthood affects the size of several components of the medial preoptic area in the male rat. *Journal of Comparative Neurology, 275,* 613 622.

Breedlove, S. M. (1992) Sexual differentiation of the brain and behavior. In J. B. Becker, S. M. Breedlove, & D. Crews (Eds.), *Behavioral endocrinology* (pp. 39–68). Boston: MIT Press.

Broverman, D., Vogel, W., Klaiber, E., Majcher, D., Shea, D., & Paul, V. (1981). Changes in cognitive task performance across the menstrual cycle. *Journal of Comparative and Physiological Psychology, 95,* 646–654.

Brown, T. J., MacLusky, N. J., Shanabrough, M., & Naftolin, F. (1990). Comparison of age- and sex-related changes in cell nuclear estrogen-binding capacity and progestin receptor induction in the rat brain. *Endocrinology, 126,* 2965–2972.

Buchanan, L., Pavlovic, J., & Rovet, J. (1998). A re-examination of the visuo-spatial deficit in Turner syndrome: Contributions of working memory. *Developmental Neuropsychology,* Special issue (Berenbaum, S., Ed.), *14,* 341–368.

Burke, A., & Broadhurst, P. (1966). Behavioural correlates of the oestrous cycle in the rat. *Nature, 5019,* 223–224.

Caldwell, B., & Watson, R. (1952). An evaluation of psychological effects of sex hormone administration in aged women I. Results of therapy after six months. *Journal of Gerontology, 7,* 228–244.

Castner, S. A., & Becker, J. B. (1990). Estrogen and striatal dopamine release: A microanalysis study. *Society for Neuroscience Abstracts, 16,* 130.

Chiarello, C., McMahon, M. A., & Schaefer, K. (1989). Visual cerebral lateralization over phases of the menstrual cycle: A preliminary investigation. *Brain Cognition, 11,* 18–36.

Clark, A.S & Goldman-Rakic, P. S. (1989). Gonadal hormones influence the emergence of cortical function in nonhuman primates. *Behavioral Neuroscience, 103,* 1287–1295.

Collaer, M. L., & Hines, M. (1995). Human behavioral sex differences: A role for gonadal hormones during early development? *Psychological Bulletin, 118,* 55–107.

Cowell, P. E., Allen, L. S., Zalatimo, N. S., & Denenberg, V. H. (1992). A developmental study of sex and age interactions in the human corpus callosum. *Developmental Brain Research, 66,* 187–192.

Cowell, P. E., Turetsky, B. I., Gur, R. C., Shtasel, D. L., Grossman, R. I., & Gur, R. E. (1994). Sex differences in aging of the human frontal and temporal lobes. *Journal of Neuroscience, 14,* 4748–4755.

Daniel, J., Fader, A., Spencer, A., & Dohanich, G. (1997). Estrogen enhances performance of female rats during acquisition of a radial arm maze. *Hormones and Behavior, 32,* 217–225.

Daniel, J. M., Roberts, S. L., & Dohanich, G. P. (1999). Effects of ovarian hormones and environment on radial maze and water maze performance of female rats. *Physiology and Behavior, 66,* 11–20.

Dawson, J., Cheung, Y. M., & Lau, R. T. S. (1975). Developmental effects of neonatal sex hormones on spatial and activity skills in the white rat. *Biological Psychology, 3,* 213–229.

DeLacoste-Utamsing, C., & Holloway, R. L. (1982). Sexual dimorphism in the human corpus callosum. *Science, 216,* 1431–1432.

Denti, A., & Negroni, J. (1975). Activity and learning in neonatally hormone treated rats. *Acta Physiologica Latinoamerica, 25,* 99–106.

Diamond, M. C. (1991). Hormonal effects on the development of cerebral lateralization. *Psychoneuroendocrinology, 16,* 121–129.

Diamond, M., Dowling, G., & Johnson, R. (1981). Morphologic cerebral cortical asymmetry in male and female rats. *Experimental Neurology, 71,* 261–268.

Diamond, M., Johnson, R. E., & Ehlert, J. (1979). A comparison of cortical thickness in male and female rats—Normal and gonadectomized, young and adult. *Behavioral Neurology, 26,* 485–491.

Diaz-Veliz, G., Soto, V., Dussaubat, N., & Mora, S. (1989). Influence of the estrous cycle, ovariectomy and estradiol replacement upon the acquisition of conditioned avoidance responses in rats. *Physiological Behavior, 46,* 397–401.

Diaz-Veliz, G., Urresta, F., Dussaubat, N., & Mora, S. (1991). Effects of estradiol replacement in ovariectomized rats on conditioned avoidance responses and other behaviors. *Physiological Behavior, 50,* 61–65.

Dohler, K. (1991). The pre- and postnatal influence of hormones and neurotransmitters on sexual differentiation of the mammalian hypothalamus. *International Reviews in Cytology, 131,* 1–57.

Dohler, K. D., Hancke, J. L., Srivastava, S. S., Hofmann, C., Shryne, J. E., & Gorski, R. A. (1984a). Participation of estrogens in female sexual differentiation of the brain: Neuroanatomical, neuroendocrine and behavioral evidence. In G. J. De Vries, J. P. C. De Bruin, H. B. M. Uylings, & M. A. Corner (Eds.), *Progress in brain research,* Vol. 61 (pp. 99–117). Amsterdam: Elsevier Science.

Dohler, K. D., Srivastava, S., Shryne, J., Jarzab, B., Sipos, A., & Gorski, R. A. (1984b). Differentiation of the sexually dimorphic nucleus in the preoptic area of the rat brain is inhibited by postnatal treatment with an estrogen antagonist. *Neuroendocrinology, 38,* 297–301.

Drachman, D., & Leavitt, J. (1974). Human memory and the cholinergic system: A relationship to aging? *Archives of Neurology, 30,* 113–121.

Eckerman, D. A., Gordon, W. A., Edwards, J. D., MacPhail, R. C., & Gage, M. I. (1980). Effects of scopolamine, pentobarbital, and amphetamine on radial arm maze performance in the rat. *Pharmacology, Biochemistry, and Behavior, 12,* 595–602.

Eicher, E., & Washburn, L. (1983). Inherited sex reversal in mice: Identification of a new primary sex determining gene. *Journal of Experimental Zoology, 228,* 297–304.

Fader, A., Hendricson, A., & Dohanich, G. (1998). Estrogen improves performance of reinforced T-maze alteration and prevents the amnesic effects of scopolamine administered systemically or intrahippocampally. *Neurobiology of Learning and Memory, 69,* 225–240.

Farr, S., Flood, J., Scherrer, J., Kaiser, F., Taylor, G., & Morley, J. (1995). Effect of ovarian steroids on footshock avoidance learning and retention in female mice. *Physiology and Behavior, 58,* 715–723.

Favreau, O. E., & Everett, J. C. (1996). A tale of two tails. *American Psychologist, 51,* 268–269.

Feingold, A. (1995). The additive effects of differences in central tendency and variability are important in comparisons between groups. *American Psychologist, 50,* 5–13.

Fedor-Freybergh, P. (1977). The influence of oestrogen on the well being and mental performance in climacteric and postmenopausal women. *Acta Obstetrics and Gynecology Scand, 64,* 5–69.

Fillit, H. (1994). Estrogen in the pathogenesis and treatment of Alzheimer's disease in postmenopausal women. *Annals of the New York Academy of Sciences, 743,* 233–239.

Fillit, H., Weinreb, H., Cholst, I., Luine, V., McEwen, B., Amador, R., & Zabriskie, J. (1986). Observations in a preliminary open trial of estradiol therapy for senile dementia—Alzheimer's type. *Psychoneuroendocrinology, 11,* 337–345.

Finucci, J. M., Isaacs, S. D., Whitehouse, C. C., & Childs, B. (1983). Classification of spelling errors and their relationship to reading ability, sex, grade placement, and Intelligence. *Brain and Language, 20,* 340–345.

Fitch, R. H., Cowell, P. E., Schrott, L. M., & Denenberg, V. H. (1991). Corpus callosum: Ovarian hormones and feminization. *Brain Research, 542,* 313–317.

Fitch, R. H., & Denenberg, V. H. (1998). A role for ovarian hormones in sexual differentiation of the brain. *Behavioral Brain Sciences, 21,* 311–352.

Fleming, D., Anderson, R. H., Rhees, R., Kinghorn, E., & Bakaitis, J. (1986). Effects of prenatal stress on sexually dimorphic asymmetries in the cerebral cortex of the male rat. *Brain Research Bulletin, 16,* 395–398.

Forgie, M. L., & Stewart, J. (1994). Effect of prepubertal ovariectomy on amphetamine-induced locomotion in adult female rats. *Hormones and Behavior, 28,* 241–260.

Frankfurt, M., Gould, E., Woolley, C. S., & McEwen, B. S. (1990). Gonadal steroids modify dendritic spine density in ventromedial hypothalamic neurons: A Golgi study in the adult rat. *Neuroendocrinology, 51,* 530–535.

Frye, C. (1995). Estrus-associated decrements in a water maze task are limited to acquisition. *Physiology and Behavior, 57,* 5–14.

Galea, L., Kavaliers, M., Ossenkopp, K., & Hampson, E. (1995). Gonadal hormone levels and spatial learning performance in the Morris water maze in male and female meadow voles, Microtus pennsylvanicus. *Hormones and Behavior, 29,* 106–125.

Geschwind, N., & Galaburda, A. M. (1985). Cerebral lateralization: Biological mechanisms, associations, and pathology, Pts. I, II, & III. *Archives of Neurology, 42,* 428–654.

Gordon, H. W., & Lee, P. A. (1993). No difference in cognitive performance between phases of the menstrual cycle. *Psychoneuroendocrinology, 18,* 521–531.

Gorski, R. (1984). Critical role for the medial preoptic area in the sexual differentiation of the brain. In G. J. De Vries, J. P. C. De Bruin, H. B. M. Uylings, & M. A. Corner (Eds.), *Progress in brain research,* Vol. 61, (pp. 129–145). Amsterdam: Elsevier Science.

Gouchie, C., & Kimura, D. (1991). The relationship between testosterone levels and cognitive ability patterns. *Psychoneuroendocrinology, 16,* 323–334.

Goudsmit, E., Van de Poll, N. E., & Swaab, D. F. (1990). Testosterone fails to reverse spatial memory decline in aged rats and impairs retention in young and middle-aged animals. *Behavioral and Neural Biology, 53,* 6–20.

Gould, E., Woolley, C. S., Frankfurt, M., & McEwen, B. S. (1990). Gonadal steroids regulate dendritic spine density in hippocampal pyramidal cells in adulthood. *Journal of Neuroscience, 10,* 1286–1291.

Grimshaw, G. M., Sitarenios, G., & Finegan, J. K. (1995). Mental rotation at 7 years: Relations with prenatal testosterone levels and spatial play experiences. *Brain and Cognition, 29,* 85–100.

Gualtieri, T., & Hicks, R. (1985). An immunoreactive theory of selective male affliction. *Behavioral and Brain Sciences, 8,* 427–441.

Hagger, C., & Bachevalier, J. (1991). Visual habit formation in 3-month-old monkeys (*Macaca mulatta*): Reversal of sex difference following neonatal manipulations of androgens. *Behavioral Brain Research, 45,* 57–63.

Halpern, D. F. (1992). *Sex differences in cognitive abilities.* Hillsdale, NJ: Lawrence Erlbaum.

Hampson, E. (1990a). Estrogen-related variations in human spatial and articulatory motor skills. *Psychoneuroendocrinology, 15,* 97–111.

Hampson, E. (1990b). Variations in sex-related cognitive abilities across the menstrual cycle. *Brain and Cognition, 14,* 26–43.

Hampson, E., & Kimura, D. (1988). Reciprocal effects of hormonal fluctuations on human motor and perceptual-spatial skills. *Behavioral Neuroscience, 102,* 456–459.

Haskell, S., Robinson, E., & Horwitz, R. (1997). The effect of estrogen replacement therapy on cognitive function in women: A critical review of the literature. *Journal of Clinical Epidemiology, 50,* 1249–1264.

Henderson, V. W., Paganini-Hill, A., Emanuel, C. K., Dunn, M. E., & Buckwalter, J. G. (1994). Estrogen replacement therapy in older women. Comparisons between Alzheimer's disease cases and nondemented control subjects. *Archives of Neurology, 51,* 896–900.

Henderson, V. W., Watt, L., & Buckwalter, J. G. (1996). Cognitive skills associated with estrogen replacement in women with Alzheimer's disease. *Psychoneuroendocrinology, 21,* 421–430.

Hendricks, S. E. (1992). Role of estrogens and progestins in the development of female sexual behavior potential. In A. A. Gerall, H. Moltz, & I. L. Ward (Eds.),

Handbook of behavioral neurobiology, Vol. 11: Sexual differentiation (pp. 129–155). New York: Plenum.

Ho, H. Z., Gilger, J. W., & Brink, T. M. (1986). Effects of menstrual cycle on spatial information-processes. *Perceptual and Motor Skills, 63*(2 Pt 2), 743–751.

Honjo, H., Tanaka, K., Kashiwagi, T., Urabe, M., Okada, H., Hayashi, M., & Hayashi, K. (1995). Senile dementia-Alzheimer's type and estrogen. *Hormone Metabolism Research, 27,* 204–207.

Ikegami, S. (1994). Behavioural impairment in radial-arm maze learning and acetylcholine content of the hippocampus and cerebral cortex in aged mice. *Behavioral Brain Research, 65,* 103–111.

Jaffard, R., & Meunier, M. (1993). Role of the hippocampal formation in learning and memory. *Hippocampus, 3,* 203–218.

Janowsky, J. S., Oviatt, S. K., & Orwoll, E. S. (1994). Testosterone influences spatial cognition in older men. *Behavioral Neuroscience, 108,* 325–332.

Jarrard, L. (1995). What does the hippocampus really do? *Behavioral and Brain Research, 71,* 1–10.

Joseph, R., Hess, S., & Birecree, E. (1978). Effects of hormone manipulations and exploration on sex differences in maze learning. *Behavioral Biology, 24,* 364–377.

Judd, H. (1984). Normal physiology during menopause. In P. Besch, J. Goldzieber, & S. Gibbons (Eds.), *The biochemistry of the reproductive years.* Washington, DC: American Association for Clinical Chemistry.

Kail, R., Carter, P., & Pellegrino, J. (1979). The locus of sex differences in spatial ability. *Perception & Psychophysics, 26,* 182–186.

Kampen, D. L., & Sherwin, B. B. (1994). Estrogen use and verbal memory in healthy postmenopausal women. *Obstetrics and Gynecology, 83,* 979–983.

Kawas, C., Resnick, S., Morrison, A., Brookmeyer, R., Corrada, M., Zonderman, A., Bacal., C., Donnell Lingle, D., & Metter, E. (1997). A prospective study of estrogen replacement therapy and the risk of developing Alzheimer's disease: The Baltimore longitudinal study of aging. *Neurology 48,* 1517–1521.

Kimura, D., & Hampson, E. (1994). Cognitive pattern in men and women is influenced by fluctuations in sex hormones. *Psychological Science, 3,* 57–61.

Kolb, B., & Cioe, J. (1996). Sex-related differences in cortical function after medial frontal lesions in rats. *Behavioral Neuroscience, 110,* 1271–1281.

Kolb, B., & Stewart, J. (1991). Sex differences in dendritic branching of cells in the prefrontal cortex of rats. *Journal of Neuroendocrinology, 3,* 95–99.

Kolb, B., Sutherland, R. J., Nonneman, A. J., & Whishaw, I. Q. (1982). Asymmetry in the cerebral hemispheres of the rat, mouse, rabbit and cat: The right hemisphere is larger. *Experimental Neurology, 78,* 348–359.

Komnenich, P., Lane, D., Dickey, R., & Stone, S. (1978). Gonadal hormones and cognitive performance. *Physiological Psychology, 6,* 115–120.

Kuhnemann, S., Brown, T. J., Hochberg, R. B., & MacLusky, N. J. (1994). Sex differences in the development of estrogen receptors in the rat brain. *Hormones & Behavior, 28,* 483–491.

Kulynych, J., Vladar, K., Jones, D., & Weinberger, D. (1994). Gender differences in the normal lateralization of the supratemporal cortex. *Cerebral Cortex, 4,* 107–118.

Leret, M. L., Molina-Holgado, F., & Gonzalez, M. I. (1994). The effect of perinatal exposure to estrogens on the sexually dimorphic response to novelty. *Physiology and*

Behavior, 55, 371–373.

Leveroni, C., & Berenbaum, S. (1998). Early androgen effects on interest in infants: Evidence from children with congenital adrenal hyperplasia. *Developmental Neuropsychology, 14,* 1998.

Lisk, R., & Suydam, A. (1967). Sexual behavior patterns in the prepubertally castrate rat. *Anatomical Records, 157,* 181–190.

Lord, T., & Garrison, J. (1988). Comparing spatial abilities of collegiate athletes in different sports. *Perceptual and Motor Skills, 86,* 1016–1018.

Lord, T., & Leonard, B. (1997). Comparing scores on spatial-perception tests for intercollegiate athletes and nonathletes. *Perceptual and Motor Skills, 84,* 299–306.

Lubinski, D., & Benbow, C. P. (1992). Gender differences in abilities and preferences among the gifted: Implications for the math-science pipeline. *Current Directions in Psychological Science, 1,* 61–66.

Luine, V., & Rodriguez, M. (1994). Effects of estradiol on radial arm maze performance of young and aged rats. *Behavioral and Neural Biology, 62,* 230–236.

Luine, V. N., Richards, S. T., Wu, V. Y., & Beck, K. D. (1998). Estradiol enhances learning and memory in a spatial memory task and effects levels of monoaminergic neurotransmitters. *Hormones and Behavior, 34,* 149–162.

Mack, C. M., Fitch, R. H., Cowell, P. E., Schrott, L. M., & Denenberg, V. H. (1993). Ovarian estrogen acts to feminize the rat's corpus callosum. *Developmental Brain Research, 71,* 115–119.

Mannan, M. A., & O'Shaughnessy, P. J. (1991). Steroidogenesis during postnatal development in the mouse ovary. *Journal of Endocrinology, 130,* 101–106.

Markus, E., & Zecevic, M. (1997). Sex differences and estrous cycle changes in hippocampus-dependent fear conditioning. *Psychobiology, 25,* 246–252.

McCarthy, M. (1994). Molecular aspects of sexual differentiation of the rodent brain. *Psychoneuroendocrinology, 19,* 415–427.

McCarthy, N. M., Schlenker, E. H., & Pfaff, D. W. (1993). Enduring consequences of neonatal treatment with antisense oligodeoxynucleotides to estrogen receptor messenger ribonucleic acid on sexual differentiation of rat brain. *Endocrinology, 133,* 433–439.

McEwen, B., Alves, S., Bulloch, K., & Weiland, N. (1997). Ovarian steroids and the brain: Implications for cognition and aging. *Neurology, 48(Supplement 7),* S8–S15.

McGlone, J. (1980). Sex differences in human brain asymmetry: A critical survey. *Behavioral and Brain Sciences, 3,* 215–263.

Meites, J., & Lu, J. (1994). Reproductive ageing and neuroendocrine function. In H. Charleton (Ed.), *Oxford reviews of reproductive biology* (pp. 215–239). Oxford: Oxford University Press.

Miles, C., Green, R., Sanders, G., & Hines, M. (1998). Estrogen and memory in a transsexual population. *Hormones and Behavior, 34(2),* 199–208.

Miranda, R. C., & Toran-Allerand, C. D. (1992). Developmental expression of estrogen receptor mRNA in the rat cerebral cortex: A nonisotopic *in situ* hybridization histochemistry study. *Cerebral Cortex, 2,* 1–15.

Morley, J., Kaiser, F., Hajjar, R., & Perry, H. (1997). Testosterone and frailty. *Clinics in Geriatric Medicine, 13,* 685–695.

Munoz-Cueto, J. A., Garcia-Segura, L. M., & Ruiz-Marcos, A. (1990). Developmental sex differences and effect of ovariectomy on the number of cortical pyramidal cell dendrite spines. *Brain Research, 515,* 64–68.

Murphy, D. M., DeCarli, C., McIntosh, A. R., Daly, E., Mentis, M. J., Pietrini, P., Szczepanik, J., Schapiro, M. B., Grady, C. L., Horwitz, B., & Rapoport, S. I. (1996). Sex differences in human brain morphometry and metabolism: An *in vivo* quantitative magnetic resonance imaging and positron emission tomography study on the effect of aging. *Archives of General Psychiatry, 53,* 585–594.

Murphy, D. M., DeCarli, C., Daly, A. R., Haxby, J. V., Allen, G., White, B. J., McIntosh, A. R., Powell, C. M., Horwitz, B., Rapoport, S. I., & Schapiro, M. B. (1993). X-chromosome effects on female brain: A magnetic resonance imaging study of Turner's syndrome. *The Lancet, 342,* 1197–1200.

Nappi, R. E., Sinforiani, E., Mauri, M., Bono, G., Polatti, F., & Nappi, G. (1999). Memory functioning at menopause: Impact of age in ovariectomized women. *Gynecologic Obstetric Investigation, 47,* 29–36.

Neils, J. R., & Aram, D. M. (1986). Handedness and sex of children with developmental language disorders. *Brain and Language, 28,* 53–65.

Nyborg, H. (1983). Spatial ability in men and women: Review and new theory. *Advances in Behavioural Research and Therapy, 5*(2), 89–140.

O'Neal, M. F., Means, L. W., Poole, M. C., & Hamm, R. J. (1996). Estrogen affects performance of ovariectomized rats in a two-choice water-escape working memory task. *Psychoneuroendocrinology, 21,* 51–65.

Ohkura, T., Isse, K., Akazawa, K., Hamamoto, M., Yaoi, Y., & Hagino, N. (1995). Long-term estrogen replacement therapy in female patients with dementia of the Alzheimer type: 7 case reports. *Dementia, 6,* 99–107.

Packard, M., & Teather, L. (1997). Posttraining estradiol injections enhance memory in ovariectomized rats: Cholinergic blockade and synergism. *Neurobiology of Learning and Memory, 68,* 172–188.

Paganini-Hill, A., & Henderson, V. W. (1994). Estrogen deficiency and risk of Alzheimer's disease in women. *American Journal of Epidemiology, 140,* 256–261.

Paganini-Hill, A., & Henderson, V. W. (1996). Estrogen replacement therapy and risk of Alzheimer disease. *Archives of Internal Medicine, 156,* 2213–2217.

Pappas, C. T. E., Diamond, M. C., & Johnson, R. E. (1979). Morphological changes in the cerebral cortex of rats with altered levels of ovarian hormones. *Behavioral and Neural Biology, 26,* 298–310.

Phillips, S. M., & Sherwin, B. B. (1992a). Effects of estrogen on memory function in surgically menopausal women. *Psychoneuroendocrinology, 17,* 485–495.

Phillips, S. M., & Sherwin, B. B. (1992b). Variations in memory function and sex steroid hormones across the menstrual cycle. *Psychoneuroendocrinology, 17,* 497–506.

Postma, A., Winkel, J., Tuiten, A., & van Honk, J. (1999). Sex differences and menstrual cycle effects in human spatial memory. *Psychoneuroendocrinology, 24,* 175–192.

Raynaud, J. P., Mercier-Bodard, C., & Baulieu, E. E. (1971). Rat estradiol binding plasma protein. *Steroids, 18,* 767–788.

Raz, S., Lauterbach, M. D., Hopkins, T. L., Glogowski, B. K., Porter, C. L., Riggs, W. W., & Sander, C. G. (1995). A female advantage in recovery from early cerebral insult. *Developmental Psychology, 31,* 958–966.

Reid, S. N., & Juraska, J. M. (1992). Sex differences in neuron number in the binocular area of the rat visual cortex. *Journal of Comparative Neurology, 321,* 448–455.

Reid, S. N., & Juraska, J. M. (1995). Sex differences in the number of synaptic junctions in the binocular area of the rat visual cortex. *Journal of Comparative Neurology, 352,* 560–566.

Reiss, A. L., Mazzacocco, M. M., Greenlaw, R., Freund, L. S., & Ross, J. L. (1995). Neurodevelopmental effects of X monosomy: A volumetric imaging study. *Annals of Neurology, 38,* 731–738.

Resnick, A., Perry, W., Parry, B., Mostofi, N., & Udell, C. (1998). Neuropsychological performance across the menstrual cycle in women with and without premenstrual dysphoric disorder. *Psychiatry Research, 77,* 147–158.

Resnick, S., Metter, E., & Zonderman, A. (1997). Estrogen replacement therapy and longitudinal decline in visual memory: A possible protective effect? *Neurology, 49,* 1491–1497.

Rhees, R. W., Shryne, J. E., & Gorski, R. A. (1990a). Onset of the hormone-sensitive perinatal period for sexual differentiation of the sexually dimorphic nucleus of the preoptic area. *Journal of Neurobiology, 21,* 781–786.

Rhees, R. W., Shryne, J. E., & Gorski, R. A. (1990b). Termination of the hormone-sensitive period for differentiation of the sexually dimorphic nucleus of the preoptic area in male and female rats. *Developmental Brain Research, 52,* 17–23.

Rissanen, A., Puolovali, J., Van Groen, T., & Riekkinen, P. (1999). In mice tonic estrogen replacement therapy improves non-spatial and spatial memory in a water maze task. *NeuroReport, 10,* 1369–1372.

Rodriguez-Sierra, J. (1986). Extended organizational effects of estrogen at puberty. *Annals of the New York Academy of Sciences, 474,* 293–307.

Roof, R. L. (1993a). The dentate gyrus is sexually dimorphic in prepubescent rats: Testosterone plays a significant role. *Brain Research, 610,* 148–151.

Roof, R. L. (1993b). Neonatal exogenous testosterone modifies sex difference in radial arm and Morris water maze performance in prepubescent and adult rats. *Behavioural Brain Research, 53,* 1–10.

Roof, R. L., Duvdevani, R., & Stein, D. G. (1993). Gender influences outcome of brain injury: Progesterone plays a protective role. *Brain Research, 607,* 333–336.

Roof, R. L., & Havens, M. (1992). Testosterone improves maze performance and induces development of a male hippocampus in females. *Brain Research, 572,* 310–313.

Ross, J. L., Stefanatos, G., Roeltgen, D., Kushner, H., & Cutler, G. B., Jr. (1995). Ullrich-Turner syndrome: Neurodevelopmental changes from childhood through adolescence. *American Journal of Medical Genetics, 58,* 74–82.

Schneider, L. S., Farlow, M. R., Henderson, V. W., & Pogoda, J. M. (1996). Effects of estrogen replacement therapy on response to tacrine in patients with Alzheimer's disease. *Neurology, 46,* 1580–1584.

Scouten, C. W., Grotelueschen, L. K., & Beatty, W. W. (1975). Androgens and the organization of sex differences in active avoidance behavior in the rat. *Journal of Comparative and Physiological Psychology, 88,* 264–270.

Seeman, M. V., & Lang, M. (1990). The role of estrogens in schizophrenic gender differences. *Schizophrenia Bulletin, 16,* 185–194.

Seymoure, P., & Juraska, J. M. (1992). Sex differences in cortical thickness and the dendritic tree in the monocular and binocular subfields of the rat visual cortex at weaning age. *Developmental Brain Research, 23,* 185–189.

Shaywitz, B. A., Shaywitz, S. E., Pugh, K. R., Constable, R. T., Skudlarski, P., Fulbright, R. K., Bronen, R. A., Fletcher, J. M., Shankweiler, D. P., Katz, L., & Gore, J. C. (1995). Sex differences in the functional organization of the brain for language. *Nature, 373,* 607–609.

Shaywitz, S., Shaywitz, B., Fletcher, J., & Escobar, M. (1990). Prevalence of reading diability in boys and girls. *Journal of the American Medical Association, 264,* 998–1002.

Sherwin, B. B. (1988). Estrogen and/or androgen replacement therapy and cognitive functioning in surgically menopausal women. *Psychoneuroendocrinology, 13,* 345–357.

Sherwin, B. B. (1994). Estrogenic effects on memory in women. *Annals of the New York Academy of Sciences, 743,* 213–230; discussion, 230–231.

Sherwin, B. (1998). Estrogen and cognitive functioning in women. *Proceedings of the Society for Experimental Biology and Medicine, 217,* 17–22.

Sherwin, B., & Phillips, S. (1990). Estrogen and cognitive functioning in surgically menopausal women. *Annals of the New York Academy of Sciences, 592,* 474–475.

Silverman, I., Kastuk, D., Choi, J., & Phillips, K. (1999). Testosterone levels and spatial ability in men. *Psychoneuroendocrinology, 24,* 813–822.

Silverman, I., & Phillips, K. (1993). Effects of estrogen changes during the menstrual cycle on spatial performance. *Ethology and Sociobiology, 14,* 257–270.

Simpkins, J. W., Singh, M., & Bishop, J. (1994). The potential role for estrogen replacement therapy in the treatment of the cognitive decline and neurodegeneration associated with Alzheimer's disease. *Neurobiology of Aging, 15*(Suppl 2), S195–S197.

Singh, M., Meyer, E. M., Millard, W. J., & Simpkins, J. W. (1994). Ovarian steroid deprivation results in a reversible learning impairment and compromised cholinergic function in female Sprague-Dawley rats. *Brain Research, 644,* 305–312.

Slabbekoorn, D., Van Goozen, S. H., Megens, J., Gooren, L. J., & Cohen-Kettenis, P. T. (1999). Activating effects of cross-sex hormones on cognitive functioning. A study of short-term and long-term hormone effects in transsexuals. *Psychoneuroendocrinology, 24,* 423–447.

Sokka, T. A., & Huhtaniemi, I. T. (1995). Functional maturation of the pituitary–gonadal axis in the neonatal female rat. *Biology of Reproduction, 52,* 1404–1409.

Spinillo A., Fazzi, E., Orcesi, S., Accorsi, P., Beccaria, F., & Capuzzo, E. (1995). Perinatal factors and 2-year minor neurodevelopmental impairment in low birth weight infants. *Biology of the Neonate, 67,* 39–46.

Stackman, R., Blasberg, M., Langan, C., & Clark, A. (1997). Stability of spatial working memory across the estrous cycle of Long-Evans rats. *Neurobiology of Learning and Memory, 67,* 167–171.

Stephenson, J. (1996). More evidence links NSAID, estrogen use with reduced Alzheimer risk. *Journal of the American Medical Association, 275,* 1389–1390.

Stewart, J., & Cygan, D. (1980). Ovarian hormones act early in development to feminize open field behavior in the rat. *Hormones and Behavior, 14,* 20–32.

Stewart, J., & Kolb, B. (1988). The effects of neonatal gonadectomy and prenatal stress on cortical thickness and asymmetry in rats. *Behavioral and Neural Biology, 49,* 344–360.

Stewart, J., & Rajabi, H. (1994). Estradiol derived from testosterone in prenatal life affects the development of catecholamine systems in the frontal cortex of the male rat. *Brain Research, 646,* 157–160.

Stewart, J., Kuhnemann, S., & Rajabi, H. (1991) Neonatal exposure to gonadal hormones affects the development of monoamine systems in rat cortex. *Journal of Neuroendocrinology, 3,* 85–93.

Stewart, J., Skavarenina, A., & Pottier, J. (1975). Effects of neonatal androgens on open-field behavior and maze-learning in the prepubescent and adult rat. *Physiology and Behavior, 14,* 291–295.

Tang, M. X., Jacobs, D., Stern, Y., Marder, K., Schofield, P., Gurland, B., Andrews, H., & Mayeux, R. (1996). Effect of oestrogen during menopause on risk and age at onset of Alzheimer's disease [see comments]. *The Lancet, 348,* 429–432.

Tobet, S. A., & Fox, T. O. (1992). Sex differences in neuronal morphology influenced hormonally throughout life. In A. A. Gerall, H. Moltz, and I. L. Ward (Eds.), *Handbook of behavioral neurobiology, Vol. 11: Sexual differentiation,* (pp. 41–83). New York: Plenum.

Toran-Allerand, A. (1976). Sex steroids and the development of the newborn mouse hypothalamus and preoptic area in vitro: Implication for sexual differentiation. *Brain Research, 106,* 407–412.

Toran-Allerand, D. (1986) Sexual differentiation of the brain. In W. T. Greenough & J. M. Juraska (Eds.) *Developmental Neuropsychology,* (pp. 175–121). London: Academic Press.

Toran-Allerand, D. (1992). Organotypic culture of the developing cerebral cortex and hypothalamus: Relevance to sexual differentiation. In P. Tallal & B. McEwen (Eds.) *Psychoneuroendocrinology Vol. 16,* New York: Pergamon.

Toran Allerand, C., Singh, M., & Setalo, G. (1999). Novel mechanisms of estrogen action in the brain: New players in an old story. *Frontiers in Nueroendocrinology, 20,* 97–121.

Van Goozen, S., Cohen-Kettenis, P., Gooren, L., Frijda, N., & Van de Poll, N. (1994). Activating effects of androgens and cognitive performance: Causal evidence in a group of female-to-male transsexuals. *Neuropsychologia, 32,* 1153–1157.

Van Goozen, S., Cohen-Kettenis, P., Gooren, L., Frijda, N., & Van de Poll, N. (1995). Gender differences in behavior: Activating effects of cross-gender hormones. *Psychoneuroendocrinology, 20,* 343–363.

Van Haaren, F., Van Hest, A., & Heinsbroek, R. P. W. (1990). Behavioral differences between male and female rats: Effects of gonadal hormones on learning and memory. *Neuroscience and Biobehavioral Reviews, 14,* 23–33.

Vogel, S. (1990). Gender differences in intelligence, language, visual-motor abilities, and academic achievement in students with learning disabilities: A review of the literature. *Journal of Learning Disabilities, 23,* 44–52.

Wagner, C. K., & Clemens, L. G. (1989). Perinatal modification of a sexually dimorphic motor nucleus in the spinal cord of the B6D2F1 house mouse. *Physiology and Behavior, 45,* 831–835.

Ward, I., & Weisz, J. (1980). Maternal stress alters plasma testosterone in fetal males. *Science, 207,* 328–329.

Warren, S. G., & Juraska, J. M. (1997). Spatial and nonspatial learning across the rat estrous cycle. *Behavioral Neuroscience, 111,* 259–266.

Weniger, J. P., Zeis, A., & Chouraqui, J. (1993). Estrogen production by fetal and infantile rat ovaries. *Reproduction, Nutrition, and Development, 33,* 129–136.

Williams, C. (1996). Short-term but not long-term estradiol replacement improves radial-arm maze performance of young and aging rats. *Society for Neuroscience Abstracts, 22,* 1164.

Williams, C. L. (1986a). Estradiol benzoate facilitates lordosis and ear wiggling of 4- to 6-day-old rats. *Behavioral Neuroscience, 101,* 718-23.

Williams, C. L. (1986b). A reevaluation of the concept of separable periods of organizational and activational actions of estrogens in development of brain and behavior. *Annals of the New York Academy of Sciences, 474,* 282–292.

Williams, C. L., Barnett, A. M., & Meck, W. H. (1990). Organizational effects of early gonadal secretions on sexual differentiation in spatial memory. *Behavioral Neuroscience, 104,* 84–97.

Williams, C. L., & Meck, W. H. (1991). The organizational effect of gonadal steroids on sexually dimorphic spatial ability. *Psychoneuroendocrinology, 16,* 155–176.

Wilson, J., George, F., & Griffin, J. (1981). The hormonal control of sexual development. *Science, 211,* 1278–1284.

Witelson, S. F. (1991). Neural sexual mosaicism: Sexual differentiation of the human temporo-parietal region for functional asymmetry. *Psychoneuroendocrinology, 16,* 131–153.

Wood, F. B., Flowers, L. D., & Naylor, C. E. (1991). Cerebral laterality in functional neuroimaging. In F. L. Kitterle (Ed.), *Cerebral laterality: Theory and research, the Toledo symposium* (pp. 103–115). Hillsdale, NJ: Lawrence Erlbaum.

Woolley, C. (1998). Estrogen-mediated structural and functional synaptic plasticity in the female rat hippocampus. *Hormones and Behavior, 34,* 140–148.

Woolley, C. S., Gould, E., Frankfurt, M., & McEwen, B. S. (1990). Naturally occurring fluctuation in dendritic spine density on adult hippocampal pyramidal neurons. *Journal of Neuroscience, 10,* 4035–4039.

Woolley, C. S., & McEwen, B. S. (1992). Estradiol mediates fluctuation in hippocampal synapse density during the estrous cycle in the adult rat. *Journal of Neuroscience, 12,* 2549–2554.

Yaffe, K., Sawaya, G., Lieberburg, I., & Grady, D. (1998). Estrogen therapy in post menopausal women: Effects on cognitive function and dementia. *Journal of the American Medical Association, 279,* 688–695.

Zimmerberg, B., & Farley, M. J. (1993). Sex differences in anxiety behavior in rats: Role of gonadal hormones. *Physiology and Behavior, 54,* 1119–1124.

CHAPTER 4

Sex Differences in Motivation, Self-Concept, Career Aspiration, and Career Choice: Implications for Cognitive Development

Allan Wigfield
Ann Battle
Lisa B. Keller
Jacquelynne S. Eccles

In this chapter we discuss gender differences in motivation, self-concept, self-esteem, career aspirations, and occupational choice. We also consider how parents and teachers influence these variables and link these differences to sex differences in cognitive development. We focus on these personality constructs and social influences because we strongly believe that any observed sex differences in cognition (and participation in different careers) are due in part to sex differences in motivation, self-concept, and views on what are appropriate activities for males and females. As we discuss in more detail later, these constructs can have causal influences on cognitive outcomes, such as school achievement, and other important outcomes such as occupational choice. To understand gender differences in crucial outcomes in children's lives, motivation and self-concept need to be considered, along with the evolutionary and neurobiological factors considered by Geary, Fitch, and Bimonte in chapters 2 and 3 in this book, as well as the constructs considered by the other authors in this book. We primarily concentrate on sex differences in these constructs during the elementary and secondary school years.

We begin the chapter with a word of caution. As other authors have pointed out, drawing conclusions about sex differences must be done carefully (see Eisenberg, Martin, & Fabes, 1996; Ruble & Martin, 1998). Although such differences often are observed, in general they tend to be relatively small, in terms of the amount of variance explained (e.g., Marsh, 1989). Thus there often is substantial overlap between boys and girls and men and women in the many different variables measured in studies of sex differences. Individual differences *within* groups of males and females often are stronger than differences *between* the two groups. Having said that, however, there do appear to be reliable sex differences in many of the motivation and self-concept constructs we and others study.

First, we briefly discuss sex differences in achievement and performance; this review is brief because many other authors in this book provide complete discussions of such differences. Then, we discuss work on sex differences in motivation, self-concept, career plans, and occupational choice. Issues regarding stereotype and stereotype threat could have been presented here; these topics instead are covered by Martin and Dinella in chapter 8. We conclude the chapter with a consideration of how parents, teachers, and factors in school environments influence the sex differences in motivation, self-concept, career plans, and occupational choice. Throughout the chapter, we note how these sex differences can influence developing sex differences in cognitive outcomes.

SEX DIFFERENCES IN ABILITIES, ACHIEVEMENT, AND PERFORMANCE

Sex differences in abilities, achievement, and performance in different areas are of longstanding interest in developmental and educational psychology. In their classic volume on sex differences, Maccoby and Jacklin (1974) concluded that there are gender differences favoring girls in verbal abilities and performance, favoring boys in mathematics ability and performance (particularly in problem solving rather than computation, during adolescence), and favoring boys in spatial ability. In their more recent reviews of gender differences in these areas, Hyde and Linn (1988) and Linn and Hyde (1989) argued that many of these differences have decreased to the point where they are negligible (see also Eisenberg et al., 1996). However, in the mathematics ability area boys continue to be more highly represented in the highest performing groups of children and adolescents (see Royer, Tronsky, & Chan, 1999). Gender differences in physical skills also have been observed. After puberty boys do better than girls on activities that involve strength and power; girls continue to be less likely to participate in activities requiring these skills (see chapter 6 for a more complete review of these findings).

There also are interesting academic performance differences between boys and girls. In general, girls earn higher grades than boys across the school years, even in mathematics and science, despite not doing as well on tests of mathematical ability during adolescence (see Royer et al., 1999). Although the overall mathematics ability differences favor boys, in certain mathematical areas, such as counting and computation, girls perform better, especially in elementary school. Further, differences in problem solving in math vary some depending on what kinds of problems are presented.

To conclude this section, gender differences in abilities and performance remain. Especially with respect to various abilities, however, gender differences appear to have decreased over the last 25 years (but see Ruble and Martin, 1998 for some cautions about this conclusion). Girls continue to outperform boys in school, if grades are the indicator of performance. How do these differences compare to the observed sex differences in motivation and self-concept?

SEX DIFFERENCES IN MOTIVATION, SELF-CONCEPT, AND CAREER ASPIRATIONS

Gender Differences in Motivation

Motivation is crucial to cognition and performance because motivation directs individuals' behavior. More specifically, motivation influences individuals' choices of which activities to do, level of engagement in them, and degree of persistence at them (Weiner, 1992). Researchers studying achievement motivation have examined a variety of motivational constructs posited to influence choice, engagement, persistence, and performance (see Eccles, Wigfield, & Schiefele, 1998; Pintrich & Schunk, 1996, for complete review). Broadly, these constructs can be broken down into those having to do with children's sense of competence, efficacy, and control; and those having to do with children's purposes and reasons for engaging in different activities. Competence-related beliefs are motivational because when children believe they can accomplish a given task or activity, they are more likely to continue to do the activity, overcome obstacles to complete it, and choose more challenging activities on subsequent occasions.

Constructs related to purposes and reasons for action include achievement values, achievement goals, and intrinsic and extrinsic motivation. Children's reasons or purposes for engaging (or not engaging) in achievement activities also are crucial to their motivation. Simply believing one is competent often is not enough reason for the individual to engage in an activity. Individuals must value the activity, have goals for doing it, or find it intrinsically or extrinsically motivating in order to engage in it. Thus, to understand choice and performance, the purposes and reasons for action also must be understood.

We have taken an expectancy-value theoretical perspective on motivation in our own work, and have developed a model of achievement choice based in this perspective (e.g., Eccles, 1987; Eccles et al., 1983; Wigfield & Eccles, 1992). The essence of this perspective is that individuals' competence-related beliefs along with their valuing of achievement are the strongest motivational predictors of task engagement, choice, and performance. Individuals' competence-related beliefs and values are influenced by children's goals, their previous experiences, by parents, and by experiences they have in school. We organize our review of sex differences in motivation around these two broad sets of constructs, incorporating some of the other constructs mentioned previously into our review. Because there have been few, if any, studies of sex differences in achievement goals, we do not discuss that construct in detail in this section.

Beliefs About Competence and Control

Gender differences in competence beliefs during childhood and adolescence often are reported, particularly in gender-role stereotyped domains and on novel tasks. For example, boys hold higher competence beliefs than girls for mathematics and sports, even after all relevant skill-level differences are controlled. By contrast, girls have higher competence beliefs than boys for reading, English, and social activities (Eccles, 1984; Eccles et al., 1989, Huston, 1983; Wigfield et al., 1991; Wigfield et al., 1997). These differences emerge remarkably early. Wigfield and colleagues (1997) conducted a longitudinal study of children's competence beliefs and valuing of different activities, including mathematics, reading, and sports. They began when the children were in first, second, and fourth grade, and followed them for three years. The results showed that boys had higher competence beliefs for mathematics and sports, and girls for English, even among the first graders. The age differences in beliefs did not change over time. Jacobs et al. (2000) followed these same children through the end of high school and found that gender differences in mathematics competence beliefs narrow by the end of high school. Gender differences in English competence beliefs favoring girls remain at the end of high school, but also are smaller than during the earlier school years.

The extent to which children endorse the cultural stereotypes regarding which sex is likely to be most talented in each domain predicts the extent to which girls and boys distort their ability self-concepts and expectations in the gender stereotypic direction (Early, Belansky, & Eccles, 1992; Eccles & Harold, 1991). That is, boys who believe that in general boys are better in mathematics are more likely to have more positive competence beliefs in mathematics. However, these sex differences are not always found (e.g., Dauber & Benbow, 1990; Schunk & Lilly, 1982) and, when found, are generally quite small (Marsh, 1989).

These sex differences in beliefs about competence are important with respect to sex differences in cognition because competence beliefs relate strongly to individuals' performance on different tasks or activities and choices of which activities to do (Bandura, 1997; Eccles et al., 1998). When individuals believe they are competent, they are more likely to continue participating in an activity; when they are less confident, they are more likely to discontinue the activity. Such choices could impact cognitive development, as continuing participation in an activity likely fosters cognitive growth, and discontinuing hampers it.

Attributions for success and failure concern children's understanding of their achievement activities. In general, attributing success to one's ability and effort and failure to lack of effort is seen as positive for subsequent motivation, whereas attributing success to luck and failure to lack of ability has negative connotations for motivation (see Weiner, 1985). Findings regarding gender differences in attributions are also mixed. Some researchers (e.g., Dweck & Goetz, 1978) find that girls are less likely than boys to attribute success to ability and more likely to attribute failure to lack of ability. Others have found that this pattern depends on the kind of task used: occurring more with unfamiliar tasks or stereotypically masculine achievement task and sometimes does not occur at all (see Parsons, Adler, & Kaczala, 1982; Yee & Eccles, 1988). More generally, sex differentiated attributions can impact males' and females' subsequent motivation, which can influence cognitive outcomes such as achievement.

Gender differences are also sometimes found for locus of control, another construct related to the individual's sense of whether he or she can accomplish a task or activity. For example, Crandall, Katovsky, and Crandall (1965) found that girls tended to have higher internal locus of responsibility scores for both positive and negative achievement events and the older girls had higher internality for negative events than did the younger girls. The boys' internal locus of responsibility scores for positive events decreased from tenth to twelfth grade. These two developmental patterns resulted in the older girls accepting more blame for negative events than the older boys (Dweck & Repucci, 1973; Dweck & Goetz, 1978). Similarly, Connell (1985) found that boys attributed their outcomes more than girls to either powerful others or unknown causes in both the cognitive and social domains.

This greater propensity for girls to take personal responsibility for their failures, coupled with their more frequent attribution of failure to lack of ability (a stable, uncontrollable cause), has been interpreted as evidence of greater learned helplessness in females (see Dweck & Licht, 1980). However, evidence for gender differences on behavioral indicators of learned helplessness is quite mixed. In most studies of underachievers, boys outnumber girls two to one (see McCall, Evahn, Kratzer, 1992). Similarly, boys are more likely than girls to be referred by their teachers for motivational problems and are more likely to drop out of school before completing high school. More consistent evidence exists that females, compared to males, select easier laboratory tasks, avoid challenging and competitive situations, lower their expectations more following failure, shift more quickly to a different college major when their grades begin to drop, and perform more poorly than they are capable of on difficult, timed tests (see Dweck & Licht, 1980; Ruble & Martin, 1998; Spencer & Steele, 1995).

In sum, reliable sex differences in beliefs about competence for different activities have been found. As noted earlier, these differences are important with respect to sex differences in cognition because competence-related beliefs are strong predictors of performance (Bandura, 1997; Eccles et al., 1983; Meece, Wigfield, & Eccles, 1990). Researchers looking at relations of competence beliefs to performance do not find sex differences in these relations; the links are as strong for girls as for boys (Meece et al., 1990). But given that the sexes differ in their level of competence beliefs for different activities, their locus of control, and (to a lesser extent) their attributions for success and failure, their performance may in part reflect these beliefs. Two examples can be used to illustrate this point. Girls doubt their competence in mathematics more than boys do, and this likely influences their performance in that subject. Boys doubt their competence more in reading, again likely influencing their performance.

Achievement Task Values

Achievement values refer to different purposes or reasons individuals have for engaging in different activities. Eccles et al. (1983) defined four components of task value: attainment value, intrinsic value, utility value, and cost. They defined attainment value as the personal importance of doing well on the task. They also linked attainment value to the relevance of engaging in a task for confirming or disconfirming salient aspects of one's self-schema. Because tasks provide the opportunity to demonstrate aspects of one's actual or ideal self-schema, such as masculinity, femininity, and/or competence in various domains, tasks will have higher attainment value to the extent that they allow the individual to confirm salient aspects of these self-schemata (see Eccles, 1984, 1987). Intrinsic value is the enjoyment the individual gets from performing the activity or the subjective interest the individual has in the subject. This component of value is similar to the construct of intrinsic motivation as defined by Harter (1981), and by Deci and his colleagues (e.g., Deci & Ryan, 1985; Ryan, Connell, & Deci, 1985). Utility value is determined by how well a task relates to current and future goals, such as career goals. A task can have positive value to a person because it facilitates important future goals, even if he or she is not interested in task for its own sake. In one sense then this component captures the more "extrinsic" reasons for engaging in a task (see Harter, 1981 for further discussion of extrinsic motivation). But it also relates directly to individuals' internalized short- and long-term goals. Finally, cost is conceptualized in terms of the negative aspects of engaging in the task, such as performance anxiety and fear of both failure and success as well as the amount of effort that needed to succeed and the lost opportunities that result from making one choice rather than another.

Eccles, Wigfield, and their colleagues have found gender-role stereotypic differences in both children's and adolescents' valuing of sports, social activities, and English (e.g. Eccles et al., 1989; Eccles et al., 1993; Wigfield et al., 1991, Wigfield et al., 1997). They primarily have studied the attainment, intrinsic, and utility aspects of value. Across these studies, boys value sports activities more than girls do, although girls also value them highly. Relative to boys, girls value reading and English more, and also value music more. Interestingly, in earlier work, gender differences in the value of mathematics did not emerge until high school (Eccles, 1984); in a recent study, high school girls and boys reported valuing mathematics equally (Jacobs et al., 2000). Although it is encouraging that boys and girls value mathematics equally, the fact that adolescent girls have less positive views of their mathematics ability is problematic because these differences likely contribute to girls' lower probability of taking optional advanced-level mathematics courses and physical science and entering mathematics-related scientific and engineering fields, thus contributing to sex-differentiated cognitive outcomes (see Eccles, 1994). We return to career choice issues later in this chapter.

Values also can be conceived more broadly to include things such as notions of what are appropriate activities for males and females to do. Sometimes such values can conflict with engagement in achievement. The role of conflict between gender roles and achievement in gifted girls' lives is well illustrated by results of an ethnographic study of group of gifted elementary school girls. Bell (1989) interviewed a multiethnic group of third to sixth grade gifted girls in an urban elementary school regarding the barriers they perceived to their achievement in school. Five gender-role related themes emerged with great regularity:

1. concern about hurting someone else's feelings by winning in achievement contests;

2. concern about seeming to be a braggart if one expressed pride in one's accomplishments;

3. over reaction to nonsuccess experiences (apparently not being the very best is very painful to these girls);

4. concern over their physical appearance and what it takes to be beautiful; and

5. concern with being overly aggressive in terms of getting the teacher's attention.

In each case, the gifted girls felt caught between doing their best and either appearing feminine or caring.

Academic Interests and Intrinsic Motivation

There is an extensive literature on gender differences in activities and interests during the preschool years (see chapter 8 as well as Eisenberg et al., 1996; Ruble & Martin, 1998). Very early, boys and girls engage in very different activities and play with quite different toys. In research done prior to the 1980s, elementary school-aged children often classified school subjects as either masculine or feminine (see Huston, 1983). Mathematics and science were viewed as masculine, and reading/English and the arts as feminine. This no longer appears to be the case, as gender stereotyping of school subjects now is less consistent (see Etaugh & Liss, 1992).

Although school subjects no longer appear to be clearly gender stereotyped, boys and girls do vary in their interest in different subject areas. In Eccles' and

Wigfield's work just reviewed (e.g., Eccles et al., 1993; Wigfield et al., 1997), boys and girls differed in their interest in reading, music, and sport in gender stereotypic ways. However, boys' and girls' interest in mathematics did not differ during elementary school (see also Folling-Albers & Hartinger, 1998). During secondary school, boys appear to be more interested in mathematics than are girls. Similar findings have been reported for science and other technical fields (see Gardner, 1998, for review). By adolescence, girls report less interest in science than do boys, and are much less likely to enroll in science and technically oriented classes or pursue these areas for their careers.

Explanations for these differences in interests and activity preferences focus on several things, including children's understanding of what is appropriate for each sex to do. Children's understanding of stereotypes about what are gender-appropriate activities increase across the childhood years (see chapter 8; Eisenberg et al., 1996; Ruble & Martin, 1998 for further discussion). From the perspective of the constructs discussed in this chapter, perhaps children develop more positive competence-related beliefs and values for activities they believe are appropriate for their gender, and thus engage in those activities more. Parents likely contribute to these differences through the toys they provide and activities they encourage children to do (see further discussion later). Peers have a strong role as well (Eisenberg et al., 1996).

The differences in patterns of interest potentially are crucial for understanding differences in cognitive performance. Various researchers have documented how interest impacts comprehension and performance (e.g., Krapp, Hidi, & Renninger, 1992; Renninger, 1992, 1998; Schiefele, 1999). When individuals are interested in the activity they are working on, they often process the information received more deeply, retain it better, and stay engaged with it for a longer period of time (although the effects of interest sometimes are complex) (see Renninger, 1992, 1998). Individuals' interests play strong roles in their choices of which activities to pursue, both in and out of school. For instance, interest has strong implications for decisions such as occupational choice, as we discuss later. Thus, to understand gender differences in cognition and performance, it is crucial to consider interest as a motivational variable.

Intrinsic motivation is another important motivational construct that is related to the interest construct. When individuals are intrinsically motivated they do activities because they enjoy them and of their own volition (see Deci & Ryan, 1985; Ryan & Deci, 2000). Although much has been written about intrinsic motivation, researchers assessing it rarely have examined sex differences in it. Gottfried's (1990) study of young elementary school-aged children's intrinsic motivation for mathematics and reading is one exception; she found no gender differences in intrinsic motivation for either subject.

In summary, as with competence beliefs, there are gender differences in children's and adolescents' valuation of different activities and their interest in them.

These differences are important for understanding the development of gender differences in cognition and performance. In our research, children's and adolescents' valuation of different activities relates strongly to their choices of whether or not to continue to pursue the activity (Eccles et al., 1983; Meece, Wigfield, & Eccles, 1990). Such choices can have an impact on actual competence and subsequent performance. The choice to participate in an activity likely will increase one's performance; choosing not to do the activity will decrease performance.

Gender Differences in Self-Concept and Self-Esteem

The literature on self-concept (SC) and self-esteem (SE) is voluminous, and cannot be reviewed completely here (see Harter, 1998, for a thorough review of the development of self-representations). However, because SC and SE both have been tied to achievement and motivation, it is important to consider them in this chapter. Further, there have been numerous studies of gender differences in SC and SE.

The literature on SC and SE has been plagued by definitional and measurement problems. Often the two terms are used interchangeably. We define SC as individuals' understanding of their roles and characteristics. SE can be defined as individuals' affective reactions to their characteristics, and overall evaluation of themselves as persons (see Wigfield & Karpathian, 1991). So for example, part of one's SC could be "I am a good tennis player." If tennis is a central activity to this individual, then her SE may be enhanced. We believe it is useful to distinguish between these two terms, to attach a specific meaning to each.

Historically, measures of SC often were global, with one overall score derived (see Harter, 1998). Global measures often relate only weakly to other constructs, such as achievement; this is due in large part to the difficulty in determining exactly what influences a construct as general as global SC. Modern theorists posit that SC is multidimensional, and thus argue that specific aspects of SC should be measured rather than measuring it globally (e.g., Harter, 1990, 1998; Marsh, 1993). For instance, if a researcher is interested in relations of SC to mathematics performance, he or she should measure SC in this domain, rather than just using a general SC measure. Popular questionnaire measures of SC developed by researchers such as Harter and Marsh focus on perceived competence as the crucial aspect of self-concept, and these measures assess this construct in several domains. Interestingly, because of this focus on perceived competence, these measures have some overlap with the measures of competence and expectancies just discussed.

By contrast, because SE reflects one's overall affective appraisal, it tends to be measured more generally. Although there are important theoretical reasons for considering SE as an overall self-evaluation, by measuring SE generally, researchers often find relatively weak relations of SE to different aspects of performance. This is because SE is influenced by so many different factors.

Historically, research on sex differences in general SC produced a conflicting pattern of findings, with some studies showing that boys have higher SCs, some studies showing that girls do, and others finding few differences (see Wylie, 1979). The more recent work utilizing specific measures of SC has produced more consistent findings that are in line with those reviewed earlier in the section on perceived competence: boys have higher SCs for physical activities and mathematics, and girls do so for reading and music (Harter, 1982; Marsh, 1989). Marsh noted, however, that these differences were not very substantial in terms of the amount of variance explained. However, such differences could have an impact on the development of cognitive differences between the sexes, as was discussed earlier in the section on competence beliefs.

One interesting group to consider is gifted children, who obviously are advanced in their cognitive skills. Research on gifted boys' and girls' perceived competence, SC, and SE also produced a conflicting set of findings, particularly when researchers studied general SC and SE. Some researchers find that gifted girls have higher general SC and SE than gifted boys do (Bartell & Reynolds, 1986; Coleman & Fults, 1982), whereas others find no such differences between gifted boys and girls (Karnes & Wherry, 1981; Loeb & Jay, 1987). The conflicting results could be the result of using different measures of SC and SE, although several of these researchers have used the same measure in their work.

The picture is clearer when researchers use measures that tap specific aspects of SC. Siegle and Reis (1998), in a large scale study of gifted boys' and girls' SC in different areas, found that girls rated their competence in language arts higher than boys did, and also valued language arts more than did the boys. Boys rated their competence as higher in mathematics, science, and social studies. These results are similar to those in "non-gifted" samples of children reviewed previously; even within gifted populations, girls and boys differ in their views of their competence in sex stereotypical ways. Again, these differences have implications for males' and females' continued involvement in different kinds of activities. Based on their sense of competence, gifted boys and girls may gravitate toward different achievement domains, with implications for their cognitive development in the different domains. Continued involvement in an academic subject area likely means stronger cognitive growth in that area.

It is important to consider what research has shown about the relations of SC to achievement. Although the causal direction in this relationship has been long debated and likely is reciprocal by middle childhood (see Marsh & Yeung, 1997; Wigfield & Karpathian, 1991), it has been clearly documented. When children have positive SCs in a given area they also achieve better, and vice versa. Moreover, there is intriguing evidence that there are sex-differentiated patterns in relations of specific aspects of SC to achievement and to general academic SC. Skaalvik and Rankin (1990) found that for boys, mathematics SC and verbal achievement predicted general academic SC. For girls, verbal SC and mathematics achievement most strongly predicted general academic SC. Skaalvik and Rankin interpreted these results in terms of gender stereotypes about who has better mathematics and verbal abilities. They suggested that if the stereotypes that boys are better at mathematics and girls are better at verbal skills are accepted, then girls' mathematics SCs would not influence their general academic SC, and the same would be true for boys' verbal SCs. These fascinating findings need to be replicated, but show how stereotypes and beliefs about specific aspects of self relate to both general SC and achievement. Such stereotypes could impact sex differences in cognitive development.

Work on gender differences in SE also has produced some interesting findings. During the middle childhood years, boys and girls report similar levels of SE. By the early adolescent years, however, girls tend to report lower SE than boys. Although in general SE rises as children move through adolescence (Dusek & Flaherty, 1981), the gender difference remains (Kling, Hyde, Showers, & Buswell, 1999). Further, young women seem more likely than young men to develop more serious negative self-evaluations, such as depression, during the adolescent years (see Eisenberg et al, 1996; Harter, 1998; Nolen-Hoeksema & Girigus, 1994).

A variety of explanations have been offered for these sex differences in SE and depression. Boys have been described as being more likely to handle difficulties by engaging in "externalizing" behavior, such as aggression. Girls, by contrast, tend to "internalize" problems to a greater extent (see Eisenberg et al., 1996). Nolen-Hoeksema and Girigus (1994) suggested that females' SE is based more on the approval of others and on pleasing others, making it more difficult for them to maintain self-approval, especially when they encounter difficulties.

Physical appearance issues likely are central as well. Harter (1990, 1998) made three essential points about physical appearance and SE, based on her own work and that of others. First, as boys and girls go through childhood and move into adolescence, girls (relative to boys) are increasingly less satisfied with their own appearance. Second, society and the media place an incredibly strong emphasis on physical appearance as a basis for self-evaluation, and this is especially true for women. There are clear (and often unrealistic) standards for women's appearance that young women strive to attain, often unsuccessfully. Third, Harter's empirical work clearly has shown that for both boys and girls (and men and women as well), satisfaction with physical appearance is the strongest predictor of SE. Taking these three points together, girls are increasingly unhappy about an aspect of themselves that seems to be the primary predictor of SE. Hence girls are more likely to develop lower SE at this time.

Another explanation for girls' lower SE during adolescence concerns socialization into male and female roles. A variety of authors have argued that interest in gender-appropriate behavior becomes pivotal at early adolescence, with both boys and girls wanting to conform to appropriate roles (see Harter, Waters,

Whitesell, & Kastelic, 1997, for review). Hill and Lynch (1983) called this phenomenon "gender intensification." For females, traditionally appropriate feminine behaviors include caregiving, pleasing others, being agreeable, and wanting to maintain connections between self and other. Note that high achievement is not on this list. Gilligan (1993) discussed these issues extensively (see also Pipher, 1994). She argued that because of the importance of these things, particularly the importance of maintaining relations to others, many young women become hesitant to express themselves fully, for fear of disrupting their relations with others. Gilligan referred to this phenomenon as "losing voice." Because stifling one's voice means presenting oneself falsely, lower SE may result. Gilligan has conducted interviews with early adolescent girls and found that many expressed concerns about these issues and felt that their voices indeed were stifled at adolescence.

Harter and colleagues (1997) conducted a series of questionnaire-based studies to examine the extent to which young women indeed do lose their voice at adolescence. They first assessed with whom adolescents felt they could express themselves fully. Not surprisingly, adolescent boys and girls felt that they could express themselves the most with same-gender friends and classmates, and less with opposite-gender classmates, parents, and teachers. Of particular relevance to this chapter, they found no decreases across sixth through twelfth grade in females' sense of being able to express their voice. They did not find overall gender differences in voice at these ages. Instead, they found that adolescents (both male and female) most likely to lose voice were those who felt they lacked social support from parents and others. Also, girls who perceived themselves as strongly feminine were more likely to lose voice, especially in the classroom setting.

Harter and her colleagues' intriguing findings showed, as Harter et al. (1997) stated "no evidence that girls, in general, lose their voices at adolescence. Rather, they suggest that Gilligan's analysis speaks primarily to a particular subset of adolescent females, namely, feminine girls who report lower levels of voice in public contexts" (p. 169). So although Gilligan's analysis appears to be too sweeping, it does appear that some girls are more at risk for losing voice at adolescence. Believing that one cannot express oneself in a public setting such as a classroom has strong implications for school performance; these girls perhaps are more likely to begin to do less well in school than their male counterparts, and female peers who do not share this gender orientation.

The findings about sex differences in SE potentially have important implications for sex differences in cognitive development. Girls focusing on social approval and physical appearance as the means to attain SE may be less invested in achieving in school, with consequences for their cognitive development. Depression and achievement also are negatively correlated. It is important to reiterate, however, that children's general SE does not relate as strongly to achievement as do specific aspects of SC. Thus the more powerful effects on cognitive development likely come from the latter variables.

Gender Differences in Career Choice
and Occupational Aspirations

We now turn to a consideration of gender differences in career choice and occupational aspirations. We begin by summarizing recent statistics on gender differences in occupations, and then discuss some of the individual and social factors likely contributing to the observed gender differences in career choice.

Gender Differences in Career Choice

The U. S. Census Bureau statistics (U. S. Census Bureau, 1999) indicate that women persist in choosing jobs that conform to the cultural stereotype of female occupations. Between the years 1983 and 1998, there was no appreciable change in the extent to which women dominated fields such as nursing, teaching and caring for young children, clerical positions, minor accounting jobs, ancillary health care workers, and food service.

During these same years, there were modest increases in female employment in some typically male-dominated, professional occupations associated with higher educational attainment. The percentage of women in the roles of physician, dentist, architect, lawyer, and engineer nearly doubled. However, considering the remarkably low female participation in these careers in 1983, the 15-year increase yields women no more than a 30% overall inclusion rate in 1998, leaving these prestigious and higher-paying careers still largely occupied by men. Even those jobs requiring little education beyond high school, but which have a stereotypical male orientation (e.g., fire fighting, police work, auto mechanics, construction trades, and truck driving), continue to draw few women into their ranks.

There are also persistent trends in men's and women's choices about mathematics and science careers. In 1998, male participation in professions based on proficiency in mathematics and science continued to be much higher than women's. These include professions such as chemists and biological scientists (67–70% male); aerospace, chemical, civil, electrical, industrial, and mechanical engineers (80–93% male); computer systems analysts (73% male); and drafting, surveying, and mapping specialists (80–87% male). Furthermore, when women choose professional careers, they continue to gravitate toward those that are helping, or relationally oriented, far outweighing men's participation rates in areas such as personnel and labor relations (66% female); educational administration (63% female); educational and vocational counseling (69% female); social work (68% female); and public relations (68% female) (U. S. Census Bureau, 1999).

Finally, women continue to occupy lower ranking positions within broad categories of occupational fields. For instance, when health careers are considered, men dominate the more prestigious diagnosing occupations such as physician and dentist (74% male), whereas women overpopulate the less autonomous assessment or treating occupations such as nurse, dietitian, and respiratory or physical therapist (73–93% female). Within the category of sales occupations, men in 1998 are over-represented in supervisory and proprietorship jobs (60% male), securities and financial service sales (71% male), and sales of commodities (74% male). Women tend to dominate in retail sales (65% female) and cashiering (78% female) (U. S. Census Bureau, 1999).

Given the evidence that sex differences in abilities are slight (see chapter 6; Eisenberg et al., 1996; Ruble & Martin, 1998), there is little evidence to suggest that the overall relegation of women to lower paying and less prestigious jobs has much, if anything, to do with their ability to perform in other areas. What then, are the developmental processes that help shape boys' and girls' differential attitudes about occupational attainment, and their occupational choices?

Gender Differences in Career Aspirations

Boys and girls share the process of coordinating their self-beliefs, values, and career aspirations. Indeed, researchers have found that both boys and girls use thoughts about future occupation to refine their developing SCs, thereby using the career domain as one important domain to test salient personal traits (Bregman & Killen, 1999; Mullis, Mullis, & Gerwels, 1998). Also, McCullough, Ashbridge, and Pegg (1994) found that regardless of gender, adolescents who had aspirations to attain a high-status career demonstrated leadership in school, high SE, and an internal locus of control. These adolescents also tended to come from cohesive families.

Despite these similarities, studies suggest that broad gender differences in career-related self-determinants exist. Gifted boys, for example, embody the investigative nature of scientists and architects in their career choice profiles, whereas gifted girls are more at ease with the ambiguity, idealism, and imagination associated with writers and artists (McGinn, 1982; Shamai, 1996). Boys also demonstrate stronger interests and corresponding career preferences for realistic themes (working with objects, working outdoors, and a need for structure), whereas girls score higher on social (interest in people and the helping professions) and conventional (preference for traditional chain-of-command work environments) themes (Mullis et al., 1998). Adolescent females who value themselves in future roles as family caretakers have been shown to place high importance on occupational choices that will allow them the time to reinforce that important self-trait in their adult lives (Eccles, 1987; Curry, Trew, Turner, & Hunter, 1994).

Similarly, the young women in a study by Jozefowicz, Eccles, and Barber (1993) placed more value than the young men on a variety of female-stereotyped career-related skills and interests such as doing work that directly helps people and meshes well with child-rearing responsibilities. These values, along with ability SCs, predicted the gender stereotyped career plans of both males and females (see Eccles & Harold, 1992, for further review).

Gender Stereotyping of Career Roles

Young children tend to have fairly inflexible belief systems about male-only participation in masculine occupations and female assignment to feminine adult roles and demonstrate sex-stereotyped ideas about adult occupations that closely mirror the actual distribution of men and women in the labor force. Reid (1995) studied first, third, and fifth grade children's beliefs about who can occupy specific adult occupations. Children's answers were very much in accordance with who does occupy these roles. These results suggested that in general, young children may be limited in thinking about possibilities that conflict with what they actually see happening in the world of work. Some gender differences emerged in this study. Fifth grade boys, for instance, expressed stronger sex-stereotyped beliefs about male occupations than did fifth grade girls. The older girls also were less sex stereotypical about male occupations than were the youngest girls; however, all groups stereotyped traditionally female careers as more appropriate for women. Thus fifth grade girls in this study may have been moving away from sex stereotyping of male occupations.

Other research suggests that as girls get older they are less likely to believe that certain careers should be occupied by males only. Sandberg, Ehrhardt, Mellins, Ince, and Meyer-Bahlburg (1987) found that 18-year-old females demonstrated a wider diversity of career options than they did at age 8, suggesting that for girls, there exists an age-related trend away from self-limiting gender notions about potential career opportunities. Jackson and Tein (1998) found that high school-aged males had more strongly sex-stereotyped beliefs about parenting and career roles than did adolescent females.

Furthermore, girls appear to contemplate a wider range of possible outcomes than do boys when it comes to career planning. Eccles (1987) found that adult men exhibit single-minded devotion to one particular goal, whereas women are more likely to place equal value on a greater number of potential adult roles, predisposing them to plan more diverse life-paths that reflect the interface of family and career. In support of Eccles, Fiorentine's (1988) longitudinal study demonstrated that from the late 1960s to the mid 1980s, college women were engaged in a process of adding to their life goals, rather than becoming single-minded about careers like males do. That is, the women were in fact adding status/prestige occupational goals to their strong adult family orientation, thereby expanding the number of life domains to which they saw themselves committed as adults. Interestingly, Curry et al. (1994) found evidence of these trends in sixth grade girls, who were found to have higher levels of concern about fulfilling multiple life domains than did their male peers.

Although adolescent girls now seem to believe they have the ability to perform a wider variety of occupations and believe that it is appropriate for females to enter these occupations, they still tend to aspire to careers that traditionally have attracted females. One main reason for this likely is adolescent girls' concerns about committing to careers that are costly in terms of time away from family. Indeed, the choice of traditional careers often is based on the concern that less traditional careers will mean too much time spent away from family (Corder & Stephan, 1984; Curry et al., 1994; Leslie, 1986). Thus it seems to be girls' valuing of different life roles rather than their ability to perform certain occupations that are driving their career choices.

Effects of Sex Differences in Career Aspiration on Gender Differences in Cognition

Cognitive developmental theory suggests that children incorporate salient sex role knowledge gained from social interaction into existing mental schemas about the self; prompting, in this context, the reorganization of thinking over time about gender, careers, and related aspirations to accommodate new data. The integration of new knowledge into preexisting, organized sets of ideas (schemas) also has the effect of making the information more retrievable, or accessible in memory, than other kinds of information that is not as readily assimilated into the child's schema (Bjorklund, 2000). This social-cognitive feedback loop perpetuates gender stereotypes when a young girl decides, based on consistent gender-stereotyping social feedback, for instance, that it is not appropriate for her to become a physician. When that occurs, future information that is consistent with that dominant nonphysician self-schema is more likely to be attended to and encoded than information that challenges the belief. Conversely, the young boy who receives regular social reinforcement (or tacit permission from the environment) to consider "physician" as a possible future self, constructs over time an increasingly more elaborate physician self-schema that is cognitively primed to receive and encode supporting information. These different self-schema in turn can impact specific aspects of cognitive development in different achievement areas. To continue this example, the girl's choice not to consider becoming a physician may limit her cognitive development in areas of study related to medicine, while potentially increasing development in other areas she does choose to pursue. The boy's cognitive development regarding things medical would increase, at the expense of other things. Thus sex-differentiated self-schemas, like other motivational constructs discussed earlier, drive choices of activities, indirectly affecting cognitive development.

SOCIAL FACTORS IN THE HOME AND AT SCHOOL INFLUENCING THESE GENDER DIFFERENCES

Parental Influences

Parents have a strong impact on many aspects of children's development, despite some recent claims to the contrary (see Collins, Maccoby, Steinberg, Hetherington, & Bornstein, 2000). These influences extend to the constructs we discuss in this chapter. How do parents influence the observed sex differences in motivation, self-concept, and occupational plans? There has been debate in the literature over the years on how differently parents treat boys and girls. Maccoby and Jacklin (1974) concluded that there were few such differences, and Lytton and Romney (1991), in a meta-analysis of the effects of parental treatment, also concluded that in general boys and girls are treated similarly. Others disagreed with these conclusions, arguing that parents do treat boys and girls differently in a number of important ways, particularly in terms of play and toy experiences provided, degree of independence allowed, beliefs about sons' and daughters' abilities, and expectations for their achievement (see Beal, 1994; Eccles et al. 1993, Eisenberg et al., 1993; Ruble & Martin, 1998). Parents also may influence how much children value different activities. In this section, we discuss parental influences on the major constructs we have been discussing: competence-related beliefs, task values, and career aspirations.

Parents' Influence on Children's Competence-Related Beliefs

Researchers have found that parents of elementary and middle-school aged children believe boys have more ability in sports than girls do, and girls have more ability in reading than boys do. Overall, parents do not differ in beliefs about boys' and girls' mathematics ability. They also appear to offer similar amounts of encouragement to boys and girls in mathematics. However, those mothers who do believe males have more natural talent in mathematics believe boys have greater competence in mathematics. Mothers thinking males and females have equal natural talent in mathematics believe sons and daughters to be equally talented in mathematics. By adolescence, parents continue to believe sons and daughters are equally competent in mathematics. However, they also begin to believe that mathematics is harder for girls to do, and that boys will do better in careers requiring mathematics (see Eccles et al., 1993, for further discussion). These differences exist even when actual performance differences between boys and girls are controlled (e.g., Eccles et al., 1989; Eccles & Harold, 1991; Jacobs, 1992; Jacobs & Eccles, 1992; see Eccles et al. 1993, for more complete review). That is, the child's sex influences parents' judgments about their abilities independently of the child's actual performance.

Researchers have also assessed sex of child effects on parents' attributions for their children's performance on academic and non-academic activities. Yee and Eccles (1988) found that parents of boys rate natural talent as a more important reason for their children's mathematics successes than parents of girls. In contrast, parents of girls rate effort as a more important reason for their children's mathematics successes than parents of boys (see also Dunton et al., 1988 and Holloway, 1986). Similarly, in Eccles et al. (1992), mothers gave gender-role stereotypic causal attributions for their adolescent children's successes and failures in mathematics, reading, and sports: sons' successes in mathematics and sports were more likely to be attributed to natural talent than daughters'; daughters' success in English was more likely to be attributed to natural talent than sons'. Furthermore, as predicted, the sex differences in these mothers' ratings of their adolescents' abilities in each domain were substantially reduced once these sex difference in the mothers' causal attributions was controlled. These findings support the hypothesis that parents' gender-role stereotyped causal attributions mediate parents' gender-role stereotyped perceptions of their children's mathematics competence.

What are some of the mechanisms by which parents' beliefs and behaviors might impact children's own motivation and achievement? One possibility is parental role modeling. Interestingly, Eccles and her colleagues have found that parents' influence on children's mathematics achievement through role modeling of engagement in mathematics does not seem to have strong effects on children's motivation and achievement. Instead, parents' beliefs and interpretations of children's experience seem more important (see Eccles et al., 1993). Many researchers have focused on parents' general beliefs and practices, and levels of involvement with their children. These researchers have found that these parental variables influence the development of children's competence-related beliefs, SE, and motivation (see Eccles et al., 1998; Goodnow & Collins, 1990; Sigel, McGillicuddy-De Lisi, & Goodnow, 1992, for reviews).

Parents' specific beliefs about their children's abilities also have been shown to influence children's motivation and performance. One well-established link is that between parents' educational expectations and children's academic motivation and performance; parents who have higher expectations for their children tend to have children who do better in school (e.g., Alexander & Entwisle, 1988; Brooks-Gunn, Guo, & Furstenberg, 1993; Gottfried, 1991; Kandel & Lesser, 1969; Schneider & Coleman, 1993). Parents' perceptions of their children's competencies and likely success also have been shown to influence children's motivation and achievement behavior (e.g., Alexander & Entwisle, 1988; Parsons, Adler, & Kaczala, 1982; Pallas et al., 1994; Phillips, 1987). For example, parents' perceptions of their adolescents' abilities are significant predictors of adolescents' estimates of their own ability and interest in mathematics, English, and sports, even after the significant positive relation of the child's actual performance to both the parents' and adolescents' perceptions of the adolescents' domain specific abilities is controlled (Jacobs, 1992; Jacobs & Eccles, 1992; Parsons, Adler, & Kaczala, 1982). Furthermore, Eccles and her colleagues found support for the hypothesized causal direction of this relationship using longitudinal panel analyses (Eccles et al., 1993; Yoon, Wigfield, & Eccles 1993). The impact of parents' specific beliefs on boys' and girls' expectation was shown by Baker and Entwisle (1987). They found that mothers' sex-differentiated expectations for boys' and girls' success in mathematics contributed to grade school boys' and girls' differential expectations for their own mathematics success.

Of particular relevance to this chapter is evidence that parents' broad gender-role stereotypes influence their views of their own children's abilities and interests.

Using path analytic techniques, Jacobs and Eccles (1992) tested whether parents' gender-role stereotypes generalized to their perceptions of their own children's ability. They found that parents who endorsed gender-role stereotypes regarding which sex is most interested in, and has the most natural talent for, mathematics, English, and sports also distorted their ratings of their own children's abilities in each of these domains in the gender-role stereotypic direction (cf., Jacobs, 1992). This did not occur for parents who did not hold these gender stereotypes.

Parents likely convey these beliefs to their children in a variety of ways. For example, they may make causal attributions for their children's performance, praising their child for that "A" in mathematics by pointing out either the child's natural talent or great diligence. As noted, there appear to be gender differences in the kinds of attributions parents make for boys' and girls' performance in different areas. They may also communicate their impression of their children's relative abilities by telling them what they are good at, or, more subtly, by encouraging them to try or discouraging them from trying, particular activities. Finally, they may make more general comments to their children about the importance of talent versus effort in accounting for individual differences in competence- statements such as "you have to be born with music talent" or "anyone can be good at sports if they just work hard enough."

Parents' Influence on Children's Valuation of Different Activities

The messages parents provide regarding the value they attach to various activities also ought to influence children's motivation and achievement. Parents may convey differential task values through explicit rewards and encouragement for participating in some activities rather than others. Also, parents may influence children's interests and aspirations, particularly with regard to future educational and vocational options, through explicit and implicit messages they provide as they counsel children. For example, parents, teachers, and counselors are more likely to encourage boys than girls to pursue mathematics-related interests (see Eccles & Harold, 1992; Eccles & Hoffman, 1984). They also may have sex-differentiated beliefs about the external barriers to success coupled with beliefs regarding both effective strategies to overcome these barriers and their own sense of efficacy to implement these strategies for each child.

Whether parents' own values and encouragement directly affect either the value the children attach to mathematics or their participation in mathematics activities has not been established. Some researchers' work suggests rather weak relations between parents' own task value and adolescents' task value for mathematics (Parsons, Adler, & Kaczala, 1982). The relations may be stronger for younger children and when a wider range of activities are included. The relation may also be curvilinear. Work in the area of intrinsic motivation suggests that excessive attempts to influence a child's interest in a specific activity can backfire and lead to a decrease in interest and involvement (e.g., Deci & Ryan, 1985; Lepper & Green, 1978).

Specific Experiences Provided by Parents

There is evidence that parents influence their children's motivation through the specific types of learning experiences they provide for their children. Parents expose children to different toys and activities, which provides children with the opportunity to develop different competencies. As noted, these kinds of experiences vary greatly for boys and girls. For instance, boys get exposed to far more manipulative toys and large-space play activities. This exposure likely affects the development of such basic cognitive skills as spatial facility (Casey, Nuttall, & Pezaris, 1997). Indeed, researchers have discussed the complex interplay of environmental and biological factors in influencing toy and activity preferences, and ultimately, cognitive development (see Halpern, 1995). From our perspective, having specific success experiences and acquiring specific skills likely influences motivation to engage in related activities through their influence on children's perceptions of competence for these activities, as well as their valuing of them. As discussed earlier, these motivational factors then can influence children's achievement.

Parents also provide different achievement-related experiences for sons and daughters (Eccles & Hoffman, 1984; Huston, 1983). For example, parents are less likely to nominate their daughters for gifted programs at school and to enroll their daughters in computer and competitive sports programs (see Eccles & Harold, 1992). Similarly, families with limited economic resources are more willing to invest these resources in their sons than in their daughters (Eccles & Hoffman, 1984). It is likely that the sex differences we see in children's competencies, self-perceptions, interests, and aspirations result in part from these kinds of differences in the experiences parents provide for their sons and daughters (see also Huston, 1983). Children's cognitive skills likely are affected too; for example, those in gifted programs should be more likely to gain cognitive skills more quickly.

How might parents' beliefs and their provision of specific experiences be related to one another? Eccles and colleagues (1993) discussed the interactions of parents' gender stereotypes, beliefs about their children, and provision of specific experiences to them. They proposed that gender stereotypes influence parents' beliefs about children's competencies and interests. Stereotypes also influence a number of mediating factors, including parents' attributions for children's performance, the importance parents attach to children acquiring skills in different areas, encouragement of involvement in different activities, and provision of toys and activities. These mediators then influence children's own sense of competence, their interest in different activities, and the amount of time they devote to different things. Eccles and her colleagues have found that parents do provide quite different achievement-related experiences to their boys and girls, and that parents' beliefs about their children's competencies and interests, rather than the child's sex per se, influences the experiences they provide children.

Parental Influences on Occupational Interests and Career Choice

Parents can contribute to the development of children's cognitive schema for gender-appropriate academic and career aspirations in various ways, including direct parental suggestion (Trice, McClellan, & Hughes, 1992), cultural socialization and parental modeling of careers (Mullis, Mullis, & Gerwels, 1998), perceived parental involvement in early learning (Marjoribanks, 1995), and parental expectations for children's success in various academic domains (Eccles, 1984; Baker & Entwisle, 1987).

Trice and colleagues (1992) found that parents make direct verbal suggestions as a means of transmitting their own occupational preferences to children. Their study demonstrated that the number of parental career suggestions increased over time between kindergarten and the sixth grade year, while children's tendency to list their parents' suggestions as a probable career choice decreased over the same time period. This was particularly true for girls. It is possible that as children move away from the sole influence of parents during the school years, they expand their social convoys to include teachers and peers who provide them with added social opportunities to consider as yet, unexplored possible career selves.

Mullis and colleagues (1998) found that gender and parental occupation were related to the stability of adolescents' career interests over a three-year period. Females scored significantly and consistently higher than males on interest measures for careers traditionally reinforced by Western culture as appropriate for women: those with social, artistic, and conventional themes. Regardless of gender, adolescents with parents in professional careers broadened their career interests over the three-year period, suggesting that children of professional parents were intellectually challenged to remain open to new career options.

Peer Support

Adolescents begin to use the pro-social, egalitarian nature of peer relationships as an adjunct to the more authority-dominated relationships they experience with parents (who sometimes have career agendas for their children). According to Young, Antal, Basset, Post, DeVries, & Valach (1999), both male and female adolescents' conversations about career reveal a mutually beneficial, intentional, goal-directed process whereby the participants aid each other in exploring personal futures, formulating educational plans, and validating and/or challenging career selection. These organized exchanges of information favorably contribute to adolescents' growing banks of knowledge about who and what they are, where they are going, and how to get there; creating yet another mechanism for cognitively equilibrating a sense of self with important life outcomes such as career choice.

Effects of School Experiences

The literature on differential effects of schooling on boys and girls is quite large, and so we only can present a brief summary here (see AAUW, 1992; Beal, 1994; Eisenberg et al., 1996; Sadker & Sadker, 1994, for further discussion). Many have argued that teachers treat boys and girls quite differently, and in ways that often are not beneficial to girls' motivation and achievement. Boys demand and get more attention for both their academic and nonacademic activities. They get called on more, and often are given more elaborate questions to answer, questions that may be more likely to facilitate their cognitive development. Part of the reason boys get called on more is that they often are more assertive in class, so that teachers simply respond to them more.

Sadker and Sadker (1994) argued that girls often are rewarded for compliant, quiet behaviors in the classroom; behaviors that are not necessarily associated with higher achievement. Some research has suggested that when girls' academic work is criticized they receive more comments about lacking ability, whereas the academic criticism boys receive focuses more on lack of effort, or on their poor behavioral conduct (Dweck, Davidson, Nelson, & Enna, 1978). Receiving more negative feedback about one's ability lowers individuals' sense of their own competence; thus these findings suggest that girls may be more likely to lack confidence in their abilities in different areas (see Beal, 1994, for further discussion). However, these findings have not always been replicated and so must be interpreted with some caution (see Parsons, Kaczala, & Meece, 1982).

Some teachers also appear to have different expectations for boys and girls, particularly in mathematics and science (Beal, 1994; Jussim, Eccles, & Madon, 1996). Research on teacher expectancies shows that these expectancies can influence students' performance; thus teachers holding lower expectancies for girls in areas like mathematics and science could negatively impact their cognitive development in these areas (see Eccles & Wigfield, 1985, for review). However, recent evidence on teacher expectancy effects suggests that such effects may be less strong than was once believed. (Jussim & Eccles, 1992; Jussim et al., 1996). Much of the association between teacher expectations for individual students and subsequent student motivation and performance reflects the "accurate" association between teacher expectations and student characteristics like prior achievement levels and behavioral patterns. However, small teacher expectancy effects over time can have a large cumulative effect on both motivation and achievement (Jussim et al., 1996), particularly if these effects begin in kindergarten and the first grade (Entwisle & Alexander, 1993).

Differences in performance in mathematics and science between males and females used to be explained in part in terms of differential course taking patterns of males and females (e.g., see Kimball, 1989). Males were more likely to take more classes in these areas. However, these patterns have changed; at least during high school girls and boys now are taking similar numbers of mathematics and science courses. The gender differences in mathematics and science course taking remain strong at the college level, however (see Royer et al., 1999).

What might be more important for understanding gender differences in performance in these areas is not course taking per se but what occurs in the classes. Instructional practices can vary widely in the same content areas. Further, there are sex differences in children's preference for different types of instructional practices, which likely interact with subject area to produce sex differences in interest in different subject areas (Casserly, 1980; Eccles, 1989; Kahle, 1984). Females appear to respond more positively to mathematics and science instruction if it is taught in a cooperative or individualized manner rather than a competitive manner; if it is taught from an applied/person-centered perspective rather than a theoretical/abstract perspective; if it is taught using a hands-on approach rather than a "book learning" approach; and if the teacher avoids sexism in its many subtle forms. These effects likely reflect the fit between the teaching style, the instructional focus, and females' value, goals, motivational orientation, and learning styles.

The few relevant studies have found support for this idea (e.g., Eccles, 1994; Eccles & Harold, 1992). If such classroom practices are more prevalent in one subject area (e.g., physical science) than another (e.g., biological or social science), then one would expect gender differences in motivation to study these subject areas. Researchers studying classroom practices have found that mathematics and physics are especially likely to be taught in a manner least preferred by females. Consequently, it is not surprising that many girls are less interested in these subject areas than in other subject areas that are taught in a manner more consistent with their preferences. It should also be noted that mathematics and physical science do not have to be taught in these ways; more "girl friendly" instructional approaches can be used. And when they are, both girls and boys are more likely to continue taking courses in these fields and to consider working in these fields when they become adults.

Although it does appear that boys and girls are treated differently, Harter et al. (1997) noted a number of problems in the research on this topic. One is that a number of the studies showing these differences are not methodologically rigorous. Perhaps most important for our concerns in this chapter, Harter et al. stated that there is almost no evidence on how the differential teacher treatment actually influences important outcomes, such as students' cognitive development, performance, and motivation. This topic is a priority for future research in this area.

Teacher and School Influences on Career Choice

Adolescent girls appear to be particularly susceptible to the impact of classroom social support systems as mediators of academic performance. Teacher support and classroom belongingness have a stronger association with expectancy and value orientations for adolescent girls than for boys (Goodenow, 1993), and females demonstrate a greater desire for approval in classroom settings than do males (Igoe & Sullivan, 1991). Farmer (1985) analyzed the effects of background, personal, and environmental influences on the aspirations, mastery and long-range career commitment of 9th through 12th grade males and females. Females scored higher than males on measures of aspirational goals; with both aspiration and mastery being enhanced for females when they perceived support from teachers for their achievements. The mediating effect of all environmental factors (parent and teacher support, perceived support for women working) on career commitment was higher for girls than for boys, suggesting once again, that long-range career planning is a more complex process for women; one that is more susceptible to the impact of opposing role priorities than for men.

CONCLUSION

We reviewed work on sex differences in motivation, self-concept, career aspirations, and career choices. Reliable sex differences in the first three of these variables emerge early in children's lives. Career choices remain strongly sex typed, despite some change in occupational patterns observed over the last 15 years. We also reviewed work on how parents, teachers, and schools influence these sex differences. We made the case that the observed sex differences in motivation, self-concept, and career aspirations can impact sex differences in cognitive development. Based in part on their motivation and aspirations, boys and girls perform differently on different academic tasks and activities. When choices become available they will choose to continue to do certain activities, and stop doing others. The greater (or lesser) involvement in these activities impacts their developing cognitive skills in these different areas. Looking beyond the individual child or adolescent, parents and teachers provide different kinds of experiences and feedback to boys and girls that also leads them to pursue sex-differentiated activities, with ultimate effects on their cognitive development. We have learned a lot about these sex differences, but the complex interplay of social, biological, and personal factors influencing these differences needs further investigation. One particular reason this is the case is that sex roles, as a culturally defined construct, are always in flux. Therefore, it is essential to revisit sex differences in these various constructs, as well as their relations to outcomes such as achievement and career choice.

REFERENCES

Alexander, K. L., & Entwisle, D. (1988). Achievement in the first two years of school: Patterns and processes. *Monographs of the Society for Research in Child Development, 53*(2, Serial No. 218).

American Association for University Women (AAUW) Report (1992). *How schools shortchange girls.* New York: American Association of University Women Educational Foundation.

Baker, D., & Entwisle, D. (1987). The influence of mothers on the academic expectations of young children: A longitudinal study of how gender differences arise. *Social Forces, 65*(3), 670–694.

Bandura, A. (1997). *Self-efficacy: The exercise of control.* New York: W. H. Freeman.

Bartell, N. P., & Reynolds, W. M. (1986). Depression and self-esteem in academically gifted and non-gifted children: A comparison study. *Journal of School Psychology, 24,* 55–61.

Beal, C. (1994). *Boys and girls: The development of gender roles.* New York: McGraw-Hill.

Bell, L. A. (1989). Something's wrong here and it's not me: Challenging the dilemmas that block girls success. *Journal for the Education of the Gifted, 12,* 118–130.

Bjorklund, D. F. (2000). *Children's thinking: Developmental function and individual differences.* Belmont, CA: Wadsworth.

Bregman, G., & Killen, M. (1999). Adolescents' and young adults' reasoning about career choice and the role of parental influence. *Journal of Research on Adolescence, 9*(3), 253–275.

Brooks-Gunn, J., Guo, G., & Furstenberg, F. F., Jr. (1993). Who drops out of and who continues beyond high school? A 20-year follow-up of black urban youth. *Journal of Research on Adolescence, 3,* 271–294.

Casey, M. B., Nuttall, R. L., & Pezaris, E. (1997). Mediators of gender differences in mathematics college entrance test scores: A comparison of spatial skills with internalized beliefs and anxieties. *Developmental Psychology, 33,* 669–680.

Casserly, P. (1980). An assessment of factors affecting female participation in advanced placement programs in mathematics, chemistry, and physics. In L. Fox, I. Brody, & D. Tobin (Eds.), *Women and the mathematical mystique* (pp. 138–163). Baltimore: Johns Hopkins University Press.

Coleman, J. M., & Fults, B. A. (1982). Self-concept and the gifted classroom: The role of social comparisons. *Gifted Child Quarterly, 26*(3), 116–120.

Collins, W. A., Maccoby, E. E., Steinberg, L., Hetherington, E. M., & Bornstein, M. H. (2000). Contemporary research on parenting: The case for nature and nurture. *American Psychologist, 55,* 218–232.

Connell, J. P. (1985). A new multidimensional measure of children's perception of control. *Child Development, 56,* 1018–1041.

Corder, J., & Stephan, C. (1984). Females' combinations of work and family roles: Adolescents' aspirations. *Journal of Marriage and the Family, May,* 391–402.

Crandall, V. C., Katovsky, W., & Crandall, V. J. (1965). Children's beliefs in their own control of reinforcements in intellectual-academic achievement situations. *Child Development, 36,* 91–109.

Curry, C., Trew, K., Turner, I., & Hunter, J. (1994). The effect of life domains on girls' possible selves. *Adolescence, 29*(113), 133–150.

Dauber, S. L., & Benbow, C. P. (1990). Aspects of personality and peer relations of extremely talented adolescents. *Gifted Child Quarterly, 34,* 10–15.

Deci, E. L., & Ryan, R. M. (1985). *Intrinsic motivation and self-determination in human behavior.* New York: Plenum Press.

Dunton, K. J., McDevitt, T. M., & Hess, R. D. (1988). Origins of mothers' attributions about their daughters' and sons' performance in mathematics in sixth grade. *Merrill-Palmer Quarterly, 34,* 47–70.

Dusek, J. B., & Flaherty, J. (1981). The development of the self during the adolescent years. *Monographs of the Society for Research in Child Development, 46* (Whole No. 191), 1–61.

Dweck, C. S., Davidson, W., Nelson, S., & Enna, B. (1978). Sex differences in learned helplessness: II. The contingencies of evaluative feedback in the classroom, and III. An experimental analysis. *Developmental Psychology, 14,* 268–276.

Dweck, C. S., & Goetz, T. E. (1978). Attributions and learned helplessness. In J. H. Harvey, W. Ickes, & R. F. Kidd (Eds.), *New directions in attribution research* (Vol. 2). Hillsdale, NJ: Lawrence Erlbaum.

Dweck, C. S., & Licht, B. G. (1980). Learned helplessness and intellectual achievement. In J. Garber & M. E. P. Seligman (Eds.), *Human helplessness: Theory and applications.* New York: Academic Press.

Dweck, C. S., & Repucci, N. D. (1973). Learned helplessness and reinforcement responsibility in children.   109–116.

Early, D. M., Belansky, E., & Eccles, J. S. (March, 1992). *The impact of gender stereotypes on perceived ability and attributions for success.* Poster presented at the Biennial Meeting of the Society for Research on Adolescence, Washington D.C.

Eccles, J. S. (1984). Sex differences in achievement patterns. In T. Sonderegger (Ed.), *Nebraska Symposium on Motivation* (Vol. 32, pp. 97–132). Lincoln, NE: University of Nebraska Press.

Eccles, J. S. (1987). Gender roles and women's achievement-related decisions. *Psychology of Women Quarterly, 11,* 135–172.

Eccles, J. S. (1989). Bringing young women to math and science. In M. Crawford and M. Gentry (Eds.), *Gender and thought: Psychological perspectives* (pp. 36–57). New York: Springer-Verlag.

Eccles, J. S. (1994). Understanding women's educational and occupational choices: Applying the Eccles et al. model of achievement-related choices. *Psychology of Women Quarterly, 18,* 585–609.

Eccles, J. S., Adler, T. F., Futterman, R., Goff, S. B., Kaczala, C. M., Meece, J. L., & Midgley, C. (1983). Expectancies, values, and academic behaviors. In J. T. Spence (Ed.), *Achievement and achievement motivations* (pp. 75–146). San Francisco: W. H. Freeman.

Eccles, J. S., Arbreton, A., Buchanan, C., Jacobs, J., Flanagan, C, Harold, R., Mac Iver, D., Midgley, C., Reuman, D., & Wigfield, A. (1993). School and family effects on the ontogeny of children's interests, self-perceptions, and activity choice. In J. Jacobs (Ed.), *Nebraska Symposium on Motivation, 1992: Developmental perspectives on motivation* (pp. 145–208). Lincoln: University of Nebraska Press.

Eccles, J. S., & Harold, R. D. (1991). Gender differences in sport involvement: Applying the Eccles' expectancy-value model. *Journal of Applied Sport Psychology, 3,* 7–35.

Eccles, J. S., & Harold, R. D. (1992). Gender differences in educational and occupational patterns among the gifted. In N. Colangelo, S. G. Assouline, & D. L. Amronson (Eds.), *Talent development: Proceedings from the 1991 Henry B. and Jocelyn Wallace National Research Symposium on Talent Development* (pp. 3–29). Unionville, NY: Trillium Press.

Eccles, J. S., & Hoffman, L. W. (1984). Socialization and the maintenance of a sex-segregated labor market. In H. W. Stevenson & A. E. Siegel (Eds.), *Research in child development and social policy* (Vol. 1, pp. 367–420). Chicago: University of Chicago Press.

Eccles, J. S., & Wigfield, A. (1985). Teacher expectations and student motivation. In J. B. Dusek (Ed.), *Teacher expectations* (pp. 185–217). Hillsdale, NJ: Lawrence Erlbaum.

Eccles, J. S., Wigfield, A., Flanagan, C., Miller, C., Reuman, D., & Yee, D. (1989). Self-concepts, domain values, and self-esteem: Relations and changes at early adolescence. *Journal of Personality, 57,* 283–310.

Eccles, J. S., Wigfield, A., Harold, R., & Blumenfeld, P. B. (1993). Age and gender differences in children's self- and task perceptions during elementary school. *Child Development, 64,* 830–847.

Eccles, J. S., Wigfield, A., & Schiefele, U. (1998). Motivation to succeed. In N. Eisenberg (Ed.), *Handbook of child psychology* (5th ed., Vol. 3, pp. 1017–1095). New York: Wiley.

Eisenberg, N., Martin, C. L., & Fabes, R. A. (1996). Gender development and gender effects. In D. C. Berliner & R. C. Calfee (Eds.), *Handbook of educational psychology* (pp. 358–396). New York: Macmillan.

Entwisle, D. R., & Alexander, K. L. (1993). Entry into school: The beginning school transition and educational stratification in the United States. *Annual Review of Sociology, 19,* 401–423.

Etaugh, C., & Liss, M. B. (1992). Home, school, and playroom: Training grounds for adult gender roles. *Sex Roles, 26,* 129–147.

Farmer, H. (1985). Model of career and achievement motivation for women and men. *Journal of Counseling Psychology, 32*(3), 363–390.

Fiorentine, R. (1988). Increasing similarity in the values and life plans of male and female college students? Evidence and implications. *Sex Roles, 18*(3/4), 143–158.

Folling-Albers, M., & Hartinger, A. (1998). Interest of boys and girls in elementary school. In L. Hoffmann, A. Krapp, K. A. Renninger, & J. Baumert (Eds.), *Interest and learning* (pp. 175–183). Kiel, Germany: Institute for Science Education.

Gardner, P. L. (1998). The development of males' and females' interests in science and technology. In L. Hoffmann, A. Krapp, K. A. Renninger, & J. Baumert (Eds.), *Interest and learning* (pp. 41–57). Kiel, Germany: Institute for Science Education.

Gilligan, C. (1993). Joining the resistance: Psychology, politics, girls, and women. In L. Weis & M. Fine (Eds.), *Beyond silenced voices* (pp. 143–168). Albany, NY: State University of New York Press.

Goodenow, C. (1993). Classroom belonging among early adolescent students. *Journal of Early Adolescence, 13,* 21–43.

Goodnow, J. J., & Collins, W. A. (1990). *Development according to parents: The nature, sources, and consequences of parents' ideas.* London: Lawrence Erlbaum.

Gottfried, A. E. (1990). Academic intrinsic motivation in young elementary school children. *Journal of Educational Psychology, 82,* 525–538.

Gottfried, A. E. (1991). Maternal employment in the family setting: Developmental and environmental issues. In J. V. Lerner & N. L. Galambos (Eds.), *Employed mothers and their children* (pp. 63–84). New York: Garland.

Halpern, D. F. (Ed.) (1995). Special issue: Psychological and psychobiological perspectives on sex differences in cognition. I. *Theory and research. Learning and Individual Differences, 7.*

Harter, S. (1981). A new self-report scale of intrinsic versus extrinsic orientation in the classroom: Motivational and informational components. *Developmental Psychology, 17,* 300–312.

Harter, S. (1982). The Perceived Competence Scale for Children. *Child Development, 53,* 87–97.

Harter, S. (1990). Causes, correlates and the functional role of global self-worth: A lifespan perspective. In J. Kolligian & R. Sternberg (Eds.), *Perceptions of competence and incompetence across the life-span* (pp. 67–98). New Haven, CT: Yale University Press.

Harter, S. (1998). The development of self-representations. In W. Damon (Series Ed.) & N. Eisenberg (Vol. Ed.), *Handbook of child psychology* (5th ed., Vol. 3, pp. 553–618). New York: Wiley.

Harter, S., Waters, P., Whitesell, N. R., & Katstelic, D. (1997). Lack of voice as a manifestation of false-self behavior among adolescents: The school setting as a stage upon which the drama of authenticity is enacted. *Educational Psychologist, 32,* 153–173.

Hill, J. P., & Lynch, M. E. (1983). The intensification of gender-related role expectations during early adolescence. In J. Brooks-Gunn & A. Petersen (Eds.), *Girls at puberty: Biological and psychosocial perspectives* (pp. 201–228). New York: Plenum Press.

Holloway, S. D. (1986). The relationship of mothers' beliefs to children's mathematics achievement: Some effects of sex differences. *Merrill-Palmer Quarterly, 32,* 231–250.

Huston, A. (1983). Sex-typing. In P. H. Mussen (Ed.), *Handbook of child psychology* (4th ed., Vol. 2, pp. 387–467). New York: Wiley.

Hyde, J. S., & Linn, M. C. (1988). Gender differences in verbal ability: A meta-analysis. *Psychological Bulletin, 104,* 53–69.

Igoe, A., & Sullivan, H. (1991, April). *Gender and grade-level differences in student attributes related to school learning and motivation.* Paper presented at the annual meeting of the American Educational Research Association, Chicago.

Jackson, D. W., & Tein, J. (1998). Adolescents' conceptualization of adult roles: Relationships with age, gender, work goal, and maternal employment. *Sex Roles, 38,* 987–1008.

Jacobs, J. E. (1992). The influence of gender stereotypes on parent and child math attitudes. *Journal of educational Psychology, 83,* 518–527.

Jacobs, J. E., & Eccles, J. S. (1992) The influence of parent stereotypes on parent and child ability beliefs in three domains. *Journal of Personality and Social Psychology, 63,* 932–944.

Jacobs, J. E., Hyatt, S., Eccles, J. S., Osgood, D. W., & Wigfield, A. (2000). *The ontogeny of children's self beliefs: Gender and domain differences across grades one through twelve.* Manuscript submitted for publication.

Jozefowicz, D. M., Barber, B. L., & Eccles, J. S. (1993, March). *Adolescent work-related values and beliefs: Gender differences and relation to occupational aspirations.* Paper presented at the Biennial Meeting of the Society for Research in Child Development. New Orleans, LA.

Jussim, L., & Eccles, J. S. (1992). Teacher expectations II: Construction and reflection of student achievement. *Journal of Personality and Social Psychology, 63,* 947–961.

Jussim, L., Eccles, J. S., & Madon, S. (1996). Social perception, social stereotypes, and teacher expectations: Accuracy and the quest for the powerful self-fulfilling prophecy. In L. Berkowitz (Ed.), *Advances in experimental social psychology.* New York: Academic Press.

Kahle, J. (1984). *Girl-friendly science.* Paper presented at the meeting of the American Association for the Advancement of the Sciences, New York.

Kandel, D. B., & Lesser, G. S. (1969). Parental and peer influence, on educational plans of adolescents. *American Sociological Review, 34,* 213–223.

Karnes, F. A., & Wherry, J. N. (1981). Self-concepts of gifted students as measured by the Piers-Harris Children's Self-Concept Scale. *Psychological Reports, 49,* 903–906.

Kimball, M. M. (1989). A new perspective on women's math achievement. *Psychological Bulletin, 105,* 198–214.

Kling, K. C., Hyde, J. S., Showers, C. J., & Buswell, B. N. (1999). Gender differences in self-esteem: A meta-analysis. *Psychological Bulletin, 125,* 470–500.

Krapp, A., Hidi, S., & Renninger, K. A. (1992). Interest, learning, and development. In K. A. Renninger, S. Hidi, & A. Krapp (Eds.), *The role of interest in learning and development* (pp. 3–26). Hillsdale, NJ: Lawrence Erlbaum.

Lepper, M., & Green, D. (1978). *The hidden cost of rewards: New perspectives on the psychology of human motivation.* Hillsdale, NJ: Lawrence Erlbaum.

Leslie, L. (1986). The impact of adolescent females' assessments of parenthood and employment on plans for the future. *Journal of Youth and Adolescence, 15*(1), 29–49.

Linn, M. C., & Hyde, J. S. (1989). Gender, mathematics, and science. *Educational Researcher, 18,* 17–19, 22–27.

Loeb, R. C, & Jay, G. (1987). Self-concept in gifted children: Differential impact in boys and girls. *Gifted Child Quarterly, 31*(1), 9–14.

Lytton, H., & Romney, D. M. (1991). Parents' differential socialization of boys and girls: A meta-analysis. *Psychological Bulletin, 109,* 267–296.

Maccoby, E. E., & Jacklin, C. N. (1974). *The psychology of sex differences.* Stanford, CA: Stanford University Press.

Marjoribanks, K. (1995). Birth order, family environment, and young adults' occupational aspirations. *Psychological Reports, 77,* 666–628.

Marsh, H. W. (1989). Age and sex effects in multiple dimensions of self-concept: Preadolescence to early adulthood. *Journal of Educational Psychology, 81,* 417–430.

Marsh, H. W. (1993). Academic self-concept: Theory, measurement, and research. In J. Suls (Ed.), *Psychological perspectives on the self* (Vol. 4, pp. 59–98). Hillsdale, NJ: Lawrence Erlbaum.

Marsh, H. W., & Yeung, A. S. (1997). Causal effects of academic self-concept on academic achievement: Structural equation models of longitudinal data. *Journal of Educational Psychology, 89,* 41–54.

McCall, R. B., Evahn, C., & Kratzer, L. (1992). *High school underachievers: What do they achieve as adults?* Newbury Park, CA: Sage Publications.

McCullough, P.M., Ashbridge, D., & Pegg, R. (1994). The effect of self-esteem, family structure, locus of control, and career goals on adolescent leadership behavior. *Adolescence, 29*(115), 605–611.

McGinn, P. (1982). Verbally gifted youth: Selection and description. In D. Keating (Ed.), *Intellectual talent: Research and development* (pp. 160–182). Baltimore: Johns Hopkins University Press.

Meece, J. L., Wigfield, A., & Eccles, J. S. (1990). Predictors of math anxiety and its consequences for young adolescents' course enrollment intentions and performances in mathematics. *Journal of Educational Psychology, 82,* 60–70.

Mullis, R. L., Mullis, A. K., & Gerwels, D. (1998). Stability of vocational interests among high school students. *Adolescence, 33*(131), 699–707.

Nolen-Hoeksema, S., & Girigus, J. S. (1994). The emergence of gender differences in depression during adolescence. *Psychological Bulletin, 115,* 424–443.

Pallas, A. M., Entwisle, D. R., Alexander, K. L., & Stluka, M. F. (1994). Ability-group effects: Instructional, social, or institutional? *Sociology of Education, 67,* 27–46.

Parsons, J., Adler, T., & Kaczala, C. (1982). Socialization of achievement attitudes and beliefs: Parental influences. *Child Development, 53,* 310–321.

Parsons, J., Kaczala, C. M., & Meece, J. L. (1982). Socialization of achievement attitudes and beliefs: Classroom influences. *Child Development, 53,* 322–339.

Phillips, D. A. (1987). Socialization of perceived academic competence among highly competent children. *Child Development, 58,* 1308–1320.

Pintrich, P. R., & Schunk, D. H. (1996). *Motivation in education: Theory, research, and applications.* Englewood Cliffs, NJ: Merrill-Prentice Hall.

Pipher, M. (1994). *Reviving Ophelia: Saving the selves of adolescent girls.* New York: Ballantine.

Reid, G. M. (1995). Children's occupational sex-role stereotyping in 1994. *Psychological Reports, 76,* 1155–1165.

Renninger, K. A. (1992). Individual interest and development: Implications for theory and practice. In K. A. Renninger, S. Hidi, & A. Krapp (Eds.), *The role of interest in learning and development* (pp. 361–396). Hillsdale, NJ: Lawrence Erlbaum.

Renninger, K. A. (1998). The roles of individual interest(s) and gender in learning: An overview of research on preschool and elementary school-aged children/students. In L. Hoffmann, A. Krapp, K. A. Renninger, & J. Baumert (Eds.), *Interest and learning* (pp. 165–174). Kiel, Germany: Institute for Science Education.

Royer, J. M., Tronsky, L. N., & Chan, Y. (1999). Math-fact retrieval as the cognitive mechanism underlying gender differences in math test performance. *Contemporary Educational Psychology, 24,* 181–266.

Ruble, D. N., & Martin, C. L. (1998). Gender development. In N. Eisenberg (Ed.), *Handbook of child psychology* (5th Ed., Vol. 3, pp. 933–1016). New York: Wiley

Ryan, R. M., Connell, J. P., & Deci, E. L. (1985). A motivational analysis of self-determination and self-regulation in education. In C. Ames & R. Ames (Eds.), *Research on motivation in education. Vol. 2: The classroom milieu* (pp. 13–51). London: Academic Press.

Ryan, R. M., & Deci, E. L. (2000). Intrinsic and extrinsic motivations: Classic definitions and new directions. *Contemporary Educational Psychology, 25,* 54–67.

Sadker, M., & Sadker, D. (1994). *Failing at fairness: How America's schools cheat girls.* New York: Scribner.

Sandberg, D., Ehrhardt, A., Mellins, C., Ince, S., & Meyer-Bahlburg, F. (1987). The influence of individual and family characteristics upon career aspirations of girls during childhood and adolescence. *Sex Roles, 16*(11/12), 649–668.

Schiefele, U. (1999). Interest and learning from text. *Scientific Studies of Reading, 3,* 257–280.

Schneider, B., & Coleman, J. S. (1993). *Parents, their children, and schools.* Boulder, CO: Westview Press.

Schunk, D. H., & Lilly, M. V. (1982, April). *Attributional and expectancy change in gifted adolescents.* Paper presented at the annual meeting of the American Educational Research Association. New York.

Siegle, D., & Reis, S.M. (1998). Gender differences in teacher and student perceptions of gifted students' ability and effort. *Gifted Child Quarterly, 42*(1), 39–47.

Sigel, I. E., McGillicuddy-De Lisi, A. V., & Goodnow, J. J. (Eds.). (1992). *Parental belief systems* (2nd ed.). Hillsdale, NJ: Lawrence Erlbaum.

Shamai, S. (1996). Elementary school students' attitudes toward science and their course of studies in high school. *Adolescence, 31*(123), 677–689.

Skaalvik, E. M., & Rankin, R. J. (1990). Math, verbal, and general academic self-concept: The internal/external frame of references model and gender differences in self-concept structure. *Journal of Educational Psychology, 82,* 546–554.

Spencer, S., & Steele, C. M., (1995). *Under suspicion of inability: Stereotype vulnerability and women's math performance.* Submitted for publication.

Trice, A., McClellan, N., & Hughes, A. (1992). Origins of children's career aspirations: II. Direct suggestions as a method of transmitting occupational preferences. *Psychological Reports, 71,* 253–254.

United States Census Bureau. (1999). *Statistical abstract of the United States: 1999.* Washington, DC: U. S. Census Bureau.

Weiner, B. (1985). An attributional theory of achievement motivation and emotion. *Psychological Review, 92,* 548–573.

Weiner, B. (1992). *Human motivation: Metaphors, theories, and research.* Newbury Park, CA: Sage Publications.

Wigfield, A., & Eccles, J. (1992). The development of achievement task values: A theoretical analysis. *Developmental Review, 12,* 265–310.

Wigfield, A., Eccles, J., Mac Iver, D., Reuman, D., & Midgley, C. (1991). Transitions at early adolescence: Changes in children's domain-specific self-perceptions and general self-esteem across the transition to junior high school. *Developmental Psychology, 27,* 552–565.

Wigfield, A., Eccles, J. S., Yoon, K. S., Harold, R. D., Arbreton, A., Freedman-Doan, K., & Blumenfeld, P. C. (1997). Changes in children's competence beliefs and subjective task values across the elementary school years: A three-year study. *Journal of Educational Psychology, 89,* 451–469.

Wigfield, A., & Karpathian, M. (1991). Who am I and what can I do? *Educational Psychologist, 26,* 233–262.

Wylie, R. C. (1979). *The self-concept* (Vol. 2). Lincoln, NE: University of Nebraska Press.

Yee, D., & Eccles, J. S. (1988). Parent perceptions and attributions for children's math achievement. *Sex Roles, 19,* 317–333.

Yoon, K. S., Wigfield, A., & Eccles, J. S. (1993 April). *Causal relations between mothers' and children's beliefs about math ability: A structural equation model.* Paper presented at the Annual Meeting of the American Educational Research Association.

Young, R., Antal, S., Bassett, M., Post, A., DeVries, N., & Valach, L. (1999). The joint actions of adolescents in peer conversations about career. *Journal of Adolescence, 22*, 527–538.

part III

Domains of Human Cognition

CHAPTER 5

Gender Differences in Language Development

Jean Berko Gleason
Richard Ely

In this chapter we explore gender differences in the development of language. Our primary aim is to describe how and why differences appear in the speech of young girls and boys. After this introduction, we undertake a short description of the language system itself, and its various components that might reflect gender differences. We then turn our attention to gender differences in the language of adults, because adult language represents the final target or endpoint for children's language development. In looking at the language of adults, we consider both stereotypical ideas that are commonly held about gender differences, as well actual differences that have been described in the literature. We also briefly discuss the varying theoretical perspectives that have been advanced to explain differences in men's and women's language. The next section presents data on the role biology may play in the development of gender differences in language. Here, we pay particular attention to differences in children's temperament, because these differences may play an important role in leading boys and girls to engage in divergent behaviors, which, in turn, lead to different experience with language.

We then review a number of studies that document differences in children's emerging language. We include individual studies, as well an important meta-analysis, to give the reader a sense of what the empirical data reveal. Our presentation is more illustrative than comprehensive, with the goal of providing clear examples of the current state of the field. Finally, we examine the social bases of gender differences, by looking at the role that parents and others play in creating and fostering gender differences in children's language in some instances, and attenuating them in others. For instance, gender differences in politeness may be accentuated by adults' preferential encouragement of polite speech in girls; by contrast, differences in reading ability are mitigated by special instructional programs for children (mostly boys) with dyslexia.

THE LANGUAGE SYSTEM

Gender differences in language could be pervasive, or they could occur in just some parts of the system. The languages of all human communities are remarkably complex symbolic modes of communication (Gleason, 2000). They are hierarchically organized and composed of a number of subsystems; these include *phonology*, *morphology*, the *lexicon* and *semantics, syntax, pragmatics*, and *discourse*. Gender differences have been claimed for each of these areas. We give an example or two of possible gender differences for each of the language subsystems, and discuss many of them further in later sections of the chapter.

Phonology

Phonology refers to the sound system of a language. It includes all the significant sounds used in the language, and the rules for combining them—for example, in English, a word can end with the consonant cluster *-sks*, as in *asks*, but it would be "illegal" to coin a new word beginning with this combination. When we say "rules" in discussing linguistic phenomena here, we are referring to the rule-governed way that speakers behave, and not to actual explicit knowledge of any rules: Speakers know how to make appropriate forms such as plurals, but would be hard-pressed to explain why, for instance, the plural on the ends of some words sounds like an "s," whereas on others it sounds like a "z."

Phonology also includes intonation and stress patterns. In English, a simple declarative sentence becomes a question if its final word is pronounced with a rising intonation: "You've had lunch?" The sounds that the speakers of a language regard as different from one another are its *phonemes*. In English, we produce many slightly different "p" sounds in words like *pot*, where the "p" is followed by a puff of air (aspiration), or in words like *spot*, where there is no puff of air. For us, these are just one sound, the phoneme "p," but in some languages, such as Hindi, aspirated and unaspirated "p" are different phonemes, and can signal differences in meaning. Hindi has words like *phal* (*fruit*) and *pal* (*moment*) that speakers can tell apart because they begin with two different phonemes. Infants can learn any language, but beginning in the second half of the first year, they begin to lose the ability to make fine distinctions among the phonemes of languages other than their own (Kuhl, Williams, Lacerda, Stevens, & Lindblom,

1992). Although many features of the sound system, such as using the right phonemes in words, are obligatory for communication, the sound system can also be modulated for expressive purposes, for instance to show that one is angry or being emphatic. Individuals, and sometimes even families, also have characteristic ways of speaking that make them recognizable. Phonology may also reflect group membership, including social class and gender. Some of the gender markers that have been claimed for phonology include the suggestion that women, unlike men, sometimes use rising intonation at the ends of sentences, even when they are not asking a question, and that they use more variety in the intonation of sentences, whereas men are more monotonic.

Morphology

The morphology of a language includes rules for word formation and variation. *Morphemes* are the smallest units in a language that carry definable meaning—the word *dog*, or the plural ending *-s* , for example. Morphemes are used to change words from singular to plural, or to indicate person and tense in verbs. Other morphological rules dictate how a word can be transformed into another word *(caring > uncaring)* or even into another part of speech *(care >careful)*. During the preschool years, children develop a systematic knowledge of morphology. One area in which morphological gender differences has been found is in the use of diminutives: the little *-y* or *-ie* morpheme that transforms a word into a baby-talk word like *doggie* or *footie*. Women use more of these when talking to children, and more are used to little girls than to little boys.

Lexicon and Semantics

The lexicon and semantics of a language are its individual words (lexicon) and the meanings attached to them (semantics). Speakers of a language have a remarkably large and complicated mental lexicon or dictionary. Children have about 14,000 words in their vocabulary by the age of 6, and adults may have as many as 50,000 that they produce, and many more that they recognize (Clark, 1993). Many claims—including stereotypical ones—have been made about gender differences in vocabulary: Women use a greater variety of color words. Men use stronger expletives. Women use more intensifiers, such as *very, really really*, and *such*. Some studies have reported that men use more complex vocabulary when speaking to children.

Syntax

Syntax includes the rules in a given language for arranging words to produce different kinds of utterances: declarative sentences, passives, imperatives, questions, and negatives, for example. Children who are acquiring English soon learn to interpret syntax—such as the difference between *The cat chases the dog* and *The dog chases the cat*. In English syntax, word order carries meaning. Typically, the first noun in a sentence is the subject, and the next is the object; some languages, such as Latin, mark subjects and objects with case endings and word order is not so important. We also expect subject nouns to be followed closely by verbs. There are other sentence patterns, of course, and speakers must learn to interpret more complex constructions, such as passives. Gender differences in syntax may be found in such things as the use of sentences containing tag questions, which are little requests for affirmation that are appended to the ends of sentences. Women are thought to produce more of these, utterances such as "It's a beautiful day, *isn't it?*"

Pragmatics

Language can be used to threaten, praise, inform, promise, request, query, blame, and even lie. Pragmatics refers to the use of language to accomplish various ends. Speakers must tailor their language to use it appropriately in different social situations. Pragmatic rules dictate the choice of wording and the interpretation of language in these social contexts. Depending on the situation, speakers vary the politeness of their utterances according to a complex set of rules, and they also vary their speech depending on the person they are addressing (a baby, for instance), as well as on their current role (minister perhaps, or mother). Research on pragmatics has suggested that women are more polite than men in comparable situations, that they are more likely to avoid direct imperatives, and that they phrase their requests in question form ("Could you take your plate off the table?").

Discourse

Discourse refers to connected speech. Speakers of a language must understand how sentences are related to one another. For instance, in English, a pronoun cannot be used unless the noun to which it refers was used first. One cannot begin a conversation with a stranger on a train by saying "*She* lives in Gloucester." But it makes sense if it follows the statement, "I'm on my way to visit my *grandmother*." Conversations and other verbal or written interactions longer than single utterances are governed by discourse conventions that dictate their form. Gender differences in discourse have been reported for narrative style; women, among other things, tell stories (narratives) that include more directly quoted speech, whereas men's stories are more likely to use an indirect way of indicating what someone has said.

From this discussion, it should be clear that each of the different components of language might reflect gender differences, and that many of those differences are expressive and stylistic in nature—the choice of a particular word, for instance, or a level of politeness. We explore this further in the section that follows.

GENDER DIFFERENCES IN THE LANGUAGE OF ADULTS

Stereotypical and Observed Differences

Stereotypical notions of gendered speech are widely held. It is commonly thought that males and females use language in distinctly different ways, comprising two separate and gender-marked ways of speaking. Some researchers regard these different ways of speaking as dialects; a dialect reflects an enduring characteristic of speakers, such as their social class or regional origins. According to this view, the very fact that one is a female or male will pervasively mark language, and males and females have obvious dialects (*genderlects*), just as Northerners and Southerners do. A contrasting, and somewhat more convincing, view is that role and situation, rather than gender, account for many differences that may be detected; the different ways males and females speak are *registers*, because such differences as may exist vary with the social situation, and are not as constant or pervasive as the features that characterize a dialect. A register is a way of speaking that reflects the speaker's current role, the topic, the context, the medium of communication, and the addressee. Speakers of a language all know a number of registers, which are marked by specific linguistic features. Baby talk, or speech to babies, for instance, is marked by the use of exaggerated stress, special vocabulary, diminutives, and frequent repetition. The baby-talk register is found most typically in parents' speech to infants (and sometimes between lovers) and would be quite inappropriate in most other communicative situations (such as in a board meeting). In a similar manner, we might expect to see gender-marked registers in situations in which males and females fulfill traditional sex roles, such as when they are fathers or mothers.

In her well-known book *Language and Woman's Place*, Robin Lakoff (1975) identified a number of linguistic features that, she claimed, were characteristic of female speech. According to Lakoff, women's speech is more hedged and uncertain than men's speech, and, at the same time more grammatical and "proper." She said that women are more polite and deferential and use certain adjectives (e.g., *adorable, divine*) as well as intensifiers (*such* and *so*.) They use special syntactic features, such as tag questions that modulate or weaken their assertions by asking for support and confirmation. Women were also thought to possess expertise in domains that men consider frivolous: for instance in discriminating among colors by using terms like *mauve, lavender*, and *taupe*. Lakoff's hypotheses were based on informal observations and introspection, and subsequent empirical work has supported some, but not all, of her predictions, in some, but not all, contexts (e.g., Crosby & Nyquist, 1977; Rasmussen & Moely, 1986; Simkins-Bullock & Wildman, 1991). The stereotypic notions persist and have sometimes been reinforced in popularized treatments of the topics (Tannen, 1990a). But few of these claims have been supported unequivocally by empirical research. Clearly, simple notions about all-encompassing gender-distinct speech patterns need to be tempered by an appreciation of the complexity of real world interactions, as well as by findings from data-driven analyses.

This gap between stereotypical models and actual data can be exemplified in work that has focused on interruptions and talkativeness, two additional features of adult language that have been identified as marked for gender. The conventional or stereotypic belief in our society is that men interrupt more than women, and that women talk more than men. Both of these claims have been examined extensively, and major reviews of these literatures (James & Clarke, 1993; James & Drakich, 1993) come to conclusions that are not compatible with the simplistic models embodied in the popular stereotypes. In fact, there is often little empirical support for the stereotypes themselves. For example, in their review of talkativeness, James and Drakich (1993) reported that only 2 of 56 studies of mixed-sex conversations found women to be more voluble than men. By contrast, in 24 of the same 56 studies men talked more than women. Other studies have shown that men and women are equally likely to interrupt one another when their age, status, and knowledge are commensurate (Redeker & Maes, 1996.)

More importantly, analyses of spontaneous discourse across a wide variety of settings suggest that interruptions and talkativeness serve different functions in different contexts, and only when careful attention is paid to the context, status, and role of interactants can meaningful inferences about gender differences be drawn. For instance, an interruption can serve to prevent someone from making an embarrassing disclosure, or it can be used to cut short another person's speaking turn in order to dominate a conversation. The person doing the interrupting might, therefore, be motivated by empathy and considerateness in the first instance and by narcissism and inconsiderateness in the second.

Where gender differences in adult language have been found, they are most likely to occur between men and women in same sex settings. Men's and women's social groups are constituted differently, and language serves different purposes within these groups. For example, women, in women's groups, emphasize personal relationships, cooperation, and rapport: Women use more back channeling (little nods of the head and other signals that they are actively listening), as well as more personal and inclusive pronouns (*we*, rather than *I*) (Maltz & Borker, 1982; Treichler & Kramarae, 1983). This emphasis on inclusiveness has also been found in studies of women's joke telling (Jenkins, 1986) and gossip (Jones, 1980). Many of the other differences that have been reported have been based on very small samples and stereotypical views, and have been advanced by researchers who already have strong theoretical ideas about the differences between the sexes.

Theoretical Explanations

Different Cultures

Two theoretical explanations based on social organization have been proposed to account for gender differences in the speech of men and women. As we have just noted, the "cultural" or "difference" approach argues that males and females grow up in separate worlds (Maltz & Borker, 1982; Tannen, 1993). Advocates of this view note that gender-specific enculturation begins in the first weeks of life, despite the absence of pronounced early behavioral differences in the sexes. By the time children enter preschool, they self-select same-sex peers as playmates to ensure compatible play partners. Boys' groups are hierarchically organized and emphasize power relationships, whereas girls' groups, like women's, are more affiliative. Girls are unable to break into the male hierarchy and, therefore, pull away into their own groupings, thus creating separate social and cultural worlds (Maccoby, 1998). The "different culture" view holds that the social separation of males and females continues in one form or another throughout the life span, generating different social experiences that, in turn, produce different, but equally functional, gender-marked ways of using language.

Dominance

An alternate (and not mutually exclusive) social-organization explanation for observed gender differences takes a very different approach. In the "power" or "dominance" model (Lakoff, 1990; Thorne, Kramarae, & Henley, 1983), differences in the speech of males and females can be traced to differences in status and power. Women are basically powerless, and their speech reflects their perceived weaknesses or deficiencies, whereas the speech of men shows their strengths. Thus, male and female speech registers should contain features that primarily reflect status. Furthermore, these features should be especially evident in mixed-sex interactions, particularly where there is a pronounced difference in the status of male and female interlocutors, for instance where a male physician and a female nurse are speaking to one another. Although some theorists have argued that both difference and dominance models are needed (Coates & Cameron, 1988), others have claimed that the two approaches are inextricably intertwined (Uchida, 1992, p. 563), a position that accurately reflects the fact that gender and status are frequently confounded.

Essential Differences

In addition to the cultural difference and the dominance or status explanations, there is a biologically based, "essentialist" rationale for gender differences in language. Such an approach argues that basic biological sex differences (e.g., hormones, brain organization) are responsible for observed differences in language. According to some evolutionary psychologists, present day women and men are controlled by gender-differentiated brains that developed during our prehistory as a species, when early humans lived in small, hunter-gatherer communities. The stereotypic differences between men's and women's communication styles are attributed to differences in neural organization; males, for instance, are seen as relying on action mediated through the primitive regions of the limbic system; females are seen as relying on language, and having more access to emotions and other right hemisphere phenomena (Nadeau, 1997.) However, as we describe in the next section, current evidence suggests that biology plays a direct explanatory role in only a few select domains of language, although it may contribute indirectly by influencing behaviors that, in turn, are reflected in language.

BIOLOGICAL BASES OF GENDER DIFFERENCES IN LANGUAGE

Innate Differences

There are a small number of gender differences in language that can be directly linked to underlying biological sex differences. These differences include the fundamental frequencies at which males and females speak and the incidence of language disorders, including dyslexia. Nevertheless, even though the origins of these differences are more clearly traced to biology, there remains large within-sex variation, and much overlap between the sexes in the pitch of speakers' voices and in the occurrence of language disorders.

With puberty, the male vocal tract undergoes rapid change, leading to characteristic voice cracking. Postpubescent males have longer vocal cords than postpubescent females, giving adolescent and adult males the ability to speak at lower fundamental frequencies (Tanner, 1989). This basic biological difference is, however, not the sole determinant in voice pitch (nor, obviously, are all adult male voices lower than all adult female voices). The degree to which males and females "place" their voice is as much stylistic, reflecting linguistic convention, as it is based on differences in vocal-tract size (Mattingly, 1966). In our society, women tend to speak in relatively high voices, at the upper end of their frequency range, whereas many men place their voices at the low end of their range. This magnifies the effects of the underlying biological difference between male and female vocal tracts. Mattingly notes that women sound as if they are smaller than they actually are, and men speak as if they are larger than they are. In traditional Japanese society, this difference may be even more exaggerated, with females showing deference by speaking in a breathy, quiet, and extremely high, squeaky, voice (Austin 1965).

Even though there are no physiological differences in the vocal tracts of pre-pubescent males and females, adults are able to identify the sex of prepubescent children (ages 4 to 14) based only on listening to their recorded voices (Sachs, Lieberman, & Erickson, 1973). This finding reflects in part the control that children exert on formant frequencies through the shape and size of their vocal tracts as they speak, not their fundamental frequencies (which are determined by the length of their vocal cords.) Because it is unlikely that young children are consciously altering their voices, the results suggest that children have unconsciously adopted some basic features of the speech registers associated with gender. Interestingly, girls who were characterized as "tomboys" were often misidentified. We know that even very young children are aware at some level of the phonological differences between men's and women's voices from research that had them role play with puppets: When children between the ages of 4 and 7 spoke for a father puppet they used voices with a pitch significantly lower than when they played a mother (Andersen, 1990, 1996). Thus differences in voice pitch, which clearly have a biological component, are also affected by social factors.

The second area in which a gender difference appears to have a strong biological basis is in the incidence of language disorders, including disfluencies (e.g., stuttering) and dyslexia. Dyslexia is a compelling example. Dyslexia is a term used to describe reading failure in children who are otherwise unimpaired. Children with dyslexia are of average or above-average intelligence; they have no significant social-emotional or cognitive deficits; and they have received adequate instructional support. Although they may also have trouble reading sentences and deriving inferences from them, dyslexic children characteristically have problems in phonological processing (e.g., segmenting words) (Stanovich, 1993). There is evidence that suggests that females outperform males across a range of phonological tasks (Lewis, 1992; Majeres, 1999). Thus, it is not surprising that the reported incidence of dyslexia is much greater in boys than in girls, with ratios varying between 2:1 and 5:1, although some of this difference may be due to referral bias (Badian, 1999; Miles, Haslum, & Wheeler, 1998; Shaywitz, Shaywitz, Fletcher, & Escobar, 1990). Possible reasons for the sex differences in the incidence of dyslexia include differences in brain lateralization and organization (Beaton, 1997). This brings us to a brief description of language areas in the brain.

Language Areas in the Brain

Human language is clearly biologically determined, even though it is just as clear that in the absence of social support it does not develop. Language relies on specialized structures in the brain and in the neurological system that appear to be particular to humans. Even the precursors of language, the social and affective characteristics of infants that tie them to the adults around them and lead them to want to communicate, have a biological basis. For instance, the infant brain contains neurons that are specialized for the identification of human faces and for the recognition of affect in faces (Locke, 1993). Long before they begin to talk, infants attend to those around them and communicate in preverbal ways.

The human brain contains a number of areas that are known to be associated with language. The two hemispheres of the brain are not symmetrical (Galaburda, LeMay, Kemper, & Geschwind, 1978). The majority of the populace is lateralized for language in the left hemisphere; about 85 percent of the population are right handed and, with rare exceptions, have their language functions represented in the left hemisphere. About one half of the left-handed population also have their language areas in the left hemisphere. The right hemisphere participates in some aspects of language processing, however, for instance in interpreting intonation and in recognizing the emotional tone of speech. Major left hemisphere areas that are known to underlie language include:

• *Broca's area* in the left frontal region, at the foot of the motor strip, near the area that controls the tongue and lips. Damage to Broca's area in adults results in Broca's aphasia, characterized by good comprehension but much articulatory difficulty and agrammatism.

• *Wernicke's area* is located near the auditory association areas of the brain, in the posterior left temporal lobe. Damage to this area results in an aphasia that is characterized by poor comprehension and fluent speech.

• *The arcuate fasciculus* connects Wernicke's area with Broca's area and is a band of subcortical fibers. According to classical models of language processing, in order to repeat a word that is heard, the incoming word is first processed in Wernicke's area and then sent out over the arcuate fasciculus to Broca's area, where it is programmed for production. Lesions in the arcuate fasciculus result in conduction aphasia—patients are unable to repeat what they have heard.

There are other areas of the brain known to be associated language as well, including the angular gyrus, which is involved in reading (Gleason & Goodglass, 1984).

In young children, the language areas are not so strongly dedicated, and the nonlanguage hemisphere can usually take over in case of damage to the dominant hemisphere. If a child of 5 or 6 suffers left-brain damage and subsequent aphasia, complete recovery of language can be expected, whereas adults who become aphasic have a more guarded prognosis, especially if substantial recovery has not been made in the first half-year after their injury. Although there is much hypothesizing among linguists about innate wiring for language, the brains of infants are not fully formed and organized at birth. Infant brains have many fewer synapses than those of adults. The number of synapses grows rapidly, and reaches adult levels by about the age of 2. By the age of 10, children have far more brain connections than adults. By the age of 16, the number of synapses is at typical adult levels. Concomitant with this remarkable synaptic growth, there is a vigorous pruning process that eliminates unused connections. This process of synaptic proliferation and pruning helps to explain the neurological bases of language and other phenomena that take place during sensitive or critical periods in development. If an infant is not exposed to language, the neural connections that underlie language may be weakened (Gleason, 1997). By the same token, this can explain in part the powerful effects of early socialization, including gender role socialization, because experiences that are repeated and reinforced will develop enduring neural representations.

Gender Differences in Language Organization in the Brain

An extended discussion of sex differences in the brain is beyond the scope of this chapter; as Fitch and Bimonte (chapter 3) have shown, however, there are a number of differences between male and female brains that may have some implications for language development, processing, and loss. As noted earlier, the human brain is asymmetrical. In particular, the left *planum temporale*, which in later life develops into Wernicke's area, is larger than the homologous region on the right. Some research has shown that this difference between the hemispheres exists in fetuses, but that it is more likely to be seen in females than in males (Witelson & Palie, 1973). The implication (which is, nonetheless conjectural) is that girls may thus have an earlier start with language. Other research has shown that the splenium of the corpus callossum in females is thicker, and that females have more interhemispheric connections than males, thus giving rise to the claim that women have better access to right hemisphere functions such as emotional and intonational sensitivity while they are processing the other, predominantly left hemisphere, components of language. In general, males' language appears to be more strongly lateralized. Females' language appears to be more heavily buffered and more broadly represented (Beaton, 1997). Relatively new technologies, such as functional magnetic resonance imaging, have made it possible to study the brain in action as well. Females activate areas in both hemispheres during phonological processing, whereas males use a comparatively restricted area of the left hemisphere (Shaywitz et al., 1995). These studies have helped to explain the possible neurological bases of gender differences in language, but must be regarded with caution as well. The presence of a particular anatomical structure does not guarantee its function. Some of the asymmetries thought to be associated with language occur in chimpanzees as well, who do not have articulate speech (Rourke, Bakker, Fisk, & Strang, 1983). There is considerable variation across individuals in brain organization in general.

Temperamental Differences

There are surprisingly few broad gender differences in temperament in children. Some studies have found that boys are significantly more active than girls, a difference that appears to become more pronounced in same-sex play (Eaton &

Enns, 1986; Eaton & Keats, 1982; Goldsmith, Buss, & Lemery, 1997; Kohnstamm, 1989; Martin, Wisenbaker, Baker, & Huttenen, 1997; Prior, 1992). Thus, boys playing with boys are likely to be more active than girls playing with girls. In addition, although females and males do not appear to differ in basic levels of physiological arousal, they do become aroused by distinctly different stimuli. Fabes (1994) reported that boys experienced higher levels of arousal in the face of competition and threats. In contrast, girls experienced higher levels of arousal in sympathy-inducing contexts.

Gender differences such as these have relevance for how children learn and use language. The language that accompanies high levels of active and competitive play (e.g., running, roughhousing) is likely to be very different from the language that accompanies quieter, more sociable play (e.g., dress up, make believe). To the degree that boys are more active and physically competitive than girls, their experience in, and expertise with, the language of active play is likely to be broader and more advanced than that of girls. Conversely, girls' reported greater propensity to engage in somewhat less active and more socially cooperative play suggests that they are more likely than boys to possess richer and more refined interpersonal discourse skills. Girls, in our society, for instance, engage in a number of activities that emphasize fine motor control (jumping rope, hopscotch, counting-out games, etc.) and are more likely than boys to learn the complex rhymes that accompany such activities. Just such patterns have been found in a number of studies that have examined the spontaneous discourse that accompanies the play of preschool and early school-age children (Maccoby & Jacklin, 1987; Opie & Opie, 1959; Tannen, 1990b). Gender differences in play contexts do appear to lead to very different patterns of language use: generations of little girls have taught one another to recite "Teddy bear, teddy bear, turn around . . ." while jumping rope, and "Miss Mary Mack . . . all dressed in black . . ." while clapping their hands.

Temperament may also affect interactive processes when children are infants. Brody (1999) argues that early differences in sociability may affect infant–caregiver interactions. For example, some research suggests that infant girls are more sociable than boys, and more likely be visually and verbally engaged with adult caregivers (e.g., Gunnar & Donahue, 1980). That is, within the first year or so of life, girls are more likely to be people oriented and concerned with others. However, we need to treat such findings cautiously, because adults also have preexisting gender stereotypes that lead them to interact preferentially with female infants (Stern & Karraker, 1989).

It is important to stress that there is little evidence that temperament alone directly affects the basic components of the language system (Bates, Bretherton, & Snyder, 1988). It is more likely that subtle gender differences in temperament foster particular play styles in children, or elicit particular caregiving styles in parents, which, in turn, are associated with particular patterns of language use (Slomkowski, Nelson, Dunn, & Plomin, 1992; Smolak, 1987). Thus, biological dispositions that affect temperament can be said to play an important, but indirect, role in the evolution of gender differences in language.

Finally, it is important to stress that although biology may play an important role in the genesis of some gender differences in language, there are social and cultural factors that can either accentuate or mitigate whatever differences exist. The presence of even a few biological differences, however slight, may also bolster the stereotypic belief that females and males are essentially different. Adults' stereotypic beliefs about children may then play a role in their perception of further gender differences.

EMERGING DIFFERENCES IN THE LANGUAGE OF CHILDREN

Children's Knowledge of Gender Stereotypes

As noted earlier, even very young children are aware of the stereotypic linguistic features that are associated with gender in our society. Sachs (1987) observed same-sex 2- to 5-year-old child dyads in pretend play as "doctors." Boys almost always chose the role of doctor for themselves, and "assigned" their partners to other roles, whereas girls usually asked their partners what role they would like to play. Regardless of the role played, however, boys used more imperatives and prohibitions (e.g., "Don't touch nothing" and "Gimme your arm") than girls, and girls made more use of tag questions and "joint utterances" (e.g., "Let's sit down").

Further evidence that children have acquired knowledge and mastery of gender-specific language can be found in young children's ability to role play adult males and females. As noted earlier, when children between the ages of 4 and 7 were asked to enact parents' speech, their pitch was significantly deeper as fathers than as mothers (Andersen, 1990, 1996). In addition, when they spoke for the father puppet they modified their language across domains. They altered their phonology as fathers by using deeper voices, were louder (sometimes yelling), and used back and lower vowels to produce an accent Andersen described as "sinister" (1996, p. 128). When they pretended to be mothers they used higher pitch, exaggerated intonation, and chose stereotypically female vocabulary. In their discourse, pretend fathers spoke about work, business meetings, how tired they were from working at the computer, and how they had to fire their secretary. In the role of mother, they complained about being exhausted from their errands.

Children enacting pretend child speech used many more direct imperatives to mothers ("Gimme Daddy's flashlight") than to fathers, and far more modified imperatives ("Would you button me?") to fathers than to mothers. When children played the roles of female nurses and male doctors in conversation, the "nurses" used more polite requests talking to "doctors" than doctors talking to nurses. For instance:

Nurse: Doctor, would you like to look at it?

Doctor: Oh, ok, Nurse. Go get the operating machine.

(Andersen, 1996, p.130)

It should be noted that children's knowledge of varying types of speech is not limited to gender differences. In this same series of studies, Andersen found that children also have stereotypic notions about the speech of babies, children, and foreigners. In other work, Edelsky (1977) asked somewhat older children to judge samples of speech as having been said by males or females, and found that, although first graders did not have exactly the same stereotypic beliefs as sixth graders and adults, they nevertheless were aware of gender differences. Salient markers for first graders were the use of *adorable* as having been said by a woman, and *dammit* as a male utterance. By third grade, children were identifying *oh, dear, my goodness*, and *won't you please* as female. For both sixth graders and adults, tag questions (*That was a great show, wasn't it?*), and the intensifiers *so, very,* and *just* were reliably judged to be female expressions.

Gender Differences in Children's Language

Young children's mastery of gender-specific speech registers suggests that they are sensitive to gender differences in the language they hear at home, in the community, and in the media (Tepper & Cassidy, 1999). Not surprisingly, at a fairly young age, their own language begins to reflect that of the larger world. In this section, we discuss a number of studies that document gender differences in children's language. Although much of our attention is focused on examining gender differences in the spontaneous speech of children, we turn first to a brief look at a major meta-analysis that examined gender differences in children's "verbal ability" (Hyde & Linn, 1988).

Meta-analyses represent an important advance over traditional narrative reviews. They allow researchers to evaluate effect sizes over a large number of individual studies, thereby generating quantitative, as opposed to qualitative, judgments as to the real world significance of a particular effect such as gender. Hyde and Linn's (1988) meta-analysis included 165 studies of children's and adults' verbal ability, a term that encompassed a wide range of primarily formal verbal tasks, including, for example, speech production, analogies, vocabulary tests, and reading comprehension. Overall, they found effect sizes to be small, with girls slightly outperforming boys in most domains. The largest effect size favoring females was for speech production, a finding that is reflected in the lower incidence of disfluencies in females. Their findings regarding gender effects by age across three general categories of tasks (all tests, vocabulary, and reading comprehension) indicate a very modest advantage for females in all three categories at all ages, with only one noticeable exception : Males ages 6 to 10 had superior performance on vocabulary tests. Their data offer no consistent support for the stereotypic notion that school-age girls are *significantly* more advanced than school-age boys. The authors concluded that the overall effect sizes were so small as to be considered negligible.

Because most of the studies analyzed by Hyde and Linn assessed basic cognitive capacities involved in language processing (word recall, verbal problem solving), this conclusion is important; it suggests that there are no underlying sex differences in how language is processed. The findings render moot any strong essentialist explanation that is based on underlying biological differences in verbal ability.

The null findings on gender differences in basic ability do not mean that gender differences in children's language do not exist. On the contrary, in a number of subtle and not so subtle ways, girls and boys speak in ways that can, at times, be markedly different. Many of the studies that document gender differences are based on naturalistic data, such as naturally occurring discourse, and thus cannot disambiguate among potential causal factors. Nevertheless, reliable patterns emerge, particularly across studies, and these patterns suggest areas where future research should focus.

Differences in the Language of Young Children

In studies conducted on early school age children in the United States, in both mixed- and same-sex interactions, boys bragged more and proffered more insults than girls (McCloskey, 1996). Sheldon (1990) reported gender differences in children as young as 3, where girls' arguments were more mitigated, whereas boys' arguments were more coercive and competitive. In a study of help-seeking behavior while solving puzzles, Thompson (1999) found that even though there were no gender differences in their ability, preschool girls were more likely than boys to involve others by asking for help while working on the puzzle. In fact, the most general difference between the styles of young American girls and boys appears to be that girls are somewhat more affiliative and collaborative in their speech, whereas boys use language in a more controlling and less modulated way (Austin, Salehi, & Leffler, 1987; Cook, Fritz, McCornack, & Visperas, 1985; DeHart, 1996; Leaper, 1991; Miller, Danaher, & Forbes, 1986; Sachs, 1987).

There is considerable variance among preschoolers in the extent to which they use gender-marked styles, and context makes a difference as well. As with adults, gender differences are seen most clearly in the contexts of same-sex groups. Boys in all-boy groups are more likely to interrupt one another, and to use threats and direct orders to one another. They are also more likely than girls to refuse to comply with another child's request, to boast, tell jokes, try to top one another's stories, call one another unpleasant names, and heckle a speaker. Girls in all-girl groups are more likely to express agreement with what another speaker has said and to pause to give another child a turn to speak. Girls are also more likely to acknowledge a point made by another speaker (Killen & Naigles, 1995; Leaper, 1991; Maccoby, 1998; Miller, Danaher, & Forbes 1986).

These differences among American preschoolers do not, however, signal universal tendencies, and dissimilar patterns can be found in other societies. For instance, among mixed-sex groups of Chinese preschoolers, it is common for girls to set the play agenda and to cast themselves in dominant roles, with boys willingly playing subservient roles, such as that of incompetent baby (Kyratzis & Guo, 1996.) It is important to consider these cross-cultural observations, because it is all too easy to assume that the play groups seen in the United States represent ineluctable conformations determined by our hunter–gatherer ancestors.

Differences in Middle Childhood and Adolescence

During the school years, children continue to self-segregate by gender. School-age girls and boys tend to socialize in same sex peer groups, although mixed-sex interactions become more frequent in adolescence. Boys and girls also continue to have somewhat different interactional goals, with girls emphasizing affiliation and boys expressing more concern with power and autonomy (Gilligan, 1982; Maltz & Borker, 1982). This can be seen, for example, in same-sex friendships, where middle-class adolescent girls show a preference for sharing conversation (Aukett, Ritchie, & Mill, 1988). In these conversations, adolescent girls are more likely than boys to talk about emotions and feelings (Barth & Kinder, 1988; Martin, 1997).

This pattern does not hold for all teenagers who have been studied in our society. Urban African American teenage girls were as likely to compete as they were to cooperate, and were as interested in justice and rights (supposedly male concerns) as they were in care and responsibility (Goodwin, 1990). In another study of adolescents in same sex groups, Filardo (1996) examined gender stereotypical speech forms in the white and African American communities. In their use of three stereotypically female patterns, white females produced more back-channeling expressions (e.g., "yeah" and "uh-huh") than white males, but were no different from males in their use of utterances that sought input from others, or in their use of mitigated speech. By contrast, African American females asked for more input from others than black males, and used more mitigated speech than black males. Thus, in American society, gender markers are not used uniformly across different cultural groups.

Gender differences have been found in a variety of domains of language during the school years. Although some studies have shown that boys swear more than girls (Jay, 1992; Martin, 1997), others have found that girls are as proficient in their use of taboo or pejorative language as are boys (de Klerk, 1992). In their personal narratives, girls are more likely than boys to refer to what someone has said, and they are more likely to recreate the speech by acting it out, or quoting it directly (Ely & McCabe, 1993; Ely, Gleason, & McCabe, 1996).

Girls' greater attention to language (as indicated by their more frequent references to speech itself) appears to carry over to their greater involvement in literacy. Attitudinal differences may account for the small but measurable gender differences in reading. For example, some boys view reading and writing as quiet, passive activities with little intrinsic appeal, and some consider the content and subject matter of many reading and writing tasks in school to be more suitable for girls than for boys (Swann, 1992). Girls on average score somewhat higher than boys in measures of reading, writing, and spelling, and these differences persist through high school (Allred, 1990; Hedges & Nowell, 1995; Hogrebe, Nest, & Newman, 1985; Swann, 1992).

THE SOCIAL BASES OF GENDER DIFFERENCES IN LANGUAGE

As we have seen, there are differences in the emerging language of boys and girls. Most of the differences that observers note are more stylistic than structural, and reflect the cultural values, social organization, and interactional preferences of young males and females. Where differences in linguistic ability are apparent, they are slight, and usually favor girls, but few differences in linguistic ability or in language use can be directly linked to biology.

Although language has a biological base, it can only develop in a social context, through interaction with others. While children are interacting with others and learning the language, they are also being socialized through the language to think and act like appropriate members of society. Part of that socialization includes learning to speak in a way that reflects their evolving status as children and their gender roles. Socialization can be explicit and conscious, as when parents say to a child, "Say 'Please, may I be excused' if you want to leave the table," or "Nice girls don't swear." Socialization can also be unconscious and indirect, as when parents speak more gently to little girls than to little boys, reflecting their beliefs that little girls are more sensitive and delicate (Rubin, Provenzano, & Luria, 1974). Parents may hear themselves speak, but they are typically not aware of the ways they modify their speech when talking to boys or girls. While we were in our local market taking a break from writing this chapter, we heard a parent say the following to a somewhat whiny 3-year-old: "You're really pushin' it there, Buster." It is unlikely that the father who said this to his son was conscious of the prototypical gender-marked register in which he was speaking (using a "tough" tone, saying "pushin'," calling the little boy "Buster") but the lesson was there nonetheless.

Linguistic socialization includes more than an emphasis on form. Parents transmit their own world views in the way they speak about things, and in the things to which they call attention. Gender is a construct that colors parents' views of their children and of themselves; their speech as mothers or fathers reflects their own gender roles and serves as models for their children. They interact somewhat differently with daughters and sons, often in subtle ways that are not immediately apparent. For instance, when parents and children are having dinner together they often produce brief narratives describing the events of the day. Analysis of dinner table conversations with preschoolers reveals that mothers quote the speech of others far more frequently than fathers and that girls quote others at twice the rate of boys (Ely, Gleason, Narasimhan, & McCabe, 1995).

The Speech of Mothers and Fathers to Boys and Girls

Meta-Analysis

Studies of parents' speech to children have proliferated during the past 25 years. Much of this research is centered on the relation between the input language and children's acquisition of language as a system, and is beyond the scope of our discussion. Most input studies have not included fathers, but there are now enough such studies for fathers' speech to be considered in meta-analyses. Leaper and his colleagues (1998), in an investigation of gender effects, analyzed a group of studies that looked at parents' speech to children. These researchers found some parent effects (mothers versus fathers) and some effects of child gender on mothers' speech, but there were too few studies available to investigate child effects on fathers' speech. Some of the effects that met their statistical criterion were that mothers, compared with fathers, talked more, and provided their children with more supportive speech, including more praise, approval, acknowledgment, and collaboration. The largest effect for fathers was that they used more directive speech than mothers. The largest child effects were, nevertheless, considered small, and included mothers talking more to daughters than to sons and mothers directing more supportive speech to daughters than to sons. Although the effects of child gender on mothers' speech were small, we would expect larger effects on fathers' speech, in line with research that shows fathers' greater emphasis on gender stereotypical behavior. For instance, in our own work we have found that fathers used more inner-state words (*happy, angry*) with girls than with boys and that fathers called their sons (but not their daughters) jocular names like *tiger, buster, dingaling,* and *nutcake.* They were also more directive and threatening with their sons than with their daughters (Gleason, 1975; Schell & Gleason, 1989).

The meta-analysis results on the effects of age and context were also revealing. For example, effect sizes were larger in speech directed to infants and toddlers than in speech directed to older children, reflecting how parents accentuate gender differences early on, during a period when the child is forming basic gender schemas. By the age of 3 or 4, children have already established clear notions of the gender-typical behavior of their culture (Bem, 1993), presumably as a result of interaction with their parents and others. For example, using home observations of children between 1 and 5 years of age, Fagot and Hagan (1991) examined parents' reactions to children's behaviors. They found that at age 18 months, boys received more negative feedback to communicative attempts than did girls. Conversely, girls received more positive feedback than did boys for making attempts to engage in conversation. Mothers encouraged children's communicative attempts more than did fathers, and were especially solicitous of girls' communicative initiations.

Thus, mothers were more likely to encourage talk in their children, and girls received more encouragement to talk then did boys. By the time the children were 5 years old, there were no gender-based differences in how parents related to the communicative behaviors of their children, presumably because by age 5 the children had already attained gender-appropriate behaviors.

In the meta-analysis conducted by Leaper and his colleagues (1998), context effects included location, the degree to which observations were structured (e.g., parent–child problem solving tasks) or unstructured, and the presence of, or type of, toys. The fewest gender effects were seen in laboratory settings with older children, where the experimenter had structured the observation and provided the toys to be used. The greatest gender effects were observed at home when young children engaged in free play with a toy they had chosen. From this it can be seen that many of the gender differences that occur routinely in the home may not always be evident when families participate in laboratory studies.

Individual Domains

A number of intriguing gender differences have been found in studies that have looked at one particular domain of language.

• *Interruptions:* Parents interrupt girls more than boys (Greif, 1980).

• *Prohibitions:* Parents direct more prohibitives ("no, no, no") to boys than to girls (Gleason, Ely, Perlmann, & Narasimhan, 1996).

• *Inner-state words:* At home and in the laboratory, parents use more inner state words (*happy, sad, angry*) with girls, and girls begin to use them at very early ages (Dunn, Bretherton, & Munn, 1987; Schell & Gleason, 1989).

• *Endearments and diminutives:* When speaking to girls, parents use more endearments ("Sweetie" or "Honey") and diminutives ("doggie" and "blankie") than to boys (Gleason, Perlmann, Ely, & Evans, 1993; Warren-Leubecker, 1982).

Parents also use diminutives over a longer period of time to girls. Use of a diminutive calls a child's attention to the referent and, in our culture, adds an important affective coloring to the referent. Parents diminutize pets, favorite objects, and, in general, things toward which they are favorably disposed. For instance, a parent may say, "See the birdie?" to a toddler, but would be unlikely to point out a "roachie," however small and cute. The pattern that emerges from the brief listing above, suggests that parents are speaking in a warmer and gentler way with little girls, using diminutives and talking about emotions, whereas with little boys they are assuming a lack of interest in the world of feelings, and the need to be particularly forceful and directive.

Context

An example of the effects of context can be found in a comprehensive study of spontaneous speech at home. Wells (1985) found that there were significant differences in *when* children spoke. Girls' speech was found most frequently in the contexts termed *Helping* and *General Activity*. On the other hand, boys spoke most frequently when engaged in play, either alone or with an adult. An examination of parents' conversational initiations revealed that they preferentially began conversations with girls when they were engaged in *Helping* or *General Activity*; parental initiations with boys occurred during boys' play activities. Although these gender-based differences in conversational contexts appear to have little effect on children's acquisition of language in the narrowly defined sense, they invariably have broad effects on children's understanding of the social uses of language (Gleason, Hay, & Cain, 1988).

Fathers' Speech

Because most research has concentrated on the speech of mothers, we have a better description of linguistic socialization by mothers than by fathers. Data on fathers indicate that mothers and fathers are similar in the basic linguistic features of their speech to young children (Mannle & Tomasello, 1987) but that their interactive and communicative styles differ, particularly in the pragmatics of their child-directed speech.

In the traditional middle-class families that have been studied, mothers are the primary caretakers. Fathers spend less time talking with children than mothers do (Stoneman & Brody, 1981) and are less in tune with their children's language. For instance, they have more difficulty understanding their children than mothers (Weist & Kruppe, 1977), and as a result, ask for clarification more than mothers (Rondal, 1980). Fathers are also not as well attuned to their children's levels of syntactic development as are mothers (Pratt, Kerig, Cowan, & Cowan, 1992). This finding suggests that, for children, fathers' discourse is more complex and, presumably, more demanding. Rarer terms are also found in fathers' speech. Conversation with preschoolers may contain complex concepts and words like *construction site*, *carburetor*, *aggravating*, and *focus knob* (Gleason, 1975, 1987; Ratner, 1988). Fathers' speech also contains many direct imperatives as well as more play with language (Bellinger & Gleason, 1982). Fathers tend to be more linguistically and pragmatically challenging when they speak with their children. Moreover, as noted previously, fathers' speech to boys and girls differs in a number of rather stereotypical ways. Thus, through interaction with their children, parents express and perpetuate specific gender-based standards, providing models of gender-marked speech themselves, and, at the same time, subtly shaping children's language in gender-marked ways.

CONCLUSION

Despite the existence of extremely popular stereotypical views of the differences between men's and women's language, it turns out that there are actually few pervasive differences that can be documented. This goes counter to our intuitions. Gender dimorphic beliefs are strong, and we are able to seize upon the availability heuristic: When we see a man refuse to ask for directions, this confirms our belief that "men won't ask for directions," even though we may have overlooked similar instances of female obdurateness.

If we regard gender differences in language as primarily a matter of registral variation, we should not be surprised to find that it is difficult and an oversimplification to claim that men always speak one way, and women another. A man may employ many more features of the male register when talking with his son, or with friends at the pub (e.g., using words like "fishin'") than when taking out a bank loan. A woman drill sergeant is unlikely to say to a recruit, "Oh dear, your rifle is sooo dirty!" Research that has looked at language in only one kind of situation is unlikely to reveal the great stylistic range that women and men employ every day. At the same time, the very fact that linguistic stereotypes exist is of great interest, because they are common, and not restricted to models of male and female speech. Everyone in our society knows that cowboys say "Howdy, pardner," even if no cowboy has ever said that. Young children are aware of the gender stereotypes and can produce some of their features when they are still preschool age. These aspects of linguistic performance do not appear to be solely products of their socialization within the family, but are no doubt also transmitted through books and the media, where stereotypic language is frequently used to delineate a character.

Although most differences appear to be of a social nature, arising from the roles that individuals play, or from the kinds of social groups they form, there remains some evidence of a biological base to gender differences in language. Male voices are certainly, on the whole, lower than female voices, even though the differences may be enhanced by social norms. Males are evidently more vulnerable neurologically, and suffer more language disability than females, even though the differences in, for example, dyslexia may not be as great as we thought. Boys with dyslexia may be noticed more readily than dyslexic girls because they are more likely than girls also to have hyperactivity disorder. Male and female brains are somewhat different in organization, and language is more highly buffered and less lateralized in females according to many studies. A more tenuous claim is that of the evolutionary psychologists, who see our ancient history as a species as overdetermining our current personalities and social organization. Average differences between the sexes in many ways obscure the great within-sex variation on all measures of language.

When we have looked at the incidence of gender differences in the speech of children, it has been fairly clear that the differences that have been observed reflect the kinds of social groups that children in our society form. In the United States, children self-segregate by gender early on, and boys and girls appear to use language for somewhat different social purposes and to accompany somewhat different activities. As we have seen, these observations do not hold for all segments of our society. In other cultures (Chinese, for instance), children's groups and their language reflect different social values and concerns.

We live in a gender dimorphic society, and parents have strong beliefs about differences between the sexes (for instance that infant boys are alert and "bouncing" and that girls are sensitive and delicate). Parents' speech to boys and girls reflects cultural values and beliefs, often in remarkably subtle ways. Fathers and mothers also speak in somewhat different ways to their children, who thus see different models of language behavior while also being spoken to in ways that vary according to their gender. Gender-role socialization includes learning to speak in gender-marked ways when it is appropriate. These observations may help to explain the appearance of gender differences in children's language. In sum:

• Most sweeping claims about gender differences in the language of adults are overstated and based on stereotypes that have not been supported by empirical research.

• Very few of the documented gender differences in children's language can be traced directly to biological sex differences, although there are a few that can be.

• Social and cultural factors contribute significantly to the development and maintenance of gender dimorphic patterns of behavior in general, and this is true of language behavior as well.

• Early in the child's life, parents and other adults, such as teachers, are important socializing agents; later, adults are supplanted by peers, particularly in same-sex groups. Much of the socialization that children experience takes place indirectly, beyond the awareness of the socializing agents themselves. Practices that are out of awareness may be deeply embedded in a culture and not easily amenable to change. This may help to explain the phenomenon of cultural continuity in gender-role socialization and in socialization of the speech that marks gender.

• Finally, where gender differences in language occur, they are likely to be situation and context sensitive. Thus, a small but nevertheless real difference found in one context may not be observed in another. This is an important consideration to bear in mind when evaluating empirical research that reports either significant or null findings.

REFERENCES

Allred, R. A. (1990). Gender differences in spelling achievements in grades 1 through 6. *Journal of Educational Research, 83,* 187–193.

Andersen, E. S. (1990). *Speaking with style: The sociolinguistic skills of children.* New York: Routledge.

Andersen, E. S. (1996). A cross-cultural study of children's register knowledge. In D. I. Slobin, J. Gerhardt, A. Kyratzis, & J. Guo (Eds.), *Social interaction, social context, and language: Essays in honor of Susan Ervin-Tripp* (pp. 125–142). Mahwah, NJ: Lawrence Erlbaum.

Aukett, R, Ritchie, J., & Mill, K. (1988). Gender differences in friendship patterns. *Sex Roles, 19,* 57–66.

Austin, A. M., Salehi, M., & Leffler, A. (1987). Gender and development in children's conversations. *Sex Roles, 16*, 497–510.

Austin, W. M. (1965). Some social aspects of paralanguage. *Canadian Journal of Linguistics, 11*, 31–39.

Badian, N. A. (1999). Reading disability defined as a discrepancy between listening and reading comprehension: A longitudinal study of stability, gender differences, and prevalence. *Journal of Learning Disabilities, 32*, 138–148.

Barth, R. J., & Kinder, B. N. (1988). A theoretical analysis of sex differences in same-sex friendship. *Sex Roles, 19*, 349–363.

Bates, E., Bretherton, I., & Snyder, L. (1988). *From first words to grammar: Individual differences and dissociable mechanisms*. New York: Cambridge University Press.

Beaton, A. A. (1997). The relation of planum temporale asymmetry and morphology of the corpus callosum to handedness, gender, and dyslexia: A review of the evidence. *Brain and Language, 60*, 255–322.

Bellinger, D., & Gleason, J. B. (1982). Sex differences in parental directives to young children. *Journal of Sex Roles, 8*, 123–129.

Bem, S. (1993). *The lenses of gender*. New Haven, CT: Yale University Press.

Brody, L. (1999). *Gender, emotion, and the family* Cambridge, MA: Harvard University Press.

Clark, E. V. (1993). *The lexicon in acquisition*. New York: Cambridge University Press.

Coates, J., & Cameron, D. (Eds.). (1988). *Women in their speech communities*. New York: Longman.

Cook, A. S., Fritz, J. J., McCornack, B. L., & Visperas, C. (1985). Early gender differences in the functional usage of language. *Sex Roles, 12*, 909–915.

Crosby, F., & Nyquist, L. (1977). The female register: An empirical study of Lakoff's hypotheses. *Language in Society, 6*, 313–322.

DeHart, G. B. (1996). Gender and mitigation in 4-year-olds' pretend play talk with siblings. *Research on Language and Social Interaction, 29*, 81–96.

de Klerk, V. (1992). How taboo are taboo words for girls? *Language in Society, 21*, 277–289.

Dunn, J., Bretherton, I., & Munn, P. (1987). Conversations about feeling states between mothers and their young children. *Developmental Psychology, 23*, 132–139.

Eaton, W. O., & Enns, L. R. (1986). Sex differences in human motor activity. *Psychological Bulletin, 100*, 19–28.

Eaton, W. O., & Keats, J. G. (1982). Peer presence, stress, and sex differences in the motor activity levels of preschoolers. *Developmental Psychology, 18*, 534–540.

Edelsky, C. (1977). Acquisition of an aspect of communicative competence: Learning what it means to talk like a lady. In S. Ervin-Tripp & C. Mitchell-Kernan (Eds.), *Child discourse* (pp. 225–243). New York: Academic Press.

Ely, R., Gleason, J. B., & McCabe, A. (1996). "Why didn't you talk to your Mommy, Honey?": Parents' and children's talk about talk. *Research on Language and Social Interaction, 29*, 7–25.

Ely, R., & McCabe, A. (1993). Remembered voices. *Journal of Child Language, 20*, 671–696.

Fabes, R. A. (1994). Physiological, emotional, and behavioral correlates of gender segregation. In C. Leaper (Ed.), *Childhood gender segregation: Causes and consequences* (pp. 19–34). San Francisco: Jossey-Bass.

Fagot, B. A., & Hagan, R. (1991). Observations of parent reactions to sex-stereotyped behaviors: Age and sex effects. *Child Development, 62*, 617–628.

Filardo, E. K. (1996). Gender patterns in African American and White adolescents' social interactions in same-race, mixed-gender groups. *Journal of Personality and Social Psychology, 71*, 71–82.

Galaburda, A. M., LeMay, M., Kemper, T. K., & Geschwind, N. (1978). Right-left asymmetries in the brain. *Science, 199*, 852–856.

Gilligan, C. (1982). *In a different voice: Psychological theory and women's development.* Cambridge, MA: Harvard University Press.

Gleason, J. B. (1975). Fathers and other strangers: Men's speech to young children. In D. P. Dato (Ed.), *Developmental psycholinguistics: Theory and applications.* Washington, DC: Georgetown University Press.

Gleason, J. B. (1987). Sex-differences in parent-child interaction. In S. U. Phillips, S. Steele, & C. Tanz (Eds), *Language, gender, and sex in comparative perspective* (pp. 178–188). New York: Cambridge University Press.

Gleason, J. B. (1997). The development of language: An overview and a preview. In J. Berko Gleason (Ed.), *The Development of language*, 4th ed., (pp. 1–39). Boston: Allyn & Bacon.

Gleason, J. B. (2000). Language. In A. E. Kazdin (Ed.), *Encyclopedia of psychology* (Vol. 4; pp. 473–476). New York: American Psychological Association and Oxford University Press.

Gleason, J. B., Ely, R., Perlmann, R. Y., & Narasimhan, H. (1996). Patterns of prohibition in parent-child discourse. In D. I. Slobin, J. Gerhardt, A. Kyratzis, & J. Guo (Eds.), *Social interaction, social context, and language: Essays in honor of Susan Ervin-Tripp* (pp. 205–217). Mahwah, NJ: Lawrence Erlbaum.

Gleason, J. B., & Goodglass, H. (1984). Some neurological and linguistic accompaniments of the fluent and nonfluent aphasias. *Topics in Language Disorders, 4*, 71–81.

Gleason, J. B., Hay, D., & Cain, L. (1988). Social and affective determinants of language acquisition. In M. L. Rice & R. L. Schiefelbusch (Eds), *The teachability of language* (pp. 171–186). Baltimore: Paul H. Brookes.

Gleason, J. B., Perlmann, R. Y., Ely, R., & Evans, D. (1993). The babytalk register: Parents' use of diminutives. In J. F. Sokolov & C. E. Snow (Eds.), *Handbook of research in language development using CHILDES* (pp. 50–76). Hillsdale, NJ: Lawrence Erlbaum.

Goldsmith, H. H., Buss, K. A., & Lemery, K. S. (1997). Toddler and childhood temperament: Expanded content, stronger genetic evidence, new evidence for the importance of environment. *Developmental Psychology, 33*, 891–905.

Goodwin, M. H. (1990). *He-said-she-said: Talk as social organization among black children.* Bloomington: Indiana University Press.

Greif, E. B. (1980). Sex differences in parent-child conversations. In C. Kramarae (Ed.), *The voices and words of women and men* (pp. 253–258). New York: Pergamon Press.

Gunnar, M. R., & Donahue, M. (1980). Sex differences in social responsiveness between six months and twelve months. *Child Development, 51*, 262–265.

Hedges, L. V., & Nowell, A. (1995). Sex differences in mental test scores, variability, and numbers of high-scoring individuals. *Science, 269*, 41–45.

Hogrebe, M. C., Nest, S. L., & Newman, I. (1985). Are there gender differences in reading achievement? An investigation using the high school and beyond data. *Journal of Educational Psychology, 77,* 716–724.

Hyde, J. S., & Linn, M. C. (1988). Gender differences in verbal ability: A meta-analysis. *Psychological Bulletin, 104,* 53–69.

James, D., & Clark, S. (1993). Women, men, and interruptions: A critical review. In D. Tannen (Ed.), *Gender and conversational interaction* (pp. 231–280). New York: Oxford University Press.

James, D., & Drakich, J. (1993). Understanding gender differences in amount of talk: A critical review of research. In D. Tannen (Ed.), *Gender and conversational interaction* (pp. 281–312). New York: Oxford University Press.

Jay, T. (1992). *Cursing in America.* Philadelphia: J. Benjamins.

Jenkins, M. M. (1986). What's so funny? Joking among women. In S. Bremner, N. Caskey, & B. Moonwomon (Eds.), *Proceedings of the first Women and Language Conference* (pp. 135–151), Berkeley, CA: Women and Language Group.

Jones, D. (1980). Gossip: Notes on women's oral culture. In C. Kramarae (Ed.), *The voices and words of women and men* (pp. 193–198). Oxford: Pergamon.

Killen, M., & Naigles, L. R. (1995). Preschool children pay attention to their addressees: Effects of gender composition on peer disputes. *Discourse Processes, 19,* 329–346.

Kohnstamm, G. A. (1989). Temperament in childhood: Cross-cultural and sex differences. In G. A. Kohnstamm, J. E. Bates, & M. K. Rothbart (Eds.), *Temperament in childhood* (pp. 483–508). Chichester, UK: Wiley.

Kuhl, P. K., Williams, K. A., Lacerda, F., Stevens, K. N., & Lindblom, B. (1992). Linguistic experience alters phonetic perception in infants by 6 months of age. *Science, 255,* 606–608.

Kyratzis, A., & Guo, J. (1996). "Separate worlds for girls and boys?" Views from U.S. and Chinese mixed-sex friendship groups. In D. I. Slobin, J. Gerhardt, A. Kyratzis, & J. Guo (Eds.), *Social interaction, social context, and language: Essays in honor of Susan Ervin-Tripp* (pp. 555–577). Mahwah, NJ: Lawrence Erlbaum.

Lakoff, R. T. (1975). *Language and woman's place.* New York. Harper & Row.

Lakoff, R. T. (1990). *Talking power: The politics of language.* New York: Basic Books.

Leaper, C. (1991). Influence and involvement: Age, gender, and partner effects. *Child Development, 62,* 797–811.

Leaper, C., Anderson, K. J., & Sanders, P. (1998). Moderators of gender effects on parents' talk to their children: A meta-analysis. *Developmental Psychology, 34,* 3–27.

Lewis, B. A. (1992). Pedigree analysis of children with phonology disorders. *Journal of Learning Disabilities, 25,* 586–597.

Locke, J. L. (1993). *The child's path to spoken language.* Cambridge, MA: Harvard University Press.

Maccoby, E. E. (1998). *The two sexes: Growing up apart, coming together.* Cambridge, MA: Harvard University Press.

Maccoby, E. E., & Jacklin, C. N. (1987). Gender segregation in children. In H. W. Reese (Ed.), *Advances in child development and behavior* (Vol 20, pp. 239–287). New York: Academic Press.

Majeres, R. L. (1999). Sex differences in phonological processes: Speeded matching and word reading. *Memory and Cognition, 27,* 246–253.

Maltz, D. N., & Borker, R. A. (1982). A cultural approach to male–female miscommuni-cation. In J. J. Gumperz (Ed.), *Language and social identity* (pp. 196–216). Cambridge, UK: Cambridge University Press.

Mannle, S., & Tomasello, M. (1989). Fathers, siblings, and the Bridge Hypothesis. In K. Nelson & A. Van Kleeck (Eds.), *Children's language* (Vol. 6, pp. 23–41). Hillsdale, NJ: Lawrence Erlbaum.

Martin, R. (1997). "Girls don't talk about garages!": Perceptions of conversation in same- and cross-sex friendships. *Personal Relationships, 4*, 115–130.

Martin, R. P., Wisenbaker, J., Baker, J., & Huttenen, M. O. (1997). Gender differences in temperament at six months and five years. *Infant Behavior and Development, 20*, 339–347.

Mattingly, I. C. (1966). Speaker variation and vocal-tract size. *Journal of the Acoustical Society of America, 39*, 1219.

McCloskey, L. A. (1996). Gender and the expression of status in children's mixed-age conversations. *Journal of Applied Developmental Psychology, 17*, 117–133.

Miles, T. R., Haslum, M. N., & Wheeler, T. J. (1998). Gender ratio in dyslexia. *Annals of Dyslexia, 48*, 27–55.

Miller, P. M., Danaher, D. L., & Forbes, D. (1986). Sex-related strategies for coping with interpersonal conflict in children aged five and seven. *Developmental Psychology, 22*, 543–548.

Nadeau, R. (1997). Brain sex and the language of love. *The world & I*, November, (pp. 330–339). Washington, DC: Washington Times Corporation.

Opie, I., & Opie, P. (1959). *The lore and language of schoolchildren*. Oxford: Clarendon Press.

Pratt, M. W., Kerig, P. K., Cowan, P. A., & Cowan, C.P. (1992). Family worlds: Couple satisfaction, parenting style, and mothers' and fathers' speech to young children. *Merrill-Palmer Quarterly, 38*, 245–262.

Prior, M. (1992). Childhood temperament. *Journal of Child Psychology and Psychiatry, 33*, 249–279.

Rasmussen, J. L., & Moely, B. E. (1986). Impression formation as a function of the sex role appropriateness of linguistic behavior. *Sex Roles, 14*, 149–161.

Ratner, N. B. (1988). Patterns of parental vocabulary selection in speech to very young children. *Journal of Child Language, 15*, 481–492.

Redeker, G., & Maes, A. (1996). Gender differences in interruptions. In D. I. Slobin, J. Gerhardt, A. Kyratzis, & J. Guo (Eds.), *Social interaction, social context, and language: Essays in honor of Susan Ervin-Tripp* (pp. 597–612). Mahwah, NJ: Lawrence Erlbaum.

Rondal, J. (1980). Fathers' and mothers' speech in early language development. *Journal of Child Language, 7*, 353–369.

Rourke, B. P., Bakker, D. J., Fisk, J. L., & Strang, J. D. (1983). *Child neuropsychology: An introduction to theory, research, and clinical practice*. New York: Guilford Press.

Rubin, J. Z., Provenzano, F. J., & Luria, Z. (1974). In the eye of the beholder. *American Journal of Orthopsychiatry, 44*, 512–519.

Sachs, J. (1987). Preschool boys' and girls' language use in pretend play. In S. U. Phillips, S. Steele, & C. Tanz (Eds.), *Language, gender, and sex in comparative perspective* (pp. 178–188). New York: Cambridge University Press.

Sachs, J., Lieberman, P., & Erickson, D. (1973) Anatomical and cultural determinants of male and female speech. In R. W. Shuy & R. W. Fasold (Eds.), *Language attitudes: Current trends and prospects* (pp. 74–84). Washington, DC: Georgetown University Press.

Schell, A., & Gleason, J. B. (1989, January). *Gender differences in the acquisition of the vocabulary of emotion.* Paper presented at the annual meeting of the American Association of Applied Linguistics, Washington, D.C.

Shaywitz, B. A., Shaywitz, S. E., Pugh, K. R., Constable, R. T., Skudlarski, P., Fulbright, R. K., Bronen, R. A., Fletcher, J. M., Shankweiler, D. P., Katz, L., & Gore, J. C. (1995). Sex differences in the functional organization of the brain for language. *Nature, 373 (6515),* 607–609.

Shaywitz, S. E., Shaywitz, B. A., Fletcher, J. M., & Escobar, M. D. (1990). Prevalence of reading disability in boys and girls. *Journal of the American Medical Association, 264*, 998–1002.

Sheldon, A. (1990). Pickle fights: Gendered talk in preschool disputes. *Discourse Processes, 13*, 5–31.

Simkins-Bullock, J. A., & Wildman, B. G. (1991). An investigation into the relationship between gender and language. *Sex Roles, 24*, 149–160.

Slomkowski, C. L., Nelson, K., Dunn, J., & Plomin, R. (1992). Temperament and language: Relations from toddlerhood to middle childhood. *Developmental Psychology, 28*, 1090–1095.

Smolak, L. (1987). Child characteristics and maternal speech. *Journal of Child Language, 14*, 481–492.

Stanovich, K. E. (1993). A model for studies of reading disability. *Developmental Review, 13*, 225–245.

Stern, M., & Karraker, K. H. (1989). Sex stereotyping of infants: A review of gender labeling studies. *Sex Roles, 20*, 501–522.

Stoneman, Z., & Brody, G. H. (1981). Two's company, three makes a difference: An examination of mothers' and fathers' speech to their young children. *Child Development, 52*, 705–707.

Swann, J. (1992). *Girls, boys, and language.* Cambridge, MA: Blackwell.

Tannen, D. (1990a). *You just don't understand: Women and men in conversation.* New York: Ballantine Books.

Tannen, D. (1990b). Gender differences in topical coherence: Creating involvement in best friend's talk. *Discourse Processes, 13*, 73–90.

Tannen, D. (Ed.). (1993). *Gender and conversational interaction.* New York: Oxford University Press.

Tanner, J. M. (1989). *Fetus into man: Physical growth from conception to maturity.* Cambridge, MA: Harvard University Press.

Tepper, C. A., & Cassidy, K. W. (1999). Gender differences in emotional language in children's picture books. *Sex Roles, 40*, 265–280.

Thompson, B. R. (1999). Gender differences in preschoolers' help-eliciting communication. *Journal of Genetic Psychology, 160*, 357–368.

Thorne, B., Kramarae, C., & Henley, C. (Eds.). (1983). *Language, gender and society.* Rowley, MA: Newbury House.

Treichler, P. A., & Kramarae, C. (1982). Women's talk in the ivory tower. *Communication Quarterly, 31* (Spring), 118–132.

Uchida, A. (1992). When "difference" is "dominance": A critique of the "anti-power-based" cultural approach to sex differences. *Language in Society, 21,* 547–568.

Warren-Leubecker, A. (1982). *Sex differences in speech to children.* Unpublished Master's thesis, Georgia Institute of Technology, Atlanta.

Wells, G. (1985). Preschool literacy-related activities and success in school. In D. R. Olson, N. Torrance & A. Hilyard (Eds.), *Literacy, language, and learning* (pp. 229–255). New York: Cambridge University Press.

Weist, R. M., & Kruppe, B. (1977). Parent and sibling comprehension in children's speech. *Journal of Psycholinguistic Research, 6,* 49–58.

Witelson, S. F., & Palie, W. (1973). Left hemisphere specialization for language in the newborn: Neuroanatomical evidence of asymmetry. *Brain, 96,* 641–647.

CHAPTER 6

Sex Differences in Mathematical Abilities and Achievement

Richard De Lisi
Ann McGillicuddy-De Lisi

This chapter presents a selective review of psychological studies of sex differences in mathematical abilities and achievement conducted from 1990 to 2000. The past ten years were examined because of space constraints and because a few influential papers published around 1990 provided cogent summaries of work up to that time and raised issues that became the focus of work that followed. An overview of these influential papers is presented.

RESEARCH FINDINGS ON SEX DIFFERENCES THROUGH 1990

Meta-Analysis Findings

In the 1980s, investigators came to recognize the importance of using precise statistical techniques rather than subjective summaries of published studies to obtain an accurate summary of sex differences research findings. For the most part, these meta-analytic studies came to rely on examining standardized average score differences (d) as the key index to summarize findings across studies. Using this approach, Hyde, Fennema, & Lamon (1990) conducted a meta-analysis of research on gender differences in mathematical performance. They concluded that the average overall effect size for sex differences was near 0; differences favoring male participants were more likely to be found as samples became more selective; and patterns varied somewhat according to the age and constructs sampled—a slight female advantage in early computation skills, a larger male advantage in high school and college for mathematical problem solving. The Scholastic Aptitude Test-Mathematics (SAT-M; now Scholastic Assessment Test-Mathematics) was identified as an area in which the male advantage seemed large enough to be of concern.

Hyde, Fennema, Ryan, Frost, and Hopp (1990) conducted a meta-analysis of gender differences for attitudes and affect relevant to mathematics. The review showed that female participants had more mathematics anxiety and less self-confidence than male participants, but these differences were small. One large difference was the tendency by male participants to stereotype mathematics as a male domain much more than female participants.

These two meta-analyses painted a minimalist picture of sex differences in mathematical abilities, school achievement, and affect. This picture was not consistent with the large differences that existed and still exist in occupational attainment in careers that require advanced training in mathematics. For example, Snyder and Hoffman (2000, Table 258) report that in the United States in 1996–1997, women earned 47% of the bachelor's degrees in mathematics, 40% of the master's degrees, but only 22% of the doctoral degrees in mathematics. Women earned less than 10% of all the bachelor's degrees in engineering fields in 1996–1997. In that same year, across all fields of study, women earned 55% of the bachelor's degrees, 57% of the master's degrees, and 41% of the doctoral degrees (Snyder & Hoffman, 2000, Table 249).

Some Unresolved Issues

Perhaps these differences in advanced study and occupational attainment in mathematics stem from a male advantage at the high end of the ability distribution. Benbow (1988) summarized 16 years of research on intellectually talented 12- and 13-year-old students in which large differences favoring male over female students on the SAT-M were evident. In particular, the imbalance favoring male students with respect to very high levels of performance on the SAT-M seemed important to explain. These data from precocious youth as well as Benbow's analysis of environmental and biological correlates/causes of sex differences were vigorously debated in 42 commentaries. For example, Benbow's report discounted differential course taking as an explanation for sex differences in mathematical aptitude, but some commentators disagreed. Another possibility discussed in the article was that more male students are found at the upper tail of the distribution because they are more variable in performance than females. The issue of greater male variability, its source and meaning, had been raised by Maccoby and Jacklin (1974) in their seminal book on sex differences. Many other factors in addition to differential course taking and differences in variability were considered by Benbow (1988) but these two have been carefully considered in the past 10 years.

Kimball (1989) made a different point about gender differences in mathematics achievement. On the one hand, female students receive either the same or better grades in mathematics classes than male students. On the other hand, male students tend to outperform female students on tests like the SAT-M. Is there a difference in learning styles or cognitive processes that renders an advantage in the classroom but a disadvantage on high-stakes tests? Is there a difference in reactions to high-stakes testing situations as contrasted with classroom testing situations? These and other issues have been addressed in recent years in an attempt to solve the puzzle brought to light by Kimball (1989).

This completes the summary of gender differences in mathematics as it existed around 1990. There appeared to be few differences that would be considered large or of practical significance, except perhaps, for differences in higher-level problem solving, especially among select samples. It was not clear whether these findings could account for very large differences in advanced study and occupational attainment. Finally, differences between classroom grades and performance on large-scale tests seemed important to understand. Before we review the research that followed, we situate the research on sex differences within the larger context of research on mathematical abilities.

Sex Differences in a Larger Context:
The Development of Mathematical Abilities

The many studies reviewed by Benbow (1988), Kimball (1989), Hyde, Fennema, and Lamon (1990), and Hyde, Fennema, Ryan, Frost, and Hopp (1990) were quite varied in their definition of mathematical abilities and achievement. In fact, in commenting on Benbow (1988), Sternberg (1988) noted that psychologists and educators have not reached a consensus on the exact nature of mathematical reasoning. Mayer (1988) asserted that we need a theory of mathematical ability, we need to know what mathematical ability is, and how to measure it. This lack of definitional consensus does not stem from a paucity of theoretical approaches. In fact, quite the opposite is true. Psychologists have been interested in and have studied mathematical abilities and achievement for at least 100 years.

During the twentieth century, studies of mathematical abilities and achievement have been conducted from a psychometric perspective (including research in education with large-scale testing); from the perspective of Gestalt psychology; from a cognitive-developmental perspective based on Piagetian, neo-Piagetian, or Vygotskian theory; and from various perspectives from modern, cognitive psychology (see Ginsburg, Klein, & Starkey, 1998 for a historical summary). Much of this work has not been concerned with sex differences and is beyond the scope of this chapter. Said another way, the study of sex differences in mathematical abilities and achievement represents a small subset of work in a much larger field. Because of the large volume of published work and this eclecticism in theoretical approaches, it is virtually impossible to present a comprehensive list of mathematical abilities. We can, however, make a few general points that will help to situate the literature on sex differences in a larger framework.

First, there is general agreement that mathematical ability is multidimensional, consisting of abilities that pertain to number, geometry, probability, and measurement. Table 6.1 presents a list of mathematical content areas and mathematical processes developed by The National Council of Teachers of Mathematics (2000). Sex differences research has not been evenly distributed across the various types of mathematical content areas and processes. For example, there has been much more work on arithmetic computation and problem solving in algebra and geometry than in statistical reasoning and proof.

Second, some mathematical abilities overlap with other cognitive abilities such as verbal, spatial, and general reasoning abilities. Relationships among cognitive abilities have been of interest to sex differences investigators. For example, Friedman (1995) presented a review of correlational studies that examined performance across measures of mathematics performance, verbal performance, and spatial performance between 1950 and 1990. In general, for both females and males alike, mathematical performance was found to be more highly correlated with verbal performance than with spatial performance. However, for students under high school age, the average difference between these correlations was found to be larger for female than for male students. In addition, Friedman (1995) reported that the correlations between mathematical and spatial performance were greater for female than for male students in moderately to highly selective samples. We review additional studies of the relationship between gender, spatial ability, and mathematical problems solving later in this chapter.

A third area of general agreement is that some forms of mathematical cognition are evident in the very early years of infancy through early childhood,

Table 6.1

Ten School-Based Standards for Mathematical Content and Mathematical Processes

Standards	
Mathematical Content	**Mathematical Processes**
Number and operation	Problem solving
Patterns, functions, and algebra	Reasoning and proof
Geometry and spatial sense	Communication
Measurement	Connections
Data analysis, statistics, and probability	Representation

Note: The standards are intended for grades K–12. The content standards are what students should know. The process standards are ways of acquiring and using knowledge.

Source: National Council of Teachers of Mathematics. (1998). *Principles and Standards for School Mathematics—Electronic Version.* Discussion Draft.

whereas other forms of mathematical cognition develop later, from middle childhood through early adulthood, and are based on these earlier forms. For example, Ginsburg et al. (1998) made a distinction between informal and formal mathematical knowledge according to whether or not the knowledge is taught in school. These authors describe forms of informal mathematical cognition that are evident in young infants and appear to be independent of language and cultural influences. Examples include early enumeration, number relations, and arithmetic reasoning. Later forms of informal mathematical thinking develop during the preschool years and are therefore influenced by language and cultural factors, even though they may not be formally taught in school. Examples include subitizing and counting and informal addition, subtraction, and division. Finally, there are mathematical processes and concepts that are taught in school, such as arithmetic computation and problem solving (Geary, 1995; Ginsburg et al., 1998).

Sex differences are more likely to be found in the later-developing forms of mathematical cognition than in the early-developing forms (Geary, 1996). As an example, consider that Piaget offered a comprehensive theory of mathematical cognition and its development that was not focused on either individual or sex differences. Piaget's research program treated logical-mathematical knowledge as a biologically based, species-wide acquisition (Piaget, 1971) and was not concerned with identification of individual differences in performance. Decades of research based on Piaget's theory examined sensorimotor, preoperational, and concrete operational abilities. This work did not reveal consistent or significant sex differences on mathematical tasks such as number conservation, transitive inference reasoning, or class inclusion. However, research did reveal sex differences on formal operational tasks that involve mathematical thinking such as proportional reasoning (Meehan, 1984).

Does the fact that sex differences in mathematical abilities and achievement are more consistently found for later-developing abilities rather than earlier-developing abilities rule out biological factors in favor of sociocultural factors as causal agents? Geary (1996) presented a theoretical model of sexual selection and sex differences in mathematical abilities that maps out contributions of, and relations between, biological and sociocultural factors. In one component of the model, for example, sexual selection is argued to have caused differences in proximate biological influences such as sex hormones. Sex hormones, in turn, are associated with sex differences in the cognitive systems that support habitat navigation (see chapter 7). Sex differences in habitat navigation, in turn, are viewed as responsible for sex differences in mathematical problem solving and geometry. In another component of Geary's (1996) model, sex differences in sex hormones are viewed as causally related to sex differences in social preferences and social styles, which, in turn, affect stereotypes and perceived competence. Differences in stereotypes and perceived competence affect sex differences in mathematics course taking and related activities, which can cause sex differences in general mathematical development. See Geary (1996, Figure 1) and the many lively commentaries this model provoked. Gallagher (1998) discusses many of these same experiential factors from a social role perspective.

Summary of Past Knowledge about the Development of Mathematical Abilities

We summarized the major findings of psychological research on sex differences in mathematical abilities and achievement as it existed in 1990. We indicated that this work is a subarea of a much larger literature on the development of mathematical abilities and achievement, much of which has been concerned with describing and explaining the course of development or the nature of individual differences in functioning. A comprehensive account of "developmental diversity" that combines insights from developmental theories such as Piaget's with psychometric accounts of individual differences, has yet to be developed (Keating, 1993). Research on sex differences might contribute to a larger, more comprehensive account, even though at present, the work is more focused on a limited range of the lifespan years (ages 6–22) and a limited number of mathematical abilities and achievements (typically, those taught in school). The next sections of this chapter present a selective review of the literature on sex differences in mathematical abilities and achievements from 1990 to early 2000.

RECENT FINDINGS ON SEX DIFFERENCES IN MATHEMATICAL ABILITIES AND ACHIEVEMENT

Early School-Based Strategies and Beliefs

Children are asked to solve addition and subtraction problems in the early elementary school grades. Such problems require children to work with symbolic representations of quantities and operations (e.g., $3 - 1 =$ __), and as such, require formal mathematical knowledge as discussed by Ginsburg et al. (1998). Carr and Jessup (1997) found gender differences in the strategies that boys and girls attempted and correctly used during the course of first grade to solve addition and subtraction problems. Gender differences in overall numbers of correct responses did not occur, but differences in strategies were evident. Boys were more likely than girls to use retrieval from memory as a solution strategy, even though their use of retrieval often led to incorrect answers early in the school year. Girls were more likely than boys to use overt algorithmic strategies (either counting on fingers or using counters) to solve problems. When children worked in mixed-gender groups, the use of retrieval increased for girls when compared to their preferred strategies when working alone. These patterns were replicated by Carr, Jessup, and Fuller (1999)—first grade boys correctly used retrieval from memory more than girls; girls correctly used overt strategies more than boys.

Boys' but not girls' strategy use was found to be correlated with their belief that adults (parents and teachers) prefer strategies that indicate mathematical ability, and was also correlated with teachers' reports of instruction on use of retrieval. Adult instruction seemed beneficial to boys' but not girls' performance.

These sex differences in strategies for solving arithmetic problems in the early elementary grades may be important in terms of the larger literature. For example, they may help to explain other recent findings that boys are faster than girls in mathematics fact retrieval by the middle elementary school grades (Royer, Tronsky, Chan, Jackson, & Marchant, III, 1999). Royer and colleagues' (1999) work is addressed in more detail in the section on advanced mathematical problem solving. The fact that first-grade girls tended to be more algorithmic in approach than boys is also consistent with findings reported by Hopkins, McGillicuddy-De Lisi, and De Lisi (1997) for third- and fifth-grade children.

Hopkins and colleagues (1997) conducted an experiment in which groups of third- and fifth-grade boys and girls, matched for arithmetic competence within grade levels, were randomly assigned to either a didactic or a constructivist teaching intervention that lasted about 30 minutes. Immediately following the teaching interventions, students completed a mathematics test that assessed addition, subtraction, multiplication, division, and dual operation problems. The test consisted of problems that were both familiar and novel in the sense that they had not yet been covered in class. As expected, fifth graders outperformed third graders, in part because more of the problems were familiar for fifth graders than third graders. A student gender × teaching condition interaction was observed. Girls in the didactic group outperformed each of the other three groups, who did not differ from each other. This interaction was reliable when performance on familiar and novel items was analyzed separately. Instruction in the use of algorithms was beneficial for girls but not for boys.

Seong, Bauer, and Sullivan (1998) analyzed grade four and six public school 1996 California Achievement Test data for the state of Louisiana in 1996. Performance of 7,000 students who scored in the top 5% according to national norms was examined. The 44-item mathematics computation test and the 50-item mathematics concepts/applications tests were analyzed for gender differences. Significant gender differences were observed on both tests at both grades. Girls outperformed boys on the computation tests; boys outperformed girls on the concepts/applications tests. This held for both black and white students. These findings for gender differences are consistent with the summary offered by Hyde, Fenemma, and Lamon (1990).

Stipek and Gralinski (1991) had third-grade and middle school students complete questionnaires related to mathematics achievement beliefs just prior to taking a test and after they received a grade on the test. Several significant gender differences were reported, but in general, girls' achievement-related beliefs were lower than boys' beliefs. At the pretest, girls rated their ability lower and expected to do less well on the test than did boys. At the posttest, girls were more likely than boys to attribute poor performance to a lack of ability and less likely to attribute success to high ability. The latter attributional findings are consistent with a larger pattern of sex differences that have been identified in many achievement domains (see Chapter 4 for related findings).

Wigfield et al. (1997) assessed changes in elementary school children's academic competence beliefs and subjective task values in reading, mathematics, music, and sports. Boys' competence beliefs were higher than girls' for mathematics, but there was no gender difference in the degree to which mathematics was valued. The fact that achievement-related beliefs show gender differences in accordance with sex-role stereotypes in the early elementary school years suggests that children are aware of and influenced by these social stereotypes. Recall the finding of Hyde and colleagues (1990) that males stereotype mathematics as a male domain to a much greater degree than females. We are not aware of any evidence that girls actually receive lower grades or tests scores than boys in elementary school. Gender differences in early achievement-related beliefs do not seem to be based on the results of classroom report card grades or from the results of standardized tests.

Summary of Recent Research Findings

In general, findings for early school-based mathematics performance conducted over the past 10 years have been consistent with prior findings. Young girls seem more cautious in their approach to arithmetic operations and also seem to have lower achievement-related beliefs than do boys. Boys appear to be more confident and willing to use direct mathematics-fact retrieval as a solution strategy for arithmetic operations. Perhaps as a result of these differences, girls may be more comfortable than boys with direct instructional approaches that teach algorithms. Performance on computational tests are likely to show small differences that favor girls over boys; performance on concepts/applications tests are likely to show small differences that favor boys over girls in terms of average scores.

Average Performance, Variability, and Extreme Performance

Sex Differences in Variability

Becker and Hedges (1988), Humphreys (1988), and Jensen (1988) discussed the implications of male student performance being more variable than female student performance with respect to interpretation of average score differences. For example, Becker and Hedges (1988) constructed hypothetical distributions to show that differences in variability can cause the large "right tail" (upper end of distribution) differences reported by Benbow (1988). This would hold for unselected populations but especially for selected populations, even though mean differences in the general population are small or even reversed to favor females. A few years later, specific data on these issues were gathered and reported by Feingold (1992), Hedges and Nowell (1995), and Willingham and Cole (1997). These studies demonstrate that a complete understanding of sex differences in mathematics (or any other measured ability) must consider not only average score differences, but also differences in variability. Each of these authors discussed performance on tests that measured several mental abilities. We focus on findings for mathematics only.

Feingold (1992) made the following key point. The statistic d is informative about sex differences at the extreme low or high end of a distribution when this mean difference is based on distributions with equal variances for females and males. (It is assumed that the variable in question is normally distributed for each sex.) In cases in which one sex is more variable and has a higher mean, then d is misleading with respect to extreme scores. For example, if male performance is higher on average and more variable than female performance, then the male advantage at the right tail is greater and the male disadvantage at the left tail is smaller than would be expected from knowledge of d alone.

Feingold (1992) examined sex differences in average performance, variability, and extreme performance on measures with national norming samples. The Differential Aptitude Tests (DAT), the Preliminary Scholastic Aptitude Test (PSAT)/Scholastic Aptitude Test (SAT), the Wechsler Adult Intelligence Scales (WAIS, WAIS-R), and the California Achievement Tests (CAT) were analyzed. For each test, variance ratios (male variance divided by female variance) were computed for different points in time and/or different aged participants. Feingold (1992) found greater male than female variability on each of the mathematics tests examined. On the PSAT-M and SAT-M for example, the average male to female variance ratios were 1.20 (i.e., 1:20 to 1:00) and 1.24, respectively. In contrast, the variance ratios were 1.05 for PSAT-V and SAT-V. In addition, the higher variance ratios observed were generally constant across the time periods examined. These findings reveal that male performance is more variable than female performance on tests of mathematical ability and achievement even when based on national norming samples. Feingold then showed how this difference in variability would render average score difference estimates (d) misleading, especially at the lower and upper ends of score distributions.

Extreme Score Differences

Hedges and Friedman (1993) reanalyzed Feingold's (1992) data to present both the tail effect sizes for gender differences and the ratios of males to females at various points in the tails. For example, on the SAT-M, the average score $d = 0.42$ but d's at the 0.90, 0.95, and 0.999 right tail points, respectively are 0.30, 0.29, and 0.25. Thus, all measures of effect size favor males over females but would be considered small in magnitude. However, as a result of greater male variability and an average score difference in favor of males, Hedges and Friedman (1993) showed that there are many more males than females in the upper score ranges. At 0.90, 0.95, and 0.999, the male/female upper tail ratios for these respective points are: 2.63, 3.39, and 12.45. Thus, there are more than 12 male students for every female student in the upper 0.1% of the SAT-M distribution analyzed by Feingold (1992). On the Arithmetic subtest of the WAIS, the overall $d = 0.34$, and the d's at the 0.90, 0.95, and 0.999 right tail points, respectively, are 0.26, 0.25, and 0.22. However, the male/female ratios for these three upper tail points are 2.22, 2.74, and 8.21.

Feingold (1992) and Hedges and Friedman (1993) showed that small mean differences favoring males coupled with greater male variability can lead to large differences in the numbers of males and females whose scores are indicative of high mathematical ability or talent. Hedges and Nowell (1995) lent increasing support to this interpretation by analyzing sex differences on assessments that used representative samples of national populations. These authors asserted that meta-analyses of studies based on highly select samples, or on convenient, nonrepresentative samples may not be any more representative of the general population than the individual studies on which they are based. Even Feingold's (1992) study, which examined tests using norming samples, may not be representative of the general population. Hedges and Nowell (1995) reanalyzed the results of six national surveys conducted between 1960 and 1992. These assessments included students and nonstudents from grade 8 to age 22. For the mathematics components of these surveys, the standardized mean differences (d) were small, ranging from 0.03 to 0.26. Variance ratios ranged from 1.05 to 1.25. Sex differences in tail ratios of males to females at the top 5% ranged from 1.50 to 2.34. Sex differences in tail ratios at the bottom 10% ranged from 0.72 to 1.00 (i.e., more females than males were in the lower tails). These differences in average scores and in variances did not vary systematically with year of assessment.

For example, on the Project Talent mathematics (total) scale, the male/female ratio was 1.3 for scores in the upper 10%, 1.5 in the top 5%, 2.1 in the top 3%, and 7.0 in the top 1% of the overall distribution. When one sex has both higher average scores and is more variable, sex ratios get higher as one moves toward the upper end of the right tail of the distribution. Hedges and Nowell (1995) maintained that this evidence helps to resolve an apparent contradiction between the high ratios of males to females in highly talented samples (such as studied by Benbow, 1988) and the generally small mean differences found between the sexes in relatively unselected samples. They found that differences in the upper end of a distribution get larger with nationally representative samples. Therefore, the high sex ratios found in some highly talented samples need not be attributed to differential selection by sex. Hedges and Nowell (1995) concluded that these results might help to explain the rather large sex differences in advanced training and in occupations that require high levels of mathematical ability. Their findings serve to qualify conclusions about minimal sex differences in mathematics reached in the late 1980s and early 1990s based on summaries of average score differences alone.

Other investigators have also found differences in variability and/or in extreme scores favoring males over females in mathematical ability and achievement. For example, Robinson, Abbott, Berninger, and Busse (1996) asked parents of preschoolers and kindergarten children to nominate their child for a study of mathematically gifted children (if the parent believed the nomination to be appropriate). Initial screening using arithmetic subtests of standardized IQ tests identified a sample for further study (55% were boys) on 15 additional measures. After screening conducted by the investigators, boys scored significantly higher than girls on 8 of 11 quantitative measures. Multiple measures of counting, arithmetic, and problem solving were used. Boys were over-represented in the group that scored in the top 3% to 8% on the various tests. Specifically, boys accounted for between 71% and 100% of those who scored near the top 5% on the various mathematics tests. Thus, the ratio of boys to girls at the upper end of the distribution was quite extreme in this sample of young, gifted children. This extends the conclusions reached by Hedges and Nowell (1995) concerning differences in upper tail ratios favoring males, to a sample of young children.

Stumpf and Stanley (1996) analyzed gender differences in participation, average scores, and extreme scores on Advanced Placement and SAT achievement examinations for cohorts in the early to mid-1980s and in 1992. For two Advanced Placement Calculus tests and two SAT mathematics achievement tests, the percentages of female participants increased over time and equaled 55% for one achievement test and about 45% for each of the other three tests. Average score gender differences favoring males were evident on all four tests and changed little over time. The differences on advanced placement tests (d's = 0.17 and 0.26) were smaller than differences on the achievement tests (d's = 0.37 and 0.42 in 1992). More female students than male students had extremely low scores (defined as a score of "1" on the advanced placement exams and a score range of 200–290 on the achievement tests); more male students than female students had extremely high scores (defined as a score of "5" on the advanced placement exams and a score range of 700–800 on the achievement tests). These lower and upper tail ratio scores were also stable over time. In 1992, the lower tail ratios ranged from 1.17 to 2.31 (more females with lower scores); the upper tail ratios ranged from 1.43 to 2.52 (more males with high scores). These 1992 test score data were based on overall N's that ranged from 15,000 to 128,000 participants. These findings are consistent with one of the patterns discussed by Feingold (1992). Small differences in average scores coupled with greater male variability led to fewer male students in the extreme left tails but more male students in the extreme right tails of distributions. Stumpf and Stanley (1996) noted that gender differences were usually smaller on advanced placement as opposed to achievement tests and discussed item format (free response versus multiple choice) as a possible explanation.

Willingham and Cole (1997) presented test data that replicated these general patterns. Average score sex differences are generally small when tests of mathematical concepts and reasoning are based on nationally representative samples but male performance is more variable than female performance. As a result, when average score differences favor male students, the ratio of male to female students increases as one approaches the upper ends of distributions. "The relationship between [average score differences and standard deviation ratios] is troubling because it indicates a tendency for greater male representation among the better prepared students than one would expect from looking at overall test score means based on representative national samples" (p. 69). Willingham and Cole (1997) showed that for tests of mathematical achievement and ability, the gender difference in variability increased from grade 4 to grade 8 to grade 12. (See Beller & Gafni, 1996 for an international study in which age trends in variability from 9 to 13 years of age were found to vary by country.) The net effect of this change, coupled with slight increases in mean score differences, created dramatic differences in the ratios of males to females in the top 10% on the mathematics tests examined (Willingham & Cole, 1997, p. 82).

Bielinski and Davison (1998) made an interesting prediction about gender differences in mathematics achievement for situations in which there are no gender difference in average scores ($d = 0$) but males are more variable than females. These situations result in proportionally more males than females at the upper *and* lower tails of the distribution, and more females than males at the center of the distribution. For these situations, Bielinski and Davison (1998) predicted that a gender × item-difficulty interaction should be found. Specifically, they predicted that female and male participants should evidence differential patterns of performance on easy versus hard items. Easy items should be easier for females than for males; hard items should be harder for females than for males. The classification of items as easy or hard is based on the performance of all participants, females and males combined.

This prediction was tested in two studies that examined the scores of representative samples of eighth and ninth grade students on pilot and field tests of a state minimum competency assessment in mathematics. These tests were designed to assess competencies in mathematics skills deemed essential for all high school graduates. Items emphasized application of mathematical concepts to real-life contexts. In both studies, overall mean scores did not differ significantly by gender, d's were close to 0, but males were more variable than females (variance ratios around 1.20 to 1.36). Some gender differences were observed on subtests, but these were in accordance with predictions. For subtests with higher overall scores, that is, easier items, female students scored higher than male students. Male students scored higher than female students on the subtests with lower overall scores. The correlation between overall item difficulty and differences in difficulty for male versus female students was significant. Bielinski and Davison (1998) concluded that there may be subtle shifts in the ability being measured as items become more difficult which resulted in the observed gender × item-difficulty interaction. Specifically, easy items may require abilities for which female students are advantaged; difficult items may require abilities for which male students are advantaged. The authors also reasoned that when mathematical concepts are first introduced, male students should outperform female students, but once the concept becomes routine, the advantage shifts to female students. If we assume that students must manipulate information to solve new problems but can retrieve information from memory to solve routine problems, this prediction is consistent with Halpern's (1997) summary of cognitive sex differences.

Summary and Implications of Research on Test Performance

When mathematical abilities are assessed via paper-and-pencil tests and nationally representative samples are observed, male performance tends to be more variable than female performance. This difference in variability is found even on tests (such as mathematics computation) for which average score differences favor females (Willingham & Cole, 1997). When samples become more selective and/or average score differences favor males over females, the variability difference leads to greater proportions of males among high scorers relative to females. This difference in variability has not changed substantially over the past 40 years. The sex difference in variability may increase from middle childhood to the end of secondary school. Summaries of sex differences in mathematics performance need to include information about variability of female and male participants along with reports of standardized average score differences. Because of differences in variability, sex of student may interact with item characteristics to change the nature of the ability being measured on specific items. None of the studies reviewed previously was designed to explain why male performance might be more variable than female performance, although possibilities were discussed by the authors. It is important to note that males were found to be more variable than females on a variety of tests covering the full range of school achievement/ability areas. Thus, the explanation for greater male variability in mathematics performance is likely to be part of a more complete account of greater male variability across many domains.

High School and College Mathematics Courses

Enrollment Patterns

Using the National Assessment of Educational Progress (NAEP) data, Davenport, Jr., Davison, Kuang, Ding, Kim, and Kwak (1998) examined the transcripts of over 23,000 students who graduated from U.S. high schools in 1990 for sex differences in mathematical course enrollment. Over all types of mathematics course, male students completed 3.13 total Carnegie Units (CUs) and female students completed 3.08 CUs. This difference was not significant, the effect size was 0.01 and the male to female ratio was 1.02. A few significant differences were obtained when specific types and sequences of mathematics courses were examined. The largest difference was enrollment in the "Standard" mathematics, college preparatory sequence. The effect size in favor of females was –0.11 and the male to female ratio was 0.93. Males were enrolled in "Functional" and "Basic" sequences more than females; males were also enrolled in "Advanced" sequences more than females. The effect sizes for these differences were less than 0.10.

Snyder and Hoffman (2000, Table 141) report percentages of male and female high school graduates in 1998 who completed various mathematics courses. The percentage differences by sex are small. For example, 11.2% of male students took calculus and 7.3% took AP calculus. For female students, the comparable percentages were 10.6% and 6.4%. Dwyer and Johnson (1997) report that fewer female students than male students take honors courses in high school but the ratio is very close, about 0.95. These data came from students who completed the 1993 SAT examinations. Recall that participation in the 1992 AP and SAT II mathematics testing ranged from 45% to 55% female (Stumpf & Stanley, 1996). These percentages for test taking are consistent with patterns of minimal gender differences in course enrollments. Taken together, these results indicate that sex differences in high school mathematics enrollment are either very small or non-existent. A similar conclusion was reached by Royer et al. (1999) based on a review of two additional recent studies.

Grades in Mathematics Courses

Dwyer and Johnson (1997) analyzed high school GPAs for 1992 ACT test takers. They found that standardized mean differences favoring females ranged from slightly below 0 to –0.10 for American Indian, white, and black participants for mathematics courses. Among Mexican Americans, other Hispanic, and Asian American groups, differences of similar magnitudes favoring males were observed. This evidence suggests that male and female students differ very little in terms of the grades they receive in high school mathematics courses. Voyer (1996) studied the relationship between gender, mathematics achievement, and spatial ability. College students reported their overall grades for high school mathematics courses. In two studies, significant gender differences favoring female students in self-reported grades occurred. The magnitude of this gender difference in grades favoring female students increased when spatial ability scores were partialled out statistically.

Grades and Test Performance

Of special interest is the pattern of sex differences in mathematics course grades and on mathematics test scores in the same participants. That is, the focus is on performance when students completed the same mathematics classes and took the same ability or achievement tests. The overall pattern is that male students outperform female students on tests such as the SAT-M, but that female students attain equal or higher GPAs than the male students. For example, data presented by Wainer and Steinberg (1992), and then reanalyzed by Bridgeman and Lewis (1996), showed that at comparable score ranges on the SAT-M (for example, scoring over 700), female students had slightly higher average calculus grades in college than did male students. When taken the other way, male students were advantaged on test scores given comparable classroom grades. For example, males with an "A" course grade had higher SAT-M scores than females with an "A" average. Benbow (1992) reported that youth observed in the Study of Mathematically Precocious Youth (SMPY) who were followed longitudinally into high school showed a difference favoring female students in course grades and classroom honors but a male advantage on standardized tests.

Snyder and Hoffman (2000, Table 128) reported similar patterns from NAEP results from 1978 to 1996. Mathematics test performance of 17-year-old students examined in relation to highest mathematics course taken, show that at each level of mathematics course taking, males earned slightly higher test scores than females. Dwyer and Johnson (1997) showed that "tests higher than grades" is typically true of male students whereas "grades higher than tests" is typically true of female students. The differential sex difference pattern found for course grades versus standardized tests holds for most academic subject areas, not just mathematics. For example, in writing, females students outperform male students in both course grades and tests, but the differential is greater for course grades than for tests. As was the case for sex differences in variability, a complete explanation of the sex difference in grades versus tests may have to appeal to a wider class of factors than just those that pertain to mathematics alone.

High School Performance: Summary and Implications

When they finish high school, boys and girls complete just about the same number of mathematics courses. Boys are slightly overrepresented in the bottom and top mathematics courses, girls are slightly overrepresented in the college preparatory mathematics sequences, but each of these differences is small. Girls get slightly better grades in high school (and college) mathematics classes than boys, but attain slightly lower average scores on mathematical ability and achievement tests. This pattern is true for most academic subject areas, not just mathematics. If test score differences are to be explained by differences in experience, counting the number and type of courses taken is unlikely to be a powerful explanation. It is possible that boys have more mathematically related experiences outside of school, which could account for test score differences, but it is not clear how such a differences would also lead boys to have either the same or lower grades in school (Royer et al., 1999). Further analysis of what standardized tests such as the SAT-M and the Graduate Record Examination-Quantitative (GRE-Q) require may help to explain this puzzle.

Advanced Mathematical Problem Solving

Sex differences on tests such as the SAT-M and the GRE-Q, considered to assess advanced mathematical problem solving and reasoning, have been intensively investigated in the past 10 years. This research has been conducted in laboratories using disclosed test items and experimental manipulations, and has also examined correlates and predictors of actual test scores. In much of this research, statistical techniques such as partial correlations, multiple regressions, or path analyses have been used. These techniques often show that the significant association between sex of subject and test performance is reduced to nonsignificant levels when additional intervening variables that are also related to sex of subject and test performance are taken into account. In reviewing this work as follows, we comment on the extent to which findings for sex differences on the SAT-M and GRE-Q can also account for findings that female students either outperform or perform at similar levels as male students in high school and college mathematics courses.

Problem Solving Processes and Strategies

Byrnes and Takahira (1993) proposed a general cognitive processing model to describe how students derive a correct answer on SAT-M problems. The model included the following six steps:

1. correctly define the problem,
2. access prior knowledge,
3. assemble an effective strategy,
4. perform error-free computations,
5. avoid misleading alternatives, and
6. execute steps 1–5 in one minute or less.

The authors observed high school juniors and seniors on five disclosed SAT-M items. The major result of this study was that students' strategy scores (step 3) and prior knowledge scores (step 2) accounted for about 50% of the variance on the 5-item test. Once these variables were accounted for, sex of the participant accounted for almost no variability in performance. It is important to note that sex differences were not significant on the prior knowledge and strategy assessments. However, when male students had the requisite prior knowledge and assembled the correct strategy, they were correct 91% of the time. For female students, the same conditional probability of success was only 72%. Thus, something other than prior knowledge and effective strategies affect female student performance more than male student performance. The authors speculated that differences in step (5), avoiding misleading alternatives, might be responsible. It is possible that classroom tests contain fewer effective misleading alternatives than SAT-M tests, and that classroom tests are not as speeded (step 6), which could account for the discrepancy in sex differences across testing and classroom contexts.

Low and Over (1993) studied Australian tenth and eleventh graders on algebra word problems that varied with respect to whether they contained sufficient, irrelevant, or missing information needed for solution. Girls were less likely than boys to identify missing or irrelevant information within problems, even though overall mathematical ability was controlled. More girls than boys perceived irrelevant information within the text of a problem as being necessary for solution. Although girls were as able as boys to solve algebraic word problems containing sufficient information, they had lower solution rates than did boys on problems containing irrelevant information because they more often incorporated irrelevant information into their attempted solutions. Low and Over (1993) concluded that there was a sex difference in knowledge of problem structure. Presumably, this would relate to the first three steps in Byrnes and Takahira's (1993) general model of mathematics problem solving.

Gallagher and De Lisi (1994) and Gallagher, De Lisi, Holst, McGillicuddy-De Lisi, Morely, and Cahalan (2000) studied sex differences in SAT-M problem solving via an analysis of the types of general strategies that could be used to generate answers. SAT-M problems were classified as conventional if they could be solved by algorithmic methods, which included use of a computational approach taught in school, assigning values to variables to generate a solution, or plugging in options. SAT-M problems were classified as unconventional if they could be solved by an insightful use of an algorithm, or by logic or by estimation. Other possible strategies included guessing, misinterpreting a problem, omitting a problem, or using a solution that could not be classified. Gallagher and De Lisi (1994) observed high school students who had scored 650 or higher on a recent administration of the SAT-M as they solved a set of difficult conventional and unconventional SAT-M problems. The students verbalized their solution strategies while solving. Female students had a higher percentage correct than male students had on conventional problems; male students had a higher percentage correct than females on unconventional problems. Female students were more likely than male students to use algorithmic solutions on conventional problems; male students were more likely than female students to use insightful solutions on unconventional problems. Students' SAT-M scores were found to be positively correlated with positive attitudes towards mathematics. Use of conventional solutions was found to correlate with negative attitudes toward mathematics.

These results were replicated and extended by Gallagher and colleagues (2000). The ability to correctly solve conventional problems with algorithmic solutions and unconventional problems with insightful solutions was found to favor males students in a high ability sample (Study 1) and in a sample of the full range of abilities (Study 2). It was also found that as ability level increased, the use of guessing, omission, and misinterpretation of problems decreased. Students' favored approach, however, was to use algorithms, even when given additional time to generate solutions. Use of logic, estimation, or insight to solve unconventional problems was infrequent for students in the below-average to average ability range. In Study 3, GRE-Q test score results were examined. Sex of subject by item type interactions were predicted and observed for several samples of examinees. Male students had a greater advantage on unconventional ("male favored") items than they had on conventional ("female favored") items.

Gallagher and De Lisi (1994) and Gallagher et al. (2000) maintained that their findings could account for the sex difference in grades versus tests. Classroom tests are more likely to require solution methods that are taught. Tests such as the SAT-M and GRE-Q contain many of these same types of items but also contain a significant proportion of items that are novel and require nonalgorithmic solutions (especially given the timed nature of the test). Male students may be more confident in their own ability in the testing context to try novel approaches. Female students may be "better" students and attempt to apply teacher-taught algorithmic methods even in situations for which this is not the optimal approach.

Mathematics Fact Retrieval

Royer et al. (1999) proposed that differences in mathematics fact retrieval comprise the cognitive mechanism that underlies sex differences in mathematics performance. They proposed that males are more likely than females to develop the ability to rapidly and automatically retrieve correct answers to addition, subtraction, multiplication, and division problems. They also proposed that differences in mathematics fact retrieval that emerge in elementary school provide a basis for later-developing mathematical competencies. They called this a "funnel effect." The idea is that being advantaged in mathematics fact retrieval leads to an advantage in present learning and that this advantage grows or widens over time. In a series of nine studies, Royer et al. (1999) showed that speed of mathematics fact retrieval was associated with differences in performance on mathematics tests that measured problem solving (not just computation) for students in elementary school and college. In the latter study, differences in mathematics fact retrieval measured in college accounted for around 20% of the variance in SAT-M scores (taken in high school). The authors also reported a slight male versus female student advantage in speed of math-fact retrieval at the high end in the middle elementary school years. Differences in out-of-school experiences, coupled with the tendency for male students to be more variable with respect to engagement in schooling tasks, were argued to be responsible for the patterns observed. Differences in math-fact retrieval are probably not that relevant for school tests, but could be very relevant for speeded tests such as the SAT-M. Thus, sex differences in math-fact retrieval could account for the sex differences in grades versus tests in mathematics.

Spatial Ability

Casey, Nuttall, Pezaris, and Benbow (1995) and Casey, Nuttall, and Pezaris (1997) investigated relationships between mental rotation scores and SAT-M scores in various samples of female and male students. In the 1995 study, mental rotation and SAT-V scores were investigated in relation to SAT-M scores in four samples: college students, 13-year-old students who participated in SMPY, and a low- and a high-ability high school sample, for which ability was defined in terms of SAT-V scores. In the 1997 study, mental rotation, SAT-V scores, math anxiety, math self-confidence, and geometry grades were investigated in relation to SAT-M scores for the same high-ability sample studied 2 years earlier. With the effects due to SAT-V scores accounted for statistically, mental rotation was found to be a significant predictor of SAT-M scores for all four samples of females students and for the two samples of high school male students. Male students had higher SAT-M and mental rotation scores than female students in all but the low-ability high school sample. Two of the three SAT-M differences that favored male students were no longer significant when mental rotation scores were covaried statistically. (When mental rotation scores were adjusted for SAT-M scores, all three sex differences favoring male students remained significant.) Casey et al. (1995) concluded that mental rotation is a key mediator of the gender-SAT-M relationship. Casey et al. (1997) provided additional support for this conclusion. They found that high mathematics self-confidence was also a significant predictor of SAT-M scores, but mental rotation accounted for about twice as much variance as self confidence in explaining the gender-SAT-M relationship. However, this pattern only held for the high-ability high school sample; it did not hold for the low-ability high school sample in which SAT-V and geometry grades were the only significant predictors of SAT-M scores.

Geary, Saults, Liu, and Hoard (2000) administered tests of arithmetic computation, arithmetic reasoning, mental rotation, and general IQ (Ravens Progressive Matrices) to male and female college students. In support of both Royer et al. (1999) and Casey et al. (1995, 1997), they found that both mental rotation and arithmetic computation scores predicted performance on the arithmetic reasoning test even when IQ was statistically controlled. Arithmetic computational fluency accounted for more variance in arithmetic reasoning scores than did mental rotation. Once again, although sex of the participant was associated with differences in mental rotation and arithmetic computation, it was not associated with differences in arithmetic reasoning when the latter two factors were accounted for.

Stereotypes and Beliefs

Steele (1997) argued that stereotype threat undermines the performance of student groups in particular academic domains when a negative stereotype about the group's performance in that domain exists. The effects of stereotype threat on women's mathematical problems solving performance were investigated by Spencer, Steele, and Quinn (1999) and by Brown and Josephs (1999). Spencer et al. (1999) administered GRE mathematics items to groups of college students who participated in different experimental conditions. In one condition, an explicit reference to the fact that this test had not produced gender differences was provided. In other conditions, gender differences were either not mentioned or explicitly mentioned for this test. The test items were identical across conditions. The hypothesized sex of student by test condition interaction occurred in each of three studies. In conditions for which the stereotype threat was expected to be operative, women performed significantly worse than all other groups. In other words, male and female performance was not different in the condition in which "no gender differences" were found, but favored males in the other conditions. Spencer et al. (1999) could not pinpoint the cause of the decrement in performance associated with stereotype threat.

Brown and Josephs (1999) built on the notion of stereotype threat by hypothesizing that males and females would have different mathematics performance concerns that would have an effect on performance in specific circumstances. Specifically, women were expected to be concerned about, and do less well in, situations in which they might be shown to be weak in mathematical problem solving. Men were expected to be concerned about, and do less well in, situations in which they might be shown to not have high mathematics ability. Women would not be concerned about, and would not have performance decrements in, situations designed to assess high levels of problem solving ability. Men would not be concerned about, and would not have performance decrements in, situations designed to assess low levels of problem solving ability. The hypothesized sex of subject × test condition interaction was obtained in three separate studies in which college students completed GRE-Q test items under different conditions.

In Study 1, the important findings were within-sex condition effects such that women in the "measure of low ability" condition scored lower than women in the "measure of high ability" condition; whereas men in the "measure of high ability" condition scored lower than men in the "measure of low ability" condition. In Study 2, all participants were told that they were being screened for low ability, but half were given an external handicap to excuse poor performance and half were not. Women in the handicap condition were expected to outperform women in the no-handicap condition because the handicap should alleviate concerns about conforming to the stereotype. Because men are not concerned about being exposed for low ability in mathematics, their performance was not expected to vary across conditions. The results of Study 2 were consistent with these predictions. In Study 3, all participants were told that they were being screened for high ability; again, half were given an external handicap to excuse poor performance and half were not. Now men's performance was expected to vary across conditions because men are concerned about not showing high levels of ability. Women's performance was not expected to vary with condition. The results of Study 3 were consistent with these predictions. Brown and Josephs (1999) concluded that gender differences favoring males on mathematical problem solving may be especially evident in "high-stakes" situations. Further studies are needed to demonstrate what role, if any, stereotype threat plays in the performance of female and male students in mathematics courses in high school and college classrooms.

Shih, Pittinsky, and Ambady (1999) replicated and extended the effect of stereotype threat on mathematical performance. These authors observed performance on a 12-item, 20-minute mathematical reasoning test in conditions in which different social identities were activated prior to test completion. Participants were Asian-American female students. Prior to testing, one-third of the sample answered questions designed to activate their Asian identity, one-third answered questions designed to activate their identities as females, and one-third answered questions that did not activate any social identity. In Study 1, U.S. college students who had averaged 750 on the SAT-M participated. Because the United States has a stereotype that Asian Americans are good in mathematics, it was expected that students in the Asian-identity condition would outperform the control condition, who in turn should outperform the female-identity condition. In Study 2, Canadian high school students participated. Because the stereotype about Asian-Americans and mathematics is not as salient in Canada, the female-identity condition was expected to underperform relative to the other two groups. These predictions were upheld in the results of the experiments. The authors also reported that in Study 1, measures of motivation, liking the test, self assessments of performance, assessment of test difficulty, and self-assessment in mathematics did not differ by condition, despite the differences in levels of accuracy on the test. Shih et al. (1999) showed that activation of self-identities without explicit reference to stereotypes could have an effect on mathematical problem solving performance. Moreover, they showed that performance could be enhanced as well as decreased by this manipulation.

In the section on early school-based strategies and beliefs, it was reported that boys have higher achievement-related beliefs than girls in elementary school. Pajares and Miller (1994) examined the effects of self-efficacy and self-concept beliefs in college student performance on a mathematical problem-solving test designed to be of moderate difficulty for college students. Mathematics self-efficacy (beliefs about what one can do) was found to be predictive of performance on the test to a greater degree than mathematics self-concept and perceived usefulness of mathematics. Gender differences in self-efficacy favoring men accounted for differences in performance on the test and for differences in self-concept. Self-evaluations of competence were predictive of performance and men had higher self-evaluations than women.

Summary and Implications of Explanatory Processes

The recent research just reviewed offers several competing explanations for the sex difference favoring males on tests of advanced mathematical problems solving such as the SAT-M and the GRE-Q. If spatial ability or mathematics fact retrieval are the key mechanisms responsible for overall differences, then it would seem that studies of performance on items with high versus low spatial demands and high versus low mathematics fact demands would need to be conducted. Ability group (e.g., high–low spatial ability) by item type (e.g., high–low spatial processing demands) interactions would add further credence to these cognitive factors as explanatory variables. Such effects should occur within and well as between sex of subject groups. If female and male students differ in terms of problem-solving strategies, then it would be important to find out when and how these differences arise. Similar to the studies of spatial ability and mathematics fact retrieval, studies of problem-solving strategies have helped to pinpoint exactly where sex differences in performance are to be expected. Finally, recent findings concerning the effects of stereotype threat could radically reshape this whole area of inquiry. If mathematical performance within subjects can be found to vary to a great degree by manipulation of the context of test administration, our whole notion of how mathematical problem-solving ability is measured may need to be reexamined.

CONCLUSION

Research conducted over the past 10 years sharpened the picture of sex differences in mathematical abilities and achievement. Sex differences in mathematical problem solving strategies can be observed very early in children's academic careers. These differences in strategies for solving arithmetic problems do not necessarily lead to differences in performance on tests, but may lay the foundation for sex differences in mathematical problem solving that persist over time. Consider the similarity between first-grade girls' use of algorithmic strategies to solve arithmetic problems with high school female students' use of algorithmic strategies on the SAT-M. In both cases, getting the right answer seems to be paramount. No one would question that year after year of mathematics instruction serves to reinforce the importance of getting the correct answer. In other words, if girls do have an early tendency to be perfectionists, this approach is unlikely to be contradicted by their classroom teachers. On average then, girls do well in situations in which mathematical problem solving parameters have been clearly defined. Girls are underserved by their classroom experiences, however, in situations that call for novel approaches to mathematical problems solving.

Next consider the similarity between first-grade boys' use of covert retrieval to solve arithmetic problems with high school male students' use of logical-intuitive strategies on the SAT-M. In both cases, it takes confidence in one's ability to use a strategy that has a greater degree of uncertainty. Boys' general approach is more likely to be contradicted by their classroom teachers who will insist that certain methods of solution be learned and followed in order to derive the correct answers to problems. On average then, boys will do less well than girls in situations in which mathematical problem solving parameters have been clearly defined, but somewhat better than girls in situations that call for novel approaches to problem solving. We are suggesting that boys persist with novel, less certain approaches to mathematical problem solving in spite of classroom demands to use algorithmic approaches. Students who are comfortable with both algorithmic and insightful approaches to problem solving are surely better prepared than students who are only comfortable with one of these two general approaches.

Direct connections between problem solving approaches in elementary school and high school have not yet been demonstrated in research studies. The previous suggestions, therefore, should be understood to be highly speculative at this time. Research that examines sex differences in mathematical problem solving in the later elementary and middle school years could shed light on this important question. How boys and girls "experience" mathematics instruction would seem to be a particularly important area of study because overall differences in number and type of classroom experiences have been found to be small in the past 10 years.

Even if these conjectures are accurate, continued study of the "average" boy or girl may not be the best approach. It now seems fairly well established that the performance of males is more variable than the performance of females in a variety of academic domains. In a given classroom then, a girl chosen at random is more likely to approximate the "average" girl than is a boy chosen at random likely to approximate the "average" boy. What about boys and girls who deviate from the average and perform at extremely high or low levels? We have learned more about the high-ability problem solver in the past decade. This problem solver is more likely to be a male than a female, especially as we move from the top 5% to the top 0.1% of the score distribution. This problem solver is more flexible in approaches to problems. This flexibility may stem from the ability to more rapidly retrieve mathematics facts, higher levels of spatial ability, and less concern for "looking bad." We know very little about the problem-solving approaches used by students, especially male students, who are at the lower end of the ability distribution. The focus on identifying top talent is important for students and society as a whole. More information is now needed, however, to assist those at the opposite end of the ability distribution. There may be sex differences in the problem-solving approaches of low-ability students that would lead to differential interventions to enhance girls' versus boys' learning and achievement.

It is unlikely that research is ever going to provide definitive answers to the "ultimate" causes of sex differences in mathematical abilities and achievement. To show that performance is a function of biological factors does not eliminate experiential factors as playing either a prior or a subsequent causal role as well.

Similarly, to show that experiential factors are causal agents does not eliminate biological factors as playing either a prior or a subsequent causal role as well. This is one of the major points of the chapter on spatial abilities by Newcombe, Mathason, and Terlecki (chapter 7)—as psychologists and educators it is of interest to study the extent to which performance can be modified through interventions. In the United States at this time, any such research must take place in a context in which mathematics is not only an integral part of the formal preschool through grade 12 curriculum, but is also examined on state-wide or national examinations. These high-stakes examinations are supposed to provide additional checks on classroom instruction and student learning. This system has led to a slight advantage for girls in the classroom but an advantage for boys on high stakes tests. Recent findings reviewed in this chapter might lead to additional work that can eliminate this sex-difference discrepancy between classroom grades and tests for mathematics performance.

REFERENCES

Becker, B. J., & Hedges, L. V. (1988). The effects of selection and variability in studies of gender differences. *Behavioral and Brain Sciences, 11,* 183–184.

Beller, M., & Gafni, N. (1996). The 1991 International Assessment of Educational Progress in Mathematics and Science: The gender differences perspective. *Journal of Educational Psychology, 88,* 365–377.

Benbow, C. P. (1988). Sex differences in mathematical reasoning ability in intellectually talented preadolescents: Their nature, effects, and possible causes. *Behavioral and Brain Sciences, 11,* 169–232.

Benbow, C. P. (1992). Academic achievement in mathematics and science of students between ages 13 and 23: Are there differences among students in the top one percent of mathematical ability? *Journal of Educational Psychology, 84,* 51–61.

Bielinski, J., & Davison, M. L. (1998). Gender differences by item difficulty interactions in multiple-choice mathematics items. *American Educational Research Journal, 35,* 455–476.

Bridgeman, B., & Lewis, C. (1996). Gender differences in college mathematics grades and SAT-M scores: A reanalysis of Wainer and Steinberg. *Journal of Educational Measurement, 33,* 257–270.

Brown, R. P., & Josephs, R. A. (1999). A burden of proof. Stereotype relevance and gender differences in math performance. *Journal of Personality and Social Psychology, 76,* 246–257.

Byrnes, J. P., & Takahira, S. (1993). Explaining gender differences on SAT-Math items. *Developmental Psychology, 29,* 805–810.

Carr, M., & Jessup, D. L. (1997). Gender differences in first-grade mathematics strategy use: Social and metacognitive influences. *Journal of Educational Psychology, 89,* 318–328.

Carr, M., Jessup, D. L., & Fuller, D. (1999). Gender differences in first-grade mathematics strategy use: Parent and teacher contributions. *Journal for Research in Mathematics Education, 30,* 20–46.

Casey, M. B., Nuttall, R. L., & Pezaris, E. (1997). Mediators of gender differences in mathematics college entrance test scores: A comparison of spatial skills with internalized beliefs and anxieties. *Developmental Psychology, 33,* 669–680.

Casey, M. B., Nuttall, R., Pezaris, E., & Benbow, C. P. (1995). The influence of spatial ability on gender differences in mathematics college entrance test scores across diverse samples. *Developmental Psychology, 31,* 697–705.

Davenport, Jr., E. C., Davison, M. L., Kuang, H., Ding, S., Kim, S-K, & Kwak, N. (1998). High school mathematics course-taking by gender and ethnicity. *American Educational Research Journal, 35,* 497–514.

Dwyer, C. A., & Johnson, L. M. (1997). Grades, accomplishments, and correlates. In W. W. Willingham & N. S. Cole (Eds.), *Gender and fair assessment* (pp. 127–156). Mahwah, NJ: Lawrence Erlbaum Associates.

Feingold, A. (1992). Sex differences in variability in intellectual abilities : A new look at an old controversy. *Review of Educational Research, 62,* 61–84.

Friedman, L. (1995). The space factor in mathematics: Gender differences. *Review of Educational Research, 65,* 22–50.

Gallagher, A. (1998). Gender and antecedents of performance in mathematics testing. *Teachers College Record, 100,* 297–314.

Gallagher, A. M., & De Lisi, R. (1994). Gender differences in scholastic aptitude test-mathematics problem solving among high ability students. *Journal of Educational Psychology, 86,* 204–211.

Gallagher, A. M., De Lisi, R., Holst, P. C., McGillicuddy-De Lisi, A. V., Morely, M., & Cahalan, C. (2000). Gender differences in advanced mathematical problem solving. *Journal of Experimental Child Psychology, 75,* 165–190.

Geary, D. C. (1995). Reflections of evolution and culture in children's cognition. Implications for mathematical development and instruction. *American Psychologist, 50,* 24–37.

Geary, D. C. (1996). Sexual selection and sex differences in mathematical abilities. *Behavioral and Brain Sciences, 19,* 229–284.

Geary, D. C., Saults, S. J., Liu, F., & Hoard, M. K. (2000). Sex differences in spatial cognition, computational fluency, and arithmetical reasoning. *Journal of Experimental Child Psychology, 77,* 337–353.

Ginsburg, H. P., Klein, A., & Starkey, P. (1998). The development of children's mathematical thinking: Connecting research with practice. In W. Damon (Series Ed.) & I. E. Sigel & K. A. Renninger (Vol. Eds.), *Handbook of child psychology: Vol. 4. Child psychology in practice* (5th ed., pp. 401–476). New York: Wiley.

Halpern, D. F. (1997). Sex differences in intelligence. Implications for education. *American Psychologist, 52,* 1091–1102.

Hedges, L. V., & Friedman, L. (1993). Gender differences in variability in intellectual abilities: A reanalysis of Feingold's results. *Review of Educational Research, 63,* 94–105.

Hedges, L. V., & Nowell, A. (1995). Sex differences in mental test scores, variability, and numbers of high-scoring individuals. *Science, 269,* 41–45.

Hopkins, K. B., McGillicuddy-De Lisi, A. V., & De Lisi, R. (1997). Student gender and teaching methods as sources of variability in children's computational arithmetic performance. *Journal of Genetic Psychology, 158,* 333–345.

Humphreys, L. G. (1988). Sex differences in variability may be more important than sex differences in means. *Behavioral and Brain Sciences, 11,* 195–196.

Hyde, J. S., Fennema, E., & Lamon, S. J. (1990). Gender differences in mathematics performance: A meta-analysis. *Psychological Bulletin, 107,* 139–155.

Hyde, J. S., Fennema, E., Ryan, M., Frost, L. A., & Hopp, C. (1990). Gender comparisons of mathematics attitudes and affect: A meta-analysis. *Psychology of Women Quarterly, 14,* 299–324.

Jensen, A. R. (1988). Sex differences in arithmetic computation and reasoning in prepubertal boys and girls. *Behavioral and Brain Sciences, 11,* 198–199.

Keating, D. P. (1993). Developmental diversity in mathematical and scientific competence. In L. A. Penner, G. M. Batsche, H. M. Knoff, & D. L. Nelson (Eds.), *The challenge in mathematics and science education: Psychology's response* (pp. 315–339). Washington, DC.: American Psychological Association.

Kimball, M. M. (1989). A new perspective on women's math achievement. *Psychological Bulletin, 105,* 198–214.

Low, R., & Over, R. (1993). Gender differences in solution of algebraic word problems containing irrelevant information. *Journal of Educational Psychology, 85,* 331–339.

Maccoby, E. E., & Jacklin, C. N. (1974). *The psychology of sex differences.* Stanford, CA: Stanford University Press.

Mayer, R. E. (1988). What we really need is a theory of mathematical ability. *Behavioral and Brain Sciences, 11,* 202–203.

Meehan, A. M. (1984). A meta-analysis of sex differences in formal operational thought. *Child Development, 55,* 1110–1124.

Pajares, F., & Miller, M. D. (1994). Role of self-efficacy and self-concept beliefs in mathematical problem solving: A path analysis. *Journal of Educational Psychology, 86,* 193–203.

Piaget, J. (1971). *Biology and knowledge. An essay on the relations between organic regulations and cognitive processes.* Chicago: University of Chicago Press.

Robinson, N. M., Abbott, R. D., Berninger, V. W. & Busse, J. (1996). The structure of abilities in math-precocious young children: Gender similarities and differences. *Journal of Educational Psychology, 88,* 341–352.

Royer, J. M., Tronsky, L. N., & Chan, Y., Jackson, S. J., & Marchant, H., III. (1999). Math-fact retrieval as the cognitive mechanism underlying gender differences in math test performance. *Contemporary Educational Psychology, 24,* 181–266.

Seong, H., Bauer, S. C., & Sullivan, L. M. (1998). Gender differences among top performing elementary school students in mathematical ability. *Journal of Research and Development in Education, 31,* 133–141.

Shih, M., Pittinsky, T. L., & Abady, N. (1999). Stereotype susceptibility: Identity salience and shifts in quantitative performance. *Psychological Science, 10,* 80–83.

Snyder, T. D., & Hoffman, C. M. (2000). U.S. Department of Education National Center for Education Statistics. *Digest of Education Statistics, 1999, NCES 2000-031.* Washington, DC: Author.

Spencer, S. J., Steele, C. M., & Quinn, D. M. (1999). Stereotype threat and women's math performance. *Journal of Experimental Social Psychology, 35,* 4–28.

Steele, C. M. (1997). A threat in the air: How stereotypes shape intellectual identity and performance. *American Psychologist, 52,* 613–629.

Sternberg, R. J. (1988). The male/female difference is there: Should we care? *Behavioral and Brain Sciences, 11,* 210–211.

Stipek, D. J., & Gralinski, J. H. (1991). Gender differences in children's achievement-related beliefs and emotional responses to success and failure in mathematics. *Journal of Educational Psychology, 83,* 361–371.

Stumpf, H., & Stanley, J. C. (1996). Gender-related differences on the College Board's Advanced Placement and Achievement Tests, 1982–1992. *Journal of Educational Psychology, 88,* 353–364.

The National Council of Teachers of Mathematics. (2000). *Principles and standards for school mathematics.* Reston, VA: Author.

Voyer, D. (1996). The relation between mathematical achievement and gender differences in spatial abilities: A suppression effect. *Journal of Educational Psychology, 88,* 563–571.

Wainer, H., & Steinberg, L. S. (1992). Sex differences in performance on the mathematics section of the Scholastic Aptitude Test: A bidirectional validity study. *Harvard Educational Review, 62,* 323–336.

Wigfield, A., Eccles, J.S., Yoon, K. S., Harold, R. D., Arbreton, A. J. A., Freedman-Doan, C., & Blumenfeld, P. C. (1997). Change in children's competence beliefs and subjective task values across the elementary school years: A 3-year study. *Journal of Educational Psychology, 89,* 451–469.

Willingham, W. W., & Cole, N. C. (Eds.). (1997). *Gender and fair assessment.* Mahwah, NJ: Lawrence Erlbaum Associates.

CHAPTER 7

Maximization of Spatial Competence: More Important than Finding the Cause of Sex Differences

Nora S. Newcombe
Lisa Mathason
Melissa Terlecki

The ancient Greeks counseled people to seek moderation in all things. But the history of psychology shows that not many heeded this advice. The literature is filled with either/or debates. Some controversies are the kind only scientists worry about, such as whether memory loss results from decay or from interference. Other controversies engage the general population, such as the debate over nature and nurture as determinants of human ability and personality. One of the most contentious areas is the issue of causes of cognitive sex differences. Despite lip service to the credo of interactionism, psychologists usually divide into biological and social camps. Biologically inclined investigators typically argue that certain sex differences are large, important, immutable, observed across species, seen in young as well as mature humans, related to biological variables such as hormone levels or brain organization, and based on adaptive evolution. Socially inclined investigators, by contrast, often argue that sex differences are small, unimportant, changeable (e.g., disappearing in historical time), larger in older children (i.e., increasing with greater exposure to the culture), related to social variables such as expectations and stereotypes, and based on culturally contingent facts such as division of labor.

The purpose of this chapter is to move away from further argument about these claims. We believe that this long-standing debate concerning the causes of sex differences in certain spatial abilities, although scientifically interesting, has diverted attention from a much more important point: that there is currently plenty of evidence to conclude that spatial skill is trainable, for both sexes (Baenninger & Newcombe, 1989; Huttenlocher, Levine, & Vevea, 1998). Thus, the issue of the causes of sex differences is fundamentally beside the point. Both sexes need to optimize their spatial skills, that is, their ability to represent and reason about distance, shape, order, and frame of reference, both mentally and using visual and linguistic symbolic systems. Spatial skills have been shown to be related to success in mechanical, mathematical, and scientific arenas, as well as to ability to perform everyday tasks (e.g., hooking up a VCR, packing the trunk of a car). Society would benefit from a much larger pool of people of both sexes able to function effectively in an increasingly technological society.

Our argument can be summed up with a familiar aphorism, "A rising tide lifts all boats." More technically, what we advocate is a focus on malleability of mean levels. It is becoming increasingly well known (in discussions of individual differences as viewed through the lens of behavior genetics) that a focus on heritability (assessed by behavior geneticists through analyses of correlations) provides little evidence relevant to the potential for mean levels of a characteristic to change substantially (Collins, Maccoby, Steinberg, Hetherington, & Bornstein, 2000; Plomin & Rutter, 1998). For example, mean levels of height have risen considerably over the past century, even though individual differences in height are strongly heritable.

PRIOR WORK ON SPATIAL ACTIVITIES AND TRAINING

A lot of the existing work on experience and spatial ability, especially that completed prior to the 1990s, was conceptualized as a test of social explanations of sex differences in spatial ability. There were two guiding ideas. One hypothesis was that activities that enhanced spatial ability were largely sex-typed as masculine, and hence more likely to be engaged in by males, leading to the male advantage for certain kinds of spatial ability. This hypothesis was generally investigated through correlational work in which people were asked to report on their spatial activities, and their reports were correlated with their scores on various spatial tests. The second hypothesis was that, if females lacked spatial experience to a greater extent than males, then spatial training should benefit females to a greater extent than males. This hypothesis was generally investigated through experimental or quasi-experimental work in which the spatial scores of people given certain kinds of spatial experience were compared, before and after the experience, with the scores of people not receiving the experience. The expectation was that one should find sex by training interactions.

In this section, we review what evidence accumulated regarding each of these hypotheses. We argue that neither body of literature provided strong support for either social or biological causation. However, the work (especially the training studies) did provide encouragement for the more socially important proposition that spatial ability is relatively easy to increase from the baseline levels observed in the real world.

Correlational Studies

In a meta-analysis of the correlational research, Baenninger and Newcombe (1989) found a weak but reliable relation between spatial activity participation and spatial ability test performance. Three categories of spatial ability (mental rotation, spatial perception, and spatial visualization) were also examined separately, as suggested by Linn and Petersen (1985). Effect sizes were significant for all three categories and the effect sizes did not differ significantly from each other. When activity participation was considered separately by sex typing, masculine stereotyped activities were found to be somewhat more strongly related to performance than feminine stereotyped or neutral activities, although not significantly so. However, for males, only masculine activity participation was significantly related to spatial abilities.

An additional study published in the same year as the meta-analysis provides an illustrative example of the sort of results obtained in studies in this tradition. Signorella, Jamison, and Krupa (1989) concluded that both spatial activities and sex-typed self-concept had a significant effect on spatial performance. More specifically, Signorella et al. (1989) found that masculine spatial activities had a direct effect on spatial performance, although they were more related to the water-level task (i.e., drawing a horizontal line in a tipped container) than the card rotation test (i.e., imagining what a two-dimensional figure would look like after rotations in the plane). In addition, a more masculine and less feminine gender self-concept was related to card-rotation performance in both sexes, although related to the water-level performance in women only.

It is hard to draw strong conclusions from this research strategy. The expected correlations are present, but weaker than one would like (although they do indicate a 9% improvement rate in test scores due to spatial activity). At least some of the problem may derive from the methodology. Correlations might well be stronger if activities were assessed contemporaneously rather than retrospectively. This might be especially true if the activity measures were derived from time diaries or from direct observation, rather than global ratings. However, even if stronger data were to result from adopting these methodological improvements, it would be difficult to support a social explanation of sex differences from such studies alone, because a plausible biological explanation of the data would still be possible. In particular, the correlations might result from self-selection of spatially able people into spatial activity.

Training Studies

In another set of meta-analyses, Baenninger and Newcombe (1989) concluded that training of a variety of types and durations increases spatial test performance and that training is beneficial for both men and women. Baenninger and Newcombe (1989) divided studies into three different categories along two dimensions: content (specific, general, indirect) and duration (long, medium, and short). Specific training referred to studies that trained with repeated exposure to stimulus materials directly related to a spatial test. General training studies used a variety of spatial tests or spatial items and varied in duration from a single, brief session, to a year-long training program. Indirect training studies referred to training that provided participants with spatial experience not related to a specific spatial test. In terms of duration, short was defined as single or brief administrations of training taking place over a period of less than 3 weeks. Medium duration was defined as more than one administration over more than 3 weeks. Long duration studies were defined as training that lasted at least a semester. Both the medium- and long-duration groups included some studies of curriculum-based training. An additional group of studies that involved repeated exposure to the same test, but no specific training, was labeled the practice group.

Baenninger and Newcombe (1989) found that improvement in test performance increased as the duration of training increased and that all the differences between the groups were significant with the exception of the practice group and short-training group. (Long duration was left out due to heterogeneity of effect sizes). This suggests that training is best administered in at least three or four sessions and that brief training is no more beneficial than repeated exposure to the same test. The combined effect size for the specific training group was significantly greater than the effect size for the general training group, which was significantly greater than that of the indirect training group. This suggests that the more specific the training, the better the performance on the test in question, a common finding in the training literature (Schmidt & Bjork, 1992). However, there is also some evidence for indirect or generalized effects, a very practically important goal of training.

Turning to the hypothesis that women would benefit more than men from training, the combined effect size for women in the meta-analysis was larger than the effect size for men, but this difference was not statistically significant. Thus, training does not benefit the sexes differentially, as initially seemed to be predicted by the hypothesis that males have less need of spatial experience than females. There are, however, two problems with concluding from this evidence of equal benefit that biological explanations of sex differences are needed, that sex differences are inevitable, and that such differences will always be determinants of sex ratios in participation in spatially demanding occupations such as engineering or architecture.

The first issue to consider is the problem of asymptote, or top-level performance obtained after extensive practice. Performance on spatial tests is clearly quite far from the maximum that could be obtained on the tests, even for the most able individuals. Thus, there is plenty of room for improvement as a function of training for men as well as women. Put differently, the reasoning behind the search for sex by training interactions was flawed in that an assumption in generating the hypothesis was that males had had about as much training from their everyday environment as they needed. In fact, there typically were no such ceiling effects. Thus, the actual design needed to evaluate how males and females benefit from training is one in which people are trained until their performance no longer shows any benefit of training (i.e., until they are at asymptotic performance). Hypothetical data from such a study are shown in Figure 7.1, which shows an equality of male and female performance at ceiling. Unfortunately, we are not aware of any experiments using the training-to-asymptote design in the published literature.

The second issue to keep in mind in considering the results of training experiments brings us back to the bottom-line message of this chapter. Suppose that a training-to-asymptote design, instead of producing data such as that in Figure 7.1, produced results such as those in Figure 7.2. Here, sex differences are still evident at asymptote, with males performing better than females even though both sexes are performing very well. Such results do, indeed, probably favor the hypothesis that for some biological reason, females have less spatial potential than do males (although some investigators might argue that aspects of socialization prevent women from benefiting equally from training, for instance,

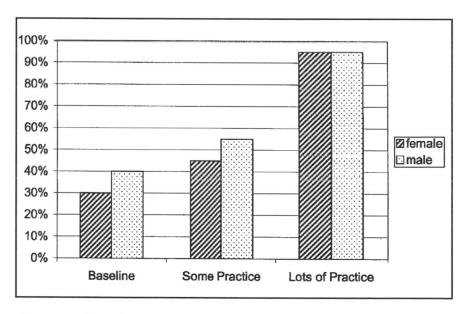

Figure 7.1. Effects of training on sex differences: One possibility.

because they see spatial skills as stereotyped masculine and as unimportant to their lives and career choices).

However, would this fact have any real-world implications, for instance, for participation in spatially demanding occupations? Consider Figure 7.3. Here, a threshold line has been superimposed on the data from Figure 7.2, to indicate that certain levels of spatial ability may be sufficient to function effectively even in spatially demanding occupations, with increments beyond this threshold unrelated to performance. If there is such a threshold, there would be no need for males to outnumber females as engineers or as architects, at least no need based on their spatial ability.

Are such threshold effects plausible? Although there has been no direct study of spatial ability and spatial occupations, it has been forcefully argued that even though mental ability predicts academic achievement, it shows fairly low relations to performance in a variety of occupations, at least above a certain threshold, with many other variables being important predictors of success (e.g., McClelland, 1973; Sternberg & Wagner, 1993; Sternberg & Williams, 1997). It takes above-average ability to enter medical school or graduate school, for instance, but once entry has been achieved there are few, if any, relations between ability and professional performance. Motivation, work habits, social skills, and so on, account for variance in success, instead.

Given these observations, it is important to determine whether training can lead to substantial improvement in two specific kinds of spatial ability that

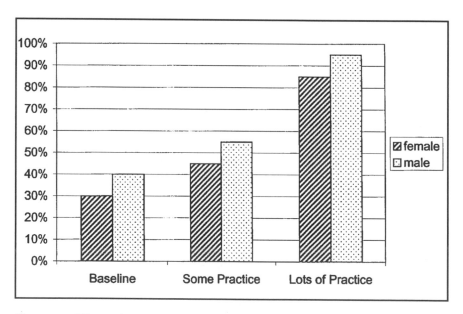

Figure 7.2. Effects of training on sex differences: Another possibility.

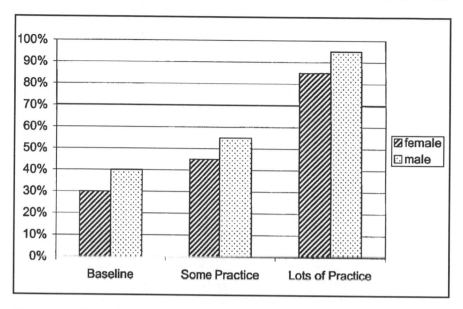

Figure 7.3. Effects of training on sex differences: A threshold effect added.

either show, or have been claimed to show, large sex differences. The Baenninger and Newcombe (1989) meta-analysis lumped spatial tests together into three fairly large categories as suggested by Linn and Petersen (1985). Looking at tests individually, as done by Voyer, Voyer, and Bryden (1995), allows us to look specifically at the two "hardest cases," the two tests that have shown the most substantial sex differences. It also provides an opportunity to consider sex-linked performance on certain other spatial tasks not central to the literature prior to the past decade.

SEX DIFFERENCES IN CERTAIN KINDS OF SPATIAL ABILITY

There are many different kinds of spatial skill that have been identified in the 100 years of work on human mental abilities. Several hundred specific spatial tests have been catalogued (Eliot & Smith, 1983), developed within several different research traditions. From the psychometric tradition dating back 100 years or so, there are paper-folding tests, embedded-figures tests, maze tasks, and two- and three-dimensional mental rotation. All of these tests and tasks have been at least suspected of showing sex differences, but not all of them seem to. Sex differences are most pronounced for three-dimensional mental rotation, although very difficult two-dimensional rotation tests seem to produce them as well (Collins & Kimura, 1997).

Horizontality and verticality tasks, coming out of the Piagetian tradition, also show substantial sex differences. More recently, several tasks have been discussed that do not have psychometric tests devoted to them (at least not yet). From cognitive and perceptual work, we have aiming and intercepting tasks, and relative velocity judgments. In animal work, there has been discussion of place learning (i.e., using distal cues to locate a target) and the relative use of geometry versus landmark cues in place learning. In recent memory work, a good deal of interest has focused on memory for object location.

In this chapter, we focus on five tasks divided into two groups. First, we examine the two kinds of test that are well accepted as showing reliable sex differences: mental rotation and horizontality–verticality tasks (Linn & Petersen, 1985). Second, we discuss less well-established and less thoroughly investigated sex differences in three other tasks, which as a group have figured importantly in sociobiological approaches to sex differences in spatial ability (Gaulin & Fitzgerald, 1986; Geary, 1998; Kimura, 1999). These areas include the male advantages seen in dynamic spatial tasks, some with a motor component, such as throwing; the proposal that males are more likely than females to use an abstract geometric or compass-determined reference frame in navigation and place finding whereas females rely on landmarks; and, the proposed female advantage in memory for object location. In each section, we discuss what is known about sex differences descriptively: the security of claims that they exist, and, if they exist, their size and whether anything is known regarding their age of first appearance or trends to increase or decrease in historical time. Most important, we examine evidence for their modifiability.

MENTAL ROTATION

Sex differences in mental rotation are arguably the strongest example for the biologically inclined. Sex differences are large (from around 0.6 to almost a whole standard deviation, or $d = 0.6$ to 1.0) (Linn & Petersen, 1985; Sanders, Soares, & D'Aquila, 1982; Voyer, Voyer, & Bryden, 1995), appear as early as the ability can be tested, at 4 years (Levine, Huttenlocher, Taylor, & Langrock, 1999), and seem not to be shrinking over time (Masters & Sanders, 1993). If anything, the differences are increasing (Voyer, Voyer, & Bryden, 1995). There is, however, dispute about whether there is age-related change in the size of the difference. Linn and Petersen (1985) found no such effect when they compared children under 13, adolescents 13–18, and adults over 18. A more recent parallel analysis by Voyer et al. (1995) did find an age-related increase in the size of the sex difference, from $d = 0.33$ for the youngest group, to 0.45 for the adolescents, and finally to 0.66 for the oldest age category. Nevertheless, to a great extent, the descriptive facts about mental rotation seem consistent with the usual conception of a biologically conditioned effect.

The sex difference in test performance on mental rotation has been localized to rate of mental rotation, rather than to the accuracy of the process or the time to code the stimulus initially (e.g., Kail, Carter, & Pellegrino, 1979; Thomas & Kail, 1991). This information has led to two kinds of investigation relevant to improving performance. One line of work has concentrated on assessing whether sex differences arise mostly because mental rotation tests are timed tests, with, indeed, a great deal of time pressure. Another line of work has focused on whether training and practice can speed the rate of mental rotation. There are three subareas of research in this general category: studies of the effect of simple practice, studies of the effect of using sign language (a visuospatial communication system), and studies of the effects of computerized practice, often game-like in nature.

Test Timing and Scoring Procedures

If rate of mental rotation is the primary difference between males and females, it would seem to follow that non-timed tests would minimize or eliminate sex differences. Goldstein, Haldane, and Mitchell (1990) reported that gender differences were no longer statistically significant when a mental rotation test was administered without a time limit or when the ratio of items solved to items attempted was used as the score. Voyer (1997) replicated the results of Goldstein et al. (1990) using a between-subjects design. He found that sex differences in performance on the Vandenberg and Kuse Mental Rotations test (MRT) were significant in the timed condition, but not in the untimed condition, and that this was not attributable to a lack of power to detect significance, as the power level was 71%. Results also indicated that a ratio score reduced the magnitude of sex differences in both timing conditions, even though they remained significant. Partial support was found for the hypothesis that sex differences in guessing behavior underlie sex differences on the MRT.

There are negative findings as well. Although Stumpf (1993) replicated the finding of Goldstein and colleagues and found that the use of ratio scores significantly decreased gender differences on the mental rotation test, results on the Eliot-Price Mental Rotations test were at odds with these findings. For most of the other spatial tests, the reduction of gender-related differences was small. Stumpf (1993) concluded that performance factors might account for some of the gender differences in spatial test performance, but that the bulk of the variance likely has to do with other factors. Findings that do not support those of Goldstein and colleagues (1990) were also reported by Delgado and Prieto (1996) and by Masters (1998).

In a meta-analysis using the Goldstein et al. data and a large group of other studies using mental rotation tests, but not including the studies specifically following up on the Goldstein et al. finding, Voyer, Voyer, and Bryden (1995) concluded that procedural factors have a strong influence on effect sizes for mental rotation. More specifically, Voyer and colleagues (1995) found that the magnitude of gender differences on the Vandenberg and Kuse Mental Rotation Test was largest ($d = 0.94$) when the test was scored out of 20. On this test, there are two variants for every referent that are correct, (i.e., that can indeed be considered rotations of the referent block figure). Scoring out of 20 involves giving credit for each of the 20 items only if both variants are identified, with no partial credit for finding one. With partial credit (scoring out of 40), the size of the sex difference was 0.70, and with unconventional scoring (including the use of ratio of correct to attempted items, as used by Goldstein and colleagues), the size of the sex difference was only 0.14.

It is not yet clear whether untimed tests reduce or eliminate sex differences in mental rotation. However, this investigational strategy is a very indirect way of looking at the locus of sex differences because overall test scores are also affected by other factors, such as guessing strategies or whether or not one rechecks one's work. Experiments using reaction time probably provide sufficient evidence to focus on rate of mental rotation as the primary, if not the only, determinant of sex differences in mental rotation, whatever the outcome of the debate on time pressure may be.

Practice and Training

There is some interesting evidence of training effects on rate of mental rotation, from three different kinds of research. In overview, the work provides some basis for optimism about improving mean levels of mental rotation ability, although much more work of this kind needs to be done. First, studies of the effects of simple practice show that improvement can be obtained. Second, naturalistic studies of the effects of communicating using sign language suggest that such communication has specific effects on spatial ability of the sort required for use of sign language, including the comparison phases of the mental rotation task, although apparently not on rate of mental rotation. Third, research on the effects of practice with spatially demanding computer games provides tantalizing evidence of robust training effects, in some cases sufficient not only to improve spatial ability but also to eliminate sex differences, perhaps because of training to asymptotic levels.

Effects of Simple Practice

Simple practice affects rate of mental rotation. Some studies concentrate on a particular set of stimuli and hence end up fundamentally changing the task. Kail (1986) had eight 9-year-olds, eight 13-year-olds, and eight 20-year-olds go through 3,840 trials of a mental rotation task. Testing occurred 4 days a week and continued for 4 weeks. The experimenter gave the participants feedback at various intervals regarding accuracy and response time, and offered cash incentives for going faster without sacrificing accuracy. Mental rotation indeed became faster over the 16 sessions in this procedure. After about 1,500 trials, age differences in rate of rotation were eliminated. Similarly, for sex differences, Kail and Park (1990) found that rates of mental rotation changed from 4.12 ms per degree for females and 2.13 ms per degree for males to 0.86 and 0.60 respectively. Unfortunately, Kail and Park found that their practice effects did not generalize to other stimuli, such as letter-like figures not used in the main experiment. The very fast "rotation" rates suggest that the task changes during practice to involve the retrieval of stored information rather than calling on mental rotation at all.

A more promising approach to training would use a variety of stimuli during training, which may allow people to experiment with changing the strategies they use in mental rotation. People adopt different strategies in mental rotation tasks, as identified by Just and Carpenter (1976), and success varies with strategy. Kail et al. (1979) suggested that females may be more likely than males to adopt a piecemeal strategy rather than rotating the whole stimulus at once. There is recent evidence showing such a strategy difference in a context where no overall sex differences exist, thus indicating the possibility of a stable preference (Naylor, Taylor, & Cross, 2000).

Adopting the varied-stimuli approach, Leone, Taine, and Droulez (1993) worked with "good" and "bad" imagers (unfortunately, without breaking out the results by sex). Participants were given 12 to 15 sessions of varied mental rotation practice over 6 weeks. Rate of mental rotation improved substantially and equally for both good and bad imagers. Rates had apparently not reached asymptotic values, even after 6 weeks. However, by the end of training, bad imagers had improved to the point that they were faster at rotating than good imagers had been initially. This pioneering study provides reason for substantial optimism about the malleability of mental rotation.

Effects of Sign Language

A strong kind of naturalistic training occurs in users of sign language. One of the requirements for a fluent signer is to be able to comprehend signs from various vantage points, requiring mental rotation of hand-arm configurations. Although practice at this task might be expected to improve mental rotation of those specific stimuli, it has also been found to generalize to mental rotation of non-hand/arm figures. Talbot and Haude (1993) found a significant relationship between experience in ASL (American Sign Language) and performance on the Vandenberg Mental Rotation Test. They found that women with extensive experience using ASL performed significantly better than either women with no experience or women with less than a year of experience with signing. No significant difference was found between the latter two groups.

Although these findings suggest that women can benefit from indirect training, such as experience and training in ASL, the question of self-selection remains. It is not clear from the data whether ASL improves spatial ability or women with high spatial aptitude gravitate toward and persist in such experiences. Also, because an overall test score was the dependent variable, Talbot and Haude could not evaluate whether better performance was due to faster rotation or better performance of the "encode" and "compare" phases of mental rotation tests.

Stronger evidence comes from research on deaf individuals. Because the occurrence of deafness is unlikely to be correlated with spatial ability, such work leads to cleaner evidence on the idea that practice with the rotational demands of sign language leads to an overall gain in mental rotation ability. Emmorey, Kosslyn, and Bellugi (1993) examined the relation between the use of ASL and performance on three visual mental imagery abilities: image generation, maintenance, and transformation. Studying deaf signers, hearing signers with deaf parents (HD), and hearing non-signers, they found that both deaf and hearing signers had an enhanced ability to generate complex images and to detect mirror image reversals in mental rotation tasks. Specifically, with regard to mental rotation, Emmorey et al. (1993) found that deaf signers performed the task more quickly than hearing participants, due to deaf participants being faster at making mirror image judgments. Signers did not appear to be faster at rotating objects in images. Deaf signers and hearing participants were equally accurate, which suggests that differences in response times were not due to a speed-accuracy trade-off. Deaf participants who were exposed to sign language from birth made fewer errors than non-native signers exposed to ASL later in childhood. HD signers performed similarly to deaf signers, suggesting that experience with ASL enhances ability on this task rather than auditory deprivation. No effect of or interaction with gender was found. In sum, the results support the idea that certain kinds of spatial experience lead to selective improvement in skills required in mental rotation, although the lack of an effect on speed of mental rotation is puzzling.

Effects of Computer Games

Another activity that might be expected to lead to improvement in mental rotation ability through practice, and that is more common than use of sign language, is the playing of certain computer games, such as Tetris. An early study of this issue found clear and interesting results (McClurg & Chaille, 1987). Fifth, seventh, and ninth grade students played one of two computer games for two 45-minute sessions per week over 6 weeks. The "Factory" game required users to mentally manipulate a three-dimensional "product" by visualizing the products movement through an assembly line of Punch, Stripe, and Rotate machines. "Stellar 7" required players to explore star systems and to recognize various three-dimensional objects that change orientation, are viewed from different positions, appear at different distances, and move at varying speeds. Students were tested 1 week before the treatment began and 1 week after treatment ended using a mental rotation test constructed from figures used by Shepard and Metzler. The Stellar 7 group and the Factory group scored significantly higher than the control group on the post-test and no significant difference was found between the Factory group and Stellar group. No significant interaction effects were found for sex or grade, which indicates that the computer games improved mental rotation for males and females at all three grade levels. These early results have been supported by Okagaki and Frensch (1994), who found that practicing Tetris for a total of 6 hours improved mental rotation time and spatial visualization skill, and that improvement in spatial skill did not differ for males and females.

Some studies involving computerized tasks have found women improving more than men, rather than the more standard finding in the training literature of parallel improvement. Saccuzzo, Craig, Johnson, and Larson (1996) examined simple practice effects on both a computerized two-dimensional mental rotation task and a paper-and-pencil rotation task. Participants were administered rotation problems in two different sessions. During the second session, both sexes improved on the paper-and-pencil test, with males still outperforming females. On the computerized rotation task, females improved at a much greater rate than males and no difference was found between male and female performance. Practice on a computerized task may differentially help females more than males. Saccuzzo et al. (1996) suggest this could be due to males having more experience with computer games. In line with this hypothesis, Roberts and Bell (1998) found that sex differences on a computerized two-dimensional rotation task disappeared when participants were simply allowed to practice a color-matching task prior to the rotation task. When there was no familiarization task, males responded quicker than females on items presented in the 180-degree and 270-degree rotation condition. This is consistent with previous literature suggesting that angle of rotation is associated with increases in reaction time to make decisions (Shepard & Metzler, 1971) and previous literature using the same gingerbread man task with an adult population (Epting & Overman, 1998). However, in the group with prior experience with the computer (color-matching group), males and females did not differ in reaction time for any of the three rotation conditions.

Summary

The exploration of how to train for improved performance on mental rotation tasks has barely begun. The lack of sustained attention to this problem likely reflects the assumption that performance is somehow fixed or innate, an assumption that investigators might rarely defend in such a simple and unvarnished form but one implicit in many discussions of the issues. Nevertheless, there is reason in the existing data to be optimistic about training. Users of sign language improve at certain aspects of the mental rotation task, likely those called on by the demands of the communication system. Properly designed training with varied stimuli, especially including computerized presentation with its attendant benefits of engaging presentation and the possibility of individually tailored interventions, has already been shown to yield substantial improvements in the mental rotation ability of both males and females, with the possibility of the elimination of sex differences at asymptote.

HORIZONTALITY–VERTICALITY

A second kind of test for which sex differences appear reliable are tests in which the aim is to draw a line or position a rod so that it is horizontal or vertical with respect to a gravitational referent, often in the presence of distracting frames of reference such as a tipped picture frame. Some aspects of sex differences in performance on these tests fit the biological model, although they come in second to mental rotation in this respect. The differences are reasonably large (Linn & Petersen, 1985) and appear as early as can be tested—although they cannot be tested before 10 years or so because children younger than that generally all show fairly extreme deviations from correct performance on horizontality–verticality tasks (Piaget & Inhelder, 1967). However, the sex differences do differ in some ways from what a biological model would predict. The differences between men and women seem to be decreasing across historical time (Voyer et al., 1995). They also seem to increase with age, from an effect size of .37 for both children and adolescents, to an effect size of .64 for adults (Linn & Petersen, 1985).

Effects of Natural Experience with Liquids

Hecht and Profitt (1995) reported a finding that presented a problem for an experiential argument regarding horizontality–verticality. Individuals with considerable experience with carrying liquid-filled containers (i.e., waiters and waitresses) were found to be worse than people without such experience on the water-level task. However, Vasta, Rosenberg, Knott, and Gaze (1997) found that individuals in occupations that provide extensive experience with water in containers, namely bartenders, waitresses, and waiters, are more accurate on two versions of the water-level task than individuals of equal age, gender, and education. Female bartenders and servers were more accurate than female sales and clerical workers, but remained significantly lower than males in the experienced group. These findings were contrary to Hecht and Profitt's (1995) conclusion that individuals in occupations that involve considerable experience with liquids in containers are less accurate on the water-level task that adults in other occupations. Finding that people working in restaurants are not impaired at judging horizontality is reassuring in more ways than one.

Effects of Training

Until recently, there were many reports that improvement in horizontality–verticality with training was hard to effect, for anyone, and did not eliminate, or even reduce, sex differences. However, recent work has now challenged this conclusion. Vasta, Knott, and Gaze (1996) found that self-discovery training erased the gender difference on the water-level problem and improved females' identification of the invariance principle on a multiple-choice test. Training consisted of solving comparatively easy problems and then going to more challenging problems that progressively incorporated competing perceptual cues (oblique lines and asymmetry). To emphasize self-discovery, participants were given no feedback, no verbal information regarding the invariance principle and only minimal modeling. (This is one of the most indirect training procedures used with this task.)

Self-discovery training significantly increased women's scores on both the paper-and-pencil water-level task and the verbal identification of the invariance principle. More interestingly, it was found that after completing problems on the self-discovery water-level task, women were just as accurate as men. These findings hold true whether the test was scored as degrees of deviation from horizontal or as number of responses falling within the 5-degree criterion range. These results did not extend to the verbal assessment of the invariance principle, as men in both conditions were significantly more accurate than women. It is also important to note that no effects of training were found for men on either of these tasks, which was not likely the result of ceiling effects because men in both conditions performed considerably below asymptote. Also, no effect of training was found on the Piaget plumb-line task and the usual gender differences were observed. This leaves open the question of generalizability.

Vasta et al. (1996) are not the only investigators to achieve successful training. Parameswaran and De Lisi (1996) found that both learner-guided instruction and tutor-guided instruction increased performance on spatial perceptual tests of horizontality and verticality. Practice alone was not sufficient. There was no gender difference in the learner-guided group and this group was the most accurate on posttest scores. Gender differences favoring males were found in both the tutor-guided group and control condition. These two recent training studies provide interesting evidence suggesting that problems with horizontality and verticality tasks, formerly considered intractable, can actually be addressed with careful training techniques.

DYNAMIC SPATIAL TASKS

In the previous two sections, we examined evidence on the trainability of two of the most impressively documented sex differences in spatial skills. We now turn our attention to a second group of spatial abilities, a group that includes three skills that have figured prominently in discussion but about which much less is known descriptively. The first of these abilities is performance on dynamic spatial tasks involving the prediction of trajectories.

One kind of dynamic spatial task involves aiming and intercepting actions. Watson and Kimura (1991) report robust sex differences that survived statistical control of strength and sports history. However, controls for strength were inadequate. Arm and shoulder strength were not directly assessed (height and weight were used as proxies). Hence, this work leaves open the issue of whether there are interesting sex differences in dynamic spatial tasks.

The idea that there are sex differences in dynamic spatial tasks that go beyond strength has, however, received support from studies using computerized dynamic displays, for which strength is irrelevant. Law, Pellegrino, and Hunt (1993) asked people to judge the relative velocities of two objects moving on a computer screen and found sex differences in performance. These differences were greatly reduced when a measure of experience with video games was entered first in a multiple regression, even though this measure was a retrospective self-report. This finding suggests that the sex difference in judging relative velocities might be secondary to sex differences in interest in video games. The sex difference in interest might in turn depend on the aggressive content of these games rather than their spatial nature. However, video game experience did not have a similar effect on sex differences in performance of a computerized ping-pong game in another study (Brown, Hall, Holtzer, Brown, & Brown, 1997).

Again though, the most important evidence concerns the effects of practice. When Law et al. (1993) gave participants feedback about their performance in a relatively brief training study, males and females benefited equally, and substantially. Because the best participants (i.e., even the males after training) were clearly not close to asymptotic accuracy, the study leaves open the question of whether the sexes would differ after more extensive training. But the main message is clear, and in line with Baenninger and Newcombe's (1989) conclusions, namely, that on many spatial tasks even the most able individuals are very far from maximized competence on the tasks.

NAVIGATION AND PLACE FINDING

In the popular press and at cocktail parties, discussion of sex differences in spatial ability rarely focuses on skills such as mental rotation or horizontality. Instead, the talk is usually of differences in finding one's way in the world. Men are better oriented than women, according to this folk knowledge—they have a sense of direction that is automatic, that involves orientation to compass points or a wider geometric space, and that does not rely on landmarks. They like to use maps and hate to ask for directions. This habit, the topic of many jokes and cartoons showing the behavior as a male foible, is also clearly seen as stemming from male superiority in navigation. Why ask for directions if generally you know where you are? In most of these discussions, the assumption is made that these differences are both innate and fixed.

Support for the proposition that sex differences in navigation are biologically rooted has come from research that shows that similar sex differences occur in various species of nonhuman mammals (e.g.Williams, Barnett, & Meck, 1990;

however, see Bucci, Chiba, & Gallagher [1995] for the possibility that sex differences may not exist at maturity, and may only reflect a different maturational course for the sexes in the growth of spatial orientation ability). The proposition has been further strengthened by being placed squarely within a sociobiological framework that links sex differences in navigation either to sex differences in the division of labor (hunting versus gathering) or to sex differences in reproductive strategy (polygamous versus monogamous) or to both. Gaulin and his associates have been influential in developing this point of view in research on nonhuman mammals (Gaulin & Fitzgerald, 1986; Sherry et al., 1992; and see chapter 3 which discusses these findings in detail). Yet another kind of support for the proposition of biological rootedness has seemed to come from studies showing that hormonal variations affect spatial ability (e.g., Galea, Kavaliers, Ossenkopp and Hampson, 1995; see Fitch & Bimonte, this volume, for extensive discussion of the role of hormones during ontogeny as well as in cyclic variation in adults).

Together, these findings seem to make a powerful case for biological causation. However, it may not be as coherent as proponents would have us believe. For instance, note that the evidence that within-sex variations in hormone levels may be significantly related to spatial learning fits oddly with sociobiological thinking (e.g., there is no obvious adaptive reason for females to have higher spatial ability during menstruation). In terms of the thesis of the chapter, however, the most important point is that evidence of biological causation of sex differences does not support the inference that levels of navigation ability are fixed and immutable.

Work with Animals

Training studies with animals have been even rarer than such work with humans, but there is one interesting relevant study of which we are aware. Perrot-Sinal, Kostenuik, Ossenkopp, and Kavaliers (1996) used the Morris water maze, a procedure in which animals are observed as they try to find a platform submerged in opaque water. These investigators gave rats initial training designed to familiarize the animals with the general situation and to address issues of sex differences in reactions to stressful situations, including swimming and environmental novelty. Following such familiarization, both male and female rats learned the location of a hidden platform faster than a control group not given such experiences and retained the information better. The improvement was more marked for females than for males; the females improved enough that no sex difference was evident in the animals given familarization. Although it would be comforting to see replications of this important study, the Perrot-Sinal et al. work provides reason to think that, even in rats, training can produce important increases in spatial ability.

Work with Humans

Direction Giving

Men and women have sometimes been found to exhibit different styles of direction giving (after examining a map and instructed to write directions from one location to another). Men tend to use more Euclidean, or abstract, terms in their directions. Females tend to be more concrete, frequently using landmarks in their descriptions (Ward, Newcombe, & Overton, 1986). Lawton (1994) found that women tend to use a route strategy, or attending on how to get from place to place (feature learning of a route, similar to landmark encoding), in their way finding, whereas men more often used an orientation strategy, or maintaining personal position in relation to environmental reference points (similar to the more abstract north, south, east, west orientation of a Euclidean approach). Evolutionary explanations have been postulated to account for such results (Dabbs, et al., 1998). Throughout prehistory, men traveled and hunted and followed "wandering paths" in seeking game, paying little attention to landmarks. Women, in contrast, stayed close to home with their children, tending house, gathering, and paying more attention to the small details of the immediate environment.

Again, however, as we have seen repeatedly in previous discussions, the facts about sex differences may be less important than the facts about malleability of mean levels of performance. Ward et al. (1986) found that participants changed their direction-giving practices substantially when given prompting to do so. In fact, in this study, it was not only that both sexes improved, but that sex differences were eliminated by instructions about the importance of using a variety of spatial terms, and cardinal direction (i.e., north, south, east, and west) in particular. Such instructions are an extremely minimal form of training, and their effectiveness suggests that one should be cautious about making too much of sex differences in this domain.

Way Finding

Several recent studies have utilized computer-generated virtual mazes for investigating sex differences in navigation and spatial route learning. The results of Moffat, Hampson, and Hatzipantelis (1998) yielded a significant male advantage for time to completion, percentage of errors, and spatial performance. Moffat et al. (1998) argue that these sex differences did not occur because of sex differences in computer game experience because its usage as a covariate did not eliminate the sex difference observed on the task. Similar sex differences were found in a study by Gibbs and Wilson (1999) of 5- to 12-year-old children. Male children were found to make significantly fewer errors, require less completion time, and demand fewer trials to reach criterion in route learning. Female children recalled more landmarks than the male children. In a study using a virtual water maze very similar to the Morris water maze, Sandstrom, Kaufman, and

Huettel (1998) found that men and women performed similarly when stable land-marks were available. However, males performed better than females when only geometric information was available or when landmarks were present but changed their position so that they were unreliable cues to the location of the hidden platform.

Nevertheless, as with other tasks we examined, training can lead to substantial improvement in performance on these tasks, and training studies give a very different picture of sex differences than is gained from static studies of baseline performance. Lawton and Morrin (1999) found males to achieve significantly better pointing accuracy than did the females in computer-simulated three-dimensional mazes, similar to the results already reported. Across various levels of maze difficulty, males outperformed females by about 20 degrees. What was interesting, however, is that with training, males and females both improved and, in fact, performed similarly in accuracy on virtually the same tasks.

Women often are found to be more anxious than men about way finding (Lawton, 1994; O'Laughlin & Brubaker, 1998). Such a difference may, of course, be either a cause or an effect of their spatial ability and style—or even an artifact of self-report style (Lawton, 1994; O'Laughlin & Brubaker, 1998). First, women who rely on a route strategy may make themselves more vulnerable to getting lost or "off track" if landmarks should no longer be available. Anxiety, in this view, is an effect of strategy and might change with instruction to adopt more effective strategies. Second, women may hold lower expectancies of their own spatial performance because most abilities are characterized as being masculine. Anxiety, in this view, is a cause of poor performance. Finally, men may simply be less likely to report or minimize their feelings of anxiety or confusion in navigational domains.

MEMORY FOR OBJECT LOCATION

Critics of sociobiology often argue that it is not a generative theoretical framework, that is, that it does not make specific and testable predictions about behavior. Rather, it offers post hoc explanations out of a set of principles flexible enough to account for almost any set of phenomena. In this context, a finding by Silverman and Eals (1992) seems to provide an important kind of support for the theory because they report a finding that females outperform males on a spatial task that they argue would be more related to gathering than to hunting. Thus, the finding seems to be indicative of the predictive and generative value of sociobiology.

The Silverman and Eals task was one in which participants were asked to look at an array of objects and memorize them. The implication was that the focus was on the objects' identities. Location was learned incidentally. Later, however, their location memory was tested and women's performance was found to significantly exceed that of men. This finding has been replicated (McBurney, Gaulin,

Devineni, & Adams, 1997; Montello, Lovelace, Golledge, & Self, 1999). However, there have also been non-replications. A recent study investigating navigational strategy (Dabbs et al., 1998) found no sex differences among male and female adults (mean age 21.7 years) concerning memory for object location. Similarly, O'Laughlin and Brubaker (1998) could not identify sex differences in location of objects in a given environment.

Probably the most serious issue concerning the Silverman and Eals research is whether the sex difference is specific to an incidental task. Adult women are frequently responsible for helping their children and their spouse locate moveable objects (e.g., "Mom, where are my shoes?" or "Honey, where are my keys?") and for this reason might be more likely to note location when it is not a task requirement. Differences between males and females might not be found with intentional learning, analogous to the Ward et al. (1986) finding that females used as many cardinal direction and distance terms as males following instructions that they are useful.

CONCLUSION

In this chapter, we examined five specific kinds of spatial ability, with a view to determining whether the conclusion that both sexes can improve substantially with training (Baenninger & Newcombe, 1989) applies to them. There is evidence that it does. Using sign language improves the comparison phase of mental rotation, and extensive practice, as well as the perhaps more palatable practice possible with computerized games, improves rotation rate as well. Appropriate training improves performance on horizontality–verticality tasks, on dynamic imagery tasks, and on navigation (even in animals). Women can easily learn to give better directions. The only unstudied sex difference is the hypothesized female advantage in object location.

We live in a society that is very concerned with rank ordering. We ask what the best ten movies of the year are, what kind of car is most reliable, or who at school is most popular. But mean levels are important too, and perhaps more important. Wouldn't we all like to have a wealth of excellent movies, reliable cars, and well-socialized children? If we could achieve those ends, how much would we care as to which was the absolute best? For instance, if asked to choose among ten kinds of automobile that were all extremely reliable, it seems that we would make a decision based on other factors (e.g., trunk space, style preferences) rather than looking at the rank ordering of reliability.

The argument in this chapter is that, as a society, our focus should be on the optimization of spatial ability in all individuals, rather than a focus on rank ordering the sexes. There is good evidence that spatial competence is not well developed in many people and that training is important. However, in many cases, not much effort has gone into delineating what kind of training works best, is most palatable, leads to most generalization, and so on. For some of the abilities we investigated, most notably object memory, training has barely been examined at all. A decade or two from now, it would be a pleasure to review a literature that would allow us to answer these socially and practically important questions.

REFERENCES

Baenninger, M., & Newcombe, N. (1989). The role of experience in spatial test performance: A meta-analysis. *Sex Roles, 20*, 327–344.

Brown, R., Hall, L., Holtzer, R., Brown, S., & Brown, N. (1997). Gender and video game performance. *Sex Roles, 36*, 793–812.

Bucci, D., Chiba, A., & Gallagher, M. (1995). Spatial learning in male and female Long-Evans rats. *Behavioral Neuroscience, 109*, 180–183.

Collins, D., & Kimura, D. (1997). A large sex difference on a two-dimensional mental rotation task. *Behavioral Neuroscience, 111*, 845–849.

Collins, W. A., Maccoby, E. E., Steinberg, L., Hetherington, E. H., & Bornstein, M. H. (2000). Contemporary research on parenting: The case for nature *and* nurture. *American Psychologist, 55*, 218–232.

Dabbs, J., Chang, E. L., Strong, R., & Milun, R. (1998). Spatial ability, navigation strategy, and geographic knowledge among men and women. *Evolution and Human Behavior, 19*, 89–98.

Delgado, A., & Prieto, G. (1996). Sex differences in visuospatial ability: Do performance factors play such an important role? *Memory and Cognition, 24*, 504–510.

Eliot, J., & Smith, I. M. (1983). *An international directory of spatial tests.* Windsor, U.K.: NFER-Nelson.

Emmorey, K., Kosslyn, S., & Bellugi, U. (1993). Visual imagery and visual-spatial language: Enhanced imagery abilities in deaf and hearing ASL signers. *Cognition, 46*, 139–181.

Epting, L. K., & Overman, W. H. (1998). Sex-sensitive tasks in men and women: A search for performance fluctuations across the menstrual cycle. *Behavioral Neuroscience, 112*, 1304–1318.

Galea, L., Kavaliers, M., Ossenkopp, K. P., & Hampson, E. (1995). Gonadal hormone levels and spatial learning performance in the Morris water maze in male and female meadow voles, *Microtus pennsylvanicus. Hormones and Behavior, 29*, 106–125.

Gaulin, S., & Fitzgerald, R. (1986). Sex differences in spatial ability: An evolutionary hypothesis and test. *American National, 127*, 74–88.

Geary, D. (1998). *Male, female: The evolution of human sex differences.* Washington, DC: American Psychological Association.

Gibbs, A., & Wilson, J. (1999). Sex differences in route learning by children. *Perceptual and Motor Skills, 88*, 590–594.

Goldstein, D., Haldane, D., & Mitchell, C. (1990). Sex differences in visuo-spatial ability: The role of performance factors. *Memory and Cognition, 18*, 546–550.

Hecht, H., & Proffitt, D. (1995). The price of expertise: Effects of experience in the water-level task. *Psychological Science, 6*, 90–95.

Huttenlocher, J., Levine, S., & Vevea, J. (1998). Environmental input and cognitive growth: A study using time-period comparisons. *Child Development, 69,* 1012–1029.

Just, M., & Carpenter, P. (1976). Eye fixations and cognitive processes. *Cognitive Psychology, 8,* 441–480.

Kail, R. (1986). The impact of extended practice on rate of mental rotation. *Journal of Experimental Child Psychology, 42,* 378–391.

Kail, R., Carter, P., & Pellegrino, J. (1979). The locus of sex differences in spatial ability. *Perception and Psychophysics, 26,* 182–186.

Kail, R., & Park, Y. (1990). Impact of practice on speed of mental rotation. *Journal of Experimental Child Psychology, 49,* 227–244.

Kimura, D. (1999). *Sex and cognition.* Cambridge: MIT Press.

Law, D., Pellegrino, J., & Hunt, E. (1993). Comparing the tortoise and the hare: Gender differences and experience in dynamic spatial reasoning tasks. *Psychological Science, 4,* 35–40.

Lawton, C. (1994). Gender differences in way-finding strategies: Relationship to spatial ability and spatial anxiety. *Sex Roles, 30,* 765–779.

Lawton, C., & Morrin, K. (1999). Gender differences in pointing accuracy in computer-simulated 3D mazes. *Sex Roles, 40,* 73–92.

Leone, G., Taine, M. C., & Droulez, J. (1993). The influence of long-term practice on mental rotation of 3-D objects. *Cognitive Brain Research, 1,* 241–255.

Levine, S., Huttenlocher, J., Taylor, A., & Langrock, A. (1999). Early sex differences in spatial skill. *Developmental Psychology, 35,* 940–949.

Linn, M., & Petersen, A. (1985). Emergence and characterization of sex differences in spatial ability: A meta-analysis. *Child Development, 56,* 1479–1498.

Masters, M. (1998). The gender difference on the mental rotations test is not due to performance factors. *Memory and Cognition, 26,* 444–448.

Masters, S., & Sanders, B. (1993). Is the gender difference in mental rotation disappearing? *Behavior Genetics, 23,* 337–341.

McBurney, D. H., Gaulin, S. J. C., Devineni, T., & Adams, C. (1997). Superior spatial memory of women: Stronger evidence for the gathering hypothesis. *Evolution and Human Behavior, 18,* 165–174.

McClelland, D. C. (1973). Testing for competence rather than "intelligence". *American Psychologist, 28,* 1–14.

McClurg, P. A., & Chaille, C. (1987). Computer games: Environments for developing spatial cognition? *Journal of Educational Computing Research, 3,* 95–171.

Moffat, S., Hampson, E., & Hatzipantelis, M. (1998). Navigation in a "virtual" maze: Sex differences and correlation with psychometric measures of spatial ability in humans. *Evolution and Human Behavior, 19,* 73–87.

Montello, D., Lovelace, K., Golledge, R., & Self, C. (1999). Sex-related differences and similarities in geographic and environmental spatial abilities. *Annals of the Association of American Geographers, 89,* 515–534.

Naylor, S. J., Taylor, H. A., & Cross, D. (2000). Gender and strategic processing differences in mental rotation. Unpublished manuscript, Tufts University.

Okagaki, L., & Frensch, P. (1994). Effects of video game playing on measures of spatial performance: Gender effects in late adolescence. *Journal of Applied Developmental Psychology, 15,* 33–58.

O'Laughlin, E., & Brubaker, B. (1998). Use of landmarks in cognitive mapping: Gender differences in self report versus performance. *Personality Individual Differences, 24*, 595–601.

Parameswaran, G., & DeLisi, R. (1996), Improvements in horizontality performance as a function of type of training. *Perceptual and Motor Skills, 82*, 595–603.

Perrot-Sinal, T.S., Kostenuik, M.A., Ossenkopp, K.-P., & Kavaliers, M. (1996). Sex differences in performance in the Morris Water Maze and the effects of initial non-stationary hidden platform training. *Behavioral Neuroscience, 110*, 1309–1320.

Piaget, J., & Inhelder, B. (1967). *The child's conception of space.* New York: Norton. (Original work published 1948)

Plomin, R., & Rutter, M. (1998). Child development, molecular genetics, and what to do with genes once they are found. *Child Development, 69*, 1223–1242.

Roberts, J. E., & Bell, M. A. (2000). Sex differences on a mental rotation task: Variations in electroencephalogram hemispheric activation between children and college students. *Developmental Neuropsychology, 17*, 199–223.

Saccuzzo, D. P., Craig, A. S., Johnson, N. E., & Larson, G. E. (1996). Gender differences in dynamic spatial abilities. *Personality and Individual Differences, 21*, 599–607.

Sanders, B., Soares, M. P., & D'Aquila, J. M. (1982). The sex difference on one test of spatial visualization: A nontrivial difference. *Child Development, 53*, 1106–1110.

Sandstrom, N., Kaufman, J., & Huettel, S. (1997). Males and females use different distal cues in a virtual environment navigation task. *Cognitive Brain Research, 6*, 351–360.

Schmidt, R., & Bjork, R. (1992). New conceptualizations of practice: Common principles in three paradigms suggest new concepts for training. *Psychological Science, 3*, 207–217.

Shepard, R. N., & Metzler, J. (1971). Mental rotation of three-dimensional objects. *Science, 171*, 701–703.

Sherry, D. F., Jacobs, L. F., & Gaulin, S. J. (1992). Spatial memory and adaptive specialization of the hippocampus. *Trends in Neurosciences, 15*, 298–303.

Signorella, M., Jamison, W., & Krupa, M. (1989). Predicting spatial performance from gender stereotyping in activity preferences and in self-report. *Experimental Psychology, 25*, 89–95.

Silverman, I., & Eals, M. (1992). Sex differences in spatial ability: Evolutionary theory and data. In J. Barkow, L. Cosmides, & J. Tooby (Eds.), *The adapted mind: Evolutionary psychology and the generation of culture* (pp. 533–549). New York: Oxford University Press.

Sternberg, R. J., & Wagner, R. K. (1993). The geocentric view of intelligence and job performance is wrong. *Current Directions in Psychological Science, 2*, 1–4.

Sternberg, R. J., & Williams, W. M. (1997). Does the Graduate Record Examination predict meaningful success in the graduate training of psychologists? A case study. *American Psychologist, 52*, 630–641.

Stumpf, H. (1993). Performance factors and gender-related differences in spatial ability: Another assessment. *Memory and Cognition, 21*, 828–836.

Talbot, K., & Haude, R. (1993). The relation between sign language skill and spatial visualization ability: Mental rotation of three-dimensional objects. *Perceptual and Motor Skills, 77*, 1387–1391.

Thomas, H., & Kail, R. (1991). Sex differences in speed of mental rotation and the x-linked genetic hypothesis. *Intelligence, 15*, 17–32.

Vasta, R., Knott, J., & Gaze, C. (1996). Can spatial training erase the gender differences on the water-level task? *Psychology of Women Quarterly, 20,* 549–567.

Vasta, R., Rosenberg, D., Knott, J., & Gaze, C. (1997). Experience and the water-level task revisited: Does expertise exact a price? *Psychological Science, 8,* 336–339.

Voyer, D. (1997). Scoring procedure, performance factors, and magnitude of sex differences in spatial performance. *American Journal of Psychology, 110,* 259–276.

Voyer, D., Voyer, S., & Bryden, M. (1995). Magnitude of sex differences in spatial abilities: A meta-analysis and consideration of critical variables. *Psychological Bulletin, 117,* 250–270.

Ward, S., Newcombe, N., & Overton, W. (1986). Turn left at the church, or three miles north: A study of direction giving and sex differences. *Environment and Behavior, 18,* 192–213.

Watson, N., & Kimura, D. (1991). Nontrivial sex differences in throwing and intercepting: Relation to psychometrically defined spatial functions. *Personality and Individual Differences, 12,* 375–385.

Williams, C., Barnett, A., & Meck, W. (1990). Organizational effects of early gonadal secretions on sexual differentiation in spatial memory. *Behavioral Neuroscience, 104,* 84–97.

CHAPTER 8

Children's Gender Cognitions, the Social Environment, and Sex Differences in Cognitive Domains

Carol Lynn Martin
Lisa M. Dinella

The goal of this chapter is to consider links between sex differences in cognitive domains, children's early social environments, and their cognitions about gender. (We use the terms "sex" to refer to any study or finding in which people are selected on the basis of demographic categories of female and male, and "gender" to refer to judgments or inferences about the sexes, such as stereotypes, roles, and concepts.) The social environment is broadly construed to include what children do with others, specifically the toys, interests, and activities children engage in, and who they interact with, specifically, experiences with same-sex peers. Two related themes will be discussed. One is how children's cognitions about gender directly influence their cognitive abilities, strategies, and motivation, and the other is how children's gender cognitions come to be influential through their indirect contributions to the children's social environment. Specifically, we propose that children's gender cognitions help shape their social environments, and their social environments, in turn, shape their beliefs, activities, skills, interactional styles, and attitudes.

The first section is a review of cognitive approaches to gender development. In the second section, an overview of the heuristic model of the interrelations among gender cognitions, the social environment, and cognitive sex differences is presented. In the third section, sex differences in children's play and activity preferences are considered and their proposed links to sex differences in cognitive domains are reviewed. In the fourth section, the direct and indirect roles of gender cognitions on children's activities and interests are described. In the next section, sex differences in children's peer preferences are reviewed and their potential socializing effects are described. In the following section, the roles of gender cognitions on children's peer preferences are outlined and the links to skill development are considered. In the final section, we summarize the links between the social environment and cognitive sex differences.

Consideration of how girls and boys develop cognitive abilities must be made with caution. Careful examination of sex differences in the cognitive domain indicates that males and females are more similar than different. Although sex differences are consistently found on certain tasks, the differences tend to be small in magnitude. Furthermore, no domain of cognitive abilities appears to be uniform in terms of sex differences. Rather than attributing a broad-based difference in cognitive abilities, these results suggest that differences exist only in certain components of some cognitive abilities and under certain circumstances. As we learn more about the nature of sex differences in cognitive abilities, it becomes increasingly obvious that no single explanation is likely to address all aspects of the issue. We are faced with the challenge of finding ways to explain differences that vary in magnitude, that change across settings, and that change across tasks. Another puzzle is the outcomes that are often associated with these cognitive abilities, especially career choices. Much larger sex differences are apparent in career choices than in cognitive abilities. Why these differences occur goes beyond ability differences. Understanding achievement-related values, academic skills, and career decisions involves considering the entire context of decision making and many sorts of influences on children's lives, including gender-related expectations (see chapter 4 and Eccles et al., 1999).

COGNITIVE PERSPECTIVES ON GENDER DEVELOPMENT: AN OVERVIEW

Although the social environment is filled with gender-related messages about what to wear, how to act, and how to relate to others, children do not passively absorb these messages. Theorists who propose cognitive perspectives concerning gender development assume that children and adults are active information processors who must gather, interpret, and then act on the information that is available to them, all within the limits imposed by human processing abilities. The advantages we derive from being able to categorize and quickly interpret information comes with some cost to accuracy. Because processing is often driven from the top downward, specific details may be lost or distorted to fit with one's expectations.

In the developmental literature, several cognitively oriented approaches have been proposed to understand children's gender development including cognitive developmental theories (Kohlberg, 1966) and gender schema theories (Bem, 1981; Martin, 1991; Martin & Halverson, 1981). Although these theories differ in a number of ways, they share the view that individuals hold gender-related cognitions and that these cognitions play an important role in behavior (see Ruble & Martin, 1998).

In his cognitive developmental theory, Kohlberg (1966) proposed an idea that was revolutionary at the time, namely, that a child's understanding of gender initiated gender development. For Kohlberg, a child's gender development becomes organized around his or her understanding of the nature of gender categories. Once this understanding has developed, children are motivated to seek out information about what is appropriate for their sex by observing the behavior of others. Research has supported the importance of children's active role in learning about gender (e.g., Slaby & Frey, 1975). The theory was not very specific about the types of gender cognitions that influence development and thus this aspect of the theory has been the center of many controversies. Nonetheless, the theory has remained central to understanding children's gender development.

The cognitive revolution in psychology spawned several other cognitive-oriented approaches, including gender schema theories. Schema theorists assume that individuals develop naïve theories about gender, which in turn, influence what individuals attend to, perceive, and remember.

One version of gender schema theory, proposed by Bem (1981), focused on the pervasiveness of gender messages in the culture and the extensive nature of the schemas that form around gender. Because gender is an important and functional aspect of our culture, individuals quickly learn to use gender as a method of categorizing and judging people (Bem, 1993). Bem also focused attention on individual differences in using gender as a processing dimension.

A developmental view of gender schemas was proposed by Martin and Halverson (1981). In this theory, we considered the developmental significance of children recognizing their own gender group and the consequences of using gender schemas. For instance, we discussed specific ways that schemas about gender organize and bias behavior, thinking, and memory. Schematic consistency—the idea that schemas guide individuals' actions and thinking so that they are consistent with their gender schemas—is central to the theory. We also proposed two forms of gender schemas, one a list-like structure akin to a stereotype and the other a more in-depth and detailed schema, which contains scripts for carrying out gender appropriate actions. Schema theories have proven successful for understanding gender development, particularly in their ability to explain how stereotypes can be maintained in the face of disconfirming evidence, why stereotypes are resistant to change, and why gender concepts may not match environmental input (Stephan, 1989).

Because the concepts we hold do not always guide our behavior, a challenge for cognitive theorists has been to refine and expand thinking about gender cognitions. Rather than arguing that one kind of cognition best captures the nature of gender schemas, another approach has been to assume that there are a variety of gender cognitions and to consider situational and individual differences in when and how they are applied (see Martin, 1999). Based on this approach, many types of gender cognitions have been identified that vary in their focus and target. Gender cognitions can be broad, such as gender stereotypes. Gender cognitions can apply to oneself, such as gender identity, a person's recognition of their own gender group and their similarity to others of their own sex. Gender cognitions can be abstract, such as gender theories about the similarities that exist within one gender group (Martin, Eisenbud, & Rose, 1995). Gender cognitions may involve scripts for gender-related activities (Boston & Levy, 1991). Gender cognitions also can be narrow, encompassing only one particular situation or event.

Gender cognitions are not necessarily consistent in their influence on children's behavior or motivation (see Deaux & Major, 1987; Martin, 1993). In some situations gender is particularly salient, thereby increasing the likelihood of children showing stereotypic behavior. In other situations, gender may not be salient and children's behavior may not be guided into stereotypic patterns. Furthermore, some children hold stronger and more rigid stereotypes whereas others hold less rigid stereotypes, and these children vary in the likelihood of their behavior being influenced by gender cognitions (Levy, 1989). Also, children differ in "gender identity," the degree to which they identify with their own gender group and in the extent to which they feel like they are typical of their group (Egan & Perry, 1999). Children's self-related concepts, such as gender identity, may also influence what they choose to do and how much effort they expend. For instance, girls who feel that they are not typical of other girls—possibly "tomboys"—may not expect to like the things other girls like; in fact, they may expect to dislike those things. Furthermore, gender cognitions need not be conscious to be influential, that is, they may become largely automatic as they are practiced again and again, therefore children need not spend excessive cognitive energy thinking about their behavior.

Although many forms of gender cognitions can be identified and researchers are beginning to recognize some of the variations across situations and across individuals that can modify their effects, most of the research on children's gender cognitions has focused on one type—gender stereotypic expectations—and that will be the emphasis in this chapter. Nonetheless, fuller understanding of when and how gender cognitions influence children's cognitive skills requires consideration of situational factors, individual differences, and multiple forms of gender conceptions (see chapter 4 and Eccles, Barber, & Jozefowicz, 1999).

CHILDREN'S SOCIAL ENVIRONMENTS

In this chapter, we focus on children's peer-related social environments, in particular, we consider what children do during play and with whom they play. The assumption that guides this review is that children's early social experiences have

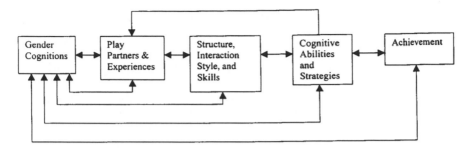

Figure 8.1. Model of social environmental influences.

long-term implications for their social and cognitive development. Specifically, children's social environments may be one source of later sex differences in cognitive abilities. To understand how children's social environments may exert an influence on cognitive abilities, it is important to outline the nature of girls' and boys' social environments and consider in some depth the types of experiences they gain in these settings.

Another goal in the chapter is to illustrate the links between children's gender cognitions and their social environments. Gender cognitions may exert influence on sex differences in several ways. As can be seen in Figure 8.1, one is through a direct path by influencing what children chose to do (e.g., academic courses, careers) and another is through an indirect path, by influencing what they do early in life (e.g., toy and activity choices) and who they play with, which then provides different learning environments. This basic model of social environmental influences is not meant to represent all influences or even all the social influences. The model is presented merely to indicate that influences can be both direct and indirect.

PLAY AND ACTIVITY PREFERENCES

In this section, we discuss the different kinds of play activities in which girls and boys engage. Then we consider how these experiences may influence children's cognitive skill development and the types of strategies they may employ.

Girls' and Boys' Activities and Interests

One possible route to developing different cognitive skills is that girls and boys spend much of their early years engaged in different activities, thereby providing them with different forms of practice, which in turn, facilitate the development of different cognitive skills. Sex differences in children's activities emerge early—between their first and second birthdays. Young girls show preferences for soft toys, dolls and doll furniture, toy animals, playing dress up, and with art supplies. Young boys enjoy transportation toys, plastic tools, and blocks. In the preschool

years, consistent sex differences are found in children's toy and activity preferences. Girls prefer dolls, art activities, kitchen play, sewing, dressing up, singing,
and listening to music. They play indoors more than boys and play more quietly
than do boys. Boys prefer transportation toys, blocks, toy weapons, and manipulating objects. Their play is more active. Individual differences in children's preferences are quite stable and boys more than girls avoid highly stereotyped cross-
sex activities (see Etaugh, 1983). Boys and girls play different types of games:
boys are more likely to play games with greater role differentiation, larger
groups, more competitiveness, and more rules than are girls (Lever, 1978).

Sex differences in interests and activities persist into middle childhood and
adolescence. Boys spend more time in outdoor chores, leisure activities, and
sports; girls spend more time socializing, shopping, doing chores (especially
indoors), and engaging in personal care (Richards & Larson, 1989; Timmer,
Eccles, & O'Brien, 1985).

The reasons that the sexes differ in their early interests is unknown. Girls and
boys may have different toy preferences due to biological factors, such as differences in activity level or in play styles, or to evolutionary pressures (see chapter
2). Infants and young girls and boys are provided with different toys by parents,
which may encourage different interests and activities. By the time children enter
preschool, peers and other social agents, such as parents and teachers, also provide pressures to conform to traditional gender stereotypic behaviors and activities (see Ruble & Martin, 1998).

ACTIVITIES, INTERESTS, AND CHILDREN'S SKILL DEVELOPMENT

Questions have existed for many years about the potential links between children's early experiences and their skill development, especially in the realms of
cognitive abilities (Liss, 1983). Playing with certain toys may provide direct
training for certain cognitive skills. Another possibility is that play provides children with opportunities to learn strategies for problem solving. The direct training argument is especially popular for explaining cognitive sex differences. For
instance, it is suggested that boys may learn visual/spatial skills through their
experience with blocks, model building, and play with other manipulative toys
(Mitchell, 1973; Sherman, 1967). Males' interest and achievement in science
may derive in part from visual/spatial skills and from the greater frequency with
which they play with science materials, such as microscopes and chemistry sets
(Astin, 1975).

Children also may learn strategies of problem solving from their play experiences. The most comprehensive view of this avenue of learning was proposed by
Block (1979, cited in Fagot & Leinbach, 1983). Block proposed that play with
girls' toys (such as dolls and domestic toys), encourages girls to learn rules, to
imitate behaviors, and to use adults as sources of help. This toy-related training

then allows girls to be good problem solvers for problems that are similar to those they have dealt with before. In contrast, boys' toys require that boys develop their own "schemas" and to find out how toys work. As compared to girls' toys, which encourage imitation of observed scenes (e.g., playing house), boys' toys more often provide feedback for correct answers rather than calling for imitation (see Fagot & Leinbach, 1983). Boys' toys are more active than girls' toys, require them to explore their environments more independently, and discourage them from using adults as information sources. As a result of differential play experiences, Block suggested that boys develop skills that allow them to restructure problems and work independently; girls develop skills that allow them to solve problems through incremental steps and with adults as information sources.

The sex difference in problem-solving strategies are similar to arguments that have been made about why sex differences in mathematics occurs for older children. Specifically, girls' greater dependence, orientation towards teachers, and the tendency to follow classroom rules have been interpreted by some researchers as indicators of girls having a "rote" learning style (e.g., Fenema & Peterson, 1985). In contrast, boys' rebellion against teachers and resistance to teachers-suggested solutions has been interpreted as an "autonomous" learning style. These styles may influence the development of additional skills and/or may influence the development of test-taking strategies. For example, even high-mathematical ability females and males use different strategies of problem solving, with males being more likely to use unconventional strategies. These strategies may be particularly effective for helping students finish time-pressured exams (Gallagher & De Lisi, 1994). Thus far, little evidence links specific learning styles and later performance in mathematics, however, research is under way to assess this hypothesis more extensively (see chapter 6 and Kimball, 1989).

For young children, the proposed links between play and cognitive skills have undergone some empirical investigation. Several studies, for instance, suggest a possible link between exposure to gender-typed toys and individual differences in spatial abilities. In one study, young boys who played more with boy-preferred toys had better spatial skills than boys who played less with boys' toys, however, the same pattern did not hold for girls (Connor & Serbin, 1977). In another study, elementary school children with more exposure to boy-preferred toys showed better visual/spatial skills than children with less experience (Serbin, Zelkowitz, Doyle, Gold, & Wheaton, 1990). In addition, both girls and boys who played more frequently with boy-preferred toys (e.g., blocks, climbing and riding toys, Lincoln Logs, Tinker Toys, puppets, ring toss, transportation toys) showed a pattern of higher spatial than verbal skills as compared to children who played more with girl-preferred toys (dolls, drawing, kitchen play, painting, board games, felt board) (Serbin & Connor, 1979). One study of young children found that both boys and girls who engaged in more boy-preferred activities in preschool showed later higher spatial, science, and mathematics skills (girls also showed higher language scores; boys showed higher art scores) (Fagot &

Littman, 1976). By adolescence, boys' science interest and girls' "interest in careers" correlated positively with first-grade scores on boy-preferred play (Tyler, 1964).

Most of the evidence supporting a link between activities and cognitive skills is correlational, leading researchers to continue to wonder whether children with particular skills are more interested in certain activities or whether particular activities promote skill development. Although training studies suggest that activities influence skill development (see Okagaki & Frensch, 1994), little is known about how extensively the play children engage in translates into differential skill development in either the cognitive or social domains. Research that tests causal mechanisms is needed to understand whether naturally occurring differences in activities play a significant role in promoting skill development. Furthermore, research is needed to more fully understand the extent to which play experiences influence direct training and/or learning style and strategies.

THE ROLE OF GENDER COGNITIONS IN INFLUENCING CHILDREN'S ACTIVITIES, INTERESTS, AND SKILLS

According to cognitive views of gender development, children's gender cognitions influence what they choose to do. Children's behavior can be guided by their beliefs about what toys, activities, and interests are appropriate for them. Thus, gender cognitions can directly influence the types of cognitive domains that children pursue and they also may influence their cognitive abilities indirectly by guiding children's early toy and activity choices, which in turn, influences the skills they develop.

Although many factors likely influence children's preferences including biological (see chapters 2 & 3 and Berenbaum & Hines, 1992; Fabes, 1994) and social factors (see chapter 4 and Fagot, 1977) the roles of gender cognitions cannot be ignored. The activities and interests that children choose can be influenced by what they think is appropriate for their sex.

The Influence of Gender Cognition on Exploration

Investigating the impact of children's beliefs about gender on their behavior and thinking requires disentangling influences due to children's prior history with toys and activities from the influence of their cognitions. The research strategies that have been most effective have involved unfamiliar, novel toys and activities. The toys and activities are either labeled as being more appropriate for one sex or the other or a more subtle suggestion is provided about the sex-appropriateness of the activities or toys.

Gender labeling of novel toys effectively directs children's behavior and memory for toys. In a study of preschoolers, children were provided with novel toys that the experimenter named and then labeled as being for boys ("I think that boys like the things in this box better than girls do"), for girls, or for both girls and boys (Bradbard & Endsley, 1983). Children were shown six objects, two with each label. After viewing each toy, the children were told that they could play with the toys. During the play period, children's touching of toys and questions about the toys were recorded. At the end of the play time and a week later, children's memory for the toys (using a recognition task), the gender labels, and toy names were assessed. Children explored own-sex labeled toys more than objects labeled for the other-sex, and both-sex toys were intermediate. Children asked more questions about both-sex labeled toys than other-sex labeled toys and there was a trend of more questions being asked for own-sex labeled toys than for other-sex toys. Children's memories were influenced by gender labels: children remembered more names of own-sex labeled toys than other-sex toys and showed intermediate levels for both-sex labeled toys. Older children were more affected by the gender labels for recall than were younger children. These results suggest that gender labels play a powerful role in children's exploration of objects and in their memory for names of objects, and it may be greater as they grow older.

In a cleverly designed study (Masters, Ford, Arend, Grotevant, & Clark, 1979), young children were shown novel toys demonstrated by either a male or female model and these toys were either labeled with gender labels or not. Children's time spent playing with the toys and their preferences for the toys were measured. By varying the sex of model and gender labels, it was possible to assess the contributions of each factor alone as well as how children integrated both sources of information. The sex of models, alone, did not influence how long children played with the toys. Gender labels, alone, did influence how long children played with toys: children were more likely to interact with the toys given same-sex labels (75% of their contact time versus 25% for other-sex labeled toys). Children's preferences followed the same pattern with no influence of models but children did show a trend to prefer same-sex labeled toys more than other-sex labeled toys. When gender labels and sex of models were considered simultaneously, gender labels again showed a stronger effect than modeling. Overall, the results suggest that labeling was more powerful than modeling and the influence was greater on children's exploration than on their preferences.

The Influence of Gender Cognitions on Motivation

Do children try harder on games or tasks that they think are appropriate for their own sex? Several studies suggest that children's motivation, accuracy, and expectancies for success are influenced by gender labeling of activities and tasks. In one of the first studies to assess the influence of gender labels on motivation (Montemayor, 1974), 6- to 8-year-old children were shown a novel game (Mr. Munchie) that involved throwing small plastic marbles into a clown's body. One third of the children were told that the game was a toy for boys, "like basketball"; one third were told the game was for girls, "like jacks"; and one third were given no information about the game. Both girls and boys performed better (got more marbles in the clown), said they liked the game more, and rated the game's attractiveness higher if the game was labeled as being for their own sex versus as being for the other sex.

Using a problem-solving task in which children made pictures of objects from cardboard shapes, researchers compared children's performance on a variety of gender measures (e.g., constancy, stereotyping) with their performance on the task that was described to children as something either boys do well on, girls do well on, or both do well on (Gold & Berger, 1978). The gender labeling effect was apparent in the boys' performance on the task but was not for the girls. The gender tasks did not relate strongly to performance.

Stein and colleagues (Stein, Pohly, & Mueller, 1971) assessed whether gender labels would influence the achievement behavior of sixth-grade children. Three paper-and-pencil tasks were used and the tasks were assigned labels (counterbalanced across children) that indicated they were for boys, for girls, or for both girls and boys. For instance, when a task was labeled as being for boys, the child was told that "this test helps to tell how good you might be at boys' school subjects like shop or industrial arts. People who are good at this test are good at building things with wood and electrical wiring and things like that." (Stein et al., 1971, p. 198). The time children spent on the task, their expectancy for success, and the attainment value of the task (how important good performance was to the child) were assessed. The gender-labeling effect was found on boys' performance on the task but not on girls' performance. Both sexes, however, showed gender labeling effects for their expectancies for success and for attainment value.

Using a perceptual-motor steadiness task, Hargreaves and colleagues (Hargreaves, Bates, & Foot, 1985) found that even relatively subtle labels influenced both girls' and boys' error rates. The task involved moving a metal loop over a 3-foot-long bent wire without touching the wire. Each time the wire was touched, a bell rang and an error was scored. Half of the 10- and 11-year-old children in the study were told that, "This is a test to see how good you would be at mechanics or at operating machinery," and the other half were told that, "This is a test to see how good you would be at needlework—sewing and knitting." Both sexes made fewer errors on the task when it was labeled as sex appropriate. For instance, boys made about 10 errors when given a same-sex label and about 18 when given an other-sex label; girls made about 13 errors in the same-sex condition and about 17 in the other-sex condition. The effect appeared to be stronger in boys than girls, although not significantly so.

Several other studies (Davies, 1986, 1989) confirm the effectiveness of subtle labels on task performance for 11-, 13-, and 16-year-old children. The tasks were given gender-related descriptions. For instance, for some children the task was described as related to "needlework" ("This task can show how good people are at needlework") and for others it was described as related to "electronics" ("This task can show how good people are at electronics"). Although the electronics label was more effective than the needlework label in illustrating a sex difference in error rates, for both girls and boys error rates on the tasks related to the labels. Specifically, girls showed more errors on the task when it was labeled electronics than when labeled needlework; boys showed more errors when the task was labeled needlework than electronics (see Davies, 1989).

Herzog and colleagues (Herzog, Enright, Luria, & Rubin, 1982) used a task similar to the Mr. Munchie game in an attempt to replicate Montemayor's (1974) results. After finding no gender-labeling results on performance or attractiveness in two studies using large samples of young children, the authors concluded that gender-label effects have been exaggerated. The authors then offered some ideas about why their results may have differed, such as the game being somewhat different from the original Mr. Munchie. They also proposed the possibility that children may construct their own labels that conflict with externally imposed labels because children are not simply passive recipients of information. The results bear out this possibility: of the 160 children interviewed after the experiment (Study 2), 63% said that this version of Mr. Munchie was a toy for both girls and boys, 7% chose a gender label opposite to that given by the experimenter, 7% said they did not know the gender label, and only 23% used the label offered by the experimenter. Thus, children in this study either did not accept or forgot the labels—only 23% could potentially show the effect of experimenter-assigned labels. It is not clear what features of this study or of this sample led to children rejecting the experimenter-assigned labels. These findings suggest that when conducting gender-labeling studies researchers need to assess children's memory for labels to ensure that the labels have been encoded by children. In the future, researchers may want to examine the situations that encourage children to reject labels so that they can decrease their susceptibility to stereotype label effects.

The results from gender-labeling research on children's exploration and motivation suggest that children, especially boys, are vulnerable to stereotypes at a young age, and that this vulnerability may have both short-term and long-term impact on them. In the short term, children may be less motivated to try tasks they believe are for the other sex, they may be less inclined to explore and touch toys that they believe the other sex prefers, and they may be less interested in activities they believe are not appropriate for their own sex. In the long term, children with vulnerability to gender labels will develop fewer skills and interests that cross gender traditional lines, thereby decreasing their range of skills.

The Influence of Gender Cognitions on Memory

Gender labels also place limits on competence by limiting the acquisition and/or retention of information relevant to a cognitive or behavioral task (see Martin & Halverson, 1981; Martin, 1991). If individuals do not pay attention to task information, and if they do not retain information about the task, then their competence to carry out the task is curtailed. To assess these types of competence restraints, it is necessary to devise a task that involves an in-depth learning procedure in which performance limitations are minimized.

In one such study, Bradbard and colleagues (Bradbard, Martin, Endsley, & Halverson, 1986) presented children with novel objects that were given one of three gender labels and, for each toy, children were told four bits of in-depth information about the functions of the objects. A week later, memory for the information was assessed. To assess the role of competence and performance limitations, some children were given incentives for remembering (a very attractive toy of their choice) and some were not. The assumption was that if only performance is influenced by gender labels, then children in the incentive condition (who should be trying particularly hard to remember the information) should remember information equally well about the same-sex and other-sex labeled toys. If only competence is influenced by labels, then children in the incentive condition should remember similarly to the nonincentive children. Specifically, both groups should remember more information about same-sex labeled toys than other-sex labeled toys because they did not originally learn the material about other-sex toys. Incentives would be ineffective for improving memory for other-sex information because children would not have learned the information in the first place. We were surprised to find only competence limitations: children showed gender-labeling effects and the incentives for remembering did not improve children's memory for in-depth information for toys labeled as being for the other-sex. Thus, children did not remember how the other-sex objects functioned but they did remember how to use the same-sex objects.

This study does not provide a definitive answer about performance and competence constraints because one could argue that a one-time incentive may not be powerful enough to override a long-term history of gender-typed tendencies. Nonetheless, this study does illustrate that children's attention to and memory for in-depth information can be influenced by their ideas about whether the task is appropriate for their sex or not.

One potential criticism of the gender-labeling studies is the demand characteristics involved in labeling the toys and activities. In many of the studies, children's play or task performance occurs in front of the person who just provided labels about sex-appropriateness. This raises the possibility that children might only conform to labels when they are in the presence of an adult or other authority figure but, when they are alone, their behavior may not be guided by labels. In an attempt to minimize demand characteristics, we (Martin et al., 1995, Study 3) developed a ruse in which one person labeled the toys but then had to leave the room. Then another person came in—a person who said she was unfamiliar with the toys—and children's preferences and behavior were assessed. When the demands of the situations were lessened in this way, gender labels continued to have a powerful effect on children's own liking of the toys and on their expectations of how much other girls and boys would like the toys. Furthermore, this study also illustrated that children must remember gender labels for them to be effective. Gender-labeling effects should only occur when children remember and accept the experimenter-assigned labels. Children were divided into groups of rememberers (those who remembered most of the labels) and nonrememberers (remembered few of the labels). Not surprisingly, the results were memory dependent such that children who remembered labels showed the expected gender-label effects whereas those who did not failed to show gender-label effects.

The gender-labeling studies about memory and attention again suggest the powerful potential of gender labels on children for both their short- and long-term development. Children who follow gender labels will avoid and not remember information about toys and activities that they believe are not for their own sex. Over time, children who are susceptible to these influences will not develop a full range of skills and abilities because they will not have developed in-depth scripts about how to carry out what they believe to be sex-inappropriate activities. With less well-developed scripts, we would then expect less well-developed behavior and less expertise in the activities. With less expertise, children may be more likely to avoid these activities when given opportunities to engage in them. A self-fulfilling pattern emerges: children initially avoid an activity because it is not considered appropriate for them, which results in not learning about the activity, which in turn leads to heightened avoidance because they avoid activities in which they feel less competent.

The research on gender labels provides strong evidence about the importance of gender beliefs for directing behavior and memory. When toys and activities that have no gender typing to begin with are given gender labels—essentially, when they are stereotyped—children respond according to whether they believe, based on the label, that the toy or activity is appropriate for their sex. The influence of gender labels is far-ranging: children's tactile exploration, question asking, name memory, in-depth memory, motivation, accuracy, and perceived importance of doing well are all influenced by how toys and activities are described.

Furthermore, the gender-labeling studies suggest that both overt and subtle markers about the sex-appropriateness of toys and activities are noticed by children. Thus, parents, teachers, and the media should exercise caution when introducing new toys and activities to children. Even unintended gender messages may be translated by children into messages about who should and should not play with a particular toy or play in a specific activity.

Gender labels are effective even in very young children, although they appear to be somewhat more effective with older children and with boys. Individual differences and developmental differences in susceptibility to gender labels needs further investigation. Some developmental factors suggest increased vulnerability for younger children whereas others suggest increased vulnerability for older children. For example, young children may be particularly vulnerable because they lack experience to counteract the labels. Older children may be more vulnerable because they are more aware and concerned about what others might think of them if and when they cross gender "boundaries." Additional research is needed to identify developmental factors that may predispose children to be more or less susceptible to gender labels. Furthermore, individual differences need to be explored in more depth. For instance, children from gender-traditional families may be more vulnerable to labels because they have experienced more disapproval for not following gender stereotypes than other children. Recent research suggests that children with perceived social constraints (e.g., they think a parent or friend will disapprove of their behavior) show more susceptibility to stereotypic toy play than other children (Raag, 1999; Raag & Rackliff, 1998). As the gender-labeling research suggests, boys seem to be more susceptible to gender labels, possibly because they, too, receive more disapproval from others for crossing gender boundaries. What is missing in this line of research, however, is an understanding as to how situations make gender labels more or less salient and how children may vary in their vulnerability to gender-labeling effects.

The implications for understanding sex differences in the cognitive domain are straightforward and involve proximal and distal influences. Children's early behavior and toy choices may be routed into gender-typed lines because of children's beliefs about what is appropriate for them, and these early experiences provide sex-differentiated contexts for learning different skills. Also, to the extent that children recognize stereotypes about cognitive domains such as mathematics and science, then we would expect that these stereotypes act as gender labels and can influence whether children pay attention to, remember, and work hard in these domains. Furthermore, the gender-labeling research suggests that the influence of gender cognitions may be more serious than simply curtailing behavior; instead, children's competence may be influenced if they pay less attention to material and remember less about the topic.

How Cognitions Influence Performance Through Stereotype Threat

Imagine that you are a girl about to take a mathematics test. If while taking the test you think about how other people assume that girls do not perform well in mathematics, your own performance might be hindered. This is an example of stereotype threat, which to date has predominantly been used to describe the underperformance of minority college students in academic areas. Stereotype threat explains differentials in performance as a combination of pressure to break out of the stereotypic mold and disidentification with domains that are stereotyped.

Stereotype threat has been described as "a situational threat . . . that, in general form, can affect the members of any group about whom a negative stereotype exists" (Steele, 1997, p. 614). When individuals are placed in an atmosphere in which they risk confirming an existing stereotype, the burden placed on them to break free of the potential stereotype can activate impairment mechanisms, such as distraction, self-consciousness, and anxiety (Steele & Aronson, 1995). Thus, individuals' preoccupation with being judged by others based on stereotypes, or of confirming the negative implications a stereotype holds for them, can actually cause a decrease in performance levels.

Individuals do not have to believe that the stereotype is true of themselves for stereotype threat to negatively affect their performance (Steele, 1997). Rather, to be worried that others will use the stereotype to identify or classify them is sufficient to cause negative outcomes. Identification with the domain in which the stereotype pertains is also necessary for stereotype threat to influence performance. If the area in which a stereotype has negative implications is not meaningful to an individual, stereotype threat will not affect their performance. For example, if one does not feel it is important to know how to solve algebraic equations, not excelling in algebra class means little and stereotype threat has no negative implications. However, if an individual places importance on doing well in algebra, for example, someone striving to become an engineer, performing badly in algebra class can be devastating. In a situation such as this one, when one feels his or her performance in an area is self-defining, stereotype threat can greatly hinder performance (Steele, 1997; Steele & Aronson, 1995).

Two main consequences of stereotype threat have been studied. The first consequence is intellectual underperformance. The second consequence is disidentification with the stereotyped domains. To explore the relevance of stereotype threat to underperformance in intellectual domains, a number of experiments have been conducted with African American and female college students. The first study, conducted by Steele and Aronson (1995), used a variety of SAT testing sessions to examine how making stereotypes salient prior to taking examinationss affected African American students' performance. The findings of this study show that subtle changes in pretest-taking conditions, such as telling test takers that the examination was diagnostic of intellectual ability or being asked to note their race before taking their examination, led to African American students achieving lower test scores than the white participants, as well as having lower scores than African American students who were not primed with stereotype salient preconditions. Individuals who had racial stereotypes primed prior to taking the test suffered from inefficient processing of the material as illustrated by their spending more time rereading the test questions before being able to answer them, expending more energy and time on each item, having higher levels of inaccuracy, and answering fewer questions. The authors suggested that these students may have vacillated between concentrating on the test items and evaluating the significance of their frustrations (whether they were having a harder time because of their race). This study also showed that, by placing individuals in situations in which they felt they may be judged by their race (in this case, simply placing them in a setting where participants expected to take a difficult ability-diagnostic test), they had greater cognitive activation of African American stereotypes, increased concerns about their ability, and had increased levels of stereotype-related self-doubts. Also, stereotype threat increased the likelihood that students distanced themselves from their group. For instance, one striking finding was that, in the session that did not prime stereotype salience, 100% of the participants indicated their race when asked. In contrast, in the condition that did prime stereotypes, only 25% of participants indicated their race (Steele & Aronson, 1995).

Stereotype threat also has been demonstrated in women taking mathematics tests (Spence, Steele, & Quinn, 1997 as cited in Steele, 1997; also see chapter 6). In the first study, male and female college students were given questions from the mathematics section of the GRE and an advanced literature test. Women were found to underperform only in the mathematics test (paralleling the stereotype that men are better at mathematics then women) and only when the mathematics section was difficult (showing that stereotype threat is more prominent when frustration levels are increased). To rule out the possibility that the women's poor performance on the harder mathematics test was due to biological limitations in women's ability, a third testing session was administered. In this session, half of the women were told that the hard test usually showed sex differences, whereas half were told that no sex differences had been found in this test. Results showed that the women who had the stereotype primed prior to taking the examination did significantly worse than the women who did not have the stereotype made salient (Spencer et al., 1997 as cited in Steele, 1997).

In a recently published study of Canadian students, stereotype threat effects were confirmed (Walsh, Hickey, & Duffy, 1999). Women underperformed on standardized mathematics examinations in comparison to men when exposed to a brief written description of stereotype threat, even when they had the same mathematics skill, interest, and perceived ability as the men. Knowledge of the effects of stereotype threat worked to raise the women's attentiveness to the existing stereotypes, and led to lower levels of accuracy. The results of these experiments support the concept of stereotype threat causing underperformance, specifically for females taking mathematical tests.

Surprisingly, the effect of stereotype threat also became apparent in an interesting, yet unexpected way. Results showed that both men and women underperformed in the gender neutral situation. This can be explained by the fact that the information given prior to the test was that the results from their scores would be compared to U.S. students' results, rather than comparing males' scores to females' scores. In this situation, both men and women have the added pressure of performing better than another group, which may have caused stereotype threat to occur in the neutral setting (Walsh et al., 1999).

Disidentification with a domain associated with a stereotype is the second implication of stereotype threat. When individuals are consistently met with increased anxiety, inability to disprove the stereotype, or underperformance due to stereotype threat, disidentification with a particular domain can alleviate these negative consequences (Steele, 1997). The main area that has been studied in terms of disidentification has been identification with school, however the concept can apply to any domain in which a stereotype is associated. Particularly for minority students, a host of barriers to school identification exist but it is hypothesized that stereotype threat imposes an additional barrier for these students (Steele, 1997). In essence, it is easier to identify with another domain in which they can excel, such as peer relations, than to continue the uphill battle of identifying with the domain associated with the stereotype. Once the disidentification process has occurred, the negative consequences (such as earning poor grades) no longer hold the personal relevance they once did. Steele (1997) uses cross-cultural statistics of gaps between stigmatized and nonstigmatized individuals to support the affect of stereotype threat and disidentification (see Steele, 1997).

So how does the concept of stereotype threat relate to performance differences in children? Although the concept has been studied mainly in adults, the process of stereotype threat can easily be applied as one possible explanation for children's sex differences in performance, even when girls and boys have the same cognitive ability. In cases in which boys and girls identify with a domain that is linked to the other sex, such as boys identifying with verbal ability or girls identifying with mathematics, even if the children know they are competent in the area, they can be affected by the pressure to perform. The added pressure of stereotypes can lead to mediating factors such as self-doubt and anxiety, which in turn reduces their actual performance in the specified area. If this pressure continues to increase, or if it is combined with other socialization pressures such as peer, parent, teacher, and media influence, it may be easier for children to disidentify with the domain and choose another arena in which to excel.

The gender-labeling studies discussed earlier can be interpreted through the lens of stereotype threat. It is possible that the underperformance in areas labeled as "for the opposite sex" may be a result of higher levels of anxiety provoked by stereotype threat, or from the process of disidentification. For example, children underperformed in the task of getting marbles into Mr. Munchie in Montemayor's (1974) study when told the task was for the opposite sex. If a task is associated with a stereotype that suggests that the task should be harder for the child, the added pressure of doing well in spite of the stereotype can cause the impairment mechanisms that lead to underperformance (e.g. anxiety, inability to focus). A second possibility is that stereotype threat causes children to disidentify with the cross-sex activity, thus, it is no longer is important to them that they excel in this area. This is suggested by the Stein et al. (1971) results in which children's attainment values and assigned importance of activities varied according to arbitrarily assigned gender labels for the tasks.

Although the findings on gender-labeling tasks and stereotype threat seem related, it is not clear how the two processes become apparent in children's developmental trajectories. However, with the information available it does seem possible to speculate about how these two processes might relate to one another. The first step in hypothesizing about the developmental component associated with these two processes is to isolate what each requires of the child, and then consider what is known about children's standard developmental progress.

Similarities exist between gender-labeling processes and stereotype threat in that both processes can lead an individual to discard a domain as "not for me" (i.e., disidentify), reducing the chances that one will gain or improve their skills in this area. Although the outcome of these two processes seem the same, the developmental requirements appear to be much different. For the process of gender labeling to occur, a child needs to have the skills and developmental readiness to categorize, label, and identify with objects or tasks as "for me" or "not for me." Without the ability to notice, encode, remember, and interpret information, the process of gender labeling could not occur. Studies suggest that children distinguish the sexes at about 1 year of age and that they can label the sexes in toddlerhood (see Ruble & Martin, 1998). Direct links between these abilities and identifying a task "for me" or "not for me" have not yet been made. Nonetheless, in a recent study (Levy, 1999), even young toddlers showed awareness of "own-sex" gender-typed categories of toys. Furthermore, the motivation to conform to one's group should increase the effectiveness of gender labels.

The developmental requirements for the stereotype threat process to be completed are a bit more complex. A child must value a domain, be aware of the existence of a stereotypic belief that applies to them, and, although they do not need to subscribe to the stereotype themselves, understand that others around them may hold these beliefs. In addition, children must be affected by a negative force, such as increased anxiety, which prevent them from reaching their potential on this task or in this area. In order for anxiety to be evoked, the individual must have the cognitive ability to understand the consequences of not performing to par or of failing to meet their own or someone else's expectations. Recognizing others' expectations, at least about gender-related activities, has been identified in preschoolers (Martin et al., 1999; Raag, 1999) but may also occur in younger children.

Children's ability to use relative standards, or in other words, to be able to compare their performance to others, also appears to be important in being susceptible to stereotype threat. For instance, children under the age of 7 often do not use social comparison in situations in which ambiguous standards exist (Ruble, 1987). Ruble's research on the prerequisite skills for social comparison showed that, by age 6, children have the basic capacities, interest, and strategies needed for social comparisons. However, children's interest and the ability to process and weigh information may increase as they grow older, and a stronger environmental pressure to use relative criteria to make judgments may account for the increased use of social comparison after the age of 6. Therefore, even though the prerequisite abilities exist in varying stages before this time, social comparison may not be used by young children very often.

The developmental findings just outlined suggest that the ability to compare exists as early as preschool years but is not used very often before the age of 6 or

7, thus susceptibility to stereotype threat may be apparent during this time, although it may occur sporadically. It also seems plausible, however, that stereotype threat may occur at different ages depending on the domain in question. For example, a child's ability to understand that boys are expected to be stronger than girls may occur at a much younger age than their understanding that boys are supposed to be better at mathematics and science. Therefore, it seems that the age in which the stereotype-threat process begins to occur may be dependent on the domain in which the child is engaging and on a child's cognitive ability to understand that a stereotype exists.

The skills required for gender labeling seem to be less complex than for the process of stereotype threat. Susceptibility to gender labeling may require only the ability to categorize into two categories, for me or not for me, although motivation to adhere to those categories may be greatly influenced by children's expectations about approval and disapproval from others. In contrast, susceptibility to stereotype threat is particularly dependent on children understanding that others hold expectations about their behavior and competencies. Therefore, it seems possible that susceptibility to gender labeling occurs earlier in a child's life than fully developed stereotype threat. Additionally, there is a striking similarity in the outcomes of these two processes, in that both include discarding a domain ("not for me" in gender labeling and disidentification in stereotype threat). In stereotype threat situations, children may reason as they do in gender-labeling situations, that is, they may consider that a particular task or domain is not "for me." When the pressure to excel in a stereotyped area leads them to lower performance, they may disengage by considering that this area is "not for me."

Further research is needed to better understand the developmental components of gender labeling and stereotype threat and the associations between these two processes. Studies also need to be conducted to test the application of the concept of stereotype threat to children specifically, even though the concepts seem highly related to earlier gender-labeling studies. The idea that stereotype threat is a barrier to the performance of cross-gender activities may help us to understand sex differences in cognitive domains in which girls and boys have similar levels of cognitive ability.

BOYS AND GIRLS IN THE SOCIAL ENVIRONMENT: PEER EXPERIENCES

The role of peers in children's development has been the subject of a lot of debate and speculation. Some authors suggested that peers constitute the major socializing agents in children's lives (Harris, 1995). It has been suggested that peers play a major role in gender development, specifically in the development of many sex differences, and that these early experiences lay the groundwork for males and females developing along different paths (see Maccoby, 1998). Thus, who children play with may be more important for the development of cognitive skills than what toys they play with. In this section, we discuss the influence of play partners on children's development and how the interactions and skills involved in playing with boys and with girls may differentially influence girls and boys.

Peers as Socialization Agents

Peers influence children's behavior in many ways. Peers play a role in children's activity choices. Peers provide sources of information about the appropriateness of activities and toys for children. Children's same-sex behavior is rewarded with positive interactions whereas cross-sex behavior is punished with fewer positive responses and with more criticism (Fagot, 1977; Fagot & Patterson, 1969; Lamb & Roopnarine, 1979; Langlois & Downs, 1980). Children report increased levels of negative responses to cross-sex play in their peers with age (Carter & McCloskey, 1984). Boys, in particular, receive more "gender-typed" training from peers than girls (Fagot, 1977). Peers model gender-typed behavior for children. In experimentally manipulated situations, the mere presence of peers—even when they did not respond negatively to the child—discouraged children from playing with cross-sex toys (Serbin, Connor, Burchardt, & Citron, 1979).

Sex Differences in Play Partner Preferences

Peers also may provide a training ground for developing many kinds of skills. Girls and boys may develop different skills because they spend so much time with other children of their own sex. Children's tendencies to prefer same-sex play partners begin around the age of 2 1/2 years of age, when girls begin to segregate from boys. By age 3, boys begin to spend more time with other boys than with girls (La Freniere, Strayer, & Gauthier, 1984). Several studies have confirmed the early emergence of sex segregation in toddlers (Fagot, 1994; Howes, 1988; Serbin, Moller, Gulko, Powlishta, & Colburne, 1994). Although the origins of sex segregation are unclear, the children who first demonstrate preferences tend to be girls who are socially sensitive and boys who are disruptive (Serbin et al., 1994). Children's interaction styles, activity level, physiological reactivity, and their cognitive understanding about who is a boy and who is a girl (and their associated beliefs about the sexes) likely contribute to the origins of sex segregation (see Leaper, 1994).

Preschool children show strong preferences for same-sex peers (e.g., Fabes, 1994; Maccoby & Jacklin, 1987; Serbin, Tonick, & Sternglanz, 1977). By the age of 6, children engage in same-sex play about half the time they are in social situations and spend less than 10% of their time with other-sex peers (Maccoby & Jacklin, 1987). Few children (about 5%) spent more time with other-sex peers than same-sex peers. Even in preschool, play partner preferences represent very large sex differences, accounting for 74% of the individual variation in the proportion of time in social interaction that children spent playing with girls and 81% of the variance in proportion of time spent playing with boys (Martin & Fabes, 2001; also see Maccoby, 1998). Children's friends tend to be of the same-sex and the number of cross-sex friends dramatically decreases from toddler-aged to preschool-aged children (Howes, 1988).

Children do not spend all of their time in same-sex groups. In their homes, children play with their siblings. In their neighborhoods, children play with the children who are available playmates and may have cross-sex friends. Furthermore, even in school settings, children's same-sex play preferences tend to be lessened in situations that are structured to include both sexes (Lockheed & Harris, 1984). Generally, sex segregation appears to be most evident in situations that are unstructured, especially situations (such as schools) where children have a choice in play partners.

The Separate Cultures of Girls and Boys Play Groups

Even with variation in sex segregation depending on settings and structure, many children spend much of their time with members of their own sex. The fact that children spend so much time playing in same-sex peer groups has led many to argue that boys and girls grow up in different social environments—in separate subcultures (Maccoby, 1988; Maccoby, 1990; Thorne & Luria, 1986). The socialization that boys and girls receive in their segregated peer groups likely contributes to their development and this contribution is likely to be above and beyond the individual difference variables that led boys and girls to initially select themselves into same-sex peer groups (Maccoby, 1990; Martin & Fabes, 2001).

Sex segregation may channel children's interests and experiences and limit the kinds of activities in which they engage (Serbin et al., 1994). The activities that are most prominent in same-sex peer groups promote certain behaviors and practices. Thus, experience within boys' and girls' same-sex peer groups is likely to foster different behavioral norms. As such, same-sex peer groups represent potentially powerful contexts for the socialization of gender-typed behavior (Carter, 1987; Leaper, 1994; Maccoby, 1988, 1998).

These separate cultures of girls' groups and boys' groups are marked by different interactional styles, which is a broad term used to describe the manner in which children relate to one another. Interactional styles encompass characteristics such as level of activity, influence styles, aggression, and independence. As children's interactional styles evolve and become more gender typed, the compatibility of cross-sex play partners decreases, and children become more comfortable choosing play partners of their own sex.

Style of influence is an area in which sex differences can be readily seen. By the age of 5, girls often use verbal persuasion and polite suggestions as a way to influence a peer's actions whereas boys more often use direct commands or physical dominance. Girls' polite style works well with other girls, but becomes increasingly less effective with boys (Serbin, Sprafkin, Elman, & Doyle, 1984). In contrast, boys' style of persuasion seems to be effective when interacting with both boys and girls (see Maccoby, 1988). Given the different results associated with boys' and girls' persuasion techniques, it follows that girls would become less willing to play with boys as time passes and may contribute to increased sex segregation.

In comparison to girls, boys' activities more often involve large gross motor skills, include rough and tumble play (Braza, Braza, Carreras, & Munoz, 1997; Di Pietro, 1981), and high levels of energy (Eaton & Enns, 1986). With girls and boys participating in pastimes that have different activity levels, sex segregation is increased. Girls and boys also play in different locations. Boys more often than girls choose to play outdoors when given a choice between indoor and outdoor activities (Pellegrini & Smith, 1993). The chance of girls and boys interacting decreases as the physical space in which they are playing becomes more distinct.

In addition to having different levels of activity in their play, the structure of boys' and girls' activities differ as well. Naturalistic observations show that when given a choice of activities, girls and boys choose activities with different structure levels (Carpenter, 1983). Girls' play has higher levels of structure than does boys' play. For example, girls are more likely to play in close proximity to mothers and have closer supervision (Lewis & Weintraub, 1974). In addition, teachers are more likely to initiate girls' activities than they are boys' activities (Fagot, 1973). Boys' play is often considered low structure because the activities have low levels of designated norms and occurs in larger groups and is less supervised. Although boys and girls consistently choose activities that correspond to their sex, children react the same when placed in high- or low-structured activities (Carpenter, 1983) suggesting that some sex differences may correspond to the structure of activities that girls and boys engage in.

Potential Links Between Interaction Styles, Peer Preferences, and Children's Skill Development

The links that have been made between children's social environments and their later skill development have centered on the general characteristics of play with boys versus play with girls. One potential link has been made through the differences in structure of girls' versus boys' play groups. In Carpenter's (1983) analysis of children's play, she argued that children use different cognitive processes when participating in high- or low-structured activities. Low-structure activities, in which boys are more likely to engage, allow children to create their own structure. This includes developing their own schemas about how to play with a novel toy or activity, which may encourage creativity. Low-structure activities also require independence, self-confidence, initiative, creative use of materials, a dis-regard of others' expectations, and persistence (Carpenter, 1983). In contrast, the high-structure activities that girls chose (Lever, 1976), require that they conform to existing guidelines and rules (Carpenter, 1983). This lessens the need to devel-op novel ideas or concepts, which may relate to the finding that girls tend to have lower levels of independence and exploration in their play than do boys (Maccoby, 1974; Maccoby & Jacklin, 1974). Carpenter (1983) also noted the cyclical nature of the consequences of interactional style. Once children become accustomed to a particular style of interaction and activities associated with this style, their skills in these areas increase. As skills increase, children are increasingly comfortable in these activities and are motivated to continue these types of activities. Thus, chil-dren develop one interactional style, and may become uncomfortable when placed in situations requiring a novel interactional style. They may avoid these situations. Therefore, the skills provided by an alternate structure level are not acquired. This process of only learning to interact and be skilled in one style may contribute to cognitive skill differences in girls and boys.

Another potential link between children's social environments and later skill development is through developing different learning styles. For instance, the interactional patterns described earlier may be one training ground for the autonomous and rote learning styles of older children. Similarly, training with peers in styles of interaction may relate to other aspects of school success. In the literature on children's achievement and success in school, some researchers have proposed that two action patterns or learning styles are important in ensuring children's success. The first is social responsibility, which involves adhering to social rules and role expectations, and from a motivational perspective, using cooperative and compliant goals. The second is independent participation, which involves autonomous, self-reliant behavior and intrinsic motivation. Each style has been found to relate to achievement and school success (see Ladd, Birch, & Buhs, 1999 for review). Furthermore, being able to use both sets of skills when they are most appropriate is probably the ideal for ensuring success in school.

From children's early social experiences, we can view girls as having many opportunities to develop a socially responsible learning style because they spend much of their time with cooperative play partners in structured situations. Research has demonstrated that girls use a more responsive and compliant style and that this style relates to better academic performance (Serbin et al., 1990). Girls may have fewer opportunities to develop autonomous and self-reliant behavior in their interactions with other girls. In contrast, boys might easily learn to be self-reliant as they spend time with other boys in competitive activities but may have fewer opportunities to learn cooperation and rule-oriented behavior. The long-term influence of developing only one skill set or in not applying skills flexibly may be evidenced in later achievement and/or career paths. In essence, then, each sex gains more experience in one set of skills but less in the other.

Linking children's social environments and their later skill development may require a more fine-tuned analysis of the nature of the social environment. Rather than simply arguing that the global differences between girls and boys' groups influence skill acquisition, we must consider the possibility that individual differences in this exposure may vary. The assumption of the separate cultures perspective is that girls and boys each learn different styles of interaction, and that individual differences in the time spent with same-sex peers plays little role in influencing the degree to which children learn same-sex patterns (Maccoby, 1998). An alternative view is that in addition to the "group" effects of peers on children's behavior, individual differences in exposure also matter. A child who experiences more time with same-sex peers has additional learning opportunities that a child who spends somewhat less time with same-sex peers might miss.

To investigate the group and individual differences in peer influence and to investigate the issue of how peer experiences might relate to children's development, a short-term longitudinal study was conducted in which many aspects of young children's (3 1/2 to 6 1/2 years) play were observed for about 6 months (Martin & Fabes, 2001). Specifically, children's tendencies to engage in gender-typed activities, to play near adults, to engage in active rough-and-tumble play, to be aggressive, and to be cooperative were assessed as were children's play partners. Data from the first 3 months were summarized to represent behavior at Time 1 and data from the second 3 months were summarized to represent behavior at Time 2. Approximately 150 observations were collected for each child during each time period. Regression analyses allowed us to examine the extent to which play in same-sex groups at Time 1 predicted behavior at Time 2 above and beyond the prediction from the level of the same behavior at Time 1.

The results showed that many aspects of children's behavior became increasingly sex-differentiated over time, and that differences in time spent with same-sex peers promoted these sex differences. For instance, the more girls played with same-sex peers at Time 1, the more they played near adults later in the term; but, for boys, the more they played with same-sex peers at Time 1, the less time they played near adults later in the term. For activity level and aggression, a similar pattern was found of girls and boys moving in opposite directions as they spent more time with same-sex peers. For example, boys who spent proportionately more time playing with same-sex peers at Time 1 were observed to be less aggressive at Time 2 than were boys who spent less time playing with same-sex peers. In contrast, girls who spent more time with other girls at Time 1 were less aggressive at Time 2. Boys (but not girls) engaged in more rough-and-tumble play over time as they played with same-sex peers. For some behaviors, both sexes moved in the same direction over time as they gained experience with same-sex peers. For instance, for both sexes, the more time children played with same-sex peers at Time 1, the greater the degree of gender-typed play at Time 2, even when initial levels of gender-typed play were controlled.

These patterns suggest that, even over a relatively short amount of time, children's behavior is significantly changed by the experiences they gain with same-sex peers. And, for both girls and boys, playing with same-sex peers moves children in a more gender-typed direction over time, congruent with the notion that peer groups, especially same-sex peers, are powerful socializers of children's behavior.

In summary, children's social environments provide a training ground for learning new skills and for developing and honing interactional styles. The social environment that many young girls experience is different from the one many boys experience. Young girls spend much of their social interaction time playing with other girls who encourage cooperation and use enabling forms of communication to promote group harmony (Maccoby, 1990). Young boys' play often is oriented around issues of dominance and the formation of a hierarchical pecking order (Maccoby & Jacklin, 1987). In these groups, girls and boys develop different interactional competencies and have exposure to different types of play experiences. Over time, whatever differences existed to begin with in the behavior of girls and boys becomes more accentuated and exaggerated due to peer-culture influences. Furthermore, the individual variations from one girl to the next and from one boy to the next in how much they play with same-sex peers influences their opportunities for learning from same-sex peers.

GENDER COGNITIONS AND SKILL DEVELOPMENT: THE EFFECTS OF EXPOSURE TO DIFFERENT INTERACTION STYLES

What roles do children's gender cognitions play in the origins, maintenance, and changes in sex segregation? Little is known thus far about the role of gender cognitions on the origins of sex segregation although the theoretical and practical implications of this knowledge are far reaching. Cognitive theorists suggest that gender-related cognitions likely influence who children chose to play with as they initially begin to segregate by sex. Children may use the very basic information about who is a boy and who is a girl to help them decide who they want to play with (Martin, 1994). Sex segregation begins at roughly the same time that children recognize and can label people by sex. However, direct links of gender knowledge and sex segregation have not yet been found (see Moller & Serbin, 1996). The issue is complicated due to the different types of gender cognitions that may be involved in these activities and because of the difficulty in assessing very young children's gender cognitions.

Although the role of gender cognitions on the origins of sex segregated play is unclear, some evidence suggests that children's beliefs about gender influence the maintenance of sex segregated play. After having experiences with girls and boys during play, children may develop a variety of gender cognitions related to their experiences with boys and girls. For instance, they develop abstract beliefs—gender theories—that girls share the same interests and boys share the same interests. These beliefs may guide new behavioral interaction as children reason that other children of the same sex are "like me" and thus, are more fun to play with no matter what they are doing, whereas children of the other sex are "not like me" and thus, are less fun to play with. In this manner, children can use social cognitions about gender as markers of expected similarities. Furthermore, children may develop ideas about the consequences associated with various types of relationships. They may come to realize that they will be teased by peers if they play with the other sex, thereby leading to avoidance of this sort of play. Girls may realize that they have difficulty influencing boys (Serbin et al., 1984). Each of these forms of social cognition may then influence the likelihood of entering a play group, selecting a playmate, and maintaining a friendship (Martin, 1994).

In a study designed to test some of these ideas (Martin, Fabes, Evans, & Wyman, 1999), young children's (41–82 months) beliefs were found to relate to their play behavior and older children's gender cognitions were stronger than younger children's. Specifically, both younger and older children had gender-related beliefs about who they liked to play with, who other girls and other boys liked to play with, and the consequences of playing with same-sex and other-sex children, and these beliefs became more gender-typed with age. Furthermore, the more strongly children held these beliefs, the more children said they preferred same-sex playmates and the more they actually played with same-sex peers over a 6-month period of observation (for a subset of the sample that was observed). Additional analyses suggested that the age and playmate preference relationship was mediated by children's beliefs about others, suggesting a possible causal link between changing gender cognitions and increased tendencies to prefer same-sex partners. In other words, as children's gender cognitions develop, they may serve to further encourage play with same-sex peers.

Children's experiences in same-sex groups influence the kinds of skills they develop. And, one important factor underlying these socialization experiences is children's gender beliefs. Children can use their knowledge of gender groupings to help them make decisions about who they think they might want to play with. Children's ideas about what others do and what others will approve of also color their choices in play partners. Additional research would be helpful for further highlighting how children's gender cognitions influence who they play with and how often they play with same-sex and other-sex peers. Also, individual differences in children's beliefs should influence patterns of sex segregated play.

LINKING SOCIAL COGNITION, THE SOCIAL ENVIRONMENT, COGNITIVE SKILLS, AND ACHIEVEMENT

Children's gender cognitions have a direct and indirect influence on skill development and performance. The direct impact is through stereotypes, which provide information about the sex-appropriateness of various activities and interests. The indirect impact flows through at least two paths: one path is through who children play with, and the other path is through influences on children's choices of toys and activities, both of which then provide sex-differentiated learning environments that may influence the development of their cognitive skills.

The impact of stereotypic beliefs on what children do, their motivation, and skill development is apparent. The existing evidence suggests that children's beliefs influence what they pay attention to, remember, and spend time exploring. Children's beliefs about what is appropriate for them influences how hard they try and their expectations for success. Thus far, much of the research on young children has been focused on how gender cognitions influence the activities they engage in rather than on their cognitive skills, but the potential links with cognitive sex differences seem obvious. If children stereotype certain domains as being "for me," they are likely to try harder, expect to succeed, pay attention to the information, and learn the information. If children label domains as "not for me," they are likely to not try as hard, expect not to succeed, pay little attention to the material, and not learn it.

Developmental changes in children's susceptibility to messages about gender inappropriate activities and interests and to stereotype threat need to be examined in much more detail. Although children understand many gender stereotypes at a young age, we do not yet know if vulnerability to gender-related stereotype threat changes with age. Gender-labeling studies suggest that accuracy in a game can be influenced by children's assumption that the game is not for them. Whether this is completely analogous to the kind of stereotype threat that is seen in adults is yet to be determined. Nonetheless, when children come to understand that skill in a particular cognitive domain is considered more likely for one group than another, these gender cognitions have the potential to hinder their performance.

The disentangling of performance and competence deficits as they relate to children's cognitive abilities, achievement, and career choices is essential if we are to maximize optimal outcomes for children and for adults. To the degree that performance is hindered by reward contingencies, these contingencies could be changed by rewarding performance on other-sex tasks. If anxiety limits performance, interventions to change the salience of stereotypes for children might be needed. If attention and memory are compromised, then the possibilities for change may seem more pessimistic because requisite knowledge has to be changed in addition to reward structures. Interventions may have to occur at an early stage—when information is first being acquired.

Additional research is needed to understand situational variability and individual differences in the influence of gender cognitions. In some situations, such as those in which a task is strongly linked to stereotypes, when one's sex is made salient, or when others' approval for one's behavior is strong, gender cognitions have great potential for influencing how children behave. Some children will develop self-concepts that strongly conform to gender stereotypic expectations, thereby making them more vulnerable to the influence of their own gender cognitions and the gendered expectations of others. Other children may develop self-concepts that differ from stereotypic expectations and they may then be less vulnerable to pressures to conform from others and less likely to develop motivations to be like others of their own sex.

Another missing piece of the puzzle is whether there are direct connections between social behavior with peers and cognitive sex differences. Specifically, we do not know whether or how the skills children learn with same-sex peers influence sex differences in cognitive domains such as mathematics and visual/spatial skills. Does practice at being in a hierarchy with others concerned with dominance relate to developing mathematical or spatial skills? Does practice with other cooperative girls contribute to the development of verbal skills? Or, does social experience contribute to the style with which children deal with academic topics? For example, does boys' experience in dominance hierarchies make them less vulnerable to time pressure on tests or more likely to use risk-taking strategies of test taking? Do girls' experiences with other girls facilitate compliant classroom behavior while also making them more anxious in test-taking situations? The long-term influences of individual variations in exposure to same-sex and other-sex peer groups is unknown. It may be that children who spend more time with same-sex peers may develop skills in one domain but not the other, whereas children who play more with both sexes may develop skills in multiple domains.

Children's development of academic interests and their movement into different career trajectories needs further consideration. The many direct and indirect influences that gender cognitions have on academic and occupational achievement are complex and worthy of more attention. Gender socialization colors the entire context associated with decision making about academic pursuits and careers (see Eccles et al., 1999).

In summary, sex differences in cognitive domains may be influenced both directly and indirectly by children's gender cognitions. Gender cognitions provide information about what toys, activities, and peers are likely to be most appealing; and experiences with toys and peers then provide sex-differentiated learning environments that influence children's skill development.

REFERENCES

Astin, H. S. (1975). Sex differences in mathematical and scientific precocity. *The Journal of Special Education, 9,* 79-91.

Bem, S. (1993). *The lenses of gender: Transforming the debate on sexual inequality.* New Haven, CT: Yale University Press.

Bem, S. L. (1981). Gender schema theory: A cognitive account of sex typing. *Psychological Review, 88,* 354-364.

Berenbaum, S. A., & Hines, M. (1992). Early androgens are related to childhood sex-typed toy preferences. *Psychological Science, 3*, 203-206.

Boston, M. B., & Levy, G. D. (1991). Changes and differences in preschoolers' understanding of gender scripts. *Cognitive Development, 6*, 412-417.

Bradbard, M. R., & Endsley, R. C. (1983). The effects of sex-typed labeling on preschool children's information-seeking and retention. *Sex Roles, 9*, 247-260.

Bradbard, M. R., Martin, L., Endsley, R. C., & Halverson, C. F. (1986). Influence of sex stereotypes on children's exploration and memory: A competence versus performance distinction. *Developmental Psychology, 22*, 481-486.

Braza, F., Braza, P., Carreras, M. R., & Munoz, J. M. (1997). Development of sex differences in preschool children: Social behavior during an academic year. *Psychological Reports, 80*, 179-188.

Carpenter, C. (1983). Activity structure and play: Implications for socialization. In M. Liss (Ed.), *Social and cognitive skills* (pp. 117–145). New York: Academic Press.

Carter, D. B. (1987). The roles of peers in sex role socialization. In D. B. Carter (Ed.), *Current conceptions of sex roles and sex typing: Theory and research* (pp. 101-121). New York: Praeger.

Carter, D. B., & McCloskey, L. A. (1984). Peers and the maintenance of sex-typed behavior: The development of children's conceptions of cross-gender behavior in their peers. *Social Cognition, 2*, 294-314.

Connor, J. M., & Serbin, L. A. (1977). Behaviorally-based masculine and feminine activity preference scales for preschoolers: Correlates with other classroom behaviors and cognitive tests. *Child Development, 48*, 1411-1416.

Davies, D. R. (1986). Children's performance as a function of sex-typed labels. *British Journal of Social Psychology, 25*, 173-175.

Davis, D. R. (1989). The effects of gender-typed labels on children's performance. *Current Psychology: Research and Reviews, 8,* 267–272.

Deaux, K., & Major, B. (1987). Putting gender into context: An interactive model of gender-related behavior. *Psychological Review, 94*, 369-389.

Di Pietro, J. A. (1981). Rough and tumble play: A function of gender. *Developmental Psychology, 17*, 50-58.

Eaton, W. O., & Enns, L. R. (1986). Sex differences in human motor activity level. *Psychological Bulletin, 100*, 19-28.

Eccles, J. S., Barber, B., & Jozefowicz, D. (1999). Linking gender to educational, occupational, and recreational choices: Applying the Eccles et al., model of achievement-related choices. In W. B. Swann, J. H. Langlois, & L. A. Gilbert (Eds.), *Sexism and stereotypes in modern society: The gender science of Janet Taylor Spence* (pp. 153–185). Washington, DC: American Psychological Association.

Egan, S. K., & Perry, D. G. (1999). *Gender identity: A multidimensional analysis with implications for children's adjustment*. Boca Raton: Florida Atlantic University.

Etaugh, C. (1983). Introduction: The influences of environmental factors on sex differences in children's play. In M. B. Liss (Ed.), *Social and cognitive skills: Sex roles and children's play* (pp. 1-19). New York: Academic Press.

Fabes, R. A. (1994). Physiological, emotional, and behavioral correlates of gender segregation. In C. Leaper (Ed.), *Childhood gender segregation: Causes and consequences. New directions for child development* (Vol. 65, pp. 19-34). San Francisco: Jossey-Bass.

Fagot, B. I. (1973). Influence of teacher behavior in the preschool. *Developmental Psychology, 9,* 198–206.

Fagot, B. I. (1977). Consequences of moderate cross-gender behavior in preschool children. *Child Development, 48,* 902-907.

Fagot, B. I. (1994). Peer relations and the development of competence in boys and girls. In L. Campbell (Ed.), *Childhood gender segregation: Causes and consequences. New directions for child development, No. 65.* (pp. 53-65). San Francisco, CA: Jossey-Bass.

Fagot, B. I., & Leinbach, M. D. (1983). Play styles in early childhood: Social consequences for boys and girls. In M. B. Liss (Ed.), *Social and cognitive skills: Sex roles and children's play* (pp. 93-116). New York: Academic Press.

Fagot, B. I., & Littman, I. (1976). Relation of preschool sex-typing to intellectual performance in elementary school. *Psychological Reports, 39,* 699-704.

Fagot, B. I., & Patterson, G. R. (1969). An in vivo analysis of reinforcing contingencies for sex-role behaviors in the preschool child. *Developmental Psychology, 1,* 563-568.

Fenema, E., & Peterson, P. (1985). Autonomous learning behavior: A possible explanation of gender-related differences in mathematics. In L. C. Wilkinson & C. B. Marrett (Eds.), *Gender influences in classroom interaction* (pp. 17-35). Orlando, FL: Academic Press.

Gallagher, A. M., & De Lisi, R. (1994). Gender differences in scholastic aptitude test—mathematics problem solving among high-ability students. *Journal of Educational Psychology, 86,* 204-211.

Gold, D., & Berger, C. (1978). Problem-solving performance of young boys and girls as a function of task appropriateness and sex identity. *Sex Roles, 4,* 183-193.

Hargreaves, D. J., Bates, H. M., & Foot, J. M. (1985). Sex-typed labelling affects task performance. *British Journal of Social Psychology, 24,* 153-155.

Harris, J. R. (1995). Where is the child's environment? A group socialization theory of development. *Psychological Review, 102,* 458-489.

Herzog, E. W., Enright, M., Luria, Z., & Rubin, J. Z. (1982). Do gender labels yield sex differences in performance, or is label a fable? *Developmental Psychology, 18,* 424-430.

Howes, C. (1988). Peer interaction of young children. *Monographs of the Society for Research in Young Children, 53.*

Kimball, M. M. (1989). A new perspective on women's math achievement. *Psychological Bulletin, 105,* 198-214.

Kohlberg, L. A. (1966). A cognitive-developmental analysis of children's sex role concepts and attitudes. In E. E. Maccoby (Ed.), *The development of sex differences* (pp. 82-173). Stanford: Stanford University Press.

La Freniere, P., Strayer, F. F., & Gauthier, R. (1984). The emergence of same-sex affiliative preferences among preschool peers: A developmental/ethological perspective. *Child Development, 55,* 1958-1965.

Ladd, G. W., Birch, S. H., & Buhs, E. S. (1999). Children's social and scholastic lives in kindergarten: Related spheres of influence. *Child Development, 70,* 1373-1400.

Lamb, M., & Roopnarine, J. (1979). Peer influences on sex role development in preschoolers. *Child Development, 50,* 1219-1220.

Langlois, J. H., & Downs, A. C. (1980). Mothers, fathers, and peers as socialization agents of sex-typed play behaviors in young children. *Child Development, 51*, 1237-1247.

Leaper, C. (1994). Exploring the consequences of gender segregation on social relationships. In C. Leaper (Ed.), *Childhood gender segregation: causes and consequences* (pp. 67-86). San Francisco: Jossey-Bass.

Lever, J. (1978). Sex differences in the complexity of children's play and games. *American Sociological Review, 43*, 471-483.

Levy, G. D. (1999). Gender-typed and non-gender-typed category awareness in toddlers. *Sex Roles, 41*, 851-873.

Lewis, M., & Weintraub, M. (1974). Sex of parent sex of child: Socioemotional development. In R. C. Freidman, R. M. Richart, & R. L. Van de Wiele (Eds.), *Sex differences in behavior* (pp. 165–190). New York: Wiley.

Liss, M. B (1983). Learning gender-related skills through play. In M. B. Liss (Ed.), *Social and cognitive skills: Sex roles and children's play* (pp. 147-166). New York: Academic Press.

Lockheed, M. E., & Harris, A. M. (1984). Cross-sex collaborative learning in elementary classrooms. *American Educational Research Journal, 21*, 275-294.

Maccoby, E. E. (1988). Gender as a social category. *Developmental Psychology, 24*, 755-765.

Maccoby, E. E. (1990). Gender and relationships: A developmental account. *American Psychologist, 45*, 513-520.

Maccoby, E. E. (1998). *The two sexes: Growing up apart, coming together*. Cambridge, MA: Belknap Press.

Maccoby, E. E., & Jacklin, C. N. (Eds.). (1974). *The psychology of sex differences*. Stanford: Stanford University Press.

Maccoby, E. E., & Jacklin, C. N. (1987). Gender segregation in childhood. In W. R. Hayne (Ed.), *Advances in child development and behavior, Vol. 20.* (pp. 239-287). Orlando, FL: Academic Press.

Martin, C. L. (1991). The role of cognition in understanding gender effects. In W. R. Hayne (Ed.), *Advances in child development and behavior, Vol. 23. Advances in child development and behavior.* (pp. 113-149). San Diego, CA: Academic Press.

Martin, C. L. (1993). New directions for investigating children's gender knowledge. Special Issue: Early gender-role development. *Developmental Review, 13*, 184-204.

Martin, C. L. (1994). Cognitive influences on the development and maintenance of gender segregation. In L. Campbell (Ed.), *Childhood gender segregation: Causes and consequences. New directions for child development, No. 65* (pp. 35-51). San Francisco, CA: Jossey-Bass.

Martin, C. L. (1999). A developmental perspective on gender effects and gender concepts. In W. B. Swann, J. H. Langlois, & L. A. Gilbert (Eds.), *Sexism and stereotypes in modern society: The gender science of Janet Taylor Spence* (pp. 45-73). Washington, DC: American Psychological Association.

Martin, C. L., Eisenbud, L., & Rose, H. (1995). Children's gender-based reasoning about toys. *Child Development, 66*, 1453-1471.

Martin, C. L., & Fabes, R. A. (2001). The stability and consequences of young children's same-sex play. *Developmental Psychology, 37*, 431–446.

Martin, C. L., Fabes, R. A., Evans, S. M., & Wyman, H. (1999). Social cognition on the playground: Children's beliefs about playing with girls versus boys and their relations to sex segregated play. *Journal of Social and Personal Relationships, 16,* 751-771.

Martin, C. L., & Halverson, C. (1981). A schematic processing model of sex typing and stereotyping in children. *Child Development, 52,* 1119-1134.

Masters, J. C., Ford, M. E., Arend, R., Grotevant, H. D., & Clark, L. V. (1979). Modeling and labeling as integrated determinants of children's sex-typed imitative behavior. *Child Development, 50,* 364-371.

Mitchell, E. (1973). The learning of sex roles through toys and books. *Young Children, 118,* 226-231.

Moller, L. C., & Serbin, L. A. (1996). Antecedents of toddler gender segregation: Cognitive consonance, gender-typed toy preferences and behavioral compatibility. *Sex Roles, 35,* 445-460.

Montemayor, R. (1974). Children's performance in a game and their attraction to it as a function of sex-typed labels. *Child Development, 45,* 152-156.

Okagaki, L., & Frensch, P. A. (1994). Effects of video game playing on measures of spatial performance: Gender effects in late adolescence. *Journal of Applied Developmental Psychology, 15,* 33-58.

Pellegrini, A. D., & Smith, P. K. (1993). School recess: Implications for education and development. *Review of Educational Research, 63,* 51-67.

Raag, T. (1999). Influences of social expectations of gender, gender stereotypes, and situational constraints on children's toy choices. *Sex Roles, 41,* 809-831.

Raag, T., & Rackliff, C. L. (1998). Preschoolers' awareness of social expectations of gender: Relationships to toy choices. *Sex Roles, 38,* 685-700.

Richards, M. H., & Larson, R. (1989). The life space and socialization of the self: Sex differences in the young adolescents. *Journal of Youth and Adolescence, 18,* 617-626.

Ruble, D. N., & Martin, C. L. (1998). Gender development. In W. Damon (Ed.), *Handbook of Child Psychology* (5th ed., Vol. 3, pp. 933–1016). New York: Wiley.

Serbin, L. A., & Connor, J. M. (1979). Sex-typing of children's play preferences and patterns of cognitive performance. *Journal of Genetic Psychology, 134,* 315-316.

Serbin, L. A., Connor, J. M., Burchardt, C. J., & Citron, C. C. (1979). Effects of peer presence on sex-typing of children's play behavior. *Journal of Experimental Child Psychology, 27,* 303-309.

Serbin, L. A., Moller, L. C., Gulko, J., Powlishta, K. K., & Colburne, K. A. (1994). The emergence of gender segregation in toddler playgroups. In L. Campbell (Ed.), *Childhood gender segregation: Causes and consequences. New directions for child development, No. 65* (pp. 7-17). San Francisco, CA: Jossey-Bass.

Serbin, L. A., Sprafkin, C., Elman, M., & Doyle, A. B. (1984). The early development of sex differentiated patterns of social influence. *Canadian Journal of Social Science, 14,* 350-363.

Serbin, L. A., Tonick, I. J., & Sternglanz, S. H. (1977). Shaping cooperative cross-sex play. *Child Development, 48,* 924-929.

Serbin, L. A., Zelkowitz, P., Doyle, A., Gold, D., & Wheaton, B. (1990). The socialization of sex-differentiated skills and academic performance: A mediational model. *Sex Roles, 23,* 613–628.

Sherman, J. A. (1967). Problem of sex differences in space perception and aspects of intellectual functioning. *Psychological Review, 74*, 290-299.

Slaby, R. G., & Frey, K. S. (1975). Development of gender constancy and selective attention to same-sex models. *Child Development, 52*, 849-856.

Steele, C. M. (1997). A threat in the air: How stereotypes shape intellectual identity and performance. *American Psychologist, 52*, 613-629.

Steele, C. M., & Aronson, J. A. (1995). Stereotype threat and the intellectual test performance of African Americans. *Journal of Personality and Social Psychology, 69*, 797-811.

Stein, A. H., Pohly, S., & Mueller, E. (1971). The influence of masculine, feminine, and neutral tasks on children's achievement behavior: Expectancies of success and attainment value. *Child Development, 42*, 195-207.

Stephan, W. G. (1989). A cognitive approach to stereotyping. In D. Bar-Tal, C. F. Graumann, A. W. Kruglanski, & W. Stroebe (Eds.), *Stereotyping and prejudice: Changing conceptions* (pp. 37-57). New York: Springer-Verlag.

Thorne, B., & Luria, Z. (1986). Sexuality and gender in children's daily worlds. *Social Problems, 33*, 176-190.

Timmer, S. G., Eccles, J., & O'Brien, K. (1985). How children use time. In J. T. Juster & F. P. Stafford (Eds.), *Time, goods, and well-being* (pp. 353-382). Ann Arbor: Institute for Social Research.

Tyler, L. E. (1964). The antecedents of two varieties of vocational interests. *Genetic Psychology Monographs, 70*, 177-227.

Walsh, M., Hickey, C., & Duffy, J. (1999). Influence of item content and stereotype situation on gender differences in mathematical problem solving. *Sex Roles, 41*, 219-240.

part IV

Summary and Conclusions

CHAPTER 9

Emergent Themes in the Development of Sex Differences in Cognition

Ann McGillicuddy-De Lisi
Richard De Lisi

In the introduction to this book, Halpern and Ikier presented some of the overarching issues in the study of cognitive sex differences. These included the question of whether we should study sex differences at all; cautionary notes on issues such as effect sizes, the context of differences, inferences based on correlational data, principles of research design, and their relationship to inferences drawn from data under various conditions; and the need for a psychobiosocial framework. The authors of the chapters that followed discussed theories, reviewed research, and presented recent data that were connected to those issues in significant ways. In this final chapter, we pick up some of the threads of Halpern and Ikier's overview and weave the many different findings and viewpoints into a tapestry that represents current knowledge of the development of sex differences in cognition.

THE NATURE OF SEX DIFFERENCES IN COGNITION

The analyses of sex differences in the domains of language, spatial ability, mathematics performance, and social cognition presented in this book revealed that there has been and continues to be a great deal of research and interest in these areas. At the same time, the causes, developmental trajectories, and implications for functioning in everyday life are multifaceted, complex, and not fully understood. A consistent pattern of development of sex differences has not been identified across the four domains. An important observation that the authors share is an acknowledgment that similarities in the performance of boys and girls and men and women outweigh findings of sex differences in performance.

This is to be expected if there is an evolutionary basis for abilities such as language, spatial abilities, mathematical reasoning, and social cognition. Due to natural selection, behaviors that were likely to facilitate survival of human beings should appear in current descendents. For example, we would expect that brain morphology would be similar in males and females of a particular species as most of their experiences in the world have a similar basis—responding to the same kinds of psychophysical energy, for example. Geary (chapter 2) expands the evolutionary model by positing that sex differences are to be expected in those sub-areas of cognitive domains that offered greater reproductive success to females as a result of their unique reproductive role as compared to males, and vice versa. Fitch and Bimonte (chapter 3) note differences occur in specific cognitive domains that appear to be related to differences in the action and effects of prenatal sex hormones, and to the circulation of hormones during childhood and adulthood. Finally, a great many social processes that have been linked to cognitive functioning have their roots in experiences that boys and girls share, such as positive outcomes for successful performance in these areas, the role of parents' expectations and teacher practices (Wigfield, Battle, Keller, & Eccles, chapter 4). In this area, too, a minority of the myriad of children's experiences that socialize them into the mores and norms of a society are systematically differentiated by sex. Regardless of the nature of causal explanations offered for observed sex differences in cognition, an overlap in the behaviors of males and females is to be expected to occur more frequently than differences.

Findings of similarity in developmental processes and trajectories notwithstanding, we have seen that behavioral sex differences in cognition do appear. In the area of language development, Gleason and Ely (chapter 5) report sex differences in the expressive use of language, the incidence of language disorders, voice pitch, and the use of gender-specific language in play that reflect gender stereotypes in language use and style, and some small effects favoring females in formal verbal tasks such as speech production, verbal tests, and reading comprehension. In the area of mathematical abilities and achievement, reliable sex differences favoring girls in computation and classroom performance in elementary school (6–10 years) were discussed in De Lisi and McGillicuddy-De Lisi's chapter 6. But higher levels of performance on mathematical problem-solving, standardized tests and a higher level of career choice in mathematical fields among males than females were observed through adolescent and adult years. Thus, there are timing differences in the appearance of sex differences across these two domains of cognition. Whereas sex differences in language appear early, that is, from 2–5 years, sex differences in mathematical abilities are more likely to be observed later in childhood, and especially in adolescence and young adulthood. Sex differences are also more likely to appear in later developing mathematical abilities such as geometry or proportional reasoning, revealing a pattern in which both timing and the particular content are important factors in understanding sex differences in mathematics achievement.

Newcombe, Mathason, and Terlecki (chapter 7) summarized research literature that showed very reliable sex differences, which favor males, occur in three areas of spatial cognition: mental rotation, representation of the horizontal/vertical coordinate, and spatial visualization. Sex differences in mental rotation appear early, often in the preschool years, and there is some evidence that suggests such sex differences, which favor boys, increase with age. Sex differences in representation of the horizontal coordinate are not typically observed until age 10 or later. Thus, in this area, the onset of sex differences seems to vary with the particular spatial ability. Although the pattern differs in some ways from that observed in the development of mathematical abilities, the patterns in these two domains are similar in that the onset and duration of sex differences varies with the particular skill or ability within the larger spatial or mathematics domain. This similarity is interesting to note given that children receive a great deal of formal instruction in mathematics but very little formal training in the use of spatial skills.

In chapter 8, Martin and Dinella revealed that sex differences in interests and activities emerge very early, at 1–2 years of age, and gender stereotypic expectations appear to be related to subsequent activities and sex differences in cognition in a variety of areas. These gender stereotypes have been proposed as one source of sex differences in other domains, including language, mathematics, and spatial performance, through their role in directing attention, guiding activities that may develop skills, and affecting memory processing in a manner that is consistent with gender beliefs.

This overview reveals that the onset and duration of sex differences varies across cognitive domains such as language, spatial performance, mathematics achievement, and social cognition. Some sex differences appear in the first year or two of life, whereas others are not observed until quite late in childhood. There is also variability within these domains when particular abilities are examined. For example, we saw that that in some areas of spatial ability, the differences appear as early as children can be assessed. For other kinds of spatial knowledge, sex differences do not appear until late childhood but then persist into adulthood. Is one sex a "winner" and the other a "loser" in terms of cognitive performance differences? There is the perception that when sex differences do occur, male advantages outweigh female advantages. Halpern (1997) and other authors in this book noted that this is not a uniform finding. For example, the direction of sex differences is not stable across content within or between domains. In mathematics performance, the advantage seems to shift from an early superiority of girls in one area to a later superiority of boys in a different area of mathematics performance. In other areas, females outperform males, as shown by school grades as well as several aspects of verbal, mathematics, and social cognition performance. Males are more likely than females to show cognitive deficits that are severe enough to warrant special intervention, presumably because of a general pattern of greater variability in performance for males than for females (for example, see Gleason & Ely's chapter 5). However, there is reason for the critics of sex difference research to be alarmed in the manner described by Halpern and Ikier in chapter 1. The sex differences that favor males appear to translate into different experiences, including career achievements and social processes that favor males over females.

In this connection, it is also important to note that recent research has identified situational factors or context as salient variables in assessments of sex differences in cognition. Many of the sex differences in language are tied to social groups and roles (chapter 5). Chapter 8 described a great variety of behaviors that appear to be similarly linked to social contexts and group membership. The content and timing of the appearance of sex differences reflect cultural beliefs about differences between boys and girls, and between men and women. In most areas, males' styles of communication are characterized as representing more power and prestige than females' expressions.

The recent work in the area of stereotype threat (reviewed in chapters 6 & 8) suggests that social groups and roles also affect mathematics performance. However, the conceptualization of the role of the social group in relation to mathematics performance is quite different than that observed in the domain of language development. Social group factors that appear to be salient in the appearance of sex differences in language have to do with the functional use of language in a social context. In the area of mathematics performance, one's identity as a member of a social group has been found to affect test performance. Mild references to issues of sex differences before administration of a challenging mathematics test results in lower performance by females even when the students are highly skilled in math. These stereotype threat findings suggest that factors such as social identity contribute to sex differences in performance on mathematics tests. Finally, spatial performance has also been shown to be vulnerable to stereotype threat. For example, McGlone, Kobrynowitcz, and Aronson (1999) found that male performance on mental rotation tasks was higher and female performance was lower when participants in late adolescence were primed with questions about gender before performing the task. Performance was compared to mental rotation performance of a control group and a comparison group that received neutral priming questions. Thus there are social group effects in the domains of language, mathematics, and spatial behaviors. Spatial performance has also been linked to experience in masculine activities and to a masculine gender-role identity.

Sex differences in mathematics performance also have been linked to different problem-solving strategies, and have been found to vary with type of assessment, and rapid processing of mathematics facts. Training in mathematics facts, which decreases response time (presumably due to increases in automaticity), raises mathematics performance levels of both boys and girls and reduces sex differences somewhat (Royer, Tronsky, Chan, Jackson, & Marchant, 1999). Parallel findings of such training effects in reading achievement provide another area in which we can note some similar patterns of effects across domains (Stanovich, 1990). Newcombe, Mathason, and Terlecki (chapter 7) report that timed testing has been implicated as a factor producing sex differences in some spatial ability studies and we have seen that processing time has been related to success on mathematics ability tests. Thus, sex differences have been minimized or eliminated with some types of practice or training in both mathematics and spatial-performance studies. However, the nature of the training that is effective differs substantially across cognitive domains.

To summarize, there are no discernible trends with respect to the onset and pattern of the development of sex differences that appear across cognitive domains. However, there are factors that cut across domains: personal-social factors such as social roles and social group membership, including effects of stereotype threat; the effect of timed assessments and possible relations to automatic processing that could affect subsequent development in a particular domain; sex differences in variability and the higher incidence of males in the tail ends of distributions of performance; and finally, the impact of practice and specific training on performance of both males and females. There has been a search for a clearly discernible pattern that suggests a single unifying principle to explain the emergence of sex differences. This approach has led repeatedly to conclusions that the causes of the observed sex differences are varied and complex, which is no doubt a valid conclusion. Often, however, the final outcome of this approach is a general statement that proposes the causal mechanism is "an interaction of biological and social forces" that does not advance research in the area.

EXPLANATORY CONSTRUCTS IN THE DEVELOPMENT OF SEX DIFFERENCES IN COGNITION: NATURE AND NURTURE

The literature reviews in this book suggest that there is some continuity in the patterns of sex differences across domains, but that the emergence of sex differences in cognition varies with domain as well as developmental period, specific content, and life experience. It seems unlikely that attempts to disentangle contributions of biology and environment will clarify the nature of sex differences in cognition. Indeed, in the opening chapter, Halpern and Ikier advocate a transformation of the question of causality from the tripartite approach of the nature versus nurture debate (i.e., explanations based on nature, on nurture, on the interaction of nature and nurture) into a psychobiosocial model in which the psychological, the biological, and the social are reciprocal processes in a seamless cloth.

The field has neglected the power of theory and a priori hypotheses in attempts to explain why sex differences in cognition occur, the particular areas in which they should be expected, and the manner in which nature and nurture form a single cloth. The organization of chapters in this book follows the current structure of explanatory models of behavior in presenting evolutionary, neurobiological, and personal-social explanations of sex differences in cognition. Within this "traditional" approach to explanation, development is often conceptualized as simply a matter of timing that is transposed over the explanatory constructs of expression of selected traits, hormonal changes, and accumulation of experiences. There appears to be no overarching biological or sociocultural theory that explains or predicts the patterns of sex differences that have been observed in the domains of language, mathematics achievement, spatial performance, or social cognitions, or in most cases, even a priori hypotheses about their appearance. However, when ontogenetic development is integrated into these explanations, we can begin to see how the biological, the psychological, and the social may be woven into Halpern and Ikier's "seamless cloth" by the threads of ontogenetic development.

To see the picture that these threads create through their interwoven patterns, we need to first examine some of the strategies we have relied on to organize perceptions of the origin of sex differences in cognition. These strategies may have led us to make inferences that limited the ability to examine the whole of the tapestry before us. For example, Halpern and Ikier noted that when we fail to find support for our hypotheses regarding social causes of an observed sex difference, we sometimes erroneously conclude that the cause is biological, in spite of a lack of evidence that biological factors were responsible. We infer that if Factor "A,"—teacher behavior, for example—did not cause the difference, then it must be due to Factor "B"; it must be inherent to the child, that is, must be biological in origin. The logically correct inference cannot include Factor B, biology, in the absence of evidence directly linking biological factors to performance of males and females. We can only conclude that the environmental effect of teacher practices (Factor A) was *not* a causal factor. Such fallacies in reasoning do not enable us to perceive the tapestry as a whole.

Similarly, there has been some tendency to assume that when sex differences appear early in life, biological processes are largely responsible. The assumption continues that when sex differences appear later in development, it is because the social or cultural processes that cause those differences require long periods of experiences during ontogeny to produce their effects. There is evidence that suggests, for example, that prenatal male hormones set a particular path of neurological development that results in differences in brain structure and function. Those morphological differences are then associated with sex differences in cognition. Fitch and Bimonte (chapter 3) directed our attention to sex differences in the size of the corpus callosum and sex differences in language and spatial performance, which are particularly lateralized abilities. Fitch and Bimonte's review of hormonal influences further suggests, however, that these assumptions about the role of male hormones during prenatal development as a mechanism that set a particular path of development in place for cognitive functioning might be too narrow. They report evidence that cognitive behaviors can be influenced by circulating hormones throughout the lifespan and also that changes in hormonal action as sexual maturity is achieved could give rise to sex differences in cognition. Biological influences can arise much later than the prenatal period and may contribute to sex differences in cognition.

The converse situation with respect to inferences about the timing of biological and environmental influences is also likely to be valid as well. That is, if children categorize events, activities, and even themselves as male or female and masculine or feminine as early as age 1–2 years, those gendered ideas are not to be taken as biologically based simply because they are accomplished early. If social processes are continually channeling attention to these differences and reinforcing gendered behavior, children could certainly learn such gendered distinctions at very young ages. It is possible that the significant biological component is an evolutionary-based tendency to classify and categorize, in this case, to attend to certain gendered events and their consequences. But note that there still must be a seamless connection between evolutionary-based attentional and categorization properties and ontogenetic sociocultural experiences to account for such gendered cognitions.

A strong theoretical basis for expecting the appearance of sex differences during a particular developmental period or on a particular task is generally lacking; many of our predilections as investigators prevent us from constructing integrative perspectives; several findings regarding sex differences are not consistently replicated; and different conditions of assessments and instruments affect the results. These factors pose a challenge for most theories, including evolutionary theory, which relies on an approach that ties currently observed sex differences back to natural and sexual selection. In this book and elsewhere, Geary (1995, 1996, 1998) shows that very specific (language, spatial, mathematical, social cognitive) abilities may have differentially advantaged males or advantaged females in terms of reproductive success. Presumably, the areas in which we observe sex differences in cognition are linked to sex differences in reproductive success in the history of human development. Some researchers who take a developmental approach do not find such evolutionary approaches useful, arguing that disconfirming evidence is nearly impossible to obtain because what exists is presumed to have been adaptive (see commentaries in Geary, 1996 for examples). On the other hand, Geary shows, in chapter 2, that a careful analysis of comparative data and evolutionary constructs can pinpoint areas in which sex differences should and should not be expected, a useful theoretical mechanism for explanations of where and why sex differences in cognition should appear. Indeed, it is difficult to imagine that evolutionary forces do not play a role in the ontogeny of sex differences in cognition. However, the biological underpinnings of sex differences in cognition do not appear to be immutably set by genes that have been selected through evolutionary pressure.

Evolutionary theory provides us with a theoretical explanation for the *ultimate* causes of behavioral differences. Geary's analyses suggest that not only are human language, spatial, mathematical, and social cognitive behaviors a result of evolutionary selection processes, but the ultimate causes of personal-social factors also have their roots in our evolutionary history. That is, it has been proposed that sexual-selection processes advantaged males who were competitive, motivated to control resources, and developed social groups based on alliances. Female humans, too, would be advantaged for particular motivational and emotional responses. Like many evolutionary theorists, he proposes that there are *proximate* causes for behavior that stem from these evolutionary bases. That is, the neurobiological correlates of sex differences, such as the morphological brain differences and hormonal differences observed by Fitch and Bimonte (chapter 3) are presumed to be the more immediate causes of spatial, mathematical, and other abilities, but the roots of these differences were derived through sexual selection.

Studies of proximate biological factors (e.g., studies of hormonal variation) that might underlie sex differences in cognition are generally more positively regarded in part because proximate biological factors are investigated through experimental methods, usually on animals. However, many of these studies rely on hypotheses derived from evolutionary theory or are post hoc explanations. There are no true neurobiological theories of sex differences in cognition that yield a priori predictions. On the other hand, developmental neurobiologists and neuropsychologists integrate studies of ontogenetic change into empirical investigations. These approaches hold the greatest potential for integrating biological and experiential processes as a result of their developmental framework and experimental methodology. In addition, there is a trend among evolutionary theorists toward experimentation as well as comparative analysis of closely related species. Further developments in these areas help to address the criticisms that such ultimate explanations of behavior cannot be disconfirmed.

It would appear that much of the sociopsychological aspects of cognitive behavior remain outside of these biological approaches, leaving us with the same old nature–nurture dichotomy that is unlikely to facilitate a deeper understanding of the causal explanations for sex differences in cognition. It is impossible to ignore the body of evidence Wigfield, Battle, Keller, and Eccles (chapter 4) present that ties sex differences in cognition to personality and social constructs (e.g., parent and teacher behaviors; expectations, self-concept; stereotypes; task values and persistence; education choices; beliefs about competency, control, and utility).

How can personal-social factors be related to biological factors to account for sex differences? In this book and elsewhere (1998), Geary proposes that sexual selection has led to particular (mathematical, spatial, verbal) abilities that are sexually dimorphic as a result of genetic and hormonal proximate, or primary, differences in biological functioning. In addition, sexual selection for certain motivational and emotional behaviors are also proposed. The reproductive success of males, for example, would be advantaged by a competitive nature, the tendency to form alliances, a motivation to control resources, and so forth. The reproductive success of females would be advantaged by different personal-social styles such a cooperative social style. Geary further suggests, however, that aspects of cognitive functioning that led to reproductive success (e.g., the spatial-navigational abilities such as those observed in male voles who must locate their female mates in high-grass areas) are coadapted, or made to apply to areas in present day life in advantageous ways. In such a model, the ultimate evolutionary causes of sex differences underlie proximate biological influences; and ultimate evolutionary causes of sex differences underlie personal-social influences that might also be considered "proximate." These ultimate evolutionary characteristics are also adapted to fit with demands of life of the twenty-first century. There is not only a seamlessness between the biological, the psychological, and the social; developmental experiences reveal the connections between the ultimate and proximate causes of behavior. Human competencies can be conceptualized not so much as the outcome of evolution but as the expression of the ongoing process of evolution and ontogeny.

In fact, even species-specific behavior across cultures does not inexorably lead to the conclusion that such behaviors are innate in the sense that they are independent of the environment or experience. In 1963, Tinbergen (1996) wrote:

A newly hatched Herring Gull pecks selectively at red objects but a human being has to learn to stop when the traffic light turns red. We have to learn the intricately co-ordinated motor patterns of speech, whereas a Whitethroat raised in isolation produces the complicated normal song of its species. It is the contrast between man and animals in the ways that they acquire either "knowledge" or "skill" which arouses in most of us an interest in the ontogeny of behaviour. (p. 127)

He noted that as psychologists and ethologists came together to establish causal explanations for behaviors, it was recognized at the outset that understanding of adult forms of behavior required investigation of the *development* of the behavior. However, he concluded that two unfortunate events occurred. First, all influences that were not environmental were subsumed under the rubric of innate factors, essentially creating a dichotomy that fostered the tendency to conclude that sources of behaviors were biological when we failed to identify an environmental or experiential cause (recall Halpern & Ikier's cautionary note on this topic in chapter 1!). Second, we lost sight of the importance of ontogenetic developmental influences necessary for physiological mechanisms to become functional. Inspection of the research literature on the developmental of sex differences suggests that we are more likely to jump to biological explanations for cognitive sex differences than for social sex differences (for example, compare explanations offered in the literature reviewed by Martin & Dinella in chapter 8 on social cognition with those offered to explain differences in spatial perform-ance reviewed by Newcombe, Mathason, & Terlecki in chapter 7).

Ontogenetic developmental experiences as well as biological factors shape innate capabilities. Tinbergen notes that the ontogenetic experience of light is necessary for the genetic "program" of light receptors to develop in the retina. We now recognize that speech categorization processes must be developed and applied for the biology of language to be instantiated. It is not simply an interac-tion of nature and nurture. In Tinbergen's words, behaviors are "at the same time innate and learned" (1996, p. 425). Recasting Halpern's references to a psy-chobiosocial model, we can say that ontogenetic experiences weave the biologi-cal, the psychological, and the social. The approach of examining outcomes, that is, sex differences in cognition, from a nature–nurture perspective will not enable understanding of those sex differences we have observed.

DESCRIPTIONS AND EXPLANATIONS OF SEX
DIFFERENCES IN COGNITIVE FUNCTIONING

In discussing main trends in psychology over 30 years ago, Piaget (1973) pro-posed that movement from descriptive to explanatory models in psychology usu-ally occurs in three stages. First, research aims to describe general facts or repeat-able relations. This first stage consists of attempts to identify patterns. Many such patterns were described in the chapters on the four domains of cognition in this book. The next stage consists of attempts to coordinate these patterns of findings in a manner that leads to logical deductions. The three chapters on explanatory constructs each examined the patterns of sex differences, examining sexual selec-tion, hormonal action, and motivational processes in an attempt to reach logical deductions. The third and final stage is the development of models that move beyond description and deduction toward explanation. Models attain the status of true explanations when their deductive operations are matched by actual changes that have taken place. In short, psychology attains an explanation when patterns of findings are matched by a possible deduction that is concretized in a model. Piaget noted that psychology abounds in explanatory hypotheses because of a wide diversity of possible models that tend to stress biological factors alone, soci-ological factors alone, or models that attempt to link biological and sociological factors by focusing on development. An important difference between models is the extent to which they are reductionistic or relational (Piaget, 1973, p. 18).

Descriptions of Cognitive Sex Differences

Piaget's taxonomy provides a convenient way to summarize the research on cognitive sex differences presented in this book. Much of the work consists of attempts to gather facts—to describe how the behavior of females and males dif-fers in terms of: (1) average levels of performance, (2) variability in performance, and (3) modifiability of performance. These descriptions become complicated by the need to include considerations of how these three types of sex differences are manifested at various points in the life cycle (infancy, early childhood, etc.), in different ethnic and cultural groups, and of course, in several domains of cognitive functioning (language, space, mathematics, etc.). Descriptions of sex differences in cognitive functioning are much more frequent for childhood, adolescence, and young adulthood (college students), than for infancy, middle adulthood, and old age. It is not clear whether researchers who study cognitive functioning in the latter age periods routinely analyze their data for sex differences and find none, or whether sex differences have not been systematically examined in these age periods.

It is clear, however, that in the age periods in which sex differences are found, patterns are complex and vary both within and across cognitive domains. As noted previously, for example, within spatial cognition, differences favoring boys over girls in mental rotations skills are observed as early as they can reliably be measured, but differences in horizontality are not reliably observed until late childhood to early adolescence. Girls outperform boys, on average, in early mathematics skill, but boys outperform girls, on average, in later mathematics skills. Thus, both the developmental period and the cognitive domain are factors in whether average score sex differences are found. Future descriptive work that addresses the ethnic-cultural groups and the age periods that have been understudied for each of the cognitive domains in question are needed to adequately include information necessary to formulate laws that can lead to explanation of the development of sex differences.

Psychologists have known for some time that sex differences in average levels of performance are small in comparison to within-sex variability in performance. Journal editors often (but not always, unfortunately) require researchers to provide measures of sex differences effect sizes and to consider whether or not findings have practical significance in addition to being statistically significant. The recent research summarized in this book has added to the description of "average" sex differences in two ways. First, it is clear that cognitive performance in a variety of domains varies with a host of factors including hormonal levels, situational contexts, and deliberate training. Such findings do more than add to a long list of descriptive findings. They require an attempt to reconcile the original "average" difference findings with demonstrations of modifiability. This is important in terms of moving to the next level of explanation; it is also vital to the focus on optimizing developmental outcomes as espoused by Newcombe, Mathason, and Terlecki (chapter 7). Second, across a variety of cognitive domains it is clear that the performance of males is more variable than the performance of females. Average score differences need to be interpreted in light of these differences in variability. As discussed in the chapter on mathematics achievement (De Lisi & McGillicuddy-De Lisi, chapter 6), for example, even small sex differences in average scores favoring males over females can result in disproportionate numbers of males being identified at the very high end of the ability distribution due to differences in variability. In addition, most psychologists do not have the means or opportunity to study the cognitive performance of samples that are statistically representative of the larger population. Instead, most psychologists work with samples that are "convenient." Note that the age ranges for which sex differences are typically found (ages 2–22) are the ones in which a researcher has a chance at obtaining a representative sample because of the near universal participation in educational programs in so many different cultures. It is unclear what effect, if any, reliance on convenient samples has on our descriptions of sex differences. For example, there may be selection factors involved in the study of infants (which ones are brought in by their parents, which ones can complete the experiments, etc.) that serve to mask findings of sex differences in cognitive functioning. More complete information about sample characteristics and selection effects will help to clarify the nature of descriptive findings about sex differences.

Coordinating Findings

There have been very few attempts to coordinate the vast array of findings of cognitive sex differences. An exception is Halpern's (1997) psychobiosocial framework that cuts across content areas and examines the underlying cognitive processes. Halpern maintained that sex differences favoring girls and women occur on tasks that require the rapid retrieval of information from memory, whereas sex differences favoring men occur on tasks that require the transformation of information in working memory. Most of the descriptive findings summarized in this book are consistent with this elegant framework. For example, the finding that females outperform males in arithmetic calculations in the early elementary school years and rely on algorithmic solutions that have been learned in school are consistent with her approach. Males, on the other hand, appear to excel on tasks that that can be accomplished through mental manipulations of visual stimuli held in working memory. As a result, we see excellent mental rotation performance in males. There are some exceptions; for example, in the recent reports that boys are faster at mathematics-fact retrieval than girls in the middle elementary school grades and that these differences persist into the college years (Royer et al., 1999). This exception notwithstanding, it remains to be explained why females and males differ in terms of the cognitive processes of speed of information retrieval versus information transformation.

Another general attempt to coordinate findings across domains is the fact that sex differences tend to be balanced in favor of female versus male students in classroom grades and school achievement, but the balance shifts toward favoring males on high-stakes tests. So, for example, sex differences in language abilities and school-related language performance favor females, but there is not a sex difference in favor of females on the SAT-V. Because only a small subset of cognitive abilities are assessed in high-stakes testing situations, this summary of findings is not as general as that offered by Halpern (1997), which includes many cognitive behaviors that have been observed only in laboratories. However, the differences in sex differences findings in classrooms versus testing contexts is important and merits further attention. Many attempts to explain sex differences in one context cannot also simultaneously explain the lack or reversal of performance differences in the other context. In our view, the present tendency to focus on differences that arise in the context of testing has neglected differences in classrooms. This has resulted in a both a failure to "give girls their due credit," and to minimize the negative impact that lower attainment in school has on boys.

Explanatory Models

Explanations of sex differences in cognitive functioning have usually been cast in terms of the nature–nurture controversy. That the human mind is a product of biological-evolutionary and social-psychological forces is disputed by very few. When it comes to explanations for sex differences in cognition, however, there have been a series of repeated attempts to emphasize one or the other "side," or to attempt to specify the relative contribution of each "separate factor." As discussed by Halpern and Ikier in the first chapter, these views are unfortunate and have not advanced the field.

A key issue is how changes due to evolutionary processes are thought to be linked to ontogeny. As discussed by Gottlieb (1992) in one model, which many view as the standard model, epigenesis is viewed as predetermined by evolutionary forces. This perspective is often packaged in biological-reductionist terms that minimize the role of experience and appeal to concepts such as "reaction range" which specifies that experience can only do so much given a specific genotype. We believe that those who object to biological-evolutionary accounts of human behavioral differences usually have such a predetermined model of epigenesis in mind. An alternative model proposed by Gottlieb (1992) views epigenesis as probabilistic. In this probabilistic model of epigenesis, individual development consists of a continuous cycle of reciprocal influences starting with components of genes and ending with the behavior of organisms in their environments. In this account, ontogenetic experience is a relational component consisting of co-actions at the horizontal (e.g., gene–gene) or vertical levels (e.g., gene–cytoplasm or cytoplasm–gene). A key, but controversial notion is that evolutionary change can start at the level of behavior and morphology without genetic alterations. The idea is that a change in the expected local ecology instigates behavioral changes that serve to activate parts of the genotype that were typically quiescent. An even more radical notion is that such behavioral changes may not necessarily be precipitated by changes in the local ecology. As Gottlieb notes:

It is appropriate to ask how the new phenotypic changes can be preserved from one gen- eration to the next if there has not been a mutation or a new genetic recombination. The answer is that the transgenerational stability of new behavioral and morphological pheno- types is preserved by the repetition of the developmental conditions that gave rise to them in the first place. Since genes are a part of the developmental system and cannot make traits by themselves, this same requirement (repetition of developmental conditions) holds for new phenotypes stemming from mutation and genetic recombination, even though that requirement often goes unrecognized or unspecified in the modern synthesis account of evolutionary change. (1992, p. 196)

This model of the relation between individual development and evolution admits of no artificial boundaries between nature and nurture and offers the prospects of fairly rapid changes in animal behaviors over successive genera- tions. How does this perspective relate to current evolutionary accounts such as that proposed by Geary (chapter 2; 1995, 1996, 1998)? Geary's model appeals to evolutionary processes, especially sexual selection processes of male–male com- petition, female choice, female–female competition, and male choice to account for sex differences in cognitive functioning. In Geary's model,

1. human cognition is viewed as modular,
2. distinctions are made between evolutionarily primary and secondary cognitive abili- ties, and
3. sex hormones are viewed as important mechanisms that cause differences in experi- ences (especially during early childhood) that help to shape cognitive functioning that is initially skeletal in nature.

Geary's model is a comprehensive account of sex differences in cognitive functioning in the sense that it links evolutionary processes with ontogeny and is broad enough to include all the major domains of cognition. We think the model deserves serious attention and offer the following comments.

It is possible to have a biological-evolutionary view of human cognition and its development without accepting modularity of cognition. This was, in fact, the life work of Jean Piaget as he attempted to describe and explain forms of human logical-mathematical thought viewed as species-wide constructions. Piaget's evi- dence for general cognitive structures (for example, object permanence) and their relations to one another (for example, object permanence ushers in symbol- ic functioning) was neither more nor less compelling than current evidence for separate cognitive modules. Our point is that an evolutionary account need not be yoked to modularity of mind. Piaget, of course, downplayed individual differ- ences in cognitive functioning, in favor of identification of general cognitive forms that were expected to be species wide, focusing on abilities common to females and males alike. With the exception of performance on measures of for- mal operational thought, this expectation was supported by literally thousands of empirical studies around the world. There have been many criticisms of Piagetian theory, but few found fault with its overtly biological-evolutionary basis. Is it acceptable to have a biological-evolutionary view only when the focus is on species-wide acquisitions but not when the focus is on individual differences? Those who dismiss an evolutionary account of sex differences in cognition, just because they are based on evolutionary models, are placing severe limits on the power of their attempts at explanations.

How does an evolutionary model relate to neurobiological and social or psychological processes described by Fitch and Bimonte and by Wigfield, Battle, Keller, and Eccles (chapters 3 & 4)? Geary's model building has appropriately emphasized how lower-level biological factors can condition experiential differences. Geary has tended to emphasize the unidirectional action of gene to cell to hormone to behavior and has not emphasized the reverse directions as discussed by Gottlieb. There is nothing inherent in evolutionary models such as Geary's, however, that precludes the study of bidirectional sets of influences. Gottlieb's concept of reaction range (which differs from the more limited norm of reaction) holds out great hope for the modifiability of human behavior in response to changes in local ecologies. Findings of sex differences that are reliable and consistent over time in specific contexts do not inform us about what might happen in other contexts. It seems highly improbable that higher-level animal behavior might be so open and responsive to changes in local ecologies, but the cognitive behavior of boys and girls, or of men and women, cannot be changed because it has an evolutionary history. Certainly, such an approach ignores the larger trend of behavioral plasticity that has evolved with larger brains and long periods of behavioral immaturity that allow for play and exploration. If evolutionary processes have conditioned females and males to be "biased" toward certain types of experiences, this does not mean that these "biases" cannot be overcome, especially when local ecologies change. Indeed, we know full well that many members of either sex are not "typical" representatives of that sex in terms of cognitive functioning (women with excellent mental rotation abilities and men with poor mental rotation abilities, for example). Findings that deliberate training can improve cognitive performance of both men and women (Newcombe, Mathasan, & Terlecki, chapter 7) are important. Findings that motivation, self-concept, and stereotype contexts affect performance are also important. We have no doubt that these "environmental" effects on cognitive performance are linked to other cognitive and affective changes at the time of their occurrence. It is interesting to speculate, however, at what level of organismic functioning these changes "stop" having an effect—behavior alone, behavior plus endocrine functioning, and so forth.

Will future work be able to link changes in environmental contexts to changes in levels of circulating hormones, or to changes in which genes are active or dormant? This remains to be seen, but the possibilities are exciting. Such work in the area of human behavior will undoubtedly require research teams as the means to measure and manipulate complex social-psychological and biological processes does not reside in most psychological laboratories. Until such time, research that is directed to biological processes alone, or to socio-psychological processes alone, should not be viewed as biased or as unimportant, but as incomplete. We caution the reader to avoid any explanation of sex differences that goes in only one direction, from biology to behavior, or from society to behavior. We have models of evolutionary and ontogenetic processes that link biology, behavior, and society. The models are general and need refinement, but this can only occur if there is a willingness to view sex differences in cognitive functioning in such terms.

REFERENCES

Geary, D. C. (1995). Sexual selection and sex differences in spatial cognition. *Learning and Individual Differences, 7,* 289-301.

Geary, D. C. (1996). Sexual selection and sex differences in mathematical abilities. *Behavioral and Brain Sciences, 19,* 229-284.

Geary, D. C. (1998). *Male, female. The evolution of human sex differences.* Washington, DC: American Psychological Association.

Gottlieb, G. (1992). *Individual development and evolution. The genesis of novel behavior.* New York: Oxford University Press.

Halpern, D. F. (1997). Sex differences in intelligence: Implications for education. *American Psychologist, 52,* 1091-1102.

McGlone, M., Kobrynowitcz, D., & Aronson, J. (1999). Grounds for stereotype threat: Social identity and test difficulty. Paper presented at the Stereotype Threat Symposium Meeting of the European Association of Experimental Social Psychology, Oxford University, London, England.

Piaget, J. (1973). *Main trends in psychology.* New York: Harper & Row.

Royer, J. M., Tronsky, L. N., Chan, Y., Jackson, S. J., & Marchant, H. (1999). Math-fact retrieval as the cognitive mechanism underlying gender differences in math test performance. *Contemporary Educational Psychology, 24,* 181-266.

Stanovich, K. E. (1990). Concepts in developmental theories of reading skill: Cognitive resources, automaticity, and modularity. *Developmental Review, 10,* 72-100.

Tinbergen, N. (1996). On aims and methods of ethology. In L. D. Houck & L. C. Drickamer (Eds.), *Foundations of animal behavior* (pp. 114–137). Chicago: University of Chicago Press.

Author Index

Abady, N., 175, 180
Abbott, R. D., 165, 180
Aboitiz, F., 64, 80
Accorsi, P., 78, 89
Adams, C., 201, 104
Adler, T. F., 96, 98, 101, 118
Adler, T., 97, 110, 111
Adolphs, R., 35, 47
Akazawa, K., 75, 87
Alberts, S. C., 33, 42
Alexander, K. L., 110, 114, 116, 119, 122
Alexander, R. D., 36, 37, 47
Ali, M., 57, 80
Allen, G., 65, 68, 87
Allen, L.S., 12, 18, 64, 67, 82
Allred, R. A., 143, 148
Altmann, J., 33, 42
Alves, S., 75, 86
Amador, R., 74, 83
Amaducci, L., 75, 80
American Association for University
    Women's (AAUW) Report, 114, 116
Andersen, E. S., 135, 139, 140, 148
Anderson, K. J., 144, 145, 151
Anderson, R. H., 62, 83
Andersson, M., 23–25, 27, 30, 40, 41, 46,
    48
Andrews, H., 75, 90
Antal, S., 113, 124
Aram, D. M., 70, 87
Arbreton, A. J. A., 162, 181

Arbreton, A., 96, 98, 100, 109, 110, 111,
    118, 123
Archer, D., 42, 43, 52
Arend, R., 215, 238
Arndt, J., 37, 44, 48
Arnold, A. P., 59, 80
Arnott, D. P., 42, 48
Aronson, J. A., 221, 239
Aronson, J., 6, 19, 246, 258
Ashbridge, D., 106, 121
Astin, H.S., 212, 234
Aukett, R., 142, 148
Austin, A. M., 141, 148
Austin, W. M., 134, 149

Bacal, C., 75, 85
Bachevalier, J., 61, 62, 67, 80, 84
Badian, N. A., 135, 149
Baenninger, M., 9, 18, 23, 48, 184, 185,
    186, 189, 198, 202, 203
Bakaitis, J., 62, 83
Baker, D., 110, 113, 117
Baker, J., 138, 152
Bakker, D. J., 137, 152
Baldereschi, M., 75, 80
Ball, G. F., 29, 48
Banaji, M.R., 7, 18
Bandura, A., 96, 98, 117
Banerjee, M., 44, 48
Barber, B., 208, 210, 234, 235
Barber, B. L., 106, 120

Barnett, A., 198, 206
Barnett, A. M., 61, 91
Baron-Cohen, S., 35, 43, 44, 48
Bartell, N. P., 102, 117
Barth, R. J., 142, 149
Barton, R. A., 32, 35, 48
Bassett, M., 113, 124
Bates, E. A., 32, 33, 49
Bates, E., 138, 149
Bates, H. M., 216, 236
Bauer, S. C., 161, 180
Baulieu, E. E., 57, 87
Beal, C., 109, 114, 117
Beaton, A. A., 135, 137, 149
Beatty, P., 59, 80
Beatty, W. W., 58, 60, 61, 76, 80, 88
Beatty, W., 59, 80
Beccaria, F., 78, 89
Beck, K. D., 72, 86
Becker, B. J., 162, 178
Becker, J. B., 59, 69, 80, 81
Behrmann, M., 35, 51
Belansky, E., 96, 118
Bell, L. A., 99, 117
Bell, M. A., 195, 205
Beller, M., 166, 178
Bellinger, D., 146, 149
Bellugi, U., 194, 203
Belzung, C., 75, 80
Bem, S., 144, 149, 209, 234
Benbow, C. P., 78, 80, 86, 96, 116, 156,
    157, 162, 164, 169, 173, 178, 179
Benenson, J. F., 44, 46, 47, 48
Bercu, B. B., 61, 80
Berenbaum, S., 60, 86
Berenbaum, S. A., 46, 48, 214, 235
Berger, C., 216, 236
Berninger, V. W., 165, 180
Berry, B., 72, 80
Berta, P., 56, 80
Best, D.L., 11, 18
Beuzen, A., 75, 80
Bielinski, J., 166, 178
Bilker, W., 12, 18
Bimonte, H. A., 55, 59, 64–66, 72, 77, 81
Birch, S. H., 229, 236
Birecree, E., 61, 85

Birge, S. J., 74, 81
Bishop, J., 72, 74, 89
Bishop, K., 60, 64, 67, 74, 81
Bjork, R., 186, 205
Bjorklund, D. F., 108, 117
Black, J. E., 33, 38, 50
Blasberg, M., 72, 89
Blizard, D., 65, 81
Bloch, G. J., 59, 66, 81
Block, R. A., 42, 48
Blumenfeld, P. B., 98, 99, 100, 119
Blumenfeld, P. C., 96, 98, 100, 123, 162,
    181
Bodenhausen, G. V., 7, 19
Bono, G., 73, 87
Borgerhoff Mulder, M., 41, 48
Borgia, G., 27, 28, 48, 49
Borker, R. A., 132, 133, 142, 152
Bornstein, M. H., 108, 117, 184, 203
Bosacki, S.L., 16, 18
Boston, M.B., 210, 235
Bracco, L., 75, 80
Bradbard, M. R., 215, 235
Braza, F., 228, 235
Braza. P., 228, 235
Breedlove, S. M., 56, 58, 59, 80, 81
Bregman, G., 106, 117
Bretherton, I., 138, 145, 149
Brickson, M., 62, 67, 80
Bridgeman, B., 169, 178
Brink, T. M., 70, 85
Broadhurst, P., 72, 81
Brody, G. H., 146, 153
Brody, L., 138, 146, 149, 153
Bronen, R. A., 67, 89, 137, 153
Brookmeyer, R., 75, 85
Brooks-Gunn, J., 110, 117
Brothers, L., 35, 48
Broverman, D., 70, 81
Brown, D. E., 36, 48
Brown, N.,198, 203
Brown, R., 44–46, 53, 198, 203
Brown, R. P., 174, 175, 178
Brown, S., 198, 203
Brown, T. J., 57, 81, 85
Brubaker, B., 201, 202, 204
Bruford, M. W., 33, 42

Bryden, M., 189, 190–192, 196, 206
Bucci, D., 199, 203
Buchanan, C., 109, 110, 112, 118
Buchanan, L., 64, 81
Buck, R. W., 42, 48
Buckwalter, J. G., 75, 84
Bugental, D. B., 36, 44, 49
Buhs, E. S., 229, 236
Bulloch, K., 75, 86
Burchardt, C. J., 226, 238
Burke, A., 72, 81
Buss, D. M., 31, 41, 42, 49
Buss, K. A., 138, 150
Busse, J., 165, 180
Buswell, B. N., 103, 121
Byrne, R., 38, 49
Byrnes, J. P., 170, 171, 178

Cahalan, C., 171, 172, 179
Cain, L., 146, 150
Caldwell, B., 74, 81
Cameron, D., 133, 149
Capuzzo, E., 78, 89
Carpenter, C., 228, 229, 235
Carpenter, P., 193, 197, 204
Carr, M., 160, 178
Carreras, M. R., 228, 235
Carter, D. B., 226, 227, 235
Carter, P., 78, 85, 191, 193, 204
Casas, J. F., 38, 41, 49
Casey, M. B., 112, 117, 173, 179
Casserly, P., 115, 117
Cassidy, K. W., 140, 153
Castner, S. A., 69, 81
Caul, W. F., 42, 48
Cavalli-Sforza, L. L., 40, 52
Cha, J., 59, 69, 80
Chagnon, N. A., 36, 41, 49
Chai, Y.M., 2, 18
Chaille, C., 194, 204
Chan, Y., 94, 95, 115, 122, 161, 168, 169,
    172, 173, 180, 247, 254, 258
Chang, E. L., 200, 202, 203
Chao, C.-C., 45, 51
Cheng, L. C., 44, 45, 49
Chessman, D. J., 33, 42
Cheung, Y. M., 61, 82

Chiarello, C., 70, 81
Chiba, A., 199, 203
Childs, B., 68, 78, 83
Choi, J., 71, 89
Cholst, I., 74, 83
Chouraqui, J., 57, 90
Cioe, J., 67, 85
Citron, C. C., 226, 238
Clark, A., 72, 89
Clark, A.S., 61, 67, 81
Clark, E. V., 129, 149
Clark, L. V., 215, 238
Clark, S., 132, 151
Clemens, L. G., 57, 90
Clutton-Brock T. H., 24, 25, 49
Coates, J., 133, 149
Cohen-Kettenis, P. T., 71, 74, 89
Cohen-Kettenis, P., 71, 74, 90
Colburne, K. A., 226, 227, 238
Cole, N. C., 163, 165, 166, 167
Cole, N. S., 14, 19
Coleman, J. M., 102, 117
Coleman, J. S., 110, 123
Collaer, M. L., 60, 82
Collins, D., 184, 189, 203
Collins, W. A., 108, 110, 117, 119
Collis, K., 27, 28, 49
Connell, J. P., 97, 98, 117, 122
Conner, J. M., 213, 226, 235, 238
Constable, R. T., 67, 89, 137, 153
Cook, A. S., 141, 149
Coote, T., 33, 42
Corder, J., 108, 117
Cornell, D. G., 12, 18
Corrada, M., 75, 85
Cosmides, L., 32, 33, 53,
Costa, D., 35, 48
Cowan, C. P., 146, 152
Cowan, P. A., 146, 152
Cowell, P. E., 64–68, 82, 83, 86
Craig, A. S., 195, 205
Crandall, V. C., 97, 117
Crandall, V. J., 97, 117
Crick, N. R., 38, 41, 49
Crosby, F., 132, 149
Cross, D., 193, 204
Curry, C., 106, 107, 108, 117

Cutler, G. B., Jr., 64, 88
Cygan, D., 65, 66, 89

D'Aquila, J. M., 190, 205
Dabbs, J., 200, 202, 203
Daly, A. R., 65, 68, 87
Daly, E., 68, 87
Danaher, D. L., 141, 152
Daniel, J. M., 72, 82
Daniel, J., 72, 82
Darwin, C., 23, 24, 27–30, 46, 49
Dauber, S. L., 97, 116
Davenport, Jr., E. C., 167, 179
Davidson, W., 114, 118
Davies, D. R., 216, 235
Davies, N. B., 24, 51
Davis, L. E., 44, 45, 49
Davison, M. L., 166, 167, 178, 179
Dawson, G., 44, 51
Dawson, J., 61, 82
de Carufel, A., 45, 53
de Klerk, V., 142, 149
De Lisi, R., 161, 171, 172, 179, 197, 205,
    213, 236
Deaux, K., 210, 235
DeCarli, C., 65, 68, 87
Deci, E. L., 98, 100, 111, 117, 122
DeHart, G. B., 141, 149
DeLacoste-Utamsing, C., 64, 82
Delgado, A., 191, 203
Delis, D.C., 13, 18
Denef, C., 65, 81
Denenberg, V. H., 57, 59, 64–66, 72, 76,
    77, 81–83, 86
Denti, A., 65, 82
Devineni, T., 201, 204
DeVries, N., 113, 124
Di Carlo, A., 75, 80
Di Pietro, J. A., 228, 235
Diamond, M. C., 59, 62, 66, 82, 87
Diamond, M., 62, 66, 82
Diaz-Veliz, G., 72, 82
Dickey, R., 70, 85
DiMatteo, M. R., 42, 43, 52
Ding, S., 167, 179
Dohanich, G., 72, 82, 83
Dohanich, G. P., 72, 82
Dohler, K., 56, 82

Dohler, K. D., 56, 66, 82
Donahue, M., 138, 150
Donnell Lingle, D., 75, 85
Dowling, G., 62, 66, 82
Downs, A. C., 226, 236
Doyle, A., 213, 229, 238
Doyle, A. B., 228, 232, 238
Drachman, D., 75, 83
Drakich, J., 132, 151
Droulez, J., 193, 204
Dubach, J., 33, 42
Duffy, J., 222, 239
Dunbar, R. I. M., 26, 32, 36, 49
Dunn, J., 138, 145, 149, 153
Dunn, M. E., 75, 84
Dunton, K. J., 109, 117
Dusek, J. B., 103, 118
Dussaubat, N., 72, 82
Duvdevani, R., 68, 78, 88
Dweck, C. S., 97, 114, 118
Dwyer, C. A., 168, 169, 179

Eagly, A. H., 23, 46, 49
Eals, M., 201, 202, 205
Early, D. M., 96, 118
Eaton, W. O., 137, 138, 149, 228, 235
Eccles, J. S., 93, 95–101, 106, 107, 109,
    110–15, 118–23, 162, 181, 208, 210,
    212, 234, 235, 239
Eckerman, D. A., 75, 83
Edelsky, C., 140, 149
Edwards, C. P., 45, 53
Edwards, J. D., 75, 83
Egan, S. K., 210, 235
Ehlert, J., 66, 82
Ehrhardt, A., 107, 122
Eicher, E., 56, 83
Eisenberg, N., 94, 99, 100, 103, 106, 109,
    114, 119
Eisenbud, L., 210, 218, 237
Eliot, J., 189, 203
Ell, P., 35, 48
Elman, J. L., 32, 33, 49
Elman, M., 228, 232, 238
Ely, R., 127, 142, 145, 149, 150
Emanuel, C. K., 75, 84
Ember, C. R., 40, 44, 52
Ember, M., 40, 44, 52

Emlen, S. T., 24–26, 49
Emmorey, K., 194, 203
Endsley, R.C., 215, 235
Enna, B., 114, 118
Enns, L. R., 228, 235
Enright, M., 217, 236
Entwisle, D., 110, 113, 116, 117
Entwisle, D. R., 110, 114, 119, 122
Epting, L. K., 195, 203
Erickson, D., 135, 153
Escobar, M. D., 135, 153
Etaugh, C., 99, 119, 212, 235
Evahn, C., 97, 121
Evans, D., 145, 150
Evans, S. M., 232, 237
Everett, J. C., 78, 83

Fabes, R. A., 94, 99, 100, 103, 106, 109,
    114, 119, 138, 149, 214, 226, 227, 230,
    232, 235, 237
Fader, A., 72, 82, 83
Fagot, B. A., 144, 150
Fagot, B. I., 212–14, 226, 228, 235, 236
Farley, M. J., 65, 91
Farlow, M. R., 64, 75, 88
Farmer, H., 99, 119
Farr, S., 72, 83
Favreau, O. E., 78, 83
Fazzi, E., 78, 89
Fedor-Freybergh, P., 70, 83
Feingold, A., 45, 49, 78, 83, 163, 164, 165,
    179
Fenema, E., 213, 236
Fennema, E., 155, 156, 157, 161, 162, 180
Filardo, E. K., 142, 150
Fillit, H., 74, 83
Finegan, J. K., 60, 84
Finucci, J. M., 68, 78, 83
Fiorentine, R., 107, 119
Fisk, J. L., 137, 152
Fitch, R. H., 55, 57, 59, 64–66, 76, 81, 83, 86
Fitzgerald, R., 190, 199, 203
Fitzgerald, R. W., 29, 30, 49, 50
Flaherty, J., 103, 118
Flanagan, C., 96, 98, 109, 119
Fleming, D., 62, 83
Fletcher, J. M., 67, 89,135, 137, 153
Flood, J., 72, 83

Flowers, L. D., 67, 91
Foley, R. A., 31, 49
Folling-Albers, M., 100, 119
Foot, J. M., 216, 236
Forbes, D., 141, 152
Forbes, M. R. L., 31, 52
Ford, M. E., 215, 238
Forgie, M. L., 65, 66, 69, 83
Fox, T. O., 58, 90
Frankfurt, M., 59, 69, 83, 84, 91
Freedman-Doan, C., 162, 181
Freedman-Doan, K., 96, 98, 100, 123
Frensch, P., 195, 204, 214, 238
Freund, L. S., 65, 88
Frey, K. S., 209, 239
Friedman, L., 158, 163, 164, 179
Frijda, N., 71, 74, 90
Fritz, J. J., 141, 149
Frost, L. A., 156, 157, 162, 180
Frye, C., 72, 83
Fulbright, R. K., 67, 89, 137, 153
Fuller, D., 160, 178
Fults, B. A., 102, 117
Furstenberg, F. F., Jr., 10, 117
Futterman, R., 96, 98, 101, 118

Gafni, N., 166, 178
Gage, M. I., 75, 83
Galaburda, A. M., 67, 78, 84, 136, 150
Galea, L., 69, 72, 83, 199, 203
Gallagher, A., 160, 179
Gallagher, A. M., 171, 172, 179, 213,
    236
Gallagher, M., 72, 80, 199, 203
Garcia-Segura, L. M., 66, 86
Gardner, P. L., 100, 119
Garrison, J., 71, 86
Gaulin, S., 190, 199, 203
Gaulin, S. J., 199, 205
Gaulin, S. J. C., 24, 29–31, 46, 49, 50,
    51, 201, 204
Gauthier, R., 226, 236
Gaze, C., 196, 197, 206
Geary, D. C., 24, 26–28, 30–34, 36–41,
    44, 45–47, 50, 159, 160, 173, 179,
    190, 203, 249, 250, 256, 258
Geffen, E., 33, 42
Gelman, R., 33, 38, 50

George, F., 56, 91
Gerwels, D., 106, 113, 122
Geschwind, N., 67, 78, 84, 136, 150
Gibbs, A., 200, 203
Gilbert, S. F., 39, 50
Gilger, J. W., 70, 85
Gilliard, E. T., 27, 50
Gilligan, C., 104, 119, 142, 150
Ginsburg, H. P., 157, 159, 160, 179
Girigus, J. S., 103, 122
Gleason, J. B., 127, 128, 136, 137, 142,
    144–146, 149, 150, 153
Glogowski, B. K., 78, 87
Goetz, T. E., 97, 118
Goff, S. B., 96, 98, 101, 118
Gold, D., 213, 216, 229, 236, 238
Goldman-Rakic, P. S., 61, 67, 81
Goldsmith, H. H., 138, 150
Goldstein, D., 191, 192, 203
Golledge, R., 202, 204
Gonzalez, M. I., 65, 85
Goodall, J., 36, 40, 50
Goodenow, C., 115, 119
Goodfellow, P. N., 56, 80
Goodglass, H., 136, 150
Goodnow, J. J., 110, 119, 123
Goodwin, M. H., 142, 150
Gooren, L. J., 71, 74, 89
Gooren, L., 71, 74, 90
Gopnik, A., 35, 50
Gordon, H. W., 70, 84
Gordon, W. A., 75, 83
Gore, J. C., 67, 89, 137, 153
Gorski, R. A., 12, 18, 56, 57, 59, 62, 66,
    81, 82, 84, 88
Gottfried, A. E., 100, 110, 119
Gottlieb, G., 255–58
Gouchie, C., 71, 84
Goudsmit, E., 69, 73, 84
Gould, E., 59, 69, 83, 84, 91
Grady, C. L., 68, 87
Gralinski, J. H., 161, 181
Grant, B. R., 29, 50
Grant, P. R., 29, 50
Green, D., 111, 121
Green, R., 74, 86
Greenberg, J., 37, 44, 48

Greenlaw, R., 65, 88
Greenough, W. T., 33, 38, 50
Greif, E. B., 145, 150
Griffin, J., 56, 91
Griffiths, B. L., 56, 80
Grigoletto, F., 75, 80
Grimshaw, G. M., 60, 84
Grossman, R. I., 68, 82
Grotelueschen, L. K., 61, 88
Grotevant, H. D., 215, 238
Gualtieri, T., 69, 73, 84
Gulko, J., 226, 227, 238
Gunnar, M. R., 138, 150
Guo, G., 110, 117
Guo, J., 142, 151
Gur, R. C., 12, 18, 68, 82
Gur, R. E., 12, 18, 68, 82
Gurland, B., 75, 90

Hagan, R., 144, 150
Hagger, C., 61, 62, 67, 80, 84
Hagino, N., 75, 87
Haines, S. A., 33, 42
Hajjar, R., 71, 86
Haldane, D., 191, 192, 203
Hall, J. A., 42, 43, 50, 52
Hall, L., 198, 203
Halpern, D. F., 5, 13, 14, 18, 23, 31, 42,
    50, 71, 77, 84, 112, 119, 167, 179, 245,
    254, 255, 258
Halverson, C., 209, 217, 238
Hamamoto, M., 75, 87
Hamilton, W. D., 33, 50
Hamm, R. J., 72, 87
Hampson, E., 15, 18, 69, 70, 71, 73, 78,
    84, 85, 199, 200, 203, 204
Hancke, J. L., 56, 66, 82
Happé, F. G. E., 44, 50
Hardin, C.D., 7, 18
Hare-Mustin, R.T., 4, 18
Hargreaves, D. J., 216, 236
Harold, R., 98, 99, 100, 109, 110, 112,
    118, 119
Harold, R. D., 96, 98, 100, 106, 109, 111,
    112, 115, 118, 123, 162, 181
Harris, A. M., 227, 237
Harris, J. R., 225, 236

Harter, S., 98, 101–4, 115, 120
Hartinger, A., 100, 119
Hartup, W. W., 33, 35, 40, 45, 51
Harvey, O. J., 37, 47, 52
Haskell, S., 73–75, 84
Haslum, M. N., 135, 152
Hatzipantelis, M., 200, 204
Haude, R., 193, 194, 205
Hauser, M. D., 29, 35, 51
Havens, M., 61, 88
Haviland, J. J., 38, 45–47, 51
Hawkins, J. R., 56, 80
Haxby, J. V., 65, 68, 87
Hay, D., 146, 150
Hayashi, K., 75, 85
Hayashi, M., 75, 85
Hecht, H., 196, 203
Hedges, L. V., 143, 150, 162–65, 178, 179
Heinsbroek, R. P. W., 61, 76, 90
Henderson, V. W., 64, 75, 84, 87, 88
Hendricks, S. E., 56, 84
Hendricson, A., 72, 83
Henley, C., 133, 153
Herrnstein, R. J., 15, 18
Herzog, E. W., 217, 236
Hess, R. D., 109, 117
Hess, S., 61, 85
Hetherington, E. H., 184, 203
Hetherington, E. M., 108, 117
Hickey, C., 222, 239
Hicks, R., 69, 73, 84
Hidi, S., 100, 121
Hill, J. P., 104, 120
Hines, M., 60, 74, 82, 86, 214, 235
Ho, H. Z., 70, 85
Hoard, M. K., 173, 179
Hochberg, R. B., 57, 85
Hoffman, C. M., 156, 168, 169, 180
Hoffman, G. E., 30, 51
Hoffman, L., 111, 112, 118
Hofmann, C., 56, 66, 82
Hogrebe, M. C., 143, 151
Holloway, R. L., 64, 82
Holloway, S. D., 109, 120
Holst, P. C., 171, 172, 179
Holtzer, R., 198, 203
Honjo, H., 75, 85

Hood, W. R., 37, 47, 52
Hopkins, K. B., 161, 179
Hopkins, T. L., 78, 87
Hopp, C., 156, 157, 162, 180
Horwitz, B., 65, 68, 87
Horwitz, R., 73–75, 84
Howes, C., 226, 227, 236
Huettel, S., 200, 205
Hughes, A., 113, 123
Hughett, P., 12, 18
Huhtaniemi, I. T., 57, 89
Hulse, S. H., 29, 48
Humphreys, L. G., 162, 180
Hunt, E., 198, 204
Hunter, J., 106, 107, 108, 117
Huston, A., 96, 99, 112, 120
Huttenen, M. O., 138, 152
Huttenlocher, J., 184, 190, 203, 204
Hyatt, S., 96, 99, 120
Hyde, J. S., 42, 51, 94, 103, 120, 121,
    140, 141, 151, 155–57, 161, 162, 180

Igoe, A., 116, 120
Ikegami, S., 75, 85
Ince, S., 107, 122
Inhelder, B., 196, 205
Insel, T. R., 35, 52
Isaacs, S. D., 68, 78, 83
Isse, K., 75, 87
Ivy, G. O., 31, 52

Jacklin, C. N., 94, 109, 121, 138, 151,
    156, 180, 226, 231, 237
Jackson, D. W., 107, 120
Jackson, S. J., 161, 168, 169, 172, 173,
    180, 247, 254, 258
Jacobs, D., 75, 90
Jacobs, J., 109, 110, 112, 118
Jacobs, J. E., 96, 99, 109, 110, 111, 120
Jacobs, L. F., 30, 51, 199, 205
Jaffard, R., 75, 85
James, D., 132, 151
Jamison, W., 185, 205
Janowsky, J. S., 71, 85
Jarrard, L., 75, 85
Jarzab, B., 56, 66, 82
Jay, G., 102, 121

Jay, T., 142. 151
Jenkins, M. M., 132, 151
Jensen, A. R., 162, 180
Jessup, D. L., 160, 178
Joffe, T. H., 32, 38, 51
Johnson, L. M., 168, 169, 179
Johnson, M. H., 32, 33, 49
Johnson, N. E., 195, 205
Johnson, R., 62, 66, 82
Johnson, R. E., 59, 66, 82, 87
Jolliffe, T., 44, 48
Jones, D., 60, 67, 85, 132, 151
Joseph, R., 61, 85
Josephs, R. A., 174, 175, 178
Jozefowicz, D. M., 106, 120
Jozefowicz, D., 208, 210, 234, 235
Judd, H., 73, 85
Juraska, J. M., 62, 63, 72, 87, 88, 90
Jussim, L., 114, 121
Just, M., 193, 197, 204

Kaczala, C., 97, 110, 111
Kaczala, C. M., 96, 98, 101, 114, 118, 122
Kahle, J., 115, 121
Kail, R., 78, 85, 191–93, 204, 205
Kaiser, F., 71, 72, 83, 86
Kampen, D. L., 64, 74, 85
Kandel, D. B., 110, 121
Kaplan, E., 13, 18
Karmiloff-Smith, A., 32, 33, 49
Karnes, F. A., 102, 121
Karpathian, M., 101, 102, 123
Karraker, K. H., 138, 153
Kashiwagi, T., 75, 85
Kastuk, D., 71, 89
Katovsky, W., 97, 117
Katstelic, D., 103, 104, 115, 120
Katz, L., 67, 89, 137, 153
Kaufman, J., 200, 205
Kavaliers, M., 69, 72, 83, 199, 203, 205
Kawas, C., 75, 85
Keating, D. P., 160, 180
Keats, J. G., 138, 149
Keeley, L. H., 36, 40, 41, 51
Kemper, T. K., 136, 150
Kerig, P. K., 146, 152
Khurgel, M., 31, 52

Killen, M., 106, 117, 141, 151
Kim, S-K., 167, 179
Kimball, M. M., 114, 121, 157, 180, 213, 236
Kimura, D., 23, 39, 42, 51, 67, 70, 71, 84, 85, 189, 190, 197, 203, 204, 206
Kinder, B. N., 142, 149
Kinghorn, E., 62, 83
Klaiber, E., 70, 81
Klein, A., 157, 159, 160, 179
Kling, K. C., 103, 121
Klinger, L. G., 44, 51
Knight, G. P., 45, 51
Knott, J., 196, 197, 206
Kobrynowitcz, D., 246, 258
Kohlberg, L. A., 209, 236
Kohnstamm, G. A., 138, 151
Kolb, B., 62, 66, 67, 69, 85, 89
Komnenich, P., 70, 85
Kosslyn, S., 194, 203
Kostenuik, M.A., 199, 205
Kramarae, C., 132, 133, 153
Kramer, J.H., 13, 18
Krapp, A., 100, 121
Kratzer, L., 97, 121
Krebs, J. R., 24, 51
Krupa, M., 185, 205
Kruppe, B., 146, 154
Kuang, H., 167, 179
Kuhl, P. K., 128, 151
Kuhnemann, S., 57, 63, 85, 90
Kulynych, J., 60, 67, 85
Kushner, H., 64, 88
Kwak, N., 167, 179
Kyratzis, A., 142, 151

La Freniere, P., 226, 236
Lacerda, F., 128, 151
Lacy, R. C., 33, 42
Ladd, G. W., 229, 236
Lakoff, R. T., 131, 133, 151
Lamb, M., 226, 236
Lamon, S. J., 155, 157, 161, 180
Lane, D., 70, 85
Lang, M., 78, 88
Langan, C., 72, 89
Langlois, J. H., 226, 236

Langrock, A., 190, 204
Larsen, R. J., 31, 49
Larson, G. E., 195, 205
Larson, R., 212, 238
Lau, R. T. S., 61, 82
Lauterbach, M. D., 78, 87
Law, D., 198, 204
Lawton, C., 200, 201, 204
Leaper, C., 141, 144, 145, 151, 226, 227, 237
Leavitt, J., 75, 83
Lee, P. A., 70, 84
Lee, P. C., 31, 49
Leffler, A., 141, 148
Leinbach, M. D., 212, 213, 236
LeMay, M., 136, 150
Lemery, K. S., 138, 150
Leonard, B., 71, 86
Leone, G., 193, 204
Lepore, V., 75, 80
Lepper, M., 111, 121
Leret, M. L., 65, 85
Lerner, M. J., 45, 53
Leslie, A. M., 35, 41
Leslie, L., 108, 121
Lesser, G. S., 110, 121
Lever, J., 41, 46, 51, 212, 229, 237
Leveroni, C., 60, 86
Levine, S., 184, 190, 203, 204
Levy, G. D., 210, 224, 235, 237
Lewis, B. A., 135, 151
Lewis, C., 169, 178
Lewis, M., 228, 237
Licht, B. G., 97, 118
Lieberburg, I., 73, 75, 91
Lieberman, P., 135, 153
Lilly, M. V., 96, 123
Lindblom, B., 128, 151
Linn, M., 185, 189, 190, 196, 204
Linn, M. C., 42, 51, 94, 120, 121, 140, 141, 151
Lisk, R., 56, 86
Liss, M. B., 99, 119, 212, 237
Littman, I., 213, 214, 236
Liu, F., 173, 179
Locke, J. L., 136, 151
Lockheed, M. E., 227, 237
Loeb, R. C., 102, 121

Lord, T., 71, 86
Loring-Meier, S., 13, 18
Lovelace, K., 202, 204
Low, R., 171, 180
Lu, J., 73, 86
Lubinski, D., 78, 86
Luine, V., 72, 74, 83, 86
Lummis, M., 17, 19
Luria, Z., 143, 152, 217, 227, 236, 239
Lynch, M. E., 104, 120
Lynch, W. C., 42, 48
Lynn, R., 11, 12, 19
Lytton, H., 109, 121

Mac Iver, D., 98, 109, 110, 112, 118, 123
Maccoby, E. E., 45, 51, 94, 108, 109, 117, 121, 133, 138, 141, 151, 156, 180, 184, 203, 225–28, 230, 231, 237
Mack, C. M., 59, 64–66, 81, 86
MacLusky, N. J., 57, 81, 85
MacPhail, R. C., 75, 83
Macrae, C. N., 7, 19
Madon, S., 114, 121
Maes, A., 132, 152
Maggi, S., 75, 80
Majcher, D., 70, 81
Majeres, R. L., 135, 151
Major, B., 210, 235
Malatesta, C. Z., 38, 45, 46, 47, 51
Maltz, D. N., 132, 133, 142, 152
Mannan, M. A., 57, 86
Mannle, S., 146, 152
Manson, J. H., 40, 51
Marchant, H., 247, 254, 258
Marchant, H., III., 161, 168, 169, 172, 173, 180
Marder, K., 75, 90
Marecek, J., 4, 18
Marjoribanks, K., 113, 121
Markus, E., 72, 86
Marsh, H. W., 94, 96, 101, 102, 121
Martin, C. L., 94, 95, 97, 99, 100, 103, 106, 109, 114, 119, 122, 209, 210, 212, 217, 218, 224, 227, 230–32, 237, 238
Martin, R., 142, 152
Martin, R. P., 138, 152

Mascie-Taylor, C. G. N., 16, 19
Masters, J. C., 215, 238
Masters, M., 190, 191, 204
Masters, S., 190, 204
Matsui, M., 12, 18
Mattingly, I. C., 134, 152
Mauri, M., 73, 87
Mayer, R. E., 157, 180
Mayeux, R., 75, 90
Mayr, E., 38, 51
Mazzacocco, M. M., 65, 88
McBurney, D. H., 201, 204
McCabe, A., 127, 142, 149
McCall, R. B., 97, 121
McCarthy, K., 38, 52
McCarthy, M., 57, 86, 86
McCarthy, N. M., 66, 86
McClellan, N., 113, 123
McClelland, D. C., 188, 204
McCloskey, L. A., 141, 152, 226, 235
McClurg, P. A., 194, 204
McCornack, B. L., 141, 149
McCullough, P.M., 106, 121
McDevitt, T. M., 109, 117
McEwen, B. S., 59, 69, 83, 84, 91
McEwen, B., 74, 75, 83, 86
McGillicuddy-De Lisi, A. V., 110, 123,
    161, 171, 172, 179
McGinn, P., 106, 122
McGlone, J., 67, 86
McGlone, M., 246, 258
McGuinness, D., 45, 51
McIntosh, A. R., 65, 68, 87
McMahan, R., 72, 80
McMahon, M. A., 70, 81
Means, L. W., 72, 87
Meck, W., 198, 206
Meck, W. H., 61, 77, 91
Meece, J. L., 96, 98, 101, 114, 118, 122
Meehan, A. M., 159, 180
Megens, J., 71, 74, 89
Meites, J., 73, 86
Mellins, C., 107, 122
Mentis, M. J., 68, 87
Mercier-Bodard, C., 57, 87
Metter, E., 74, 75, 85, 88

Metzler, J., 194, 195, 205
Meunier, M., 75, 85
Meyer, E. M., 72, 89
Meyer-Bahlburg, F., 107, 122
Midgley, C., 96, 98, 101, 109, 110, 112,
    118, 123
Miles, C., 74, 86
Miles, T. R., 135, 152
Mill, K., 142, 148
Millard, W. J., 72, 89
Miller, C., 96, 98, 109, 119
Miller, M. D., 175, 180
Miller, P. M., 141, 152
Miller, R. E., 42, 48
Milne, A. B., 7, 19
Milun, R., 200, 202, 203
Minch, E., 40, 52
Miranda, R. C., 57, 86
Mishkin, M., 62, 67, 80
Mitchell, C., 191, 192, 203
Mitchell, E., 212, 238
Moely, B. E., 132, 152
Moffat, S., 200, 204
Molina-Holgado, F., 65, 85
Moller, L. C., 226, 227, 231, 238
Montello, D., 202, 204
Montemayor, R., 215, 217, 223, 238
Moore, C., 16, 18
Mora, S., 72, 82
Morely, M., 171, 172, 179
Moriarty, J., 35, 48
Morley, J., 71, 72, 83, 86
Morrin, K., 104, 204
Morrison, A., 75, 85
Mortimore, C., 44, 48
Moscovitch, M., 35, 51
Mosher, M., 38, 41, 49
Mostofi, N., 74, 88
Mueller, E., 216, 223, 239
Mullis, A. K., 106, 113, 122
Mullis, R. L., 106, 113, 122
Munn, P., 145, 149
Munoz, J. M., 228, 235
Munoz-Cueto, J. A., 66, 86
Murdock, G. P., 41, 51
Murphy, D. M., 65, 68, 87

Murray, C., 15, 18
Muruthi, P., 33, 42
Mututua, R. S., 33, 42

Nadeau, R., 134, 152
Naftolin, F., 57, 81
Naigles, L. R., 141, 151
Nappi, G., 73, 87
Nappi, R. E., 73, 87
Narasimhan, H., 145, 150
Naylor, C. E., 67, 91
Naylor, S. J., 193, 204
Negroni, J., 65, 82
Neils, J. R., 70, 87
Nelson, K., 138, 153
Nelson, S., 114, 118
Nest, S. L., 143, 151
Newcombe, N., 9, 18, 23, 48, 184–86, 189,
    198, 200, 202, 203, 206
Newman, I., 143, 151
Nolen-Hoekesma, S., 103, 122
Nonneman, A. J., 62, 85
Nowell, A., 143, 150, 163, 164, 165
Nuttall, R. L., 112, 117, 173, 179
Nyborg, H., 70, 87
Nyquist, L., 132, 149

O'Brien, K., 212, 239
O'Laughlin, E., 201, 202, 204
O'Neal, M. F., 72, 87
O'Shaughnessy, P. J., 57, 86
O'Donnell, L., 13, 18
Ohkura, T., 75, 87
Okada, H., 75, 85
Okagaki, L., 195, 204, 214, 238
Opie, I., 138, 152
Opie, P., 138, 152
Opitz, J. M., 39, 50
Orcesi, S., 78, 89
Oring, L. W., 24–26, 49
Orwoll, E. S., 71, 85
Osgood, D. W., 96, 99, 120
Ossenkopp, K. P., 199, 203, 205
Ossenkopp, K., 69, 72, 83
Over, R., 171, 180
Overman, W. H., 195, 203

Overton, W., 200, 202, 206
Oviatt, S. K., 71, 85

Packard, M., 72, 87
Paganini-Hill, A., 64, 75, 84, 87, 88
Pajares, F., 175, 180
Palie, W., 137, 154
Pallas, A. M., 110, 122
Papas, C.T.E., 59, 66, 87
Parameswaran, G., 197, 205
Parisi, D., 32, 33, 49
Park, Y., 193, 204
Parker, G. A., 24, 26, 52
Parry, B., 74, 88
Parsons, J., 97, 110, 111, 114, 122
Pasternak, B., 40, 44, 52
Patterson, G. R., 226, 236
Paul, V., 70, 81
Pavlovic, J., 64, 81
Pegg, R., 106, 121
Pellegrini, A. D., 38, 52, 228, 238
Pellegrino, J., 78, 85, 191, 193, 198, 204
Perlmann, R. Y., 145, 150
Perrot-Sinal, T.S., 199, 205
Perry, D. G., 210, 235
Perry, H., 71, 86
Perry, W., 74, 88
Petersen, A., 185, 189, 190, 196, 204
Peterson, P., 213, 236
Pezaris, E., 112, 117, 173, 179
Pfaff, D. W., 66, 86
Phillips, D. A., 110, 122
Phillips, K., 70, 71, 89
Phillips, S. M., 59, 66, 70, 74, 87
Piaget, J., 159, 180, 196, 205, 252,
    256, 258
Pietrini, P., 68, 87
Pinker, S., 24, 32, 35, 52
Pintrich, P. R., 95, 122
Pipher, M., 104, 122
Pittinsky, T. L., 175, 180
Plomin, R., 138, 153, 184, 205
Plunkett, K., 32, 33, 49
Pogoda, J. M., 64, 75, 88
Pohly, S., 216, 223, 239
Polatti, F., 73, 87

Poole, M. C., 72, 87
Porter, C. L., 78, 87
Post, A., 113, 124
Postma, A., 70, 87
Pottier, J., 61, 90
Povinelli, D. J., 35, 52
Powell, C. M., 65, 68, 87
Powlishta, K. K., 226, 227, 238
Pratt, M. W., 146, 152
Premack, D., 35, 52
Preuss, T.M., 35, 52
Pribram, K. H., 45, 51
Prieto, G., 191, 203
Prifitera, A., 13, 18
Prior, M., 138, 152
Proffitt, D., 196, 203
Provenzano, F. J., 143, 152
Pugh, K. R., 67, 89, 137, 153
Puolovali, J., 72, 88
Pyszczynski, T., 37, 44, 48

Quigley, B., 42, 48
Quinn, D. M., 174, 180

Raag, T., 220, 224, 238
Rackliff, C. L., 220, 238
Raff, R. A., 39, 50
Rajabi, H., 63, 89, 90
Rankin, R. J., 102, 103, 123
Rapoport, S. I., 65, 68, 87
Rasmussen, J. L., 132, 152
Ratner, N. B., 146, 152
Raynaud, J. P., 57, 87
Raz, S., 78, 87
Redeker, G., 132, 152
Reid, G. M., 107, 122
Reid, S. N., 63, 87, 88
Reis, S.M., 102, 123
Reiss, A. L., 65, 88
Renninger, K. A., 100, 119, 121, 122
Repucci, N. D., 97, 118
Resnick, A., 74, 88
Resnick, S., 74, 75, 85, 88
Reuman, D., 96, 98, 109, 110, 112, 118, 119, 123
Reynolds, J. D., 25, 26, 52

Reynolds, W. M., 102, 117
Rhees, R. W., 57, 62, 88
Rhees, R., 62, 83
Richards, M. H., 212, 238
Richards, S. T., 72, 86
Richey, M.F., 12, 18
Riekkinen, P., 72, 88
Riggs, W. W., 78, 87
Rilling, J. K., 35, 52
Ring, H., 35, 48
Rissanen, A., 72, 88
Ritchie, J., 142, 148
Roberts, J. E., 195, 205
Roberts, S. L., 72, 82
Robertson, M., 44, 48
Robinson, E., 73–75, 84
Robinson, N. M., 165, 180
Rodriguez, M., 72, 86
Rodriguez-Sierra, J., 59, 66, 88
Roeltgen, D., 64, 88
Rogers, P. L., 42, 43, 52
Romney, D. M., 109, 121
Rondal, J., 146, 152
Roof, R. L., 61, 63, 68, 73, 88
Roopnarine, J., 226, 236
Rose, H., 210, 218, 237
Rosenberg, D., 196, 206
Rosenthal, R., 6, 19, 42, 43, 52
Ross, J. L., 64, 65, 88
Rotter, G. S., 43, 52
Rotter, N. G., 43, 52
Roullet, P., 75, 80
Rourke, B. P., 137, 152
Rovet, J., 64, 81
Royer, J. M., 94, 95, 115, 122, 161, 168, 169, 172, 173, 180, 247, 254, 258
Rubin, J. Z., 143, 152, 217, 236
Ruble, D. N., 94, 95, 97, 99, 100, 106, 109, 122, 209, 212, 224, 238
Ruiz-Marcos, A., 66, 86
Rutter, M., 184, 205
Ryan, M., 156, 157, 162, 180
Ryan, R. M., 98, 100, 111, 117, 122

Saccuzzo, D. P., 195, 205
Sachs, J., 135, 139, 141, 152, 153

Sadker, D., 114, 122
Sadker, M., 114, 122
Sahib, M. K., 57, 80
Saiyalel, S. N., 33, 42
Salehi, M., 141, 148
Sandberg, D., 107, 122
Sander, C. G., 78, 87
Sanders, B., 190, 204, 205
Sanders, G., 74, 86
Sanders, P., 144, 145, 151
Sandstrom, N., 200, 205
Saults, S. J., 173, 179
Savin, V. J., 42, 48
Savin-Williams, R. C., 41, 45, 46, 52
Sawaguchi, T., 32, 52
Sawaya, G., 73, 75, 91
Scarlato, G., 75, 80
Scarr, S., 38, 52
Schaefer, K., 70, 81
Schaller, M., 44, 52
Schapiro, M. B., 65, 68, 87
Schell, A., 144, 145, 153
Scherrer, J., 72, 83
Schiefele, U., 95, 96, 100, 119, 123
Schlenker, E. H., 66, 86
Schmidt, R., 186, 205
Schmitz, B., 35, 48
Schneider, B, 110, 123
Schneider, L. S., 64, 75, 88
Schofield, P., 75, 90
Schrott, L. M., 65, 66, 83, 86
Schunk, D. H., 95, 96, 122, 123
Scouten, C. W., 61, 88
Seeman, M. V., 78, 88
Seielstad, M. T., 40, 52
Self, C., 193, 204
Sellen, D. W., 41, 52
Semmelroth, J., 31, 49
Seong, H., 161, 180
Serbin, L. A., 213, 226, 227–29, 231, 232, 235, 238
Setalo, G., 75, 90
Seymoure, P., 62, 88
Shamai, S., 106, 123
Shanabrough, M., 57, 81
Shankweiler, D. P., 67, 89, 137, 153

Shaywitz, B. A., 68, 68, 89, 135, 137, 153
Shaywitz, S. E., 67, 89, 135, 137, 153
Shea, D., 70, 81
Sheldon, A., 141, 153
Shepard, R. N., 30, 52, 194, 195, 205
Sherif, C. W., 37, 47, 52
Sherif, M., 37, 47, 52
Sherman, J. A., 212, 238
Sherry, D. F., 30, 31, 51, 52, 199, 205
Sherwin, B. B., 64, 70, 73, 74, 78, 85, 87, 89
Shih, M., 175, 180
Showers, C. J., 103, 121
Shryne, J., 56, 66, 82
Shryne, J. E., 56, 57, 62, 66, 82, 88
Shtasel, D. L., 68, 82
Siegle, D., 102, 123
Sigel, I. E., 110, 123
Signorella, M., 185, 205
Silverman, I., 70, 71, 89, 201, 202, 205
Simkins-Bullock, J. A., 132, 153
Simmons, L. W., 24, 26, 52
Simpkins, J. W., 72, 74, 89
Sinclair, A. H., 56, 80
Sinforiani, E., 73, 87
Singh, M., 72, 74, 75, 89, 90
Sipos, A., 56, 66, 82
Sitarenios, G., 60, 84
Skaalvik, E. M., 102, 103, 123
Skavarenina, A., 61, 90
Skudlarski, P., 67, 89, 137, 153
Slabbekoorn, D., 71, 74, 89
Slaby, R. G., 209, 239
Slomkowski, C. L., 138, 153
Smith, I. M., 189, 203
Smith, P. K., 38, 52, 228, 238
Smolak, L., 138, 153
Snyder, E., 46, 48
Snyder, L., 138, 149
Snyder, T. D., 156, 168, 169, 180
Soares, M. P., 190, 205
Sokka, T. A., 57, 89
Solomon, S., 37, 44, 48
Soto, V., 72, 82
Spencer, A., 72, 82

Spencer, S. J., 174, 180
Spencer, S., 97, 123
Spinillo A., 78, 89
Sprafkin, C., 228, 232, 238
Srivastava, S., 56, 66, 82
Stackman, R., 72, 89
Stanley, J. C., 165, 181
Stanovich, K. E., 135, 153, 247, 258
Starkey, P., 157, 159, 160, 179
Stavnezer, A. J., 64, 65, 66, 81
Steele, C. M., 6, 15, 19, 97, 123, 173,
    174, 180, 220–23, 239
Stefanatos, G., 64, 88
Stein, A. H., 216, 223, 239
Stein, D. G., 68, 78, 88
Steinberg, L., 108, 117, 184, 203
Steinberg, L. S., 169, 181
Stephan, C., 108, 117
Stephan, W. G., 36, 37, 53, 209, 239
Stephenson, J., 75, 89
Stern, M., 138, 153
Stern, Y., 75, 90
Sternberg, R. J., 157, 181, 188, 205
Sternglanz, S. H., 226, 238
Stevens, K. N., 128, 151
Stevens, N., 33, 35, 40, 45, 51
Stevenson, H.W., 17, 19
Stewart, J., 61–63, 65, 66, 69, 83, 85, 89,
    90
Stipek, D. J., 161, 181
Stluka, M. F.,110, 122
Stone, S., 70, 85
Stoneman, Z., 146, 153
Strang, J. D., 137, 152
Strayer, F. F., 226, 236
Stricker, L. J., 7, 19
Strong, R., 200, 202, 203
Strube, M. J., 44, 45, 49
Stumpf, H., 165, 181, 191, 205
Sullivan, H., 116, 120
Sullivan, L. M., 161, 180
Sutherland, R. J., 62, 85
Suydam, A., 56, 86
Swaab, D. F., 69, 73, 84
Swann, J., 143, 153
Swim, J. K., 7, 19
Szczepanik, J., 68, 87

Székely, T., 25, 52

Taine, M. C., 193, 204
Takahira, S., 170, 171, 178
Talbot, K., 193, 194, 205
Tallal, P., 42, 53
Tanaka, K., 75, 85
Tang, M. X., 75, 90
Tannen, D., 132, 133, 138, 153
Tanner, J. M., 134, 153
Taylor, A., 56, 80, 190, 204
Taylor, G., 72, 83
Taylor, H. A., 193, 204
Teather, L., 72, 87
Tein, J., 107, 120
Tepper, C. A., 140, 153
The National Council of Teachers of
    Mathematics, 158, 181
Thomas, H., 191, 205
Thompson, B. R., 141, 153
Thorne, B., 133, 153, 227, 239
Timmer, S. G., 212, 239
Tinbergen, N., 251, 252, 258
Tobet, S. A., 58, 90
Tomasello, M., 146, 152
Tonick, I. J., 226, 238
Tooby, J., 32, 33, 53
Toran-Allerand, C., 75, 90
Toran-Allerand, C. D., 57, 86
Towson, S. M. J., 45, 53
Treichler, P. A., 132, 153
Trew, K., 106, 107, 108, 117
Trice, A., 113, 123
Trivers, R. L., 24, 25, 33, 36, 53
Tronsky, L. N., 94, 95, 115, 122, 161, 168,
    169, 172, 173, 180, 247, 254, 258
Tuiten, A., 70, 87
Turetsky, B.I., 12, 18, 68, 82
Turner, I., 106, 107, 108, 117
Tyler, L. E., 214, 239

Uchida, A., 133, 154
Udell, C., 74, 88
Ungerleider, L-G., 16, 19
United States Census Bureau, 105, 106, 123
Urabe, M., 75, 85
Urresta, F., 72, 82

Valach, L., 113, 124
Van de Poll, N., 71, 74, 90
Van de Poll, N. E, 69, 73, 84
Van Goozen, S., 71, 74, 90
van Goozen, S. H., 71, 74, 89
Van Groen, T., 72, 88
Van Haaren, F., 61, 76, 90
Van Hest, A., 61, 76, 90
van Honk, J., 70, 87
Vasta, R., 196, 197, 206
Vevea, J., 184, 203
Vincent, A.C. J., 24, 49
Visperas, C., 141, 149
Vladar, K., 60, 67, 85
Vogel, S., 68, 78, 81, 90
Vogel, W., 70, 81
Voyer, D., 168, 181, 189–92, 196, 206
Voyer, S., 189, 190–92, 196, 206

Wagner, C. K., 57, 90
Wagner, R. K., 188, 205
Wahlsten, D., 60, 64, 67, 74, 81
Wainer, H., 169, 181
Wallace, C. S., 33, 38, 50
Wallen, K., 46, 53
Walsh, M., 222, 239
Ward, I., 62, 90
Ward, S., 200, 202, 206
Warren, S. G., 72, 90
Warren-Leubecker, A., 145, 154
Washburn, L., 56, 83
Waters, P., 103, 104, 115, 120
Watson, N., 197, 206
Watson, R., 74, 81
Watt, L., 75, 84
Wayne, R. K., 33, 42
Weiland, N., 75, 86
Weinberger, D., 60, 67, 85
Weiner, B., 95, 97, 123
Weinreb, H., 74, 83
Weintraub, M., 228, 237
Weist, R. M., 146, 154
Weisz, J., 62, 90
Wellman, H. M., 35, 50
Wells, G., 145, 154
Weniger, J. P., 57, 90
Westen, D., 31, 49

Wheaton, B., 213, 229, 238
Wheeler, T. J., 135, 152
Wherry, J. N., 102, 121
Whishaw, I. Q., 62, 85
White, B. J., 37, 47, 52, 65, 68, 87
Whitehouse, C. C., 68, 78, 83
Whitesell, N. R., 103, 104, 115, 120
Whiting, B. B., 45, 53
Wigfield, A., 93, 95, 96, 98, 99–102,
    109, 110, 112, 114, 118–20, 122,
    123, 162, 181
Wildman, B. G., 132, 153
Williams, C. L., 59, 61, 77, 91
Williams, C., 72, 91, 198, 206
Williams, E. M., 33, 38, 50
Williams, G. C., 24, 53
Williams, J.E., 11, 18
Williams, K. A., 128, 151
Williams, W. M., 188, 205
Willingham, W. W., 14, 19, 163, 165–67
Wilson, J., 56, 91, 200, 203
Winkel, J., 70, 87
Winocur, G., 35, 51
Wisenbaker, J., 138, 152
Witelson, S. F., 67, 77, 91, 137, 154
Wood, F. B., 67, 91
Woodruff, G., 35, 52
Woolley, C., 75, 91
Woolley, C. S., 59, 69, 83, 84, 91
Wrangham, R. W., 39, 40, 51, 53
Wright, T. M., 42, 50
Wu, V. Y., 72, 86
Wylie, R. C., 102, 123
Wyman, H., 232, 237

Yaffe, K., 73, 75, 91
Yan, M., 12, 18
Yaoi, Y., 75, 87
Yee, D., 96, 98, 109, 119
Yee, M. D., 44, 45, 46, 53
Yeung, A. S., 102, 121
Yoon, K. S., 96, 98, 100, 110, 123,
    162, 181
Young, R., 113, 124

Zabriskie, J., 74, 83
Zalatimo, N. S., 64, 67, 82

Zecevic, M., 72, 86
Zeis, A., 57, 90
Zelkowitz, P., 213, 229, 238

Zimmerberg, B., 65, 91
Zonderman, A., 74, 75, 85, 88

Subject Index

Abilities and sex differences
  physical abilities, 94
  see also Cognitive differences by sex;
    Mathematical abilities
Aging
  menopause and memory, 73
    estrogen replacement therapy and
      Alzheimer's disease, 74–75, 78
  sex differences in neurobiological con-
    sequences of, 68
Arcuate fasciculus, 136
Autism, and gender, 44

Biological differences as research default-
    explanation fallacy, 14–15, 248
Bowerbird, 27–29, 29f
Broca's area, 136
Brown-headed cowbird, 31

Callitrichid monkeys, 26
Career choice/occupational aspirations
    and sex differences
  career aspirations, 106
  career choices, 105–106
  choices vs. differences, 208
  effects on gender differences in cogni-
    tion, 108
  gender stereotyping of career roles,
    107–108
Cloning, impact on male/female concepts, 4
Cognitive competencies
  inherent specificity question, 33

  and play, 38, 45
Cognitive difference by sex/research
  cross-cultural research, 11
  cyclicity and the female brain, 69
  descriptions, 252–254
    and coordination of findings,
      254–255
    and explanatory models, 255–258
  effects of sex differences in career
    aspirations, 108
  effects of sex differences in self-con-
    cept/self-esteem, 104
  empirically driven, 23, 31
  evaluative issues
    nomological net, 8, 12–15
    research design questions, 8–12
  from hormonally moderated epigenetic
    process theory, 39, 45
  mathematical abilities, 94
  mathematical models of group differ-
    ence/variance, 77–78
    within group variance vs. between
      group variance, 94, 243–244
  processes masked by overall perform-
    ance, 77
  psychobiosocial framework, 15–17,
    247, 252
  social issues
    biases in prior research, 6–7
    and censorship, 8
    controversy, 3–4
    media attention, 10

"women-have-less" fallacy, 5

Evolutionary theories of cognitive sex dif-
        ferences, 12–13, 244, 249–250
    impact of social complexity on evolu-
        tion, 32, 35, 79, 257
    intrasexual competition, 27–31, 40–42
    and ontogenetic development in brain
        and cognition, 38–39
    and probabilistic model of epigenesis,
        255–256
    and sexual selection studies, 31

Gender development/cognitive perspec-
        tive, 208–211, 233–234
    children
        activities/interests/skill develop-
            ment, 212–214
        "cultures" of girls'/boys' groups,
            227–228
        gender cognitions as influences on
            exploration, 214–215
        gender cognitions as influences on
            memory (gender labeling stud-
            ies), 217–220
        gender cognitions as influences on
            motivation, 215–217, 233
        and gender identity, 210
        peers as socializing agents, 225–226,
            234
        performance and stereotype threat,
            220–225
        play/activity preferences, 211–212
        sex segregation, 226–227
        social environments, 210–211, 211f
    cognitive developmental theory, 209
    gender cognitions and sex segregation,
        231
    gender cognitions and situational/indi-
        vidual differences, 210
    gender-labeling and stereotype threats,
        224–225
    interaction styles/peer
        preferences/skill development
        interaction, 228–231
    schema theories, 209
        developmental view, 209

and skill development, 232–233
Gender intensification phenomenon,
        103–104
Genderlects, 131

Hormonal mechanisms and the brain,
        248–249
    androgens, 56–57, 69
        behavioral effects in animal studies,
            60–62
        (circulating) and spatial ability in
            men, 71–72
        (circulating) and spatial ability in
            rodents, 72–73
        experiments and assumptions, 76
        neural effects in animal studies,
            62–63
    animal studies of cerebral organization,
            67–68
    estrogen
        behavioral effects in animal studies,
            65
        (circulating) and spatial ability in
            rodents, 72
        (circulating) and spatial ability in
            women, 70–71
        neural effects in animal studies,
            65–66
        neurobehavioral effects of in
            human studies, 63–65
        protective role in females, 78–79
    feminine development path, 56
    hormonally moderated epigenetic
            process theory, 39,45
    hormone replacement studies; verbal
            memory and fluency, 73–74
    and human cognitive sex differences, 66
        in cerebral blood flow patterns dur-
            ing verbal tasks, 67
        in language recovery, 67
        in right ear advantage (REA), 67
    masculine development path, 55–56
    organizational vs. activational features
            of steroid hormones, 58–59
    orthogonal developmental processes
            and qualitative/quantitative dif-
            ferences, 76–77

permanent hormone effects
   vs. activational hormone effects,
      68–69
   neurobehavioral effects of andro-
      gens, 60
   and "sexual differentiation of the
      brain," 58
   in structural asymmetries, 67
   steroid receptors/steroid effects on
      neural growth, 57–58
   transient (circulating) effects mecha-
      nisms, 75–76
   Y chromosome gene coding, 55–56

Intrasexual competition and evolutionary
      changes, 27–31

Language development/gender differences,
      127–128, 146–148, 244–245
   in adult language
      cultural differences explanation, 133
      dominance model explanation, 133
      "essentialist" rationale, 133–134
      language disorders, 135
      observed differences, 132–133
      stereotypical differences, 131–132
      voice "placing," 134
   biological basis, 147
      brain differences by gender, 137
      innate differences, 134–135
      language areas of the brain, 135–137
      temperamental differences, 137–139
   children
      gender-marked language styles,
         141–142
      knowledge of gender stereotypes,
         139–140
      language usage differences, 140–141,
         147
   language system
      discourse, 130–131
      lexicon and semantics, 129
      morphology, 129
      phonology, 128–129
      pragmatics, 130
      syntax, 129–130
   middle childhood and adolescence,
      142–143
   see also Social factors
Lynn, R., misuse of standardized instru-
      ments, 11–12

Mathematical abilities, 246–247
   advanced problem solving, 170
      cognitive processing model,
         170–171
      male/female "favored" items, 172
   development of
      in different stages of childhood,
         158–160
      theoretical approaches, 157, 159
   early school-based strategies/beliefs
      (recent findings), 160–162,
      176–177
      research summary, 162
   fact retrieval, 172
   mathematics courses enrollment pat-
      terns (high school/college),
      167–168, 169
      course grades, 168
      test performance/grades differ-
         ences, 168–169
   meta-analysis findings (through
      1990), 155–156, 160
   multidimensionality, 158, 158t
   and other cognitive abilities, 158
   and performance by gender, 177–178
      extreme score differences, 163–167
      research implications, 167
      sex differences in variability,
         162–163
      and stereotypes, 175, 176
   spatial ability, 173
   stereotypes, 159–160
      and beliefs, 173–175
Motivation differences by sex, 95
   achievement task values, 98–99
      gender-role related themes, 98
   attributions for success/failure, 97
   competence beliefs, 96–97
      parental influences, 109–111, 148
      and performance, 98
   expectancy-value theoretical per-
      spective, 95–96

and gender cognitions, 215–217
intrinsic motivation, 100–101
locus of control, 97
patterns of interest, 99–100

Nature vs. nurture debate, 15–16, 255
  vs. probabilistic model of epigenesis,
    255–256
  and psychobiosocial model, 247
Neocortex size and social system com-
    plexity, 32

Operational sex ratio (OSR), 25–27

Performance differences by sex, 95
Piaget, Jean
  descriptive to explanatory modeling in
    psychology, 252
  research in logical-mathematical
    knowledge, 159, 256
  spatial skills testing/sex differences, 190
Polygyny, in human societies, 41–42

Red-necked phalarope, 25–26
Relationships
  with friends
    and mutuality, 35
    and reciprocity, 33
  kin-based, 33
    and inclusive fitness, 33
  and language, 35
  and theory of mind, 35
    and autism, 44
    and inferences about social decep-
      tions, 43–44
Robbers Cave experiment impact, 37
Ruff, 27, 28f

Self-concept (SC)/self-esteem (SE) and
    sex differences, 101
  and achievement, 102–103
  and cognitive development, 104
  and depression in adolescence, 103
  and gender roles, 103–104
  and gifted children, 102
  global measures vs. specific aspect
    measures of SC, 101

multi-factor influences of SE, 101
Sexual selection, 24, 38
  dynamics
    operational sex ratio (OSR), 25–27
    reproductive rates, 24–25
  hominid social structure, 39–40
    coalition-based male–male intrasex-
      ual competition, 40
    and development, 45–46
    intrasexual competition, 40–42
    relational vs. physical aggression, 41
  and paternal investment in humans,
    26–27
  as a theoretical perspective, 23,46
    and testable predictions generation,
      47
Social factors influencing gender differ-
    ences, 246, 250
  and behavior development, 251–252
  children's social environments, 210–211,
    211f
  in language, 143–144, 148
  parental influences, 108–109
    on children's competence-related
      beliefs, 109–111
    on children's valuation of activities,
      111
    learning experiences provided, 112
    on occupational interests/career
      choice, 113
  parental speech to boys and girls
    context, 145–146
    fathers' speech, 146
    individual domains, 145
    meta-analysis, 144–145
  peer support, 113
    and boys'/girls' cultures, 227–228
  school experiences, 114–115
    career choice influences, 115–116
    teacher expectancy, 114
Sociocognitive modules
  evolutionary taxonomy of, 32
  group-level modules
    sex differences at early age, 44–45
    social ideologies development, 37
    social universe parsing, 36–37
  individual-level modules (one-on-one

relationships), 33, 35
sex differences (favoring men), 43
sex differences (favoring women),
    42–43
systems (individual and group-level), 33, 34t
Spatial skill, 245
    dynamic spatial tasks, 197–198
    horizontality–verticality skills/sex differ-
        ences, 196
        natural experience effects, 196
        training effects, 196–197
    mean level change potential, 184, 202–203
    mental rotation skills/sex differences,
        190–191, 195–196
        computer games (as practice activi-
            ty), 194–195
        practice and training, 192–193
        sign language (as naturalistic train-
            ing), 193–194
        test timing, 191–192
    navigation and place finding, 198–199
        animal training studies, 199
        direction giving, 200
        way finding, 200–201
    object location memory, 201–202
        sociobiological implications, 201–202

research on social explanations of
    differences (prior to 1990s),
    184–185
    correlational studies, 185
    threshold effects, 188–189, 189f
    training studies, 186–189, 187f,
        188f
    and sex differences in specific tests,
        189–190
Stereotypes
    as a categorization process, 7
    and sex research, 6–7
    and sill development, 233
    stereotype threat, 7, 220–221
        disidentification with domain,
            222–223
        domain vs. individual identifica-
            tion, 221
        underperformance consequence,
            221–222

Voles, 29–31

Wernicke's area, 136
Women's rights, and research on sex
    differences, 4

About the Contributors

ANN BATTLE is assistant director of the Department of Human Development, College of Education, University of Maryland College Park. Her research interests are in the areas of adolescent cognition and socialization processes as they relate to measures of school adjustment and overall classroom climate. Dr. Battle is also the director of the Human Development Master's in Education program for secondary education teachers.

HEATHER A. BIMONTE is currently working as a Postdoctoral Fellow under the supervision of Dr. A. Granholm at the University of South Carolina. She is interested in the role of estrogen effects on memory.

RICHARD DE LISI is a professor of educational psychology at Rutgers, The State University of New Jersey. He has written about 50 publications pertaining to cognitive development, sex differences in cognitive abilities, and sex role development. He is currently Chair of the Department of Educational Psychology and Director of the Ph.D. Program in Education at Rutgers University in New Brunswick. He is author of a recent book, co-authored with Jeffrey K. Smith and Lisa F. Smith, titled *Natural Classroom Assessment. Designing Seamless Instruction & Assessment.*

LISA M. DINELLA is a doctoral student in the Family and Human Development program at Arizona State University. She is currently finishing her master's degree in marriage and family therapy. Her master's thesis is on girls and math and science development. Her B.S. is in psychology from Trenton State College.

JACQUELYNNE S. ECCLES is the Wilbert McKeachie Collegiate Professor of Psychology, Education, and Women's Studies at the University of Michigan. Her research interests include the development of achievement beliefs, values, and motivation; gender differences in these beliefs and values; the influence of educational contexts on children's motivation and achievement; and development in the family. She received her Ph.D. from UCLA and currently serves on the Board of Editors for *Child Development.*

RICHARD ELY is an instructor in psychology at Boston University. His research has focused on the social, emotional, and linguistic development of young children. Past research projects have included studies of children's language play, children's use of quotations, and children's use of negatives. Currently, he is examining the early development of self-concept by analyzing young children's personal narratives.

ROSLYN HOLLY FITCH is an Assistant Research Professor in the Department of Psychology, Behavioral Neurosciences Division, at the University of Connecticut. Her early research focuses on the area of developmental hormones and sex differences in behavior and neuromorphology. More recent work includes research on the development of animal models of developmental disability, with a special emphasis on the role of hormones in mediating observed sex differences in the incidence of disability, as well as sex differences in response to early brain injury.

DAVID C. GEARY is director of the Ph.D. Program in Developmental Psychology and the Frederick A. Middlebush Professor of Psychological Sciences at the University of Missouri at Columbia. He has widely published across a wide range of topics, including cognitive and developmental psychology, education, evolutionary biology, and medicine. His two books, *Children's Mathematical Development* (1984) and *Male, Female: The Evolution of Human Sex Differences* (1988), have been published by the American Psychological Association. Among his many distinctions is the inclusion in the 2001 volume of *Who's Who in the World* and the Chancellor's Award for Outstanding Research and Creative Activity in the Social and Behavioral Sciences (1996).

JEAN BERKO GLEASON is a professor in the Department of Psychology at Boston University. She is also a faculty member and former director of BU's Graduate Program in Applied Linguistics. She has been a visiting scholar at Stanford University and at the Linguistics Institute of the Hungarian Academy of Sciences in Budapest. Since writing her doctoral dissertation on the child's learning of English morphology at Harvard/Radcliffe, she has continued to conduct research in the areas of language development in children, aphasia, language attrition, lexical development, and developmental sociolinguistics.

DIANE F. HALPERN is professor of psychology at California State University, San Bernardino. She is author of several books including *Sex Differences in Cognitive Abilities* and *Thought and Knowledge: An Introduction to Critical Thinking*. Dr. Halpern has served as president of the Western Psychological Association, General Psychology, Division 1 of the American Psychological Association, and the Society for the Teaching of Psychology. She has won many awards for her teaching and research including the 1999 American Psychological Foundation Award for Distinguished Teaching, the 1996 Distinguished Career Award for Contributions to Education given by the

American Psychological Association, the California State University's State-Wide Outstanding Professor Award, the Outstanding Alumna award from the University of Cincinnati, and the Silver Medal Award from the Council for the Advancement and Support of Education.

SIMAY IKIER is a doctoral student in the perception, cognition and cognitive neuroscience program at the University of Toronto, where she is studying cognitive aging. She received her master's degree in psychological sciences from Bogazici University in Istanbul, Turkey. Her thesis involved the investigation of a special memory illusion in twins' autobiographical memories.

LISA B. KELLER received a Master of Arts degree from the Department of Human Development, University of Maryland. Her research interests include sex differences in gifted children's motivation to study math and science, and identity development. She currently is studying abroad in Israel, and will pursue a Ph.D. in sociology at the University of Southern California.

CAROL LYNN MARTIN is Professor of Family and Human Development at Arizona State University. Dr. Martin's major research interests include children's gender development and the consequences of children's same-sex and other-sex peer relationships. Dr. Martin has published numerous articles and chapters on gender development. In 1998, along with Dr. Diane Ruble, Dr. Martin authored a chapter on gender development for the *Handbook of Child Psychology*, which provides state-of-the-science reviews and outlines future directions for the field. In 2000, Dr. Martin and Dr. Richard Fabes published a book on child development.

LISA MATHASON is a Ph.D. student in the educational psychology program at Temple University. For 3 years previously, she served as Study Coordinator for an Early Childhood Initiative Project, funded by the Learning and Intelligent Systems Initiative of the National Science Foundation. With Dr. Nora Newcombe as principal investigator, this project followed the spatial development of children over second and third grade.

ANN McGILLICUDDY-DE LISI is the Marshall R. Metzgar Professor of Psychology and Head of the Psychology Department at Lafayette College. She is a developmental psychologist who specializes in parent beliefs about child development and learning environments within the family as well as sex differences in cognition. Dr. McGillicuddy-De Lisi has coedited a book on parents' beliefs (with I. E. Sigel and J. J. Goodnow) as well as published numerous research articles and book chapters on children's and adults' cognitive development. She recently has been appointed coeditor of the *Journal of Applied Developmental Psychology*.

NORA S. NEWCOMBE is a Professor of Psychology at Temple University. Her research concerns spatial cognition, its development, and individual differences in spatial ability, as well as the development of memory for early childhood experiences. She is the author of a recent book, co-authored with Janellen Huttenlocher, entitled *Making Space: The Development of Spatial Representation and Reasoning.*

MELISSA TERLECKI is a graduate student in cognitive psychology at Temple University. Her major research interest is in sex differences in spatial ability. She has conducted secular studies in this area with Dr. MaryAnn Baenninger and is currently pursuing research in spatial performance with Dr. Nora Newcombe.

ALLAN WIGFIELD is Professor of Human Development at the University of Maryland. His research has focused on the development and socialization of children's and adolescents' achievement motivation in different areas, with a particular focus on sex differences in motivation. He also studies motivation for literacy. He currently is Associate Editor of the *Journal of Educational Psychology.*